# CONTEMPORARY FEMINIST POLITICS

## Women and Power in Britain

by

JONI LOVENDUSKI

AND

VICKY RANDALL

OXFORD UNIVERSITY PRESS

1993

Oxford University Press, Walton Street, Oxford OX2 6DP

Oxford New York Toronto
Delhi Bombay Calcutta Madras Karachi
Kuala Lumpur Singapore Hong Kong Tokyo
Nairobi Dar es Salaam Cape Town
Melbourne Auckland Madrid

and associated companies in
Berlin Ibadan

Oxford is a trade mark of Oxford University Press

Published in the United States by
Oxford University Press Inc., New York

British Library Cataloguing in Publication Data
Data available

Library of Congress Cataloging in Publication Data
Lovenduski, Joni.
Contemporary feminist politics : women and power in Britain / by
Joni Lovenduski and Vicki Randall.
Includes bibliographical references (p.   ) and index.
1. Women in politics—Great Britain.   2. Feminism—Great Britain.
I. Randall, Vicky.   II. Title.
HQ1236.5.G7L68   1993   305.42'0941—dc20   92-41371
ISBN 0-19-827738-5
ISBN 0-19-878069-9 (pbk.)

3 5 7 9 10 8 6 4 2

Printed in Great Britain
on acid-free paper by
Bookcraft (Bath) Ltd
Midsomer Norton, Avon

# *Preface*

WE began the research for this book during the autumn of 1988. Undertaking an account and interpretation of changes in the British women's movement since the late 1970s was an ambitious project, even more ambitious than we perhaps realized at the outset. There were so many dimensions to consider, people to talk to, sources to consult. Added to these demands were the changes in our own personal circumstances over this period. Between us we notched up two house moves, a job change, two changes of partner, and a baby. It frequently occurred to us that these experiences almost encapsulated the transformations that we met in the lives of other feminists. But, at any rate, the four years we spent on it gave us time to mull over our findings, strengthening our confidence that we have broadly got it right.

All in all, working on this book has been an inspiring experience, and one in which we have built up quite a lot of debts. Our reckoning would be incomplete if we did not pay special tribute to the commitment, wisdom, and sheer ability of the women we interviewed in countless women's projects, groups, and organizations. They are generally not the media feminists whose faces are familiar from television or the press. They really are the 'unsung heroines', pressing on in frequently adverse conditions, vigilant for what they believe to be women's interests—our interests. Problems of confidentiality mean that we cannot name them individually, but we do want to thank them all for their time and other forms of assistance, and to acknowledge the importance of what they are doing.

We have, of course, more specific acknowledgements to make. First, we should like to thank those who read and commented on the early drafts of one or more chapters of this book: Veronica Beechey, Judy Evans, Ghita Ionescu, Mary McIntosh, Elizabeth Meehan, Kate Nash, Sarah Perrigo, Carol Smart, and Alan Ware. Secondly, we were greatly assisted by a useful 'launching' grant from the Nuffield Foundation and, later, by a small grant from Loughborough University's research committee. We relied heavily on the general academic support of our employers— Loughborough University, the Polytechnic of Central London (now the University of Westminster), and Essex University. Joni Lovenduski received academic hospitality and collegial support from the Institute of Governmental Studies at the University of California at Berkeley during the summer of 1991. We also used the valuable archives of the Fawcett Library and the Women's Health Campaign.

Then we must thank all the individuals and organizations that gave us interviews or provided us with information. Because we promised confidentiality, individuals cannot be named. We met members of groups and organizations involved in health and reproductive rights campaigning, rape crisis work, the women's refuge movement, the black women's movement, equal opportunities work, women's cultural projects, the media, and education. We conducted interviews in Birmingham, Bristol, Edinburgh, Glasgow, Leeds, London, Manchester, and Nottingham. In addition, we owe thanks to Labour Party Head Office, especially to Joyce Gould and Vicky Phillips, Conservative Central Office, especially Baroness Joan Seccombe and Sir Tom Arnold, the Equal Opportunites Department of the TUC, the Equal Opportunities Commission, and the National Association of Local Government Women's Committees.

We received helpful comments when we presented papers, based on research for the book, to a postgraduate seminar in the Department of Politics at Edinburgh University in January 1991, to the Ph.D. Colloquium in the Department of Government at Essex in January 1992, to the joint conference of the Political Studies Association's Women and Politics Group and the British Sociological Association's Sexual Divisions Group in February 1992, and to the ECPR workshop on the Methodology of Studying New Social Movements at Limerick in April 1992.

Finally, many individuals were helpful. We are particularly grateful for help, information, and/or advice from Melissa Benn, Bea Campbell, Martin Durham, Janet Ford, Alice Leonard, Leonora Lloyd, and Pippa Norris. Adrienne Jamieson offered hospitality at a crucial moment. Denise McKnight provided support and technical help with word processing. Tim Barton, our editor, has been endlessly patient and encouraging. And our families and friends are to be thanked for putting up with all the fuss and bother that is part of writing a book and producing a manuscript.

Despite all the help that we received, it is of course we two who are answerable for any shortcomings. In fact, the book, as it has emerged, has been very much a joint project. Together we have felt our way towards an interpretation, and any remaining differences are matters of emphasis only. As far as separate authorship can be attributed, we have each contributed about half the final manuscript. Joni Lovenduski is largely responsible for the chapters on difference, political institutions, equal opportunities, and male violence; Vicky Randall for those on the changing economic and political context, reproductive rights, and motherhood. However, in the remaining chapters responsibility is more blurred: the Introduction is very much a joint effort; Joni Lovenduski wrote about one third of Chapter 4, on the grassroots women's movement; while Vicky Randall produced the first draft of the Conclusion and Joni Lovenduski amended it.

We do not fool ourselves that this study will find favour in all quarters. With such subject-matter, the book is bound to arouse criticism and protest. But we do hope that, by offering a relatively systematic analysis and argument, we have contributed in some way to the understanding of contemporary feminist politics.

J.L. and V.R.

*September 1992*

# Contents

# List of Abbreviations

| | |
|---|---|
| AEU | Amalgamated Engineering Union |
| ALRA | Abortion Law Reform Association |
| ARM | Association of Radical Midwives |
| ASTMS (MSF) | Association of Scientific, Technical, and Managerial Staff (Manufacturing, Science, and Finance) |
| BMA | British Medical Association |
| BPAS | British Pregnancy Advisory Service |
| BWWH | Black Women for Wages for Housework |
| CADI | Campaign for Access to Donor Insemination |
| CAP | Campaign against Pornography |
| CAPC | Campaign against Pornography and Censorship |
| CBI | Confederation of British Industry |
| CHC | Community Health Council |
| CHIRU | Community Health Initiatives Resource Unit |
| CND | Campaign for Nuclear Disarmament |
| COHSE | Confederation of Health Service Employees |
| Co-ord | Co-ordinating Committee in Defence of the 1967 Act |
| CPSA | Civil and Public Services Association |
| CRE | Commission for Racial Equality |
| DWCA | Doctors for a Woman's Choice on Abortion |
| EC | European Community |
| ELBWO | East London Black Women's Organization |
| EOC | Equal Opportunities Commission |
| FAB | Fight the Alton Bill |

| FAC | Feminists against Censorship |
|---|---|
| FACT | Feminist Anti-Censorship Task Force |
| FAST | Feminism against Sexual Terrorism |
| FINRRAGE | Feminist International Network of Resistance to Reproductive and Genetic Engineering |
| GLC | Greater London Council |
| HEA | Health Education Authority |
| ICAR | International Campaign for Abortion Rights |
| ILEA | Inner London Education Authority |
| LARC | Labour Abortion Rights Campaign |
| LBWHAP | London Black Women's Health Action Project |
| LLGC | London Lesbian and Gay Centre |
| LWAC | Labour Women's Action Committee |
| NAC | National Abortion Campaign |
| NALGO | National and Local Government Officers' Association |
| NALGWC | National Association of Local Government Women's Committees |
| NAS/UWT | National Association of Schoolmasters and Union of Women Teachers |
| NATFHE | National Association of Teachers in Further and Higher Education |
| NCC | National Child Care Campaign |
| NCCL | National Council of Civil Liberties |
| NCHR | National Community Health Resource |
| NCU | National Communications Union |
| NEC | National Executive Committee |
| NEDC | National Economic Development Council |
| NGA | National Graphical Association |
| NHS | National Health Service |
| NICs | newly industrializing countries |

| | |
|---|---|
| NIEOC | Northern Ireland Equal Opportunities Commission |
| NJACCWER | National Joint Action Campaign Committee for Women's Equal Rights |
| NSMs | 'new' social movements |
| NUM | National Union of Mineworkers |
| NUPE | National Union of Public Employees |
| NUR | National Union of Railwaymen |
| NUT | National Union of Teachers |
| OECD | Organization for Economic Co-operation and Development |
| OWAAD | Organization of Women of Asian and African Descent |
| PCA | Pro-Choice Alliance |
| PSBR | public sector borrowing requirement |
| RCOG | Royal College of Obstetricians and Gynaecologists |
| RCP | Revolutionary Communist Party |
| SAFTA | Support after Termination for Abnormality |
| SDP | Social Democratic Party |
| SERPS | State Earnings Related Pension Scheme |
| SERTUC | South-East Regional TUC |
| SNP | Scottish National Party |
| SOGAT | Society of Graphical and Allied Trades |
| SPUC | Society for the Protection of the Unborn Child |
| STAC | Stop the Amendment Campaign |
| SWAP | Scottish Women against Pornography |
| SWP | Socialist Workers' Party |
| TACT | Tories for the Abortion Act of 1967 |
| TECs | Training and Enterprise Councils |
| TGWU | Transport and General Workers' Union |
| TUC | Trades Union Congress |

| | |
|---|---|
| TUCRIC | Trade Union Community and Resource Information Centre |
| UCATT | Union of Construction, Allied Trades, and Technicians |
| UCW | Union of Communication Workers |
| USDAW | Union of Shop, Distributive, and Allied Workers |
| WAPC | Women against Pit Closures |
| WAR | Women against Rape |
| WASH | Women against Sexual Harassment |
| WAVAW | Women against Violence against Women |
| WHIC | Women's Health Information Centre |
| WHRRIC | Women's Health and Reproductive Rights Information Centre |
| WIM | Women in Medicine |
| WLM | Women's Liberation Movement |
| WNC | Workplace Nurseries Campaign |
| WRRC | Women's Reproductive Rights Campaign |

# 1

# Introduction

As we go to press at the end of 1992, the media is full of pronouncements that the British women's movement has returned or revived, that its agenda is far from completion, that a new generation of young feminists will not tolerate the conditions under which their mothers worked and lived. But only a few years ago, at the end of the 1980s, different generalizations were made. We were told that the women's movement was in decline, that, nevertheless, it was subverting local government and the caring professions, that it had been outgrown and replaced by 'post-feminism', which was often defined as 'ex-feminism'. Announcements of the death of the British women's movement may have been no more than wishful thinking on the part of an anti-feminist press, but questions about the state of the movement were difficult to answer. It was hard to come by reliable information. There seemed to be a dearth of systematic research and analysis on the subject. As feminists—and as social scientists—we found ourselves increasingly irritated and perplexed by oracular pronouncements that offered nothing in the way of substantiation or evidence. We wanted to know what had 'really' been happening. What was this 'movement' inherited from the optimistic 1970s, and how far and in what condition had it survived the difficult 1980s? How was British feminism affected by the far-reaching political and economic changes associated with Thatcherism? And what input had feminism made to those changes?

This book is our attempt to piece together some of the answers to those questions. It is based on research carried out mainly between the autumn of 1988 and the summer of 1991, but we have continued to update it right up to the writing of the final drafts in the summer of 1992. Because the subject-matter is potentially vast, we had to be selective, to make hard decisions about what definitions to adopt, what topics to cover, and who to talk to, and there was undoubtedly some element of arbitrariness in those decisions. So what we offer is not a definitive verdict, but an honest account of our findings and conclusions, an assessment on which we hope others will build. The movement that we found presents a complicated, but by no means disheartening picture. The British women's movement has changed: in some senses it has declined, but in others it has developed, and it is still very much alive.


## DEFINITIONS AND TERMS

### Feminism and the Women's Movement

The terms that we have already used—'feminist', 'women's movement'—and many of those that we will use—'politics', 'Radical feminist', 'liberal', etc.—are contentious. For example, feminists disagree about many dimensions of the term 'feminist', and many political scientists would not regard feminist politics as politics at all. This means that we need to explain the way in which we use such terms, not because we claim absolute authority over them, but because it is necessary to make our conceptual framework clear.

First, what do we mean by 'feminism'? For the purposes of this book, we have opted for an enabling, fairly open definition of the term. We describe as feminist all ideologies, activities, and policies whose goal it is to remove discrimination against women and to break down the male domination of society.[1] Such a definition raises problems. Many women who are actively in pursuit of sex equality objectives of one kind or another, or who support such objectives, explicitly refuse to be labelled as feminists. This may be because the press has succeeded in caricaturing feminism as an extreme form of man-hating by unlovable, unattractive, humourless women, because of the alienating sectarianism of some feminist groups, or simply because of the difficulties of operating simultaneously in several very different environments. Some women are 'closet' feminists; others do not think they are feminists at all—the 'I am not a feminist, but . . .'

[1] This is Drude Dahlerup's definition. See her 'Introduction' to *The New Women's Movement: Feminism and Political Power in Europe and the USA* (Sage, London, 1986), 6.

syndrome. Many of those in the black women's movement have
objected to the term because they identify it with 'white' feminism. Some prefer the term 'womanism'. We feel that, despite
such reluctance, in the very broad sense that we have defined, all
these women should be included in a study of feminist politics.

Our concept of the 'women's movement' flows from our
understanding of feminism. We see it as comprising all those
individuals, networks, organizations, ideas, and practices that
espouse feminist values and goals. It is a tremendously diverse
and fluid phenomenon which cannot be reduced to one
approach, idea, or form of activity. The diversity of the women's
movement requires some description and explanation. It is
important to understand that the women's movement is itself
made up of a number of different movements. Historically, the
revival of British feminism in the late 1960s was launched by the
Women's Liberation Movement (WLM). But the feminism of
the nineteenth century generated organizations and traditions
that persist to this day, and these too are a component of the
women's movement. In addition, one dimension of the feminist
transformation of political institutions in Britain has been its
influence on traditional women's organizations. Such organizations have been both influenced by feminist ideas and infiltrated
by feminists. As a result, traditional churchwomen's organizations, the Women's Institute, the Soroptomists, women's auxiliaries, and other women's groups in Britain organize in support
of feminist goals, and in their 'feminist' mode they are sometimes referred to as 'liberal' or 'equal rights' feminists. This
strand of feminism was, in the 1970s, far less significant than its
equivalent in the United States, but it grew in both strength and
radicalism, and is now a force to be reckoned with in the feminist politics of the 1990s. Accordingly, we define the British
women's movement as the shifting coalition that includes the
WLM and the experienced women activists from the range of
British organizations; it draws in a large number of women who
are motivated by a strong commitment to sex equality, but who
may not be active in the WLM.

At the end of the 1960s and during the 1970s the WLM transformed British feminism, giving it a radical edge and energy that
had been absent for several decades. Although its emergence is
an interesting story, we do not account for it here, and we refer

readers to its extensive documentation elsewhere.[2] Instead, the chapters that follow will describe aspects of the early development of the WLM only where it is required to explain what happened later. Here we list its component elements.

It was the WLM that gave the women's movement of the 1970s many of its most characteristic features: the proliferation of small and local groups, the rejection of 'masculine' forms of hierarchical organization, the insistence on organizational separatism, the acknowledgement of the authentic voice of subjective experience as a political value, and the politicization of 'personal' issues such as abortion, sexuality, and gender relations themselves. Despite the repeated affirmation of 'sisterhood' in slogans and manifestos, the WLM was never really united, and, as time went by, an ideological rift between Radical and Socialist feminists widened, culminating in a bruising confrontation at the 1978 annual conference in Birmingham, the last national conference of the whole of the WLM. At the end of the 1970s, then, at least three distinct strands of the women's movement were active: the two WLM tendencies of Radical and Socialist feminists, and the equal rights activists of the wider women's movement.

During the 1980s the coalition grew more complex. The black women's movement and the Greenham Common movement are seen both as 'autonomous' women's movements and as offshoots of the WLM. The radicalization of women in established organizations made them feminists, but were they part of the WLM? This is a question that is worth raising not because there are ready answers, but because asking it alerts us to the shifting boundaries of the movement, demonstrating its complexity and thereby underlining the need to be clear about which element of it is under discussion. Thus, judgements that the women's movement or feminism was in decline during the 1980s have meaning only when they specify how the terms are being used. Very often such assessments refer to the WLM. There is little doubt that the WLM as we knew it in the 1980s did decline. But it is also

---

[2] See e.g. Anna Coote and Bea Campbell, *Sweet Freedom*, new edn. (Blackwell, Oxford, 1987); Sheila Rowbotham, *The Past Is before us* (Penguin, Harmondsworth, 1990); Amanda Sebestyen (ed.), *'68, '78, '88: From Women's Liberation to Feminism* (Prism, Bridport, 1988), Michelene Wandor, *Once a Feminist: Stories of a Generation* (Virago, London, 1990).

clear that important aspects of feminism gained in strength. We therefore argue against any simple, singular formulation of what has happened to the British women's movement. It has changed; it is no longer centred on the WLM. Today, it derives its energy from a number of intellectual and political sources; rather than dying, it is in important respects evolving and growing.

## Politics

'Politics' is another term that we need to define. There is a tendency within traditional political science to define politics narrowly as a purposive activity confined to a public decision-making domain. According to such formulations, politics is observable, and takes place in the public sphere. It does not go on in the 'private' sphere. For some time, radical political theorists have challenged that understanding, arguing that politics is essentially about power, which need be neither observable nor confined to a public arena. However, they have rarely ventured beyond that critique to challenge the notion that private or personal life is not political.

Feminists have drawn on the critical strain of political theory to mount a fundamental critique of narrow, conventional ways of understanding 'politics'.[3] Feminism insists that 'the personal is political', and rejects, both in theory and in practice, the entire distinction between private and public spheres. This is because, for many feminists, the very distinction between 'public' and 'personal' life exists only because of the asymmetric power relations between the sexes. Radical feminists regard conflict between men and women as *the* fundamental power relationship in society. Most feminists would agree that the distinction between 'public' and 'private' life is a convention that serves to conceal power relations between men and women. Once the convention is rejected, feminist politics may take place anywhere, and what was formerly understood as private life may be the most political of all sites of activity. Intimate and familial relationships may be shown to have a political dimension: for example, how you dress

---

[3] See the discussion of this critique by Vicky Randall, 'Feminism and Political Analysis', *Political Studies*, 39/3 (1991); and J. Lovenduski, 'Toward the Emasculation of Political Science', in Dale Spender (ed.), *Men's Studies Modified* (Pergamon, Oxford, 1981).

your little girl, or whether you let a man open a door for you, are decisions that have a political component. Since the end of the 1960s feminist campaigns have helped to politicize and bring on to the public agenda a succession of issues formerly associated with private or personal life: abortion and reproductive rights, women's health, domestic violence, incest, sexuality, and language are examples of this.

But the argument that politics is everywhere does not mean that all feminists explicitly want to be involved in politics. Radical feminists in particular have been wary of participation in the public politics of political parties, the state, or other organizations. They have theorized public political institutions as part of the apparatus of male dominance or patriarchy. Such institutions are organized on male hierarchical principles and around masculine interests. A deep mistrust of the public political sphere characterized the WLM in its early years, and a great ambivalence towards political institutions persisted well into the 1980s. Yet, from the outset, the WLM did address political authorities and did mount public political campaigns. Since then, feminists have increasingly engaged with the state in a variety of ways. The contradiction that this suggests is more apparent than real. Early feminist understandings of the state tended to parallel the simplistic and monolithic formulations that were offered by the 'New Left' in the 1960s and 1970s. In the 1980s, alongside general trends in the ideas of the political and intellectual Left in Europe, there were important developments in socialist feminist theorizations of the state, which recognized the plural arenas of the state as meaningful sites of struggle. In other words, feminist practice has always engaged with the state, and, as it has developed, feminist theory has found ways of explaining this.

Such considerations influence the way in which we approach feminist politics in this book. For much of our analysis we adhere to the broader understanding of politics as something that embraces power relationships in all aspects of our lives. But we have also retained the notion of a public political sphere, because the relationship between the two meanings of politics has been central to the development of the women's movement.

## Radical, Socialist, and Liberal Feminism

The meaning and significance of politics in general, and appropriate feminist political strategy in particular, has also been an issue of dispute between feminists. The starting point of Radical feminism is sex–class analysis, which asserts that gender is the fundamental division in society and the major determinant of power relations. During the 1970s such assertions were unacceptable to Socialist feminists, who at that time experienced little difficulty in expressing their theories in what Michelle Barrett has called a 'confident, materialist vein'.[4] The intellectual project of Socialist feminism developed from the determination of some feminists to maintain their socialist politics. At first they considered sexual politics to be mediated by, and often secondary to, class politics. But in the course of the 1980s that view shifted to more sophisticated understandings of different elements of political identities, and it became more difficult to distinguish the political strategies of Radical and Socialist feminists. Something akin to 'liberal' feminism became more influential, a development that further blurred the distinctions between feminist political strategies. If few women claim to be Liberal feminists, many pursue Liberal feminist goals of seeking to promote and integrate women into public life in the hope that the implementation of feminist policies will follow. In the British context, Liberal feminism is perhaps better understood as a strategy rather than as a movement. We show that it is a strategy that has steadily gained support from feminists.

## Patriarchy

As we have seen, Radical feminists have understood politics to be centrally about 'patriarchy'. This is a term that we invoke at various points of our analysis, so it also requires a few words of explanation. In everyday parlance, the word 'patriarchy' is used interchangeably with 'male dominance' or 'system of male dominance'.[5] There have been numerous attempts to develop systematic theories of patriarchy, but, not surprisingly, given the

[4] Michèle Barrett, *Women's Oppression Today*, rev. edn. (Verso, London, 1988), 'Introduction'.
[5] See Vicky Randall, *Women and Politics* (Macmillan, London, 1987), ch. 2.

enormity of the task, these have not yet been entirely successful or convincing. Ambiguities remain, both about the central features of patriarchy and about the means by which it is perpetuated. One of the earliest Radical feminist accounts stated that 'the principle of patriarchy appears to be two-fold: male shall dominate female, elder male shall dominate younger'.[6] In her influential book *The Sexual Contract* feminist theorist Carole Pateman argued that, in modern contract-based societies, patriarchy in its old form appears to have been overthrown: 'Patriarchy ceased to be paternal long ago. Modern civil society is not structured by kinship and the power of fathers; in the modern world, women are subordinated to men *as men*, or to men as fraternity. The original contract takes place after the political defeat of the father and creates modern *fraternal patriarchy*.'[7] The resulting 'sexual contract' is the basis of women's subordination. Pateman's thesis has not gone unchallenged,[8] but the way in which patriarchy has changed is an important theme of contemporary feminist analysis.

Feminists disagree about the mechanisms through which patriarchy is reproduced. Radical feminists have tended to emphasize the role of hierarchy—and especially of violence—in maintaining patriarchy. Socialist feminists worked long and hard to integrate explanations of patriarchy with the analysis of capitalism, though few by now would want simply to explain the former by the latter. In another influential recent work, *Theorising Patriarchy*, Sylvia Walby sought to structure the debate about patriarchy by formulating six distinct, though interrelated, patriarchal structures through which gender relations are constructed: paid employment, household production, culture, sexuality, violence, and the state. Her argument is that, partly in response to the successes of first-wave feminism, there has been a shift in Britain from a predominantly private form of patriarchy to one in which the public structure of state and market play a preponderant role.[9]

The arguments offered by Pateman and Walby are interesting

---

[6] Kate Millet, *Sexual Politics* (Abacus, London, 1972), 25.

[7] Carole Pateman, *The Sexual Contract* (Polity, Cambridge, 1988).

[8] See Diana Coole, 'Patriarch and Contract: Reading Pateman', *Politics*, 10/1, (1990).

[9] Sylvia Walby, *Theorising Patriarchy* (Blackwell, Oxford, 1990).

and have helped to move the debate on, but many central issues remain unresolved. This is, of course, partly due to the fact that the protagonists hold different basic beliefs, and we suspect that there will never be a very satisfactory theory of patriarchy. But that does not mean that it is a term we can do without. Despite its ambiguities and inadequacies, the idea expressed by the term 'patriarchy' is a key component of much of feminist political analysis. Although we are well aware of the shortcomings of the term, we use it here simply as a shorthand for what we see as a traditional and systematic male dominance of women.

## THE RESEARCH

Although we have denied ourselves the freedoms of the post-modernist rejection of the entire epistemological basis of social science, we fully recognize the problems of attempting to conduct 'unbiased', 'scientific' social research. Indeed, we cannot imagine what such research would look like. We are not unbiased. Not only are we feminists, but we incline more towards Socialist than Radical feminism (though one of us—Vicky Randall—is probably more sympathetic to Radical feminist arguments than the other). We both also strongly believe that feminists *should* be prepared to engage in public politics. But we do not see this book as an opportunity to judge or exhort other feminists. There is, after all, little point in telling a movement what to do. Our primary concern has been to improve our understanding of what has happened to the women's movement. Indeed, to the extent that we have been successful in this aim, we believe that this study, depressing though some of its findings will be for some feminists, is of greater value than either a polemic or an uncritical celebration.

Our account is shaped by the strategies that we devised to produce it. We were anxious to work from authentic sources and voices, but also to organize our analysis in a coherent way. To fulfil both goals, we adopted a two-part research strategy. First, we drew on the original demands of the WLM to identify a number of issues around which to research and analyse developments in feminist thinking, activity, and impact; to see how far and in what ways this original impulse was carried forward. We started with the aims of the WLM as agreed at the first national conference at Ruskin College in 1970. Four demands were adopted at Ruskin: equal pay; equal education and opportunity; twenty four-hour nurseries; free contraception and abortion on demand. In 1974, at the Edinburgh conference, two further demands were added, namely 'financial and legal independence for women', and 'an end to all discrimination against lesbians and a woman's right to choose her own sexuality'. In 1978, at Birmingham, the seventh and last demand was adopted: 'freedom from intimidation by threat or use of violence or sexual coercion, regardless of marital status; and an end to all laws, assumptions and institutions which perpetuate male dominance and men's aggression towards women'. Feminist activity and groups grew up around each of these demands, and the work and ideas developed and expanded in the years that followed. We have translated them into four of the organizing themes of this book, each with its own chapter: equality at work, health and reproductive rights, motherhood and child care, and sexuality and violence. To complete our account we added a fifth theme, that of women's citizenship and political representation.

Secondly, to research our five themes we sought to interview as wide a range of feminists as possible. Although the 'stars', the high-profile spokeswomen and theorists, could not be ignored, we were anxious to talk to those involved in everyday, local feminist activities. We were also aware of the danger of generalizing from the experience of London feminists to the rest of the country. Inevitably, the sheer size of London—and the volume of feminist activity there—required us to pay it considerable attention. But we visited and used material from Birmingham, Bristol, Edinburgh, Glasgow, Leeds, Leicester, Manchester, Nottingham, and Oxford.

In the course of our research we interviewed over 120 women. We consulted the publications of numerous feminist writers and made extensive use of feminist journals, including *Feminist Review*, *Spare Rib*, *Trouble and Strife*, *Everywoman*, and *Outwrite*. And we had access to the newsletters and other documentation of many women's organizations and local government women's units. Inevitably, we had to leave some things out. We do not, for instance, include Northern Ireland, partly because it deserves a study of its own, partly because of time and resource constraints. Originally, we had intended to cover in detail the development of feminism in the traditional women's organizations and the growth of women's studies in Britain. Though these areas receive passing mention, it proved impracticable to explore them comprehensively. They are important topics that must be left for others to consider.

## CONTEMPORARY FEMINIST POLITICS: SOME EMERGING THEMES

To recap: this book is an attempt to trace developments in the British women's movement since the end of the 1970s. It also seeks to explain those developments, in terms of both the movement's own internal dynamic and changes in its political and economic environment. We cannot report any amazing surprises. We did not, unfortunately, discover that, unbeknown to everyone, there is a vibrant, youthful, grass-roots feminist culture that thrives in different parts of the country. What we have pieced together is, however, a much more complex and, in many ways, encouraging picture than that invoked by simplistic and ill-informed talk of movement 'decline'. One feature of this picture is the tremendous variation, not only between regions, but also between cities, in the scale and forms of movement activity. There are real limits to the extent to which it is possible to generalize about the British women's movement.

But there has been decline, although it is more a feature of the WLM than it is of the women's movement as a whole, and, even so, the fortunes of the WLM have varied. Not only was there a burgeoning of the black women's movement and the Greenham movement in the middle of the 1980s, but mobilization over the issue of pornography at the beginning of the 1990s marked a return to 'classical' WLM concerns.

The decline of the WLM was exacerbated by internal conflicts. The battles between Radical and Socialist feminists rumbled on into the 1980s: indeed, they are still very much with us in the form of a vigorous theoretical debate. There were also bitter conflicts between white feminists and the black women's movement. These now seem to be subsiding. The growing importance of 'identity politics' made for conflict which has also been fuelled by the dilemmas that arise from increasing involvement with the state and its agencies.

Another feature of the 1980s was deradicalization. The more extreme, separatist Radical feminist arguments lost some of their grass-roots appeal over the years. But deradicalization is also part of the price of increasing integration. Feminists had to relinquish control of the definitions of issues that found their way on to mainstream political agendas. Increasingly reliant on state support, feminist organizations had to make their decision-making procedures more hierarchical and bureaucratic. Original goals to encourage self-help and 'empowerment' were threatened by the need to accept a more traditional relationship with the women who were assisted as 'clients'.

The growing involvement of feminist groups with state agencies was a striking development of the 1980s. The reasons for this are complex, but basically they are to do with changes in the orientation both of many women's groups and of local government. Perhaps most importantly, from 1982 and the creation of the Greater London Council (GLC) Women's Committee and Unit, there was a flowering of 'municipal feminism'. But there were drawbacks to this development. Feminist volunteers came under particular pressure when resources were cut back or withdrawn. Still, the value of the services to women at large, the encouragement to new feminist initiatives, and the accumulation of experience and skills amongst the women who were engaged must not be minimized.

In a similar, but perhaps more positive vein, is the increasing feminist penetration of mainstream institutions. The obvious and crucial areas here are the Labour Party and the trade unions, but feminists have also made inroads into several professions such as medicine and the law, and their influence has grown within the media and in academic life. Such developments have led to a steady diffusion of feminist perspectives and values. Thus, despite the best efforts of the moral Right, there has been no serious government attempt to turn back the clock of women's emancipation. Even during the difficult Thatcher years there were real policy gains regarding rape, domestic violence, and taxation, and the line was held on abortion.

So, the corollary of some decline in the WLM and of feminist deradicalization was increasing feminist activity in a range of political arenas, and a radicalization of women-related issues in mainstream institutions. The two processes are clearly connected, and in some ways this is inevitable and desirable. However, we are uneasy about WLM decline. We believe that, in the long run, feminists *inside* a system are more likely to be effective and motivated if there is a strong autonomous feminist movement *outside* the system. Indeed, without a continuing impulse from the grass roots, it is not clear in what sense one can talk about a 'movement' at all. We therefore take some heart from the continuing and unpredictable eruptions of vitality from the extra-institutional part of the movement.

So far we have sketched some of the main changes in the women's movement without offering much in the way of explanation. A good part of that explanation is specific, lying in the conjuncture of processes internal to the movement with changes in its economic and political environment. Nevertheless, it could be argued that what has happened to British feminism is what you would expect to happen to an ageing social movement. There is a large literature on social movements that draws attention to the fact that they always contain a mixture of more radical informal networks and conventional system-oriented organizations, and that, over time, the tendency is for increasing 'institutionalization' of one kind or another. The women's movement as it (re-)emerged in the 1960s was identified as one of a number of qualitatively distinct 'new' social movements (NSMs), which were, initially at least, expected to behave rather differently from the 'old' social movements. The NSMs were born out of student protest, and reflected in some way a crisis in industrial society and a rejection of materialist values. Some of the first writers on NSMs emphasized the extent to which they differed from the 'old' social movements in their preoccupation with lifestyle and cultural questions, their conscious opposition to hierarchical forms of organization, and their inclination towards unconventional forms of protest.[10]

Yet observers soon came to recognize that more traditional themes and more conventional political strategies and forms of organization were present in the NSMs. Moreover, they were

---

[10] For a discussion of these writers, see Alan Scott, *Ideology and the New Social Movements* (Unwin Hyman, London, 1990).

characterized by distinct tendencies towards 'institutionalization'. As Claus Offe wrote: 'Socio-political movements are extremely ill-equipped to deal with the problems of time.'[11] Faced by the difficulties of sustaining momentum, the *de facto* movement leaders, still committed to their original goals, will find the attractions of proper funding, formalized membership, structured decision-making, and the use of professional expertise hard to resist. Opposition to these tendencies will generate fierce conflicts within the movement, which may weaken the more 'spontaneous' element still further.

Although there is considerable enlightenment to be gleaned from the social movement literature, we would still argue that the women's movement has its own particular features. For example, 'identity politics' has been more prominent here than in the peace or ecology movements. The women's movement, at least the WLM, was to a large extent defined by the desire to 'liberate' women, to reveal the real women who had been so long obscured by male oppression. The movement was based on identity, the identity of women, hence the slogan 'sisterhood'. Clearly, the search for authentic identity was a key movement motivation.[12] However, the very idea of women's authentic identity was bound eventually to raise questions about what being a woman meant, and to lead to the discovery that there are actually enormous, possibly unbridgeable, differences between women.

Differences amongst its members were an important source of the movement's internal developments, but these were acted out in a context of rapidly changing social and economic circumstances. The movement was not suspended in air, but was part of a developing society. Our next chapter considers in some detail the social and economic trends of the 1980s, and the specific contribution of 'Thatcherism'. One of our conclusions is that, in a number of ways, the combined effect of these changes was to enhance women's 'autonomy' psychologically and in terms of relationships. As a result, feminist values continued to resonate.

[11] Claus Offe, 'Reflections on the Institutional Self-Transformation of Movement Politics: A Tentative Stage Model', in Russell Dalton and Manfred Kuechler (eds.), *Challenging the Political Order: New Social and Political Movements in Western Democracies* (Polity, Cambridge, 1990), 237.
[12] This argument is developed in Jonathan Rutherford, 'A Place Called Home: Identity and the Cultural Politics of Difference', in Jonathan Rutherford (ed.), *Identity, Community, Cultural Difference* (Lawrence and Wishart, London, 1990).

Over the same period of time, however, women neither achieved nor substantially improved their equality with men in terms of employment or income. Some women did very well. The Thatcher years accentuated the class differences between women. But most women had a hard time. The precise implications of these two conflicting trends for the women's movement are not altogether clear, but we can say that divisions within the movement were probably exacerbated by intensified class differences, and that, more generally, most women's availability for political activity was reduced.

Perhaps, though, the most crucial point is that there was a change in the 'political opportunity structure' during these years. This term, which derives from the social movement literature of the 1960s, has been progressively refined and is helpfully glossed by Sidney Tarrow.[13] The way in which a social movement becomes institutionalized will, to a significant degree, depend on what opportunities or constraints are presented by the political system as a whole. Our account suggests that, by the early 1980s, the political opportunity structure for feminism in Britain had altered. Perhaps the most important manifestation of this alteration was the fact that the Labour Party and the trade unions, in their hour of need, became much more receptive to feminist arguments.

To summarize: the decline and deradicalization of the British women's movement since the end of the 1970s was accompanied by, and in many ways was a consequence of, its greater involvement with state agencies and the growing presence of feminists in mainstream institutions. These developments cannot be understood as simply the continuation of the 'natural life cycle' of the movement; they must be related to the changing social and economic environment and to the changing political opportunity structures of the 1980s and early 1990s. The chapters that follow explain and develop these themes. Chapter 2 sets the context: it examines economic and social trends in the 1980s, the specific character and import of 'Thatcherism', and its sequel. Chapters 3 and 4 focus on feminism and the women's movement. The former considers the main trends and divisions in feminist ideas that

---

[13] Sidney Tarrow, *Struggle, Politics and Reform: Collective Action, Social Movements and Cycles of Protest* (Cornell University, Western Societies Paper 21, Ithaca, NY, 1991), 32–8.

are important to the later themes of this book, while the latter highlights important developments in the movement at grass roots. The next five chapters are explorations of the themes that form the core of our investigation: political representation and citizenship, equal employment opportunities, reproductive rights and health, motherhood and child care, and male violence. In the Conclusion we attempt to draw together the various strands of our analysis and to assess the state of feminist politics in Britain at the beginning of the 1990s.

# 2

# The 1980s in Britain: Political Framework, Economic Change, and 'Thatcherism'

BEFORE we can understand what has happened to the British women's movement since the late 1970s, we need to have a clearer idea of the context within which it developed and presently persists. This chapter examines the most relevant features of that context, and the ways in which they changed in the 1980s. The first section considers the general framework of political institutions and processes that may have influenced the movement's character and have certainly helped to determine the manner and degree of its impact. In the second and third sections we focus more specifically on the 1980s, looking at both the changing economic context and the ideology and policies associated with successive Thatcher governments, in order to arrive at some preliminary assessment of their implications for women and for feminism. Finally, and briefly, we assess the significance of any developments since John Major took over the leadership of the ruling Conservative Party in November 1990.

## THE NATURE OF POLITICS IN BRITAIN

This section is directed in particular to our non-British readers, but even those familiar on a day-to-day basis with the features of Britain's political system may find it useful to be reminded of what distinguishes it from other 'liberal democracies', notably those of the United States and Western Europe, and how this may be relevant for feminist politics. There are certain widely recognized, distinctive characteristics of the British political system whose historical roots go back well into the previous century and before, and which have survived to the present. We need to note the ways in which these features were accentuated or modified during the Thatcher years.

The British governmental process is very centralized, whether considered as national policy-making or as central–local relations. Formally speaking, sovereignty resides in Parliament, as distinct, say, from a written constitution. In practice, policy is largely made by the government created by the majority party in the Lower House, the House of Commons. Largely as a result of 'the first past the post' electoral system, which encourages selection of the 'safe' male (middle-class, white) candidate, women's representation in the House of Commons has remained pathetically low. Following the 1992 general election, it reached an all-time high of 9.2 per cent. Women's representation in government has therefore been minimal, with one particularly important exception, Mrs Thatcher herself.

The absence of a written constitution has meant that Britain does not have a tradition of constitutional interpretation through the courts (as, for instance, in the United States) which could provide an alternative channel for attempts to change policy.[1] Neither is there a Bill of Rights and concomitant culture of individual freedom and rights. This point needs to be qualified. From the 1970s there was a greater tendency to involve the courts in what could be called 'constitutional' disputes which arose in the context of more polarized party political conflict. Most relevantly for feminism, from the mid-1970s the European Community (EC) has issued successive directives aimed at promoting greater equality of opportunity between the sexes, which women have been able to invoke in British courts. But changing the attitudes and procedures of the judiciary—the 'legal culture', as it were—is an arduous business.

In making policy, the national government is dependent both for advice and for policy implementation on its ostensibly 'neutral' civil service, which is also highly centralized and works under conditions of great secrecy. The neutrality of civil servants, collectively and individually, has always been open to question, and under Mrs Thatcher it has regularly been suggested that party political considerations have influenced top administrative

[1] See Joni Lovenduski, 'Implementing Equal Opportunities in the 1980s: An Overview', Public Administration 67 (Spring 1989)

appointments. None the less, as Meehan[2] argues, British feminists have had to contend with a particular type of bureaucratic culture, where, for instance, it would be extremely difficult to form the kinds of networks between women inside government and feminist groups outside that have been so important in the United States. This ethos has extended to 'quasi-government organizations' such as the Equal Opportunities Commission itself, although, as Chapter 6 will describe, there are now indications that this may be changing. In these circumstances, feminists have been better able to influence government policy if co-opted into the policy process on the basis of their 'expertise'. However, this is a painfully slow process, and raises the usual problems about the isolation and accountability of such 'femocrats'.

The insulation of the government process is reinforced by its highly unitary character. There is no significant regional level of decision-making, as in the United States, Italy, or the old German Federal Republic. Local authorities in Britain have been entirely the creations of Parliament, set up and abolished by statute, with carefully enumerated powers and duties devolved to them and as easily removed from them. Again this point needs qualification. Local authorities have always had important things to do, especially with the expansion of the Welfare State. Their responsibilities are, moreover, of particular interest to women and feminists, concerning, as they do, such areas as housing, social work, child care. The liveliness of local party politics has ensured that, in practice, local authorities have always been more than simply agents of central government. Under the terms of the 1964 London Government Act and the 1974 Local Government Act, new regional authorities were established for London and six of the major conurbations. Following the 1979 general election which led to the formation of the first Thatcher government, these 'metropolitan' authorities—and, most dramatically, the GLC—became the focus of Labour resistance to Conservative national policies. Predictably, this role was cut short when, in 1984, all the metropolitan authorities were simply abolished.

Not only have the powers of British local government traditionally been limited, but, under Mrs Thatcher, successive measures restricted them still further. Most importantly, both central

[2] Elizabeth Meehan, *Women's Rights at Work: Campaigns and Policy in Britain and the United States* (Macmillan, London, 1985).

government grants and the ability of individual local authorities to overshoot centrally determined spending levels were severely cut back. The extent of local authority discretion in specific policy areas, most notably housing, was also reduced. Yet local government has been a major, if not *the* major, arena of feminist activity in the 1980s. This is principally because of changes in the composition and attitudes of local Labour leaderships, including, as we shall see, their greater receptivity to feminist initiatives.

As the last point reminds us, our account of the British political system would be incomplete without reference to party politics. Despite all that has been said, Britain is, of course, a 'democracy'. Regular national elections are held, in which the main political parties compete to acquire control of the governmental machine that we have been describing. However, even in this regard, it could be said that British politics exhibits a degree of inflexibility, of limited choice, from a feminist perspective. Since the Second World War at least, party competition has been dominated by two parties, Conservative and Labour, which, simplifying a good deal, could be identified with the interests of business and the middle class in the first case, and labour and the working class in the other.

An important factor contributing to this effectively two-party system has been the 'first past the post' electoral system. In contrast to a great number of West European states, which enjoy some form of proportional representation, the British system means that only one candidate, the one who receives a plurality of votes, can be elected for each constituency. The effect, at least in conjunction with the geographical distribution of the parties' voters, has been to magnify the electoral majority of the winning party, in terms of seats awarded in the House of Commons. It has also reinforced the dominance of the two major parties, helping to perpetuate the present two-party system. For instance, the Conservatives won 42.4 per cent of the vote in 1983, but this gave them 397, or well over half, of the 650 parliamentary seats. The Labour Party, with 27.5 per cent of the vote, had 200 seats, again rather more than their share of the vote indicated. On the other hand, the new 'centre' Alliance, with 25.3 per cent of the vote, had no more than 4 seats. Not surprisingly, given both the difficulties faced by the Alliance and the strong policies imposed by the ruling Conservative Party with less than half of the nation's voters behind it, the issue of electoral reform attracted increasing attention in the course of the Thatcher decade.

Although the exact relationship between feminism and the Conservative Party is something that we shall want to explore and that has certainly been changing in the 1980s,[3] feminists' main hopes in this two-party scenario have clearly lain with the Labour Party. Historically, the Left has tended to be the best bet for feminists in a great number of countries, and yet it is hardly a reliable ally.[4] In Britain the Labour Party has been closely linked with a trade-union movement strongly patriarchal in its assumptions and practices, at least until recently. Both Labour Party and unions have traditionally pursued goals and been identified with constituencies to which women were perceived as quite marginal. Given the importance of the Labour Party for British feminism, we shall have much more to say about it, notably in Chapter 5.

The strength of the Left in Britain (the most obvious contrast is with the United States) has contributed to the character of the women's movement, creating, we shall argue, both opportunities and weaknesses. By the late 1970s, changes in the nature of the Labour Party leadership, especially at local level (as already noted), offered new opportunities for socialist feminists to influence party policy. But this also increased the dependence of feminist initiatives upon the fortunes and favour of the local Labour Party.

There *have* been other political parties. From the early 1970s, while the politics of the two main parties appeared to polarize, psephologists noted a significant decline in electoral support for both of them—the phenomenon of 'dealignment'. In this context, first the fortunes of the small Liberal Party appeared to revive, and later, in the early 1980s, a fragment of the Labour Party broke away, calling itself the Social Democratic Party (SDP), and formed an alliance with the Liberals. Eventually, after the 1987 general election, the Liberals and most of the Social Democrats merged to form one party, the Liberal Democrats. The rump of the old SDP, which refused to merge, finally dissolved. These centre parties did show an increasing sensitivity to a number of

[3] See e.g. Bea Campbell, *The Iron Ladies* (Virago, London, 1987).
[4] See Vicky Randall, 'Women and the Left in Europe: A Continuing Dilemma', *Western European Politics*, 9/2 (1986).

feminist issues, providing some additional limited opportunity for feminists in the Labour and Conservative Parties to pressure for more change in their own programmes. Another party to emerge in the 1980s, the Greens, never offered the same apparent electoral challenge to Labour and Conservative (contrasting in particular with experience in Germany), but took on board and helped to disseminate a number of feminist assumptions and organizational values.

We must also acknowledge here the existence of regional and (sub-)national variations. Electoral support for each of the two main parties has tended to concentrate in specific geographic areas. Under Mrs Thatcher in particular, the Conservatives were clearly strongest in the south, and especially the south-east, while Labour was strongest in the north, Wales, and Scotland. But in addition there have been significant nationalist movements and parties in Scotland and in Wales. Their heyday was perhaps in the mid-1970s, when the issue of devolution briefly assumed a prominent position in the British political agenda. After the devolution referendum was lost, in 1979, their support may have subsided for a while. However, in Scotland, in particular, the experience of Conservative rule under Mrs Thatcher soon helped to revive nationalist feelings. This is both because the Conservative Party had so few Scottish MPs and because the government pursued unpopular and centralizing policies. The Scottish National Party (SNP) itself began to demand complete political independence, in the context of fuller integration into the European Community. On the other hand, in 1989 a Scottish Constitutional Convention, including all parties except the SNP and the Conservative Party, drew up a Claim of Right demanding a Scottish Assembly. This issue raised important questions about women's representation for Scottish feminists (see Chapter 5).

None the less, the most important point to stress here is the extent to which, traditionally, the party system—and, indeed, popular political culture itself—has been dominated by notions of 'class'. That dominance has more recently been challenged. For a long time sociologists and political scientists have questioned not only conventional class distinctions, but even the utility of class as a basic analytic category for explaining social and political developments in Britain. Certainly, in the 1980s the Labour Party leadership tried to get away from its traditional 'cloth cap' working-class image, while the Conservative Party under Mrs Thatcher insisted on the irrelevance of class and succeeded in appealing across perceived class divisions, capturing around one half of the 'working-class' vote. In one sense, then, British politics is much less about class then it once was. And yet in another sense it could be argued that, after the surge of liberalism and Scottish and Welsh nationalism in the 1970s, the effect of Thatcherism was to bring class firmly back into the centre of the political agenda. The central thrust of Thatcherism has been the neo-liberal economic policies—attacking the prerogatives of trade unions, cutting welfare, and so forth (as we shall discuss shortly)—which can readily be interpreted as a move away from an emphasis on social harmony and consensus, and a move towards recognition of conflicting (class) interests. At the very least, then, we can say that the issue of class dominated the political 'discourse' of the Left within which Socialist and Radical feminists first sought to elaborate and assert their distinctive arguments. It has perhaps been easier more recently and intellectually for feminists to discount class, or at least to assign it less importance. On the other hand, the practical impact of policies under Mrs Thatcher has in some ways underlined the relevance of class differences for women.

British feminists, then, have had to operate within a remarkably centralized, unitary government system. Despite its professed intention of rolling back the state, government under Mrs Thatcher actually reinforced this centralization, especially in central–local relations. Feminists have also had to contend with a juridical tradition unused to questions of constitutional interpretation and, more pertinently, to the language of abstract 'rights', and a bureaucratic culture which is secretive and eschews any overt political association. Again, although feminism has enjoyed all the undoubted political advantages of operating within a democracy (however we might want to qualify that term), effective party competition has been largely restricted to two political parties, both of which are traditionally rather 'conservative' in their perceptions and ways of going about things. They are also both, of course, patriarchal, though, partly thanks to feminism itself, this may be beginning to change. Finally, feminists have had to operate within the parameters of a popular political culture which has been largely dominated, at least until recently, by notions of social class.

## THE CHANGING DEMOGRAPHIC AND ECONOMIC CONTEXT OF THE 1980s

Having suggested some of the long-term constraints imposed upon post-war feminism by the nature of British politics, we must now focus our attention more specifically on the context of feminism in the 1980s. In her discussion of the experience of women in Scotland, Esther Breitenbach[5] makes a useful distinction between equality and autonomy. Equality refers to women's access to opportunities and resources, as compared with men's. Autonomy focuses on the individual woman's freedom within personal relationships, for instance control over her *own* fertility, and access to housing in her *own* name. The central theme of this section will be that, during the 1980s, women in Britain have gained greater autonomy, though not greater equality.

We shall first consider relevant social and economic changes, and then examine the specific impact of Thatcherism. While we do not intend to argue that developments in the women's movement are simply the result of changes in its environment, these clearly have a tremendous bearing. Again, while it is no coincidence that the period we have selected for study includes the three Thatcher governments—and, indeed, a central concern of this book is the relationship between feminism and the Thatcher phenomenon—we do not intend to imply any simple identification of Thatcherism with the major economic, social, and political developments of these years. Later in this chapter we shall look further at what is meant by 'Thatcherism'. At this stage we want to make the more obvious but important point that many of the changes that have affected women's status and opportunities in Britain since the late 1970s have their counterpart in countries throughout the Western world. This is particularly true of the two key areas we are examining in this section: patterns of family life, and employment opportunity.

From the 1970s and continuing into the 1980s there have been a number of gradual changes in the pattern of family life in

[5] Esther Breitenbach, 'The Impact of Thatcherism on Women in Scotland', in Alice Brown and David McCrone (eds.), *The Scottish Government Yearbook (1989)* (Unit for the Study of Government in Scotland, Department of Government, University of Edinburgh, Edinburgh, 1989)

Britain which, cumulatively, have considerable implications for women. First, there has been a decline in the overall marriage rate. According to Malcolm Wicks,[6] this is partly a consequence of people marrying later—in the 25–9 age group, 31 per cent of women remained unmarried in 1987, compared with 13 per cent in 1971—although it also reflects the increasing popularity of cohabitation. By 1989, 27 per cent of children were born out of wedlock. At the same time there has been a dramatic and widely remarked increase in the rate of divorce: it is presently estimated that nearly four out of every ten new marriages will end this way, although remarriage rates are also high.

There has also been a decline in the birth rate. Between 1970 and 1987 the number of children per woman fell from 2.44 to 1.82.[7] Women are having their first child later, and more women are remaining childless. A survey recently cited in the *Guardian*[8] found that whereas ten years previously only one in fifty British adults favoured having just one child, the figure is now one in ten.

Such trends are not confined to Britain; in broad terms, they are observable in most industrial democracies over the last two to three decades. There are, of course, variations between countries. Britain has the highest rate of increase in divorce of any EC nation, while the decline in its birth rate is less than in most of its EC partners (partly because its birth rate was relatively low to start with). But the similarity in the general pattern of change points to common underlying and long-term causes: material factors such as greater affluence and improved methods and dissemination of contraception, together with cultural change, especially growing secularization.

At face value, these trends would seem to indicate greater independence and hence progress for women. But while the influence of feminist ideas on women's expectations has probably played some part in promoting them, the consequence of current demographic trends for women has not necessarily or always been benign. This is most evident in the situation of single mothers, whose numbers have steadily grown. Between 1971 and 1989 in

[6] Malcolm Wicks, 'The Battle for the Family', *Marxism Today*, Aug. 1990.

[7] Anna Coote, Harriet Harman, and Patricia Hewitt, *The Family Way* (Institute for Public Policy Research, London, 1990).

[8] See the *Guardian*, 29 July 1991.

Britain the proportion of all families with dependent children whose household was headed by a single parent increased from 8 to 17 per cent. Nearly nine out of ten single parents are women, and the growth in single-parent families was accounted for in particular by an increasing percentage of divorced or single mothers. It is true that single parenthood does not tend to be a permanent state. According to one study, 60 per cent of the single mothers were no longer without a partner by the time the child was 5.[9] None the less, Britain has one of the highest rates in Europe, although it is a trend reported from most EC countries and from the United States. Going back to Breitenbach's distinction between autonomy and equality, we could conclude that these changes in household composition and fertility rates have increased women's autonomy, but not necessarily contributed to greater equality with men.

Changes in family structure are one cause—they may also be a result—of women's more active search for paid employment. In Britain, as in other Western democracies, there has been a steady increase in women's, especially married women's, paid employment since the last war. It is helpful to contrast two main phases in the post-war development of individual Western industrialized economies which have in turn been associated with distinctive employment structures and opportunities for women.[10] After the war and lasting into the late 1960s, these economies entered an era of relative stability and prosperity, with a growth in mass production based on demand in the home market and on governments' use of 'Keynesian' methods of economic regulation. This period saw a steady rise in female employment. In particular, women were drawn into the expanding service sector, whether into the public sector of the more developed Welfare States or, as in the case of the United States, into the private service sector.

Already in the 1960s these economies were coming under pressure, and by the 1970s a major process of economic restructuring was under way. The sources of this pressure were many and

[9] See John Ermisch and R. E. Wright, 'Welfare Benefits and the Duration of Single Parenthood', *National Institute of Economics Review*, 130 (Nov. 1989).

[10] See the valuable discussion by Jane Jenson and Elizabeth Hagen, 'Paradoxes and Promises: Work and Politics in the Postwar Years', in Jane Jenson, Elizabeth Hagen, and Ceallaigh Reddy (eds.), *Feminization of the Labour Force* (Polity, Cambridge, 1988).

are disputed: a general worsening of the economies' competitive position, particularly in the face of rivals in the newly industrializing countries (NICs); energy costs exacerbated by oil price rises in the early 1970s and again in the early 1980s; changing consumer expectations. The response of business was to cut production, to rationalize, and to search for ways of increasing flexibility—through, for instance, the employment of new technology and the use of part-time workers. One consequence was rising unemployment. By 1975 there were already 15m. people out of work in all the OECD countries; by the early 1980s the figure stabilized at around 30m.

As far as can be gleaned from official figures—and the difficulties both of defining and of measuring female unemployment must especially be borne in mind—the specific implications of this restructuring for women's employment have not been entirely negative. First, as Jenson and Hagen emphasize,[11] one should not idealize the pattern of women's employment in the earlier post-war era. It entailed extensive job segregation and stereotyping, and inequality of pay. Second—and taking the OECD countries as a whole—although as unemployment grew, in the 1960s and 1970s, female rates were generally higher than male, by the early 1980s the rate of increase in female unemployment was slightly less than it was for men, although the absolute female rate remained higher than the male rate. But thirdly, and most positively, while the male economic participation rate declined slowly but steadily throughout the 1970s and the first half of the 1980s, the reverse was true for women. Despite the protracted economic 'crisis', women sought paid work in ever-increasing numbers. Their participation rate climbed from 45.6 per cent in 1970 to 55.9 per cent in 1984.[12] These differences are partly due to the relatively low numbers of women in the vulnerable manufacturing sector and to their disproportionate concentration in the service sector, which went on expanding at least into the early 1980s. They also reflect the demographic changes noted earlier. But, finally, they have to do with the new demand for part-time workers.

[11] Ibid.
[12] See Isabella Bakker, 'Women's Employment in Comparative Perspective', in Jenson et al. (eds.), Feminization.

The imperatives of restructuring, with its emphasis on flexibility, made part-time work particularly attractive for employers. From 1973, in OECD countries, there was a marked growth in part-time employment; this effectively meant in female part-time employment, since the part-time workforce is overwhelmingly female in all countries. So, the specific needs of employers for part-time workers provided employment opportunities for women. However, there are several negative implications of recent economic developments for women's employment opportunities. Most significantly, women have been increasingly concentrated in part-time work. By the mid-1980s, over 30 per cent of the female workforce in Sweden, Canada, and the United Kingdom and almost 25 per cent in the United States and Germany, worked part-time. This feminization of part-time work perpetuates patterns of job segregation. There are other disadvantages in part-time work. Bakker invokes the OECD's distinction here between 'voluntary' and 'involuntary' part-time work: its report[13] suggests that 'involuntary part-time working occurs when a worker is forced to take a part-time job instead of a full-time job because of the difficulty of finding the latter', and cites evidence for Canada and the United States which indicates that this is on the increase. Part-time work also tends to exclude employees from various forms of benefit and job protection, pro-rata pay is lower, and part-time workers are less likely to be unionized—all reasons, of course, why employers find it attractive.

The changing pattern of women's employment opportunities in Britain, then, is not unique; it has parallels in other industrialized economies, and must be understood in the context of worldwide economic change. The absolute rate of female employment climbed steadily throughout the 1970s, dipped in the early 1980s, but recovered sooner than male employment, by 1985–6. The rate of employment for married women had climbed to 50 per cent by 1975, and remained broadly at that level thereafter. But, most significantly, the rate of employment for mothers with dependent children (that is, under 16, or under 19 but in full-time education and living at home) was 52 per cent by 1979, fell during the recession to 46 per cent by 1983, but then rose to 59 per cent by

[13] OECD. *Employment Outlook* (Paris, 1983).

1989. The rate of employment for mothers with children under 5 rose from 24 per cent in 1983 to 41 per cent by 1989, though this was low in comparison with many other European countries, and only 12 per cent were in full-time employment while the remaining 29 per cent worked part-time.[14] At the same time, there was a continuous increase in the overall proportion of women in paid employment who were working part-time, from 33.5 per cent in 1971 to 42.5 per cent in 1989.[15]

As in the case of demographic trends, and especially when taken in conjunction with them, we can see that these developments do not of themselves imply greater equality for women, although they may suggest greater autonomy. The increasing numbers of women in paid employment may partly reflect their desire for greater financial independence and personal fulfilment, but it could also be a consequence of the growing number of women who need to support themselves and, in many cases, their dependants. The striking predominance of women amongst part-time workers—94 per cent in 1981—does not necessarily reflect women workers' preferences, but is equally a function of the pressures of poverty, the kind of work available, and the inadequacy of childcare provision.

Our last point demonstrates the difficulty of disentangling the outcomes of economic 'forces' from those of government policy. So far we have discussed the opportunities and difficulties posed for women by changes in the job market and as a result of broader demographic trends. We need now to consider how these interacted with government policies through the 1980s. This brings us to an examination of the phenomenon of 'Thatcherism'.

## DEFINING 'THATCHERISM'

Despite the controversy and complexities surrounding the concept of Thatcherism (see below), we do believe that it refers to a meaningful political entity. Thatcherism was an important independent factor shaping British political life in the 1980s, and it had real

[14] Figures from the 1989 General Household Survey, cited in the *Guardian*, 31 Oct. 1990.
[15] See Jane Humphries and Jill Rubery, 'Recession and Exploitation: British Women in a Changing Workplace, 1979–1985', in Jensen *et al.* (eds.), *Feminization*.

consequences both for women and the women's movement. For that reason, it merits separate discussion in this chapter.

Before seeking to characterize Thatcherism for ourselves, it is necessary briefly to refer to the ways in which it has been analysed. There is, not surprisingly, a colossal literature on the subject by now, ranging from rarified theory to anecdotal journalism. However, although the concept has been approached from enormously different viewpoints, and conclusions appear at first sight to diverge widely, on close inspection there turns out to be considerable common ground.

One of the most basic areas of disagreement amongst commentators on the Thatcher years is whether there is actually such a thing as Thatcherism, or whether it is simply the invention of academics and the media. The answer to this question, of course, depends on what one takes Thatcherism to be. Is it a style of leadership, a distinct and coherent political ideology, or, more than these, a systematic programme of action largely coterminous with government policy under Mrs Thatcher?

An important distinction here is between the 'holistic' approach adopted by a number of influential neo-Marxist writers, including Stuart Hall and Andrew Gamble, which has depicted Thatcherism as a comprehensive and powerful political 'project', and views that are more 'partial', both in their narrow understanding of Thatcherism and in their estimation of its significance. As Marxists, exponents of the 'holistic' approach have had ultimately to link Thatcherism with economic change, more specifically the changing requirements of capital, but they have rejected any simple notion of functionality. Instead they have invoked Antonio Gramsci's idea of the 'hegemonic project'. Their argument is that the process of economic restructuring begun in the late 1960s necessitated a radical restructuring of society and its values. In order to create the necessary political coalition and popular support to sustain this social transformation, appeal had to be made to a whole range of interests and 'discourses'. For a time at least, the Thatcherite project, with its distinctive blend of neo-liberal and authoritarian values, was singularly successful in achieving and maintaining this 'hegemony'. Mrs Thatcher was able to impose her agenda and to dictate the terms of political debate. Her government consistently pursued a related set of policy objectives which both drew upon and reinforced processes of social restructuring, undermining of working-class solidarities, and the 'privatization' of politics.[16]

With the passage of time, the proponents of this approach themselves became more cognizant of the political weaknesses of Thatcherism. Others were always more sceptical about its importance. For example, other Marxists took a rather more determinist line. They emphasized the extent to which Thatcherism was not unique but was part of an international trend, as states adapted to the changing requirements of capital.[17] And a number of political scientists, ranging from centre Left to centre Right, have offered their own interpretations. One widely cited paper focuses on Mrs Thatcher's 'statecraft'. It argues that what is distinctive about Mrs Thatcher is that she has been a strong leader and has successfully reasserted the independent authority of government. However, in so doing, rather than breaking radically new ground ideologically or in terms of policy, she has remained true to a basic Conservative tradition. And while Thatcherism at the level of ideology has been reasonably cohesive, its function has been to legitimize policies that have been determined largely on the basis of pragmatic considerations.[18]

Others have pointed out that political support for Mrs Thatcher was always qualified. She captured the Tory leadership in 1975 almost by default. Not only did the 'first past the post' electoral system, as usual, translate the Conservative share of the vote—only 42 per cent in 1983 and 1987—into a much larger proportion of parliamentary seats, but, at least from 1979, the trend of public opinion was away from specifically 'Thatcherite' policies. Neither the electorate nor most Conservative MPs were ever Thatcherite on a strict understanding of the term.[19]

[16] These arguments were developed in a succession of writings, but see in particular the articles by Stuart Hall and by Andrew Gamble in *Marxism Today*; Stuart Hall and Martin Jacques (eds.), *The Politics of Thatcherism* (Lawrence and Wishart, London, 1983); and Andrew Gamble, *The Free Economy and the Strong State* (Macmillan London, 1988).

[17] See e.g. Bob Jessop *et al.*, 'Authoritarian Populism: Two Nations and Thatcher', *New Left Review*, 147 (1986).

[18] See Jim Bulpitt, 'The Discipline of the New Democracy: Mrs Thatcher's Domestic Statecraft', *Political Studies*, 4/1 (1986).

[19] See Ivor Crewe and Donald Searing, 'Ideological Change in the British Conservative Party', *American Political Science Review*, 82/2 (1988); and Ivor Crewe, 'Has the Electorate Become Thatcherite?', in Robert Skidelsky (ed.), *Thatcherism* (Blackwell, Oxford, 1989).

Our own position is that Thatcherism was not simply a conjuring trick or a media fantasy, although Mrs Thatcher and her entourage showed themselves extremely adept at using the media to project a compelling image. Thatcherism refers to more than a style of leadership. The ideology of Thatcherism showed numerous inconsistencies and ambiguities, but which ideology does not? Nor was the ideology purely rhetorical. On the contrary, the 1980s witnessed a steadfast drive to implement a number of its central policy thrusts. Even though these were not always successful in their own terms, they had a major impact on people's lives, sometimes in unforeseen ways. Finally, while there is no question but that the Thatcherite programme was closely connected to the changes in Britain's economic situation and to the interests of at least a section of the business community, and that, in this, it resembled policies of the 'New Right' in the United States and elsewhere, neither the particular emphases of its ideology nor its success in dominating the political system for over a decade were inevitable.

Before we can discuss its specific implications for women in more detail, however, we do need to 'unpack' the concept of Thatcherism a little further. One question that needs to be raised is the relationship between Thatcherism and the New Right. Like 'Thatcherism', the latter term has been variously and inconsistently employed. Here, however, we will take it to refer in Britain to a surge of right-wing political groups and ideas from the 1970s. This movement clearly fed into Thatcherism's ideology and sources of political support. But the two are not synonymous. Not all New Right ideas were significantly taken up in Thatcherism, and policies under Mrs Thatcher were frequently criticized by New Right spokespersons for not going far enough.

This connects with a second important point, the lack of agreement on what 'Thatcherism' should cover. Does it relate specifically to Mrs Thatcher's own preferences and actions? Or to the values of her governments as a whole, as expressed explicitly or implied by their policies? Or is there some 'essence' of Thatcherism which is neither of these, and against which they can be measured? There are methodological problems and analytical limitations in all these approaches. In practice, it seems wisest to understand Thatcherism as referring to an ideology closely associated with Mrs Thatcher and certain of her colleagues and with the key areas of government policy which it has informed.

But beyond these definitional ambiguities, as we have already noted, it is widely agreed that, as an ideology, Thatcherism itself was in many ways contradictory and ambiguous. Most fundamentally, it is seen to have comprised two main, and possibly conflicting, strands. The first of these is variously identified as liberalism, economic liberalism, or neo-liberalism. With its more recent intellectual origins in the work of F. A. Hayek, though going back to the classical liberal economists, the core tenet of this strand, in Desmond King's words, is the 'superiority of market mechanisms as a promoter both of economic prosperity (because of the supposed greater efficiency of the market in the allocation and use of scarce resources); and of the maximisation of individual freedom through the limiting of state intervention'.[20]

With the apparent failure of Keynesian economic strategies, and influenced in particular by the writings of Milton Friedman as popularized within the Conservative Party by Keith Joseph and Mrs Thatcher herself in the 1970s, economic liberalism came for a time to be identified with the more specific philosophy of monetarism, or the view that the main—or, for the purists, the only—means by which governments should seek to influence the economy was through control of the money supply. The first Thatcher government began with a broadly monetarist approach. It restricted money supply, but also attached great importance to reducing the public sector borrowing requirement (PSBR), although King and others suggest that this does not strictly follow from monetarist principles. While this approach did succeed in reducing inflation, it was also associated with a dramatic rise in unemployment. Therafter there was much greater emphasis on 'supply-side' economic policies, supposedly freeing up the factors of production, such as deregulation, privatization, and attacking the 'restrictive practices' of trade unions.

The political dimension of economic liberalism, though never articulated in the same detail, would seem to be the importance of individual freedom, and, as a corollary, a minimal, 'nightwatchman' role for the state. Certainly, within the New Right, there are the 'libertarians' who do argue for a minimalist

---

[20] Desmond King, *The New Right* (Macmillan, London, 1987), 9.

government or state. Within Thatcherism, however, libertarian arguments are rarely invoked. Indeed, Andrew Gamble has gone so far as to suggest that, within the logic of neo-liberalism itself, there is, paradoxically, an imperative towards a strong state. This is needed, first, to intervene in the domestic economy in order to free up the market, and, secondly, to provide the military presence to protect economic interests abroad.[21] King modifies this argument, pointing out that one can distinguish between government and state. In a neo-liberal regime, measures to free up the market might require a strong government, but the state, in the sense of the public sector, including welfare services and state-run enterprise, would diminish.

Neo-liberalism itself, and particularly its political ramifications, is by no means lacking in internal ambiguities and possible contradictions. We would still feel confident in saying that, in some broad sense, it has had an enormous influence not only on economic policy, but on policies in fields such as social security and trade-union regulation, seen to have a direct bearing upon the success of economic policy. It has even been extended to areas—most notably, the health services—where any economic consequences are likely to be much less direct. The success with which the values of self-reliance and enterprise have been instilled in the public at large is much more debatable; collectivist notions appear to die hard.[22]

The other strand of Thatcherism is again variously identified as traditional authoritarianism, conservatism, or neo-conservatism. King characterizes 'conservatism' in this sense as essentially pre-capitalist in orientation, with an organic view of society and its relationship to the state. It values hierarchy and order, and regrets the threat to these values posed by the expansion of the Welfare State and social democracy. It sees the patriarchal family as the bedrock of social order. This kind of conservatism is, of course, implicitly critical of, and to be distinguished from, the values actually espoused by the post-war Conservative Party leadership. It also appears, characterized in this way, to be diametrically opposed to many aspects of neo-liberalism.

[21] Gamble, *Economy and State*.

[22] See e.g. Ivor Crewe, 'Values: The Crusade that Failed', in Dennis Kavanagh and Anthony Seldon (eds.), *The Thatcher Effect* (Oxford University Press, Oxford, 1989).

In sorting out the different areas of Thatcherite conservatism, it is helpful again to bear in mind the distinction drawn earlier between Thatcherism and the New Right. While the New Right has contained individuals and groups advocating 'conservative' policies on the whole range of issues, their penetration of Thatcherite positions has been uneven. One aspect of this conservatism apparent in Thatcherism has been a form of patriotism, nationalism, or its detractors might even want to call it neo-imperialism, which was most obviously manifest in the Falklands/ Malvinas episode. That this could conflict with the transnational logic of economic liberalism emerged in the final confrontation within the Cabinet over Britain's relationship to the EC, although, of course, Mrs Thatcher was able to argue that the EC was itself a hindrance to international free trade.

Closely allied with this, many have seen racist undertones in Thatcherism. Before she became Prime Minister, Mrs Thatcher made a television appearance, following which electoral support for the Conservatives jumped by several points, in which she talked of the danger of British family life being 'swamped' by alien cultures.[23] In the prevailing climate of race relations in Britain, it is difficult to view this remark as an innocent one. And it is often noted that the activity and electoral appeal of neo-fascist groups declined with the advent of the first Thatcher government. However, whilst it has certainly been promoted by several New Right tendencies, overt racism has not been a prominent feature of Thatcherism. Immigration policies have been discriminatory, but this was not a new departure; it was continuing a trend which Labour governments had played a significant part in fostering.

Authoritarianism is another value integral to conservatism, and one which many have detected in Thatcherism. In terms of overt pronouncements, it is most obvious in the emphasis on law and order. In the aftermath of the 1981 inner-city riots, Stuart Hall was already referring to the 'drift into a heavily-policed authoritarian democracy',[24] confirmed for many by the policing of the miners' strike in 1984. A number of Conservative MPs—but, in the government, most prominently Norman Tebbitt—regularly called for the restoration of 'decency and order'.[25]

[23] Cited in Gamble, *Economy and State*, 136–7.
[24] See *Marxism Today*, Sept./Oct. 1981.
[25] See Martin Durham, *Sex and Politics: The Family and Morality in the Thatcher Years* (Macmillan, London, 1991).

As we have already seen, a number of critics of neo-liberalism have pointed to the paradox that, in practice, its economic prescriptions require a strong state. The suggestion has been made that, lacking an adequate account of the state within its own body of theory, neo-liberalism has been able instead to invoke conservatism's much fuller and more considered account to rationalize this need. Neo-conservative writers like Roger Scruton and other contributors to the *Salisbury Review* have deplored the weakening of the state in the era of social democracy and expanding social citizenship rights. They have emphasized the authority of the state and its essential role in maintaining social order and protecting property. Thatcherism has been able to borrow from these arguments.

There is little doubt that in some respects Thatcherism has, in practice, entailed the strengthening of state authority—the attack on the unions and on local government being only two of the most obvious domestic examples of what Ralf Dahrendorf has called an 'insidious process of deinstitutionalisation'.[26] And yet it is much less clear that it *has* sought to justify this with reference to old conservative arguments about the organic link between the patriarchal family, social hierarchy, and state authority. In other respects, as we have seen, Thatcherism has been about pushing back the Welfare State, and, to a lesser extent, challenging establishment and professional privilege in the name of individual self-reliance.

If Thatcherism as an ideology has drawn only selectively on the conservative New Right's defence of the authoritarian state, it seems much more inclined to share the conservative perception of the importance of the family and its relationship to social morality and order. It can be argued that neo-liberalism itself assigns a major role to the family, as the arena in which the individual is trained in attitudes of self-reliance and enterprise, as a unit of consumption, and, more politically, as a bulwark against the encroachments of the state. It was surely from this perspective that Mrs Thatcher made her (in)famous remark that 'There is no such thing as society: there are only individuals, and families.' But such liberal concerns have been supplemented by more

[26] Ralf Dahrendorf, 'Changing Social Values under Mrs Thatcher', in Skidelsky (ed.), *Thatcherism*

patently conservative fears for the health of family life and traditional family values.

Mrs Thatcher herself and many of her colleagues have repeatedly, and almost ritualistically, celebrated the virtues of family life. For instance, in 1979 she asked: 'What is the real driving force of society? It is the desire of the individual to do the best for himself and his family.'[27] And in 1981 she declared: 'One of the most revealing things about the rhetoric of the Left is the almost total absence of any reference to the family. Yet the family is the basic unit of our society. It is within the family that the next generation is nurtured.'[28] The conception of the family tends to be traditionalist, at least to the extent of including both a mother and a father, preferably married. The importance of the family was one theme in the Conservative Party's campaign in the run-up to the 1979 general election. Following the inner-city disturbances of 1981, and again in the wake of football hooliganism in the mid-1980s, a number of senior politicans, including Mrs Thatcher herself, linked social disorder with the breakdown of traditional family values, which they attributed in particular to the permissiveness of the 1960s.[29] Rising rates of illegitimacy and divorce were regularly deplored. Leading government figures inveighed against publications like *Jenny Lives with Eric and Martin*, which, they argued, encouraged children to become homosexual. Concern about the breakdown of the family seemed to reach a new crescendo in the late 1980s, as the steadily rising rates of illegitimacy and single parenthood alarmed not only the moral conservatives, but the hitherto tolerant neo-liberals, who feared the extra strain that this potential growth in the numbers of dependent families could impose on state services and coffers.

And yet even this generalization about the importance of the family within Thatcherite ideology must be qualified (the question is also taken up in Chapter 8). First, we must note that Conservative stress on the significance of the family is not unusual. All post-war governments, even if their ideal conceptions of family life have differed, have felt obliged to sing its praises. James Callaghan, the Labour Prime Minister who preceded Mrs Thatcher, declared in 1978: 'The overriding social

---

[27] Speech made in Cardiff, 16 Apr. 1979.
[28] In *The Times*, 17 Oct. 1981.
[29] See Durham, *Sex and Politics*.

concern is to preserve and enhance the influence of the family.'[30] Secondly, despite the rhetoric, little was done under Mrs Thatcher directly to sustain the family, traditional or otherwise. Moral conservatism clashed with liberal ideas about limits to state intervention and individual freedom, and, perhaps more importantly, with economic priorities. For instance, the government's drive to replace institutional care for the frail and mentally ill by 'care in the community', with its implicit invocation of the family, was not matched by any corresponding transfer of funds. One exception to this pattern was the inclusion of Clause 28 in the 1988 Local Government Act, prohibiting the 'promotion' of homosexuality by local authorities. Perhaps the moral conservatives were allowed this important concession because it was cheap; it also afforded the opportunity to get at left-wing, Labour-controlled local councils. This apart, the only policy that might be described as positively reinforcing the family, a series of measures aimed to ensure that errant fathers pay up for their children's keep, was announced only at the very end of the Thatcher reign, in 1990, and could just as easily be seen as an attempt to reduce the burden on the state of financially supporting these families. Thatcherites would themselves claim that they had helped families by providing them with increased choice— over which school their children should go to and what they should be taught there, or through the option of buying their council house[31]—but this seems to us quite disingenuous. Thirdly, and this is a point made repeatedly by the social policy critics of Thatcherism, numerous of its policies actually made life more difficult for a great many families—for instance, benefit entitlements were reduced, child benefit was frozen, the stock of cheap accommodation was diminished by encouraging the sale of council housing. But finally, although the family was awarded a prime position in the Thatcherite liturgy, it was less than clear what this family should be like, and, above all, it was unclear what women's place within it should be.

As we shall see below, some feminists have portrayed Thatcherism as consisting centrally and essentially of an anti-

[30] See David Morgan, *The Family, Politics and Social Theory* (Routledge and Kegan Paul, London, 1985).

[31] See e.g. David Willetts, 'The Family', in Kavanagh and Seldon (eds.), *The Thatcher Effect*

feminist backlash and the reassertion of the traditional patriarchal family and its values.[32] But has Thatcherism advocated a
'patriarchal' family? Surely, it is more the case that the family
image presented has been inconsistent, or that the issue has been
fudged. Indeed, to quote Michèle Barrett and Mary McIntosh,
'Against those who argue that "Thatcherism" takes a straightforward pro-family and anti-feminist stance, it can be pointed out
that the position taken is in many ways far more contradictory
than the support for a stereotypical nuclear family embedded in
the Beveridge Report and the host of welfare policies and
reforms developed in the post-war decades.'[33] We return to this
important issue below.

Thatcherism, then, has combined elements of neo-liberal and
neo-conservative thinking. But which strand has dominated, and
to what extent has this combination given rise to tensions and
contradictions? Perhaps the most prevalent view, and the one to
which we ourselves would subscribe, is that neo-liberal values
have been in the ascendant. Above all, it is the neo-liberal *economic* agenda that has been the driving force of policy-making
under Thatcher, although conservative values and more politically pragmatic considerations have also been apparent at times.
Nor have neo-liberal and neo-conservative perspectives necessarily and always been in collision. Much of the time they have
either been compatible—for instance, invoking the importance of
community (read family) care to legitimate cuts in mental health
services—or simply compartmentalized. However, at other
times—and some policies affecting women, like abortion, are a
case in point—the tensions have been visible.

It can also be argued that the character of Thatcherism
changed over time, or, if Thatcherism is taken to be some
unchanging core, that its ability to determine policy waxed and
waned over time. For instance, Andrew Gamble[34] has suggested
that while Thatcherism was still a 'project' to build a political
coalition and maximize popular support, before Mrs Thatcher
actually became Prime Minister it was particularly ready to take

---

[32] See in particular Miriam David, 'Moral and Maternal: The Family in the
Right', in Ruth Levitas (ed.), *The Ideology of the New Right* (Polity, Cambridge,
1986).
[33] Michèle Barrett and Mary McIntosh, *The Anti-Social Family* (Verso,
London, 1982), 13.
[34] Gamble, *Economy and State*.

on conservative notions about the traditional family and morality, but that, after 1979, these ideas were less significant in real policy terms. Others have argued that it was in her third term of office, after the 1987 general election, that Mrs Thatcher began to move more determinedly into the terrain of public and private morality, most notably with the insertion of Clause 28 in the 1988 Local Government Act, and the establishment, under the auspices of the 1990 Broadcasting Act, of a Broadcasting Standards Council.[35]

To recapitulate: all attempts to define and evaluate Thatcherism are inevitably hazardous and controversial. We incline towards those interpretations which present it as more than just a matter of statecraft, as guided by a broad ideology that has influenced important areas of policy-making. That ideology has contained two, rather different, liberal and conservative strands, sometimes in opposition, but neo-liberal economic values have been paramount. As such, Thatcherism has not necessarily been 'successful' in realizing either its immediate or its long-term objectives. As Marsh and Rhodes remind us in a recent study of policy 'implementation' under Mrs Thatcher: 'the Thatcher Government, like its predecessors, failed to achieve many of the aims it set itself. In addition, as is always the case, the policies pursued sometimes had unintended consequences which undermined the effect of the policy or the achievement of some other policy objective.'[36] Nor has it succeeded in transforming public attitudes towards enterprise or the Welfare State, but it has undoubtedly had a major impact on the concrete reality of people's everyday lives and on the terms of national political debate. We must now proceed to assess its particular implications for women during the 1980s.

## Thatcherism and Women

Perhaps the very first thing to say here is that there are severe

---

[35] See Jeffrey Weeks, 'Causes for Concern', *Marxism Today*, Feb. 1987; and the critical assessment of this argument in Martin Durham, 'The Thatcher Government and the Moral Right', *Parliamentary Affairs*, Jan. 1989.

[36] David Marsh and R. A. W. Rhodes, 'The Implementation Gap: Explaining Policy Change and Continuity', in David Marsh and R. A. W. Rhodes (eds.), *Implementing Thatcherite Policies* (Open University Press, Buckingham, 1992),

limits to the extent to which one can generalize about the impact of Thatcherism on women. As developments within the women's movement have reminded us, there are enormous differences among women—class, region, race, sexual orientation, to mention some of the most obvious—and it is more than probable that Thatcherism has served to exacerbate these differences. It must also be emphasized that what follows is not intended to be comprehensive: constraints both of space and of the availability of hard information limit what can be said, though some of the issues arising in particular policy areas will be pursued in subsequent chapters. Finally, in assessing these implications, it is useful to bear in mind the autonomy–equality distinction noted earlier.

We have seen that feminists themselves are in disagreement as to the main consequences of Thatcherism for women, though few would argue that they have been good. In particular, there have been two contrasting schools of thought. One, articulated most effectively by Elizabeth Wilson, sees Thatcherism as primarily driven by neo-liberal economic aims, and its most significant effect on women as the almost incidental by-product of pursuing them.[37] The other argues that what is distinctive about both the New Right and Thatcherism is their reassertion of traditional social morality; they have been a reaction against the feminist gains of the 1960s and 1970s.[38]

Those taking the 'anti-feminist backlash' line have suggested parallels with the United States, where, under Reagan, the 'moral Right' was much more influential within the New Right and more effective in altering public policy. This approach borrows too much from the American model and from writing on the New Right. Indeed, in David's account, not only is no distinction made between the New Right and Thatcherism, but there is little attempt to differentiate between British and American experience. The anti-feminism thesis may be questionable even for America, and it is most definitely an overstatement in the British context.

[37] Elizabeth Wilson, 'Thatcherism and Women: After Seven Years', in Ralph Miliband et al. (eds.), Socialist Register 1987 (Merlin, London, 1987). For an earlier formulation of this view, see also Jean Gardiner, 'Women, Recession and the Tories', in Hall and Jacques (eds.), The Politics of Thatcherism.

[38] See David, 'Moral and Maternal'. For a more qualified form of this argument see Tessa Ten Tuscher, 'Patriarchy, Capitalism and the New Right', in Judith Evans et al. (eds.), Feminism and Political Theory (Sage, London, 1986).

Ten Tuscher develops a rather more complex argument. In the 1960s, changes in women's situation and attitudes led to a 'crisis in patriarchy' which, in turn, stimulated the mobilization of the moral Right. However, the influence of the moral Right was constrained, so long as capitalism could exploit the commercial opportunities of sexual liberation. Only with the economic crisis of the 1970s could the moral Right assert its common interest with capital. Then the anti-feminist backlash was less vehement in Britain than in the United States, because the British women's movement was weaker than its American counterpart.

In supporting this interpretation, much has been made of isolated utterances of individual Conservative ministers, and, most famously, of Patrick Jenkin's remark that 'If the Good Lord had wanted us to have equal rights to go out to work, he wouldn't have created men and women.' David attaches considerable importance to the 'secret' report of a Family Policy Group set up by the Cabinet on the eve of the 1983 general election. This apparently endorsed a very traditional family model and covered a wide range of proposals, including encouraging young mothers to stay at home and take on greater 'caring' responsibilities. Yet, in the event, such recommendations played no part in the election campaign.

Rather, as we have suggested, the Conservative government message about the proper division of labour within the family was ambiguous: at different times both egalitarian and traditionalist views were expressed, but often the problem was simply ignored. Mrs Thatcher herself has hardly been consistent. It is true, as Campbell[39] points out, that, as Prime Minister, she was forever talking about the family as the *centre* of women's lives, and tended only to refer to women's common experience in their capacity as housewives. In a recent interview with Jenni Murray on Women's Hour, she warned against the danger of a 'generation of crèche children'.[40] Yet, earlier in her career she had voiced views almost diametrically opposed to this. It is worth quoting here at length from an article she wrote in 1954 for the Conservative publication *Onward*:

[39] Campbell, *Iron Ladies*.
[40] Interview with Jenni Murray for Radio 4's Woman's Hour, reported in the *Guardian*, 18 May 1990.

For a short while after our twins were born I was without help and had to do everything myself including three-hourly feeds day and night, so I know how exhausting children and housework can be! As well as being exhausted, however, I felt nothing more than a drudge . . . I had little to talk about when my husband came home in the evening and all the time I was consciously looking forward to what I called 'getting back to work'—namely, to using some of the mental resources which I had been expressly trained to use for years.

In order for a mother of young children to go out to work, Mrs Thatcher argued, she needed, first, someone reliable to look after them (it obviously helps if you have pots of money!), but, secondly, an understanding husband—'Some men I know are far too ready with the phrase "Woman's place is in the home,"'—and this would not necessarily have a harmful effect on the family.

From my own experience I feel there is much to be said for being away from the family for part of the day. When looking after them without a break, it is sometimes difficult not to get a little impatient and very easy only to give part of one's attention to their incessant demands. Whereas having been out, every moment spent with them is a pleasure to anticipate and a definite time each day set aside to give completely to them and their problems. Later on there will not be that awful gap which many women find in their lives when their children go away to school.[41]

Despite its complacency about the economics of child care, this is a remarkably eloquent and forceful protest—with its plaintive, from the heart phrases, 'nothing but a drudge', 'incessant demands'—long before the resurgence of feminism in the 1960s, against confining women to domesticity.

There were several reasons why, under Mrs Thatcher, there was no serious or consistent attempt to turn the clock back and to drive women back into the home. Above all, there were the facts of economic life. Although the view was occasionally expressed during the recession at the begining of the 1980s that women should give up their paid jobs as a way of relieving male unemployment, it was never taken up by the government officially. For one thing, it contradicted neo-liberal belief in freedom of choice. But also the government must have been aware that female labour was cheap and flexible, not directly in competition with male, and attractive to employers. As we have seen,

[41] Reprinted in the *Guardian*, 21 Mar. 1990.

female employment figures have steadily risen during the 1980s. Talk about a woman's place being in the home seems increasingly irrelevant and anachronistic.

But these facts of life were mirrored in the complexity of internal Conservative Party politics. Campbell suggests that, in fact, Conservative women played a crucial and widely underestimated role in determining the moral agenda of the New Right after the Second World War. That agenda was incubating, as it were, during the 1950s and 1960s, and then hatched in the 1970s. Ironically, by that time many Conservative women no longer subscribed so unquestioningly to these traditionalist views. Increasing numbers of Tory women were also going out to work, and, indeed, 'many of the younger male Tory ministers were married to women with jobs outside the home'.[42] The impact of second-wave feminism cannot be discounted.

We find Mrs Thatcher's government adopting a similarly equivocal stance on questions of female sexuality and fertility, which could be seen to have a bearing on the stability of family life and women's domestic role. Despite the regular imprecations of Mrs Thatcher, Rhodes Boyson, Norman Tebbit, and others against the permissive 1960s and their legacy, and the pressures of organizations like SPUC and the Conservative Family Campaign, it is difficult to point to any concrete victories in this area for the moral conservatives. Against them were ranged not only the New Right libertarians and the hedonistic consumerism of the Conservatives' 'yuppy' constituency, but other leading Conservative figures, some of whose not so private lives would have made any other position blatant hypocrisy. Victoria Gillick's campaign to prevent girls under 16 receiving contraceptives without their parents' consent is a case in point. According to Campbell, although Mrs Thatcher was sympathetic, the Conservative Women's National Committee did not support the campaign. It was eventually defeated in the courts, although doctors may have become more cautious as a result. Abortion is another issue where the moral Right's views could have been expected to prevail, but, as we show at some length in Chapter 6, the Conservative government held off for as long as it could from involvement in the controversy about whether, under what

---

[42] Campbell, *Iron Ladies*, 162.

circumstances, and up to how many weeks of pregnancy abortion should be legal, and then intervened in a way that tended to confirm the status quo and certainly could not be presented as a victory for the anti-abortion lobby. In the event, the availability both of contraceptive aids and advice and of abortions has been much more affected by the health cuts that are the consequence of economic policies than by any anti-feminist backlash.

One partial exception to this generalization about the Conservative government's reluctance in practice to intervene in matters of sexual morality, as we have noted, is in relation to homosexuality. Although there was never any question of repealing the act passed under the Wilson Labour administration legalizing homosexual relations between consenting adults, Clause 28 does provide new sanctions against the open expression of gay values and culture. There are considerable doubts as to whether these sanctions will be backed up by the courts, and campaigns against legal expressions of homophobia appear to be well supported. At the time of writing, anecdotal evidence suggests that many councils are not prepared to risk enforcing Clause 28. But grants to gay and lesbian bookshops have been cut, and fears about the use of the law are widespread. Lesbian feminists have found the legislation threatening, both for its actual content and for the message it gives out about homosexuality.

Although we do not wish to discount the significance of the moral Right offensive, we do want to argue that economic liberalism has impacted on women in far more serious and far-reaching ways. What is more, while some of the economic policies involved have helped women, or at least some women, on balance, taken together, these policies have made women's lives harder. As already stressed, economic restructuring and long-term demographic changes have shaped the context within which women seek to survive, to work, to raise children. But government policies have not been about helping them to do so; instead, they are largely guided by the perceived imperatives of economic policy.

Some women benefited from the economic policies of the 1980s. Mrs Thatcher and Thatcherism have often been depicted as, in a sense, rationalistic or meritocratic, not respecting tradition for its own sake, but submitting institutions and privilege to a rigorous scrutiny. Dennis Kavanagh describes Mrs Thatcher as

'pre-eminently an anti-establishment figure'.[43] Though the extent
to which she actually succeeded in 'denting' establishment practices was perhaps limited[44]—and, indeed, it can be argued that
she was increasingly willing to be co-opted into the establishment
herself—in so far as Thatcherism did attack privilege, monopolis-
tic practices, and so forth, this must have directly and symbolically opened up new space and opportunities for suitably
qualified women to enter and compete.

The Thatcher government never challenged the principle of
equal opportunities head on. It could be argued that this principle is highly congruent with economic liberalism, so long as it
does not cost anything. On the other hand, an equal opportunities policy that involves no expenditure is unlikely to have much
impact. At any rate, the Equal Opportunities Commission was
not abolished, although its budget and staff were cut. And
although it is now a cliché that Mrs Thatcher only ever included
one other woman in her Cabinet, Baroness Young, briefly present as Leader of the House of Lords, she did apparently encourage the promotion of women in the civil service (see Chapter 5).

Taxation policy under Mrs Thatcher went some little way to
advance women's autonomy, notably with the 1989 provision for
separate taxation of husbands and wives. The government
imposed a tax on workplace nurseries in 1984, but, under mounting pressure, took it off again in 1990. None the less, social security arrangements, as we shall see, still largely assume and
reinforce women's economic dependence on husband or male
lover. In short, the policies were beneficial only to certain groups
of women—those who were in employment and earning enough
to pay income tax.

It is possible that some women have benefited from the whole
ethos of self-help and enterprise. There was an overall increase in
the numbers of self-employed in Britain from 1.9m. in 1979 to
3m. in 1988.[45] But Department of Employment figures cited
recently in the *Guardian* indicate that the number of independent
working women doubled, to 774,000, over the 1980s.[46] In the

[43] Dennis Kavanagh, *Thatcherism and British Politics* (Oxford University Press,
Oxford, 1987), 291.
[44] See Richard Norton-Taylor, 'Old Values Die Hard', the *Guardian*, 13 Sept.
1989.
[45] Figure cited in Crewe 'Values'     [46] The *Guardian*, 4 Dec. 1991.

interviews for this book, more than one woman activist claimed to have been influenced by the message of Thatcherism—that it was no good waiting for the government or others to help you, you had to go out and get things started yourself.

In the same way, some women may have benefited from the new emphasis on consumer rights (which subsequently, of course, became the cornerstone of John Major's brand of populism). Such an emphasis may have increased the acceptability of the demand that mothers-to-be should be able to choose how and where they want to give birth. The whole principle of 'the customer knows best', while clearly excluding those without purchasing power, means that it is less acceptable to dictate to women, whether from a moral or an 'expert' standpoint.

Against these undoubted pluses must be set a whole series of policies whose effects, taken together, appear to have increased hardship and struggle, especially for mothers either working or wanting to work, single mothers, 'carers', the elderly, and the poor. These include measures aimed directly at freeing up the economy—most importantly, deregulation, but to some extent privatization as well—and measures to reduce public spending and dependence on the Welfare State. Let us consider how these have affected key areas of women's lives.

Paid employment, we shall later argue, is an essential precondition, in today's society, for sex equality. But, for the bulk of working women, it is also necessary for economic survival, or at least for the avoidance of extreme poverty. The increase in overall unemployment rates in the early 1980s was not purely due to government economic policies, but it was almost certainly exacerbated by them. Although these rates fell somewhat in the second half of the decade, official figures overstated the recovery by constantly redrawing the criteria for inclusion, and even these official figures were still way over the 1979 level by 1988.[47] Recorded female unemployment remained well below men's during these years, but again the government may have helped to exaggerate this gap by insisting, after 1982, that mothers should only be considered as 'available for work' if they could demonstrate adequate child-minding arrangements.

[47] Samuel Brittain, 'The Government's Economic Policy', in Kavanagh and Seldon (eds.), *The Thatcher Effect*.

Government policies have affected the conditions of women's paid work. The government has been concerned to minimize restrictions upon employers. The powers of the wages councils covering the worst-paid workers (mostly women) have been reduced. An amendment to the 1974 Employment Protection Act, in 1980, made a woman's entitlement to reinstatement to her job after maternity leave dependent on her having worked for the employer concerned for at least two years. Although this was later successfully challenged in the courts, it is indicative of the government's attitude. The Thatcher government put up a stout resistance to all proposals emanating from the EC that sought to ameliorate terms of employment, including a 1983 draft directive on the conditions of part-time workers, another on parental leave, and, in 1988, another on sex discrimination, one of whose effects would have been to place a greater obligation on employers to prove that there had not been discrimination. Though it could not veto the 1976 Equal Treatment Directive, Britain produced the longest list of derogations or exceptions of any EC member country!

Government enthusiasm for privatization has likewise adversely affected the terms of women's employment. In fact, it has served as another route to deregulation. In particular, the subcontracting of local government and NHS work has frequently been associated with deterioration in job security, levels of pay, and working conditions for—predominantly female—ancillary workers. As Angela Coyle writes:

Sub-contract work alters the very nature of the employer/employee contract. Contract work often means that labour can be hired and fired at will without entitlement to redundancy or severance pay. Agreed rates of pay, hours of work and the place of work may be changed at the employer's will. And employers' legal responsibilities for providing a safe working environment can be more easily evaded.[48]

Partly as a result of these policies, women's average hourly pay has continued to lag behind men's. Following the implementation of the Equal Pay Act in 1975, the gap had closed very slightly by 1977, when women's average hourly pay was 75 per cent of men's, but by 1980 it had widened again, and the corresponding figure was 73 per cent. By 1989 it was still only 75.1 per cent.

[48] Angela Coyle, 'Going Private: The Implications of Privatisation for Women's Work', *Feminist Review*, 21 (1985), 12.

Rather than compensating for these disparities in earned income and recognizing the particular needs of unemployed women, single mothers, carers, or the elderly, social security policy has reflected the Thatcher government's desire both to hold down public expenditure and to discourage dependency on the state. (Although, ironically, the proportion of the population dependent on income support and single-parent benefits actually grew between 1981 and 1988 from 3.4m. to 5.6m.)[49] While taxation policy has gone some way towards recognizing married women's need for economic independence, the social security system still incorporates assumptions that go back to the Beveridge era. Prior to the 1986 Social Security Act, supplementary benefit was awarded to the household assessed as a single unit, and was made payable to the man rather than to his wife or cohabitee.

The Social Security Act replaced the supplementary benefit system with income support, but it did not change the system of assessment and payment. A subsequent measure provided that the couple could choose which of them received income support, but this was inadequately publicized and made little difference in practice.[50] The abolition of single payments—for instance, for items necessary for a newborn baby—was an additional blow: these have been replaced by loans from the Social Fund, which have to be repaid. The act also signalled the end of the maternity grant as a universal entitlement, and in doing away with SERPS, the State Earnings Related Pension Scheme introduced by the Labour government in 1975, it removed a provision (allowing married women's entitlement to be calculated over their twenty highest-earning years) which had gone a little way to redress the severe imbalance between men and women's retirement pensions.

When the government produced the original Green Paper outlining the new provisions, its own Social Security Advisory Committee observed that it did not

offer a comprehensive analysis of how the benefits and contributions ought to respond to social and economic changes in this area: how to reconcile greater participation in the labour force and expectation of equal treatment with the undoubted fact that women remain the principal carers and because of the interruption in their working lives, find

---

[49] Cited in Crewe, 'Values'.
[50] Cited in Ruth Lister, 'Future Insecure: Income Maintenance under a Third Tory Term', *Feminist Review*, 27 (1987).

their earning capacity reduced long after caring responsibilities have ceased.[51]

Finally, although the real amount spent on welfare has not fallen, it has failed to keep pace with need. Instead, the new government enthusiasm for 'community care', unsupported in practice by appropriate resourcing, has added to women's already considerable burden as 'carers' of the elderly and infirm. In fact, entitlements for the carers were actually reduced in the 1980s, and the government only extended the invalid care allowance, introduced in the 1970s, to married or cohabiting women carers in 1986 as a result of being challenged in the European courts.[52]

Closely related to questions of women's paid employment and income is the issue of child care. As we have seen, much of the increase in women's paid employment has been part-time, and while this may at times reflect a preference—indeed, feminists have increasingly urged unions and employers to promote more flexible working arrangements—most part-time workers have a very bad deal. There is considerable evidence that many would prefer full-time work, but that a major obstacle, one that also prevents so many single mothers from going out to work at all, is the total inadequacy of child care provision in this country. We pursue this question in Chapter 8, but while it would be quite unfair to suggest that the problems began with Thatcherism— Britain has an almost inexplicably poor record of public provision—the government under Mrs Thatcher has done virtually nothing to improve the situation. As we are often reminded, Mrs Thatcher herself, when she was Secretary of Education in 1972, pledged that the government would make nursery education available to all 3- and 4-year-olds whose parents wanted it. Yet in 1990 she made her 'generation of crèche children' remark. During the 1980s, local education departments came under pressure to cut already minimal state provision. Between 1979 and 1985, moreover, thirty-one local authorities reduced the number of places in their day nurseries, and many raised their fees.[53] Only towards the end of the decade, with the identification of the

[51] See Hilary Land, 'Time to Care', in Mavis Maclean and Dulcie Groves (eds.), *Women's Issues in Social Policy* (Routledge and Kegan Paul, London, 1991).
[52] Ibid.
[53] Barbara Webster, 'A Woman's Issue: The Impact of Local Authority Cuts', *Local Government Studies*, Apr. 1985.

so-called 'demographic time bomb'—that is, anticipation of a serious fall in the number of new school-leavers coming on to the job market—in the 1990s, did the government take up the issue with any vigour, and even then it made it clear that there was no question of increasing state provision, only of encouraging private initiatives.

Women have been hit hard by cut-backs in other vital areas of public provision. The most important of these is housing. While it is true that they have continued to benefit from the 1977 Housing (Homeless Persons) Act, which gave women in certain circumstances a stronger claim to council accommodation, the amount and quality of housing available has clearly been affected by the combination of a council house sales policy with drastic restrictions on new building. Of course, selling council houses has proved a popular policy with much of the electorate. But, for certain categories of household, its impact has been particularly severe. For instance, in Scotland more women than men, but also, according to the 1981 census, 78 per cent of single-parent families, were living in council houses (they were also most likely to be in the poorest accommodation).[54]

Health care is another critical area. Again, as the Thatcher government constantly reminded us, the level of real expenditure on the National Health Service (NHS) actually rose, though by a very modest amount, in the 1980s. Nor were the escalating costs of its own making: they reflected demographic change and technological advance, which were posing similar problems in other advanced industrial nations, possibly exacerbated by underfunding by previous governments.[55] But, given the Thatcher government's reluctance to spend more than was absolutely necessary, many areas of provision inevitably suffered. As already noted, pro-choice campaigners are now less concerned about restrictions on the legality of abortion than about the inadequacy of NHS provision. By 1990 less than 50 per cent of abortions each year were being performed under the National Health Service. A rising abortion rate none the less points to the need for proper family planning services, but these were reduced in the 1980s. By 1987 more than fifty clinics had been closed.[56]

[54] Breitenbach, 'Thatcherism in Scotland'.
[55] Charles Webster, 'The Health Service', in Kavanagh and Seldon (eds.), *The Thatcher Effect*.          [56] See the *Guardian*, 11 Dec. 1987.

Women were disproportionately handicapped by cuts in public transport. Recent research has shown that women are much less likely than men to use cars to get around: they are more likely simply to walk, but they also make greater use of public transport.[57]

How far this amounts to a 'feminization of poverty' is disputed. Over the last few years there has been a considerable argument about whether, as the Thatcher government claimed, everybody became better off in real terms during the 1980s, even though the gap between better and worse off widened, or whether, as seems intuitively correct to the present authors, some significant section of the population actually got poorer. It depends, of course, on which elements you include in the calculation. Conventional approaches do not take into account, for instance, the *time spent* on earning income, let alone on domestic tasks, or the sheer amount of stress involved in trying to juggle work and parental responsibilities. And how do you quantify the impact of deteriorating public services? However, when it comes to women, there are also difficulties about *knowing*, especially when a wife or female partner is not earning, or when a man is receiving income support for the whole family. In this situation, some have preferred to argue that the poverty of women, which has always existed, has become more visible in the 1980s because of the larger numbers of single mothers whose income is known and recognized to be below the poverty line.[58]

Before concluding this survey of the impact of Thatcherism on women, we must raise two further questions. The first is about the alleged 'privatization' of politics. Several writers have suggested that along with the emphasis on consumerism, on the individual or the family as the bulwark against the state, on enterprise and merit being their own reward, there has been a turning-away from the 'community' or collective political action. Thus Howard Newby has depicted Thatcherism both as reflecting and sharpening a process in which old communities have been disintegrating under the impact of declining traditional industries and increased geographical and social mobility. Citing indicators

---

[57] See Kristine Beuret, 'Women and Transport', in Maclean and Groves (eds.), *Women's Issues*.

[58] See Caroline Glendinning and Jane Millar, 'Poverty: The Forgotten Englishwoman', *ibid*.

such as the growth in DIY and home-ownership, he has said: 'The community has been privatised. The home is the haven in a heartless world and families retreat into the home not the community.'[59] In a rather similar vein, Zygmunt Bauman describes on the one hand the decay of the old labour politics, based on strong traditional trade unions and the centrality of 'work' and on the other, the Thatcher government, which, responding to these long-term social changes, 'offers the public a massive programme of *buying oneself out*, singly or severally, from politics'. Under Mrs Thatcher, politics has been defined negatively, as to do with taxes and petty regulations. At the same time, it has become more difficult to achieve change through politics as local government powers are stripped away and successive government functions are privatized.[60]

Again, intuitively, we recognize some truth in this analysis. Amongst the women we interviewed for this study, it was a recurrent refrain. We wonder, none the less, how far it is a perception particularly associated with political tendencies—the Left, feminism—which had been more successful in attracting mass followings in the 1970s. It certainly seems contradicted by the upsurge of political activity around peace and 'Green' issues in the Thatcher years. Perhaps Thatcherism made mass political mobilization more difficult amongst the less well off—the working class, women—but this could be explained as readily in terms of increasing hardship as by the 'privatization of politics' thesis.

The second question, which has received a good deal of attention amongst feminists and the media, concerns the impact of Mrs Thatcher as an image, a *spectacle*, on women. In a practical way, we have suggested, Mrs Thatcher did very little for other women, but did she offer some kind of inspiration? Surely, the very fact of her occupation of the supreme political office, and of the confidence and authority with which she carried out its duties, had some effect. She must have made it seem more possible for women to be powerful, to succeed in a 'man's world'.

In conclusion, then, Thatcherism was not a complete disaster for women. It brought some new opportunities, and it was not inspired by any consistent anti-feminist animus. On the other

---

[59] Cited by Madeleine Bunting, the *Guardian*, 6 Sept. 1989.
[60] Zygmunt Bauman, *New Statesman and Society*, 29 July 1988.

hand, the Thatcher governments did little positively to realize feminist objectives, in contrast to governments in a number of other European countries at the time. But, beyond this, it has to be emphasized that the impact of Thatcherism varied enormously amongst different groups of women. Some women, already in a reasonably favourable position, were able to improve on it—according to the Anglia Building Society, the numbers of women buying property doubled over the decade.[61] For others, probably the great majority, life got harder in a number of ways, and the problems were greater for women in the north than in the south, for black women than for white women, and so on.

In the chapters that follow, we go on to explore the consequences of economic and social changes, and specifically of 'Thatcherism', for the British women's movement itself. But finally, and briefly, we must consider the question of continuity and change under Mrs Thatcher's successor.

### THE POST-THATCHER CONTEXT

John Major took over the leadership of the Conservative Party from Margaret Thatcher, who was increasingly seen as an electoral liability, in November 1990. In the general election of April 1992, despite widespread predictions of a hung Parliament, the Conservative Party won a clear victory, though with a reduced majority of seats. While arguments about the reason for this electoral outcome are still raging—and one depressing aspect is that, reversing the trend of the previous two general elections, women were apparently slightly more inclined to vote Conservative than men—there is less doubt that the prospects of a future Labour government look increasingly remote. 'Majorism' is not going to be a flash in the pan. We have to take it seriously.

None the less, it is very early days to pronounce on the character of this post-Thatcher period. There is no mature body of literature to which to turn for guidance, as there is for Thatcherism; mostly, we must still rely on the newspapers. One obvious question to ask is how far the Major regime really differs from Mrs Thatcher's period of rule. Opinions differ, natur-

[61] Cited in a survey by the Henley Centre, noted in the *Guardian*, 14 Aug.

ally, but many, ourselves included, subscribe to the view that the differences are more of style than of content. Above all, there has been no serious modification of the government's economic neoliberalism. On the contrary, there are to be further privatizations, new applications of the principle of the internal market, further hivings-off of government agencies, weakening of the powers of local government, and so forth. Perhaps most important of all, economic stringency has been reinforced by the prolonged recession, with, as we write, no obvious end in sight.

At the same time, John Major seems anxious to differentiate his political vision from that of Mrs Thatcher. He has sought to project himself as more egalitarian than Mrs Thatcher. He has extolled the 'classless' society, thereby tacitly criticizing the tendency for government policies under his predecessor to sharpen class divisions. But his understanding of classlessness is a specific and limited one. Primarily, it involves extending the principle of consumer choice. As has become clear in the elaboration of the Citizen's Charter, the citizen, for John Major, is overwhelmingly a consumer; what happens to those who are not in a position to exercise consumer choice is not a problem that he is prepared to confront.

He has also sought to appear more responsive to the public's concerns. One of the constituencies of which he has been made aware—and this is, of course, one measure of the deepening impact of the women's movement in the 1980s—is women. He was rebuked, not least by women in his own party, for not appointing women to his Cabinet when he took over as Prime Minister in November 1991. Accordingly, in the new Cabinet, formed after the April general election, there are two women, Virginia Bottomley and Gillian Shepherd. He has also associated himself with Opportunity 2000, a scheme, initially involving sixteen major employers, to promote women's employment opportunities, although it has been made clear that initiatives to help women—for instance, in the child care field—must not involve significant increases in government expenditure.

What will this mean for women? It seems clear that the more morally conservative elements of the old Thatcher project will pose still less of a threat in the new era. The legitimacy of claims to equality in employment, of a mother's right to go out to work, of a pregnant woman's right to say how she wants to give birth, and so on are now well established. But the effects of continuing economic liberalism combined with the recession will ensure that it is, for the most part, only a privileged minority of women who benefit from the new opportunities that result.

# 3

# Difference, Identity, and Equality

THE diverse sources of its ideas in liberal, humanist, and socialist philosophy, psychoanalytic thought, critical theory, and contemporary social sciences are both a problem and a resource for feminism. The feminist political project may draw on a large and varied array of strategies of emancipation, and feminists may seek support and make alliances within several political traditions. But the choice thus afforded is also the source of disagreements, of conflict about preferred strategies, and of conflicting tendencies in the feminist movement. Thus, as we explained in the Introduction to this book, there were at least three identifiable tendencies in British feminism in the early 1970s: Liberal, Socialist, and Radical strategies of emancipation were supported by different and sometimes opposed groups. And these were not the only theoretical tendencies to thrive in the British WLM—ecofeminism, women's peace groups, anarchist groups, and others also commanded the loyalties of many feminists.

The purpose of this chapter is to introduce and discuss the ideas, theories, and arguments that have preoccupied and divided British feminists since 1979. Our interest is in the fragmentation of the WLM and in the accompanying differences in feminist political practice that are important to the issues and the policies that are the subject of the remainder of this book. So, the discussion in this chapter is not intended to be a comprehensive account of feminist theory, rather it is an attempt to familiarize our readers with some of the important general ideas that were in play during the developments that we discuss in the chapters that follow.

Nevertheless, we offer more than a simple list of concepts and definitions here. We identify a concern with 'difference' as a central theme of the ideas and issues that we have picked out, and explore what this has meant to British feminism. To explain our approach, we must first set out what we mean when we use the term 'discourse'. Discourses, simply defined, are the ways in which members of a society express in language the things that happen to them. Discourses may express ideas, events, actions, or relationships. According to the French philosopher Michel Foucault, experience and knowledge have no existence separate from language, thus discourses create experiences as they take place.[1] In addition, as Helen Crawley and Susan Himmelweit explain, discourses may be a form of power:

Power is exercised by the process through which any discourse constitutes its subjects. In particular, discourses of femininity always both constitute what it means to be a woman and in so doing control the behaviour of individual women, their subjects. Women are both the subjects of such discourses and subjected to control by them. This is never a simple process, . . . and at any particular time there are many competing discourses of femininity.[2]

The investigation of the way in which power is constructed in discourse has developed into quite a large scholarly industry, to which feminists have made an important contribution. However, although we readily acknowledge that the insights afforded by discourse analysis are often valuable and original, we think that the approach should be used with circumspection. We do not accept definitions of power that regard language as its only source: money, guns, physical strength, and so forth are sources of power of a kind that cannot be captured by even the most sophisticated analysis of the way in which they are constructed in language. We therefore stress our appreciation that a sensitivity to discourse *adds* to our understanding of power, and is especially useful in the analysis of how power is constituted and maintained in gender relations. Moreover, we think that the notion of competing discourses also helps us to understand

---

[1] Post-structuralist and post-modernist thought have been enormously influential on Anglo-American feminist thinking. For full discussions, see Valerie Bryson, *Feminist Political Theory* (Macmillan, Basingstoke, 1992); Chris Weedon, *Feminist Practice and Poststructuralist Theory* (Blackwell, Oxford, 1987).

[2] Helen Crawley and Susan Himmelweit, 'Biology, Society and the Female Body' in *Knowing Women* (Polity, Oxford, 1992), 64 5.

power *within* the women's movement, which is why we introduce it here.

Arguably, 'difference' is the leitmotif of modern feminist discourse. Almost immediately, the idea of difference became a well-articulated central theme of British feminist argument. At first, it was the issue in arguments about equality between men and women. At the same time as some feminists claimed equality with men in all areas of social life, others argued that equality was not an appropriate goal for feminists, because inescapable differences between men and women meant that justice required that they should receive different treatment. In other words, a problem with the early, simple demand for equality was that it assumed that differences between men and women were unimportant. Strategies based on such assumptions would inevitably actually disadvantage women, who would have to become like men if they were to benefit. This argument has waged ever since, and is still the basis of strategic disagreements between feminists. But it has changed over the years, as feminist solidarity was also tested by the realization that the effect of class, sexual, and racial differences on women's lives divided them more than sisterhood united them. Within a very short period after its inception, the WLM began to fragment. That fragmentation was expressed in competing feminist discourses about differences between women: a series of issues and experiences emerged in which class, sexuality, and race received the most sustained attention. It was about the things that divided them that feminists most talked, wrote, and argued. The meaning of difference for feminists was constituted in competing discourses in which two distinctive arguments were particularly important: first, arguments about women's equality with men, and, secondly, and subsequently, arguments about the identities of different women within an originally asserted unity of womanhood or sisterhood. Accordingly, we trace here how feminists have constructed difference as they have encountered it, described it, and discussed it. British feminism has a strong strategic dimension which, together with its intellectual and political origins, its discourse strongly reflects. We will therefore briefly sketch the immediate antecedents of the WLM in Britain, in order to set our discussion of developments since 1979 in their appropriate context.

## Intellectual Beginnings

British feminism draws on at least three intellectual traditions.[3] The main influences on feminist thought are Marxist socialism, the cultural studies movement, especially Raymond Williams's work on language and difference, and psychoanalytic thought. In the tradition of Marxist socialism are Veronica Beechey's writings on patriarchy and paid work, Sheila Rowbotham's historical writings, and the various political interventions of Bea Campbell, Lynne Segal, and Hilary Wainwright. But the early significance of the cultural studies movement is also apparent in the influence of Germaine Greer and Juliet Mitchell. Whilst later British feminist theorists were often trained in social science or cultural studies, both Greer and Mitchell were 'refugees from English departments' (Greer was at Warwick University, Mitchell at Reading). They were 'refugees' in British academic life because the English departments of the 1960s were traditional in their approaches and generally impervious to the influences of the 'new criticism' that was to be so important twenty years later. But critical theory and cultural studies influenced second-wave feminism from the outset. For example, the title of Juliet Mitchell's path-breaking essay 'Women: The Longest Revolution' was a reference to Raymond Williams' *The Long Revolution*. Mitchell's essay owes an obvious intellectual debt to Marxist thought. It appeared in *New Left Review* in 1966 and is one of the founding texts of contemporary British socialist feminism. Germaine Greer was less inclined than Mitchell to look for structural explanations of women's oppression, and took as her chief target the feminine woman rather than men or capitalism. A brilliant self-publicist, Greer had an enormous influence on popular feminism, as much through the press and broadcasting media as through her own books.

During the 1970s two other influences were American feminism and Continental European post-structuralism. Books by Betty Friedan, Shulamith Firestone, and Kate Millet were widely read and discussed by British feminists in those years. The influence of

[3] See the introductory sections in Terry Lovell (ed.), *British Feminist Thought: A Reader* (Blackwell, Oxford, 1990). We draw heavily on these essays for their discussion of the development of British feminist socialist theory.

post-structuralism took longer to be apparent, but by the beginning of the 1980s references to Derrida, Foucault, Lacan, Cixious, Kristeva, and Irigaray were hallmarks of writing by influential British and American feminist theorists.[4]

Much of the British feminist writing of the 1970s was intended as theoretical interventions into debates on the Left. They attempted to demonstrate that the analysis of women was a central condition of theory. In other words, this was intellectual work begun in a traditional manner, with interventions in theoretical debates. These interventions were mainly ignored or summarily rejected by established (male) theorists in the relevant fields.

Such rejections undoubtedly strengthened the resolve of feminist intellectuals, and by the early 1970s the project of developing feminist theory was well established. The dominant influence was that of Marxist Socialist feminists—historians, social scientists, or scholars in the new cultural studies movement—who sought to expose the material conditions of women's oppression under capitalism. Socialist feminists sought to theorize patriarchy in ways that made it compatible with Marxist thinking, an exercise that may have delayed the emergence of Radical feminism in the British movement. The 1970s were taken up with a long debate about women's labour under capitalism, in which Socialist feminists advanced a 'dual systems' theory to explain women's oppression. Patriarchy took into account traditions of male power, whilst Marxism reserved to itself the explanation of relations of production. The debate about the relative influences and nature of capitalism and patriarchy, like many of the debates that followed, brought into play different feminist understandings of sex and gender. The core disagreement was about the degree to which differences between men and women were the result of biology (sex) or social conditioning (gender).

## Political Heritages

The practice of the political Left was probably as important as its theories in shaping the British feminism which emerged from the left-wing politics of the 1960s, and a culture in which sexual

---

[4] See Weedon, *Feminist Practice*, and Bryson, *Feminist Theory*.

libertarianism was one of the dominant values. The beginnings of the WLM took place inside other, mainly socialist, groups and movements. This had an enormous effect on its politics, strategies, and theoretical development. Many of the first supporters of the WLM were committed to particular political organizations, and, naturally, they sought alliances with those organizations. For example, feminists working inside the British Left resisted its traditional bureaucratic and hierarchical practices while at the same time seeking to account for the nature of femininity and feminism in the context of other struggles against oppression. But there was little real sympathy for the feminist project either in the Labour Party or in the various 'liberatory' groups on the revolutionary Left, who regarded feminism as, at best, a possible source of new members, and, at worst, a bourgeois diversion. A central element of feminist experience of socialism was the priority that it gave to social class. So, British feminist intellectuals sought to devise a politics that prioritized the liberation of working-class women. At the same time, they sought to make alliances with socialist men.[5] But the rapid growth of the WLM meant that it mobilized large numbers of women who had not been involved in socialism, had no resulting loyalties, and who could see no reason for struggling to cope with the difficulties of negotiating the inhospitable and sexist gatherings and organizations of socialist parties and groups. Moreover, the sectarian politics of feminists from groups such as the Socialist Workers Party and the International Marxist Group were greatly disliked in the WLM. Soon, feminists began to demand separate organizations and the exclusion of men from WLM meetings. The first major argument amongst feminists was one about excluding men. Historically, the project to establish 'spaces' for women to develop their own liberatory strategies evolved out of a rejection of socialist organizations. In the course of that experience, feminists learned to be suspicious of traditional class politics. As is now well known, consciousness-raising groups and other women-only activities were highly successful in enabling women to explore their identities and to develop a feminist politics away from the influence of male oppression. The initial idea of the feminism of women's liberation was that women shared a common experience of

[5] The tensions that resulted are well described by Anne Phillips in *Divided Loyalties* (Virago, London, 1987)

subordination. It was this that would make a unified women's liberation movement possible. But the 'logic of difference' meant that, inevitably, aspirations to unity were short-lived. Thus, in the process of its own creation, feminism reproduced the same kind of universalist claims and the same suppression of difference amongst women that earlier socialist tradition had constructed in its privileging of the idealized political experience of the working class.[6]

## Strategic Influences

Initially, then, both the theory and the practice of New Left politics set the terms of feminist explorations of power, sex, and gender. But, however it was articulated, the argument about difference was, in many respects, a modern version of a very old debate. Disagreements about the significance of differences between the sexes for strategies to achieve women's equality with men were commonplace amongst first-wave feminists. They were central to the arguments about protective legislation at the end of the last century and to the rows over Eleanor Rathbone's campaigns for a 'family endowment' (to be paid to the mother) in the 1920s.[7] During the 1970s, disagreements about the practical significance of difference divided those (Liberal and Socialist) feminists who concentrated on procuring equal rights at work and equal representation in public life from those who favoured a 'pro-woman' strategy. In its extreme form, 'pro-womanism' was essentialist, in that its advocates held that differences between the sexes were innate. A feminist nature–nurture argument that has continued for more than two decades began between those who held that gender was socially constructed and those who thought that it was biologically determined. Strategically, the argument was about whether the unsatisfactory inequalities that arose from differences between men and women could be changed. One side favoured reforms of the law to establish formal equality; the other favoured special treatment for women. In its starkest 'either/or' form, the argument led into an ideological cul-de-sac. Recognizing that neither position, narrowly construed, was particularly satisfactory, most British feminists adopted intermediate

[6] Lovell (ed.), *British Feminist Thought.*
[7] See Olive Banks, *Faces of Feminism* (Martin Robertson, Oxford, 1981).

positions. Today, strategic disagreements are, more often than not, about what can be changed and how. Understanding of the need to take on such issues as conditions of maternity leave and child care, sexual harassment, and the masculinity of the workplace has been accompanied by growing recognition that formal notions of equality do not translate directly into workable policy. Throughout the 1980s there was evidence that the opposition between equality and difference was a false one, and that, in practice, both perspectives had much to offer.[8]

It is difficult to capture the precise interplay between theory and practice that led to the easing of the equality–difference opposition in feminist strategy. Of course, broadly speaking, theoretical and strategic change were closely linked processes. As we have already stated, the chronology of their constructions of difference was that British feminists began by considering differences between men and women, then proceeded to explore the relative importance of class, sexuality, and race to gender. These discourses of difference were built around *two* other concepts: equality and identity. In the context of discourses of equality, discussions of difference were about the ways in which members of a group valued the perceived differences between them. In discourses of identity, the discussions of difference were about those distinctive salient characteristics of group members which unified them and set them apart from other groups and subgroups. The recognition by feminists that identity was as important to the construction of difference as equality marked an important shift in their thinking. In both theory and in practice, it became difficult to maintain boundaries between considerations of equality and identity.

We believe that the WLM has always contained both discourses. While feminists demanded equality with men in a number of spheres and organizations, they affirmed their identity as a subordinate and oppressed group and explored the problem of whether (seemingly universal) differences between men and

---

[8] See Cynthia Cockburn, *In the Way of Women* (Macmillan, London and Basingstoke, 1991), for a full discussion of the shift from goals of equality to demands for parity in the British equality policy networks. For a discussion of similar shifts in the USA, see the chapter by Carol Bacchi, 'Pregnancy, the Law and the Meaning of Equality', in Elizabeth Mechan and Selma Sevenhuijsen (eds.), *Equality, Politics and Gender* (Sage, London, 1991).

women were innate. More than two decades later, following exhaustive discussions of gender, class, sexuality, and race, the same questions were central to feminist explorations of masculinity. These were not separate discussions; they overlapped earlier arguments and were reconsidered in discourses constructed around each kind of difference.

## FROM DIFFERENCES BETWEEN WOMEN AND MEN TO DIFFERENCES AMONGST WOMEN

The initial premiss of the WLM was that women were oppressed by men. The experience that women share, the basis of their identity as women, is their difference from men. That difference underpins a set of asymmetric power relations in which men dominate women. Feminism asserts that male domination is oppressive, and calls on women to unite to liberate themselves from this oppression. The starting-point of the WLM was the belief that women had a common interest in challenging their male oppressors.

But, almost immediately, the different political backgrounds of feminists began to fracture the movement's unity. 'Liberal' feminists, including many women in the Labour Party, in the professions, and in mainstream women's organizations, believed that liberation (a term that they did not actually use) was a matter of removing obstacles to equality between the sexes. Once institutional and legal barriers to equality were gone, women could, if they wanted to, take up the same social roles as men. Accordingly, they concentrated their efforts on obtaining legal and procedural changes to eliminate unfair discrimination against women. Socialist feminists, or Marxist feminists as they are sometimes called, struggled (notably in the debate over the dual systems theory) to develop theories and strategies that integrated differences of class and sex. The debate over the dual systems theory that took place during the early 1980s brought into feminist thinking an increasingly subtle understanding of the interplay between class and gender. It was, however, not the only influence on feminist thinking at that time. Feminist theory advanced significantly with the recognition that many aspects of women's oppression did not yield readily to Marxist categories. What was needed was a more adequate explanation of the importance of oppression to women's identity. Eventually, this intellectual quest focused on theories of 'subjectivity' whereby understanding was often sought in psychoanalytic thought. 'Subjectivity' is defined by Helen Crowley and Susan Himmelweit as 'that combination of conscious and unconscious thoughts and emotions that makes up our sense of ourselves, our relation to the world and our ability to act in that world'.[9] Subjectivity is an alternative to the 'individualist notion of people as rational, self-motivated individuals in pursuit of their own clear and stable self-interest'. Its explanatory utility is that it enables us to recognize that individuals often behave in ways that they do not intend and that may not be in their own interest. It captures the way in which people are at the same time actors in the world and subject to forces beyond their control. It underlines the fact that people are intentional subjects, and, in so doing, offers the potential to take account of individual agency amongst members of oppressed groups.[10] Here once again Juliet Mitchell was influential. Her widely read *Psychoanalysis and Feminism* was a rereading of Freud that insisted that psychoanalytic thought offered feminism the key to the psychic processes through which feminine identity was acquired and internalized.

Both Liberal and Socialist feminists regarded the power imbalances between the sexes as a social construction amenable to reorganization by reforming (in the case of Liberal feminists) or transforming (in the case of Socialist feminists) institutions. But Radical feminists stressed the universal nature of male privilege. Thus 'subjectivity' was not the only, or even the first, challenge to an initial tendency by feminists in Britain to prioritize the politics of the class struggle. An early, if indirect, attack on Marxist certainties came from American feminist Shulamith Firestone's *The Dialectic of Sex*, published in 1971, which argued (to the horror of Socialist feminists trained to accept the primacy of economic class in explaining social life) that 'sex class' was the primary social division and the source of women's oppression. In other words, men caused women's oppression. The terrain of British intellectual feminism was so well colonized by Marxist socialism that Firestone's ideas did not take hold as readily here

---

[9] Crowley and Himmelweit (eds.), *Knowing Women*, 7.
[10] Ibid.

as they did in the United States. Nevertheless, Radical feminist ideas were propounded in Britain and very rapidly became influential. Their different theoretical understandings of feminism often paralleled practical differences, and these fed back into the theory. For example, Radical feminists were influenced by work in women's refuges, on rape crisis lines, and about pornography. They became increasingly interested in explaining male violence. They were unconvinced by explanations of women's oppression that prioritized class and that were based on the relations of production. Increasingly, 'women-centred analysis' became dominant. Radical feminist theory was built around a kind of essentialism in which the belief that sexual differences are fundamental gained in explanatory status. But Radical feminism was always more than a set of simple explanations postulating a universal and malevolent 'male nature'. Language, representation, the construction of knowledge and gender were theorized in initiatives that have often been taken by Socialist feminists. One irony is that although Socialist feminists proclaimed their commitment to working-class politics and to the mobilization of working-class women, it has frequently been work by Radical feminists that is more popular, easier to understand. This has meant that the Radical feminists, who argue that feminists should avoid contact with traditional political organizations, institutions, and processes, have often been more successful in bringing their issues to the political agenda and in establishing their definitions in popular feminism.

## Difference and Sexuality: Radical Feminism

During the 1970s the emphasis of Radical feminism had shifted steadily from an assertion of women's equality to a preoccupation with male sexual behaviour and to an increasing certainty of the need for separatist strategies of liberation. This became an insistence that political lesbianism was the correct strategy for the liberation of women. This shift was accompanied by an analysis that implicated heterosexuality as the means of men's domination of women, an account that became plausible as the locus of debates about difference moved to sexuality.

The term 'sexuality' is often a euphemism for lesbianism in the contemporary feminist movement. For many feminists, lesbianism became an issue at the national conference in Edinburgh in 1974, when the demand to end discrimination against lesbians and to affirm the right of women to determine their own sexuality was adopted. The demand originated from the first national conference for lesbians, held at Canterbury the previous spring, where plans were made to insist that the next WLM conference include an afternoon of workshops and a plenary session on sexuality. The issue that caused problems at Edinburgh was the involvement of men in feminist politics. This developed into an argument about whether feminists should be involved with men at all. During 1974 and 1975 combat between the two groups in the movement became increasingly acrimonious. There were arguments about the nature of the London Women's Liberation Workshop and about the presence of men on International Women's Day marches. One outcome was that the workshop ceased to function as a centre for the movement, while another was that many women began to feel alienated from feminism. Some left the movement. In the autumn of 1974 the workshop newsletter serialized 'the Clit Statement' over ten issues. This was essentially an attack on heterosexual and bisexual women. The issue finally exploded when male heterosexuality was conflated with male violence to women and was brought up at the national conference at Birmingham in 1978. After the conference, the editorial collective of WIRES (the national WLM newsletter) began to espouse the strategy of political lesbianism, accusing heterosexual women of sleeping with the enemy. The call to political lesbianism was based on an analysis which said that heterosexuality was socially compulsory. The logic of this was that female heterosexuality was a product not of preference, but of false consciousness. Social support for heterosexuality was so strong, the analysis continued, that women who chose heterosexuality were not making a choice. In many feminist circles by the end of the 1970s it was impossible to 'choose' heterosexuality: only lesbianism could be 'chosen'.

Such an outlook underestimated women's agency—and, along with it, the degree of autonomy that women have—and almost certainly undermined the confidence of many heterosexual women. Gradually it became impossible to discuss heterosexuality, and the analysis of the sexuality of most women lost its place on the feminist agenda. That was an important shift for femi nism. Sexuality had been very much on the agenda of the consciousness-raising groups. Bea Campbell comes very close to saying that the emergence of the WLM was, in many respects, precisely about reclaiming women's sexuality.[11] She argued in 1980 that women's response to the sexual revolution of the 1960s was both an ambiguity about sexual freedom at the expense of sexual protection and an incipient critique of heterosexuality. In their discussions, women were organizing their ideas about sexual practice together, talking about sex without men around. One of the demands that women made was for sexual satisfaction. But the implied critique of heterosexuality was never made, and the exploration of the sexuality of heterosexual women was forced underground. Campbell argues (and it is hard to find a reading of the politics of that period that suggests an alternative to her view) that although most women were 'in heterosexuality', the potential to make a feminist critique was never realized, because the split between Radical and Socialist feminism 'banished heterosexual women to the swamp'.[12]

At the time of the split in 1978, Socialist feminism was far too tentative about the politics of personal life to construct much of a sexual politics. The sectarianism of the split meant that women who continued to relate to men were considered to be traitors. The *Spare Rib* collective spent much of 1980 tearing itself apart over whether a submitted article claiming that lesbians had silenced heterosexuals in the women's movement was anti-lesbian and therefore should not be printed. It was not printed. For much of the 1980s it was impossible to talk about heterosexual relations in the WLM. There was almost no exploratory, analytical feminist writing about the subject during those years. The issue did not re-emerge until the end of the decade.[13]

In short, between 1979 and 1990 the argument about sexuality became an argument about lesbianism. Although heterosexuality and masculinity are, as much as lesbianism, at the heart of the arguments over sexual difference that split the movement for more than a decade, they were barely considered in this context. Instead they were discussed mainly in the context of debates

---

[11] Bea Campbell, 'Feminist Sexual Politics', *Feminist Review*, 5 (1980), 1–18.
[12] Ibid. 14.
[13] See Athina Tsoulis, 'Heterosexuality: A Feminist Option', *Spare Rib*, June 1987: 22–6.

about the causes of male sexual violence. This might be taken as symptomatic of the problem of difference.[14]


## Political Lesbianism and Radical Feminism

Prior to the WLM, feminism was not a major reference point for British lesbians, who, if organized at all, were part of the gay rights movement. The re-emergence of feminism offered new possibilities for lesbian organization. The first national conference for lesbians was held at Canterbury on 26–7 April 1974. The conference included workshops on separatism, Radical feminist lifestyles, monogamy and jealousy, lesbianism and the women's movement, the gay movement, and the revolutionary Left. This conference was the origin of the sixth demand affirming women's right to their own sexuality which was passed at the national WLM conference in Edinburgh. From this early stage, an elision of lesbianism and feminism was apparent. Those who went to Canterbury recall that there was a feeling at the conference that Radical feminism did mean—or ultimately would mean—being a lesbian. There was an assumption that once women confronted the issues about their sexuality, they would naturally become lesbians.[15] This was a time when 'coming out' was a focus of the gay rights movement, and, undoubtedly, the arguments about gay pride influenced the emergence of political lesbianism as a political value and strategy.

The political lesbian position was articulated most clearly in 1979, in the publication of *Political Lesbianism: The Case against Heterosexuality* by Leeds Revolutionary Feminists. This pamphlet declared sexuality to be the primary source of women's oppression. Heterosexuality was imposed on women for men's benefit, and thus lesbianism is synonymous with feminism. Not all lesbian or Radical feminists accepted this argument, and not all of those who did were comfortable with the fierceness and moral certitude with which it was expressed. But gradually it became apparent that political lesbianism was central to the logic of Radical feminist politics.

The reasoning behind the Radical feminist understanding of

[14] We are grateful to the anonymous reader provided by Oxford University Press for this observation.
[15] See Trouble and Strife, 1 (Winter 1983), 27–6.

the politics of sexuality was that only lesbians could really be feminists, because only lesbians chose other women sexually, only lesbians were truly women-centred. In other words, the lesbian sexual preference for women was political. Arguably, this is a standpoint that takes the erotic away from sex. If lesbianism is a political preference, then desire is secondary. Logically, women who do not desire other women should, nevertheless, abstain from sexual relations with men. Another feature of the argument was contention about who was the most oppressed. Lesbians were more oppressed than heterosexual women, hence lesbians were politically superior. Inevitably, a hierarchy of oppression arose in which some lesbians were more oppressed than others. Later debates suggested that political lesbianism also involved 'politically correct' sexual practices. This was the implication of the lesbian sado-masochism debate of the mid- to late 1980s (see below). In other words, political lesbianism claimed both feminism and lesbianism for itself, asserting a single 'correct' feminist identity. This assertion was not accepted universally by lesbian feminists on either side of the Atlantic, many of whom objected to the removal of erotic motivation and autonomy from lesbianism by its conflation with the political philosophy of feminism. Gayle Rubin pointed out in 1982[16] that Radical feminism specifically avoided the acknowledgement of lesbian desire, because acknowledging the importance of one kind of desire logically required the acceptance of other kinds of desire. That would undermine lesbian separatist politics. The political practice of separatism required a political basis for lesbianism.

The Radical feminist response to this varied, from Sheila Jeffreys's unwavering separatism and political lesbianism (see her *Anticlimax*) to a more thoughtful, but ultimately essentialist, stance which could be found in the discussions at the Lesbian Sex and Sexual Practices conference held in London in April 1983. Jane Egerton reported how the conference confirmed a general wish to integrate rather than to choose between the political and sexual dimensions of lesbianism. It would be difficult, she remarked, to get rid of the political component so long as heterosexuality can be made 'compulsory because of men's power over

---

[16] Deidre English, Amber Hillibaugh, and Gayle Rubin, 'Talking Sex: A Conversation on Sexuality and Feminism', *Feminist Review*, 11 (1982).

us'.[17] The logic of this was inescapable. Clearly, however carefully it was expressed, at the core of Radical feminism was the view that women's continuing heterosexuality was the result of male coercive power.

Although the logic of Radical feminist politics is that only lesbians may be feminists, Radical feminists are careful not to exclude heterosexual women. Many Radical feminists actually deny that political lesbianism is at the heart of their politics. In the first issue of the Radical feminist journal *Trouble and Strife*, in 1983, the editorial collective wrote that although they were critical of heterosexuality, they did not think that only lesbians could be feminists. The same editorial set out the politics of British Radical feminism, basing it on two core ideas. First, all women are oppressed as women. This is the primary oppression, prior to race, class, ethnicity, and other bases of oppression. Secondly, men oppress women because they benefit from doing so, and change is possible only through women's collective action. It is pointless to try to convince men of the need for feminism. In other words, political separatism is necessary; political alliances with men are a diversion.

The elision of lesbianism and feminism continued to be a feature of Radical feminist writing throughout the 1980s. Davina Cooper and Didi Herman's review of the Socialist feminist journal *Feminist Review*'s special issue (34) on lesbian politics was a restatement of the political basis of lesbianism. They criticized the articles in *Feminist Review* for 'being about the primacy of pleasure, uncritically validating practices for the enjoyment they give', and objected to the reduction 'of lesbianism to nothing more than a cultural and sexual choice'. For them, 'lesbian feminism as a set of principles and practices that aims to shape our personal lives and public institutions is much broader than whom we sleep with and how . . . [It has] an important contribution to make to the way the whole of society should be restructured and developed.'[18]

During the 1980s, sexual difference was explored both in theory and in practical politics; it was an issue for Socialist as well as Radical feminists. Arguments about sexuality, desire, and

---

[17] Jane Egerton, quoted in *Trouble and Strife*, 1 (Winter 1983).

[18] Davina Cooper and Didi Herman, 'Turning us off', *Trouble and Strife*, 19 (Summer 1990), 14–18.

identity were brought by feminists to both established and new institutions. Ideas and arguments about sexuality and equality affected the politics of established institutions, and drew political battle lines between different feminisms. We offer two examples to illustrate these points: the interplay between lesbian and Labour politics in the mid-1980s, and the lesbian sado-masochism debate of the later 1980s.

The funding by the Greater London Council of lesbian projects, and the later provisions for such projects by other local authorities, helped to initiate a political presence for lesbians in the Labour Party. However, the competition to secure funding brought out the divisions between lesbian groups. The Labour Party was only just coming to terms with a politics of sexuality and was ill equipped to deal with competing demands from a community that it assumed was unitary. An already confused political position was weakened by doubts and divisions amongst feminists as to whether competing for project funding would mean co-option and a dilution of their radical energy. And as Labour began to count the costs of the 'loony Left' image that it had been given by a homophobic tabloid press, its support for lesbian feminists became more and more conditional. By the time of the 1988 campaigns to oppose Clause 28, many Labour politicians had had enough of gay issues.

According to Ann Tobin,[19] the 'loony Left' image that Labour acquired as a result of its support for gay rights led a number of local Labour politicians to dissociate the party from these politics. She quotes as evidence both the letter that Patricia Hewitt wrote to Neil Kinnock, leader of the Labour Party, which made the observation that 'the gays and lesbian issue is costing us dear', and the fact that John Cunningham, Labour's local government spokesman, initially supported Clause 28. The identification of Labour with gay rights probably helped the Conservative government to win support for its policies to reduce the powers of local government. But the fact that Labour paid a high price for its stands on gay rights did not satisfy the gay and lesbian communities. Tobin argues, with some justification, that the Labour Party never really understood what gay rights were

---

[19] Ann Tobin, 'Lesbians and the Labour Party: The GLC Experience', *Feminist Review* 34 (Spring 1990), 56–66.

about. She recalls an incident during the 1986 National Conference of Labour Women at Rothesay, in which platform speakers responded to press accusations that the conference was populated by a bunch of hairy lesbians so ugly that they would even be rejected by sailors home on leave. Speakers hastened to affirm that the majority of the women present were not lesbians, and that most were very attractive.[20] This is one of many examples of Labour disarray over the issue.

The problem was that, in the party, the politics of sexuality upset the politics of class. For example, the new women's committees undoubtedly did not give centrality to class issues, and were therefore at odds with significant parts of Labour culture. At a time of spending cuts, the new units were thriving, receiving increased (if somewhat small) budgets. The recruitment of women's committee staff was often direct from the women's movement, and the workers' loyalty was to the communities of women that they served rather than to the bureaucrats in the town halls or to the local authority trade-union hierarchies. What was often perceived as the 'flaunting' of their sexuality by gay and lesbian couples heightened a sense that Labour was abandoning its true constituency for a bunch of deviants.[21] For many Labour activists, the 'black, one-legged lesbian' syndrome became a part of the discourse as a shorthand for equality policies. Some did not understand the offensiveness of such expressions, and failed to realize that they belittled the whole equalities strategy. Others, argues Tobin, felt comfortable with the homophobia and racism in the phrase—something that they would not otherwise have been able to express.[22] Gay and lesbian lobbies and political groups failed to associate with the Labour councillors, who were as much the target of Clause 28 as were the gay groups themselves. Ultimately, Labour failed to connect to gay politics, and the gay movement failed to connect to Labour.

The issue of lesbian sado-masochism became a feature of feminist and lesbian politics in the middle of the 1980s. Although it may appear to be an obscure and rather minor issue, it is an example of the capacity of identity politics of difference to fragment both the Left and the women's movement into competing groups. The emerging groups soon discovered their own internal

[20] *Feminist Review* 34 (Spring 1990), 59.
[21] *Feminist Review* 34 (Spring 1990), 63.          [22] Ibid.

differences. This debate is about differences between lesbians and is particularly illustrative of the logic of a politics that is based upon the assertion of an oppressed identity. It surfaced in a battle about whether sado-masochist groups should be allowed to meet at the London Lesbian and Gay Centre (LLGC) once it was established in 1985. The arguments that followed were repeated in outline in many of the debates over identity politics in the feminist movement.

Susan Ardill and Sue O'Sullivan account for the debate in Socialist feminist terms.[23] They begin by setting out the conventions of feminist argument that prevailed at the time. We need to rehearse these conventions if the significance of the sado-masochism debate is to be explained properly.

One characteristic feature of the political assertion of identity is 'naming and claiming'. An individual names herself as part of a group, and that naming gives a moral authority to her words. It was common for someone to say: 'I am a lesbian and I think. . . .' Such a statement invoked a feminist ideology that said, first, that the world consisted of a hierarchy of oppressions, and, secondly, that subjective experience is the key to understanding that hierarchy. The naming places the 'named' in the hierarchy. As an insight, it has a certain resonance, but it certainly made everyday life difficult. Reflecting on this, one feminist activist told us: 'The only person you can be friends with is someone who is like your identical twin . . . cos either you'd be oppressing them or they'd be oppressing you.' Ardill and O'Sullivan are very critical of naming and claiming. 'Somehow the radical power of uncovering by describing, creating language for experiences that have previously gone unarticulated, just becomes labelling, slotting things neatly into place.'[24] Thus the 'lesbian mother', for example, will be assumed to have predictable ideas about men, money, the state, sex, etc. Their criticism appears to be twofold. First, the naming is reduced to mere labelling rather than being carefully distilled into theory, and, secondly, theoretical status is claimed for the sets of experiences articulated in the naming process. Objective experience is both reduced and overreached thereby. It is overreached both because

---

[23] Susan Ardill and Sue O'Sullivan, 'Upsetting an Applecart: Difference, Desire and Lesbian Sado-Masochism', *Feminist Review*, 23 (1986), 31–57.

[24] *Feminist Review* 34 (Spring 1990), p. 34.

people have different experiences and because they understand similar experiences in different ways. During the 1980s, one ideology of political lesbianism claimed feminism for itself. These were the feminists who opposed the lesbian sado-masochists, largely because they claimed a different lesbian feminist identity.

At first the political lesbians were successful. Lesbian sado-masochist publications were banned, or sold only under the counter at feminist bookshops. The lesbian sado-masochists were barred from A Woman's Place and the London Women's Centre, but the LLGC was inclined to be tolerant, wanting to welcome a range of groups. In a series of acrimonious meetings, one group of lesbian feminists sought to bar another group from LLGC premises.

The sado-masochism debate raised a number of issues. The practice and representation of lesbian sado-masochism was opposed by many lesbians because of the connotations of sadism and masochism, linked sometimes to actual torture and emotional suffering. Worried by the suspicion that masochism and feminity were unproblematically connected, many objected to the power relationships expressed in such practices. It was supported by others because of its affirmation of the erotic and of the place of fantasy, and also because they opposed censorship and exclusion. The debate was difficult because of the feelings involved, because of the (often prurient) curiosity it excited, and because of the absence of a language in which to discuss sexuality. Ardill and O'Sullivan believe that the debate was more muted in Britain than in the United States, where similar arguments took place, because sex is generally discussed less in Britain.

But by the end of 1982 the issue was much discussed by lesbian feminists. It brought a restatement of the revolutionary feminist position. The Leeds-based revolutionary feminist newsletter, *Revolutionary and Radical Feminist Newsletter*, set out its (opposed) views. The Leeds group also organized the Lesbian Sex and Sexual Practices conference in London in April 1983. During the winter of 1983–4 the London WLM newsletter refused to carry a notice about a meeting to discuss sado-masochism, and lesbian sado-masochists appeared with a provocative banner (a lesbian symbol wrapped in chains) at the 1984 Lesbian Strength march, a move that caused an uproar of criticism. It was in this context that the LLGC opened to letters demanding that sado-masochists be banned from the centre. The main public argument against the sado-masochists concerned the contamination of both lesbianism and the centre with a 'violent male ideology'. Feminists in Lesbians against Sado-Masochism declared that they were unwilling to tolerate the symbols of brutality that were posed by the sado-masochists; they denied that sado-masochistic practices could be chosen, and thought that they were an extension of women's subordinate status, a mirroring of heterosexual roles.

This seemingly obscure issue has considerable implications. We examine it here because it illustrates important characteristics of contemporary feminist politics. It raises for discussion issues about sexuality such as desire and fantasy, and, by extension, it politicizes the practice of sex. A distinctive feature of the debate is that it engages sexuality and sexual practice, and it develops issues about power in sexual relationships. This is the main reason why so many of the arguments about sexuality refer to it. Political lesbians[25] maintain that whenever the issue of sado-masochism is raised, the discussion soon slides into heterosexual discourse in which masculine (butch) and feminine (femme) sexual roles are re-established. The restatement of revolutionary feminism in a form virtually unchanged since its first appearance is another significant development. Equally important is the argument that sado-masochism should be opposed by feminists because it says that 'no' means 'yes', and calls pain pleasure.[26]

Eventually the lesbian sado-masochists were allowed to use the centre, but only on condition that they did not indulge in explicit representations of sado-masochistic practice. (They were not allowed to arrive leading each other on collars and chains, for example.) Radical feminists reasserted their political lesbianism in this debate, repeating the view that women's sexuality is the key to liberation and oppression, that men maintain their power specifically through sexuality. The argument shows that revolutionary feminism was still an important strand of Radical feminism in Britain at the end of the 1980s.

That sexual politics were central to the feminist agenda in the 1980s was largely due to their centrality to the Radical feminist

[25] See letter from Didi Herman and Davina Cooper in *Feminist Review*, 37 (1991).
[26] Ibid.

political agenda. The relationship between politics and sexuality was (and is) an important problem for feminists, and the accusation by Radical feminists that Socialist feminism did not offer a critique of heterosexuality is a fair one. Only at the beginning of the 1990s did a feminist literature appear that theorized masculinity, and even this paid little attention to heterosexuality. Equally valid was the complaint that heterosexuality was the assumed practice in the early years of the movement, hence it was essential for lesbians to assert their identity. The use of that identity by some Radical feminists as the core to their politics meant that many of the other implications of difference were virtually unexplored in Radical feminist theory. Race, class, ethnicity, nationality, age, ability, and other identities were simply asserted to be secondary to gender. There were no black women on the founding editorial collective of *Trouble and Strife*; the collective did not know a suitable one, and they believed that to search for one especially would be tokenism.

### Difference, Socialist Feminism, and Race

Whilst Radical feminists concentrated on sexuality as a political practice, Socialist feminists struggled for most of the 1980s to produce a theorization of difference that included a number of bases of political identity. This project necessitated a search for an adequate theorization of women's sexuality. Such issues were difficult to treat in a Marxist framework, and Socialist feminists were drawn increasingly over the decade to psychoanalytic theory, which they explored and attempted to redevelop in feminist terms. Post-structural theories were also imported from abroad, directly from the writings of French feminist intellectuals,[27] indirectly via the British New Left and, occasionally, from the writings of American feminists about French feminist thought.[28] This was theory that dealt with mind, thought, language, and representation. Often accessible only through badly translated sources, it was unnecessarily difficult to read and difficult to understand. But its exploration of language, sexuality, identity, and difference offered the possibility of the resolution of important feminist dilemmas.

[27] e.g. Cixious, Irigaray, Kristeva.
[28] See Jean Radford's review of Toril Moi, *Sexual/Textual Politics* (Methuen, London, 1985), in *Feminist Review* (1986), 114–16

No sooner had the attempt to understand sexual difference fragmented the movement, than race became a divisive issue. Black women complained that the assumed feminist identity was white, and that no account of their experience was taken by white feminists. The anti-imperialist predispositions of Socialist feminists meant that these complaints found a resonance. Socialist feminists started to address issues of race and sexuality at around the same time. Already committed to the politics of class, this meant that they began to look for a more general understanding of difference. They were not content to substitute one identity for another; rather, they wanted to understand how identities were constructed. During the 1980s the Socialist feminist journal *Feminist Review* ran numerous articles on sexuality, identity politics, race, and class. From these and other publications, we may trace the development of Socialist feminist theories of difference.

An indication of the Socialist feminist understanding of sexuality in the early 1980s is to be found in the editorial statement in the first of the *Feminist Review*'s special issues on sexuality, in the summer of 1982. The editorial begins by affirming that 'to politicise sexuality has been one of the most important achievements of the Women's Liberation Movement'. The editorial then suggests that women establishing sexuality of their own have two problems to overcome: the extent and power of the 'masculinisation of human sexuality', and the absence of intellectual and analytical concepts to assist the understanding of sexuality. Exploring sexuality is important intellectual work, work that is not well served by 'phallocratic psychoanalysis'. Neither, however, is the project well served by the common-sense sociology that tends to substitute for theorization. The same editorial notes that it is easier to discuss lesbianism in the women's movement than to discuss heterosexuality.

As the decade progressed, the interplay between different components of social explanation received more attention, and attitudes to psychoanalytic theory became more considered and 'nuanced'. By the middle of the 1980s an ambitious theoretical and political project was established. A long editorial in 1986[29] discussed disagreements in the *Feminist Review* collective, and a

---

[29] 'Editorial', *Feminist Review*, 23 (1986).

set of issues for Socialist feminists during the 1980s was itemized. These were class politics, relations with black feminists, and the feminist peace movement. The editorial affirmed the importance of class analysis to an explanation of gender relations, but asserted that relations of production could not be understood without reference to sexuality, ideology, reproduction, and culture. The importance of subjectivity was acknowledged. The collective also rejected the view that male control over sexuality and reproduction is the single or main cause of women's oppression. Finally, the political resonance of Socialist feminism was described as stemming from its recognition of the world as containing more than one system of domination. The interlinked importance of class, gender, and race was declared, and the need to develop appropriately differentiated political strategies was asserted. The development of theory was to continue, but the journal would, the editorial promised, become more political, less academic in its outlook.

## Black Women and the Politics of Difference

Just as theorists explored the politics of difference, some groups of women affirmed the importance of race to political identity. A central feature of the women's movement in the 1980s was the emergence of a much more confident and articulate black women's politics,[30] both in organizational and theoretical terms. Organizationally, this was a fragment, if a rebellious one, of the various male-dominated black campaigns against racism. Black women involved in these campaigns resented the sexism that they found amongst the male activists, and wanted a 'space' of their own in which to discuss their attitudes to issues such as racism and imperialism.

But they were also reacting against the racism and exclusivity of the white women's movement. They criticized a feminist movement which claimed to speak for all women, but which made virtually no attempt to involve black women or to reflect their special concerns. As Kum-Kum Bhavnani and Pratibha Parmar

[30] The use of the term 'black' to describe women of Asian and Afro-Caribbean descent is itself an issue amongst black feminists. Women of Asian descent feel that it does not adequately capture their experience. It does, however, point out the black–white distinction that is at the centre of British racism, and it therefore has some utility.

wrote in 1978: 'The women's movement in Britain has never taken up the question of racism in any real way and because this issue affects all black women, we feel that a failure to take it up has ensured and will continue to ensure that the Women's Liberation Movement as a whole is irrelevant to the needs and demands of most black women.'[31] *Spare Rib* refused to publish their article. Black women argued that feminism was *not* for all women; rather, it was for privileged white women. They pointed out that black women in Britain face problems that are both acute and distinctive. These cannot be understood simply as the sum of sexism and racism. And racism itself was inadequately understood by feminists. Racism affects everyone, but it is more difficult for white people to realize how they are affected, because whiteness is treated as normal; it is assumed. Thus, 'Black women cannot . . . speak of their troubles outside of the context of racism and resistance if only because their colour is never "invisible"; white feminists, on the other hand, can speak—and many do—as if that colour did not exist.'[32] In other words, a racist state is 'racist to everyone', but it is more difficult for white people to see it. This is why white feminists failed to understand their particularity and generalized their specific problems to all women.

The specific interactions of sexism and racism have created particular difficulties and forms of injustice. Thus, there are issues that are of direct concern to many black women, but not generally to white women. One notable example of such an issue is immigration. Moreover, even where the issues are of concern to both black and white women, it is not just that it is worse for black women than it is for white, but that the experience is different. Employment politics offer an example of this phenomenon. Black women were more affected by rising unemployment during the early 1980s because they were more likely to be working in the hard-hit industrial sector. Black women were much more likely than white women to take full-time jobs. This might be a reflection of the typically lower rates of pay that they might expect and of the greater possibilities for informal child care

[31] Quoted in Pratibha Parmar, 'Other Kinds of Dreams', *Feminist Review*, 31 (1978), 55–66.

[32] From Razia Aziz, 'Feminism and the Challenge of Racism: Deviance or Difference', in Crowley and Himmelweit (eds.), *Knowing Women*, 298.

arrangements. Another factor is that, within the Afro-Caribbean community, nearly one household in three with children is headed by a (normally female) single parent, and difficulties with child care mean that relatively few are able to take paid jobs, full-time or part-time.[33]

These are just a few examples of a widespread pattern. The fact is that, in virtually all the issue areas that we examine in the subsequent chapters of this book—employment, child care, reproductive rights and health, rape and domestic violence—black women will be found to have their own particular concerns which not only differ from those of white women, but, in some cases, conflict with them.

Affirmations of black identities gave black women the anger and confidence to assert themselves within feminism. Black women set up their own organizations, independent of white feminist groups. Indeed, many were reluctant to see themselves as feminists at all. Some Afro-Caribbean women preferred the term 'womanist'. That is why, in 1982, when the organizers of the fourth and last conference of OWAAD (Organization of Women of Asian and African Descent) chose 'Black Feminism' as its central theme, there was a major row.

As the 1980s progressed, black women's voices were heard more clearly and authoritatively in the national feminist press. By January 1984 three of the eight full-time members of *Spare Rib*'s editorial collective were black women, and their concerns featured prominently in the magazine, a tendency that has continued ever since. Also in 1984, the editorial collective of *Feminist Review* invited a group of black women to produce a special issue on black women in Britain, which was called 'Many Voices, One Chant'.[34] *Outwrite*, a newspaper emphasizing the concerns of black women in Britain and of Third World women, was launched in 1982. The feminist publisher Sheba was launched by six white women, but soon a majority of the collective were black women, though the collective was anxious to avoid becoming an entirely black group.[35]

Initially, the emphasis on 'blackness' was liberating and ener-

---

[33] See Irene Breugel, 'Sex and Race in the Labour Market', *Feminist Review*, 32 (1989).

[34] *Feminist Review*, 17 (Autumn 1984).

[35] See 'Can Black and White Women Work together?', *Spare Rib*, July 1986.

gizing, but Pratibha Parmar and others argue that it became counter-productive. Once asserted and recognized, the focus on 'blackness' put further obstacles in the way of black and white women working together. For example, one article in *Spare Rib* was entitled 'Ten Points for White Women to Feel Guilty about'. And the editors of one anthology of black women's writings express regret at the 'futile politics of victim and guilt tripping', or the tendency to believe in the 'moral and political superiority which is supposed to derive from the mere fact of being a Black woman'.[36]

Another problem with the assertion of the unity of blackness is that it is difficult to maintain in theory and to sustain in practice. Not only did the category 'black' obscure the important distinctions between women of Afro-Caribbean and Asian origin, but these in turn are highly differentiated communities. There are further class differences to be taken into account amongst black women, and differences of sexual orientation also emerged within the black women's movement, although less disruptively perhaps than amongst white feminsts. OWAAD itself lasted only four years. In the main, black women's groups in the 1980s brought together women of either Afro-Caribbean or Asian origin; mixed groups are the exception.

Too strong an identification with the 'black' community tended to conceal the patriarchal roots of many of the problems faced by black women. As groups such as Southall Black Sisters increasingly realized, they had to fight oppression by their own menfolk, even at the risk of being accused of exposing their communities to racist political attack.

Moreover, sexuality was on the agenda for black feminists. Black lesbians began to organize at the OWAAD conference in 1981, when they demanded autonomous space for a workshop. In the early 1980s four black lesbians described their experiences in an article in *Feminist Review*.[37] They felt that 'coming out' posed special problems for black women. The gay movement's insistence that the real 'coming out is coming out to your family' is an extra pressure on black women, who, because of the effect

---

[36] See S. Grewal *et al.*, *Charting the Journey: Writings by Black and Third World Women* (Sheba, London, 1988), preface, p. 3.

[37] 'Becoming Visible: Black Lesbian Discussions', *Feminist Review*, 17 (July 1984), 53–77.

of racism, are more dependent on their families. They can less afford to run the risk of complete rejection. Arguably, the accumulation of identities for black lesbian feminists could make this group the most radical of all oppressed groups. But it is also one of the most cross-pressured. The difficulty of responding to the imperatives of lesbian politics and of the diverse and differentiated black and women's movements is more likely to lead to political exhaustion than to a confident politics.[38]

By the beginning of the 1990s, then (as we describe more fully in Chapter 9), the polarization between white feminism and a black women's movement was diminishing. This occurred in the context of a feminist politics that had been intellectually refined, but in other ways disrupted and dispersed, by the politics of difference.

Throughout the 1980s, articles exploring race, sexuality, culture, and class offered insights into aspects of political identity. Clara Connolly recalls[39] that black women were especially hostile to political lesbians' insistence on the centrality of sexuality and on separatism. Black women brought to the women's movement their history of anti-racist struggle, their reliance on the black community and the family as a source of support. They also challenged the 'pathologizing' of the black family by white socialist intellectuals, and the lack of involvement by white women in campaigns about deportation, immigration, and other attacks on black families.

## Feminism and Masculinity

The last of our difference issues is masculinity. As we have already indicated, second-wave feminists were always interested in the relationship between biological sex and social conditioning. The problem was to determine the social significance of the biological differences between men and women. Some feminists tended to favour explanations based on biological determinism, and thought that male–female differences were innate. Others argued that gender was socially constructed. In general, Radical

[38] See also Jewelle Gomex and Barbara Smith, 'Talking about it: Homophobia in the Black Community', *Feminist Review*, 34 (Spring 1990), 47–54.

[39] Clara Connolly, 'Splintered Sisterhood: Antiracism in a Young Women's Project', *Feminist Review*, 36 (1990), 52–64.

feminists were more inclined to the former position, whilst Socialist feminists leaned towards social construction explanations. However, it is fair to say that very few Radical feminists would explicitly support an essentialist position, and very few Liberal or Socialist feminists would refuse to acknowledge that biological sex is important. Within a very short period of time, most feminists began to write and speak about gender rather than sex, a focus of attention that looked to femininity and masculinity rather than to maleness and femaleness for explanations of gender relations. The project was to understand femininity, but it soon became apparent that this would be impossible without also considering masculinity. Thus, a concern about gender and femininity led feminists to a concern with masculinity. The focus changed from '"the woman question", which saw men as the norm and women as the "other"', to questioning why men were regarded as the norm. For example, feminist studies of male violence shifted from questioning women's complicity in staying with violent men to questioning why men were violent.[40]

In the course of this continuing exploration, feminists drew on the insights of mainstream social science, contemporary psychoanalytic theory, and numerous other academic disciplines[41] to develop a project that has paid considerable attention to the competing masculinities in contemporary society. A central concern, very much influenced by feminist adaptations of Lacanian psychoanalytic thought, is with gender acquisition. This is very much work in progress, but, at the time of writing, the most convincing of these explorations, those which offer most to our discussion of the discourses of difference, stress that the acquisition of gender identity is a precarious, never-finished process. The girl/woman is disadvantaged in this acquisition because she constructs her femininity in a linguistic and cultural order that favours particular heterosexual masculinities.[42]

The insight that the acquisition of masculinity and femininity represent socially conditioned processes of developing an identity

[40] We are grateful to Gill Allwood, who has allowed us to quote from her unpublished draft Ph.D. thesis.
[41] For good accounts, see Lynne Segal, *Slow Motion: Changing Masculinities, Changing Men* (Virago, London, 1990); R. W. Connell, *Gender and Power: Society, the Person and Sexual Politics* (Polity, Cambridge, 1987).
[42] Allwood, unpubl. thesis, and see Sally Alexander, 'Women, Class and Sexual Difference', in Lovell (ed.), *British Feminist Thought*.

probably raises more important questions about power in gender relations than it answers. In so doing, it sets an intellectual agenda that is likely to preoccupy feminists for some years to come. But it does more than raise new questions: it also offers a vocabulary with which to address political disagreements between feminists. Before we take this up, however, it is necessary to pick up the threads of the discussions of difference, equality, and identity with which we began this chapter.

### Identity, Difference, and Feminism

The political and theoretical articulation of difference by particular subordinate groups turns on the recognition of their 'otherness'. The 'otherness' of a subordinate group refers to the way in which it is defined as being unlike the dominant group. For Simone de Beauvoir, women were 'the other', definable only in relation to men. There is a tendency for a dominant group to regard a subordinate group as an undifferentiated whole. It is the 'otherness' of the subordinate group—that is, the fact that they are not, say white, heterosexual, middle-class men—which gives them an appearance of unity and coherence to the dominant group, and sometimes to themselves, which does not otherwise exist. The hegemony of the dominant group means that all kinds of 'otherness' are seen as politically identical.

So, when a subordinate group makes a claim for recognition, it is likely to be a claim that arises from its experience of subordination, from the construction that has been placed on its 'otherness'. Different subordinate identities get run together because they share a common oppression, are designated by a common 'otherness', the fact that they are not part of the dominant group. For a time, conflicts of interests between different oppressed groups may be overlooked and sometimes suppressed, and a solidarity of 'others' is apparent. This process explains how it was that, initially, feminists felt able to speak for all women, or that working-class leaders claimed to represent all of the working class, white and black, male and female.

There are two dangers in this process. First, the unity originally asserted is spurious, largely conditioned by the interests and definitions of the dominant group. Secondly, the very assertion of a specific identity by a group encourages the assertion of identity by its subgroups. In other words, one element of the dynamic of identity politics is fragmentation. The moment that power is claimed by the assertion of a particular identity, other possible claims for power are born.

Analysis of identity politics was a preoccupation in Britain during the 1980s, as the Left struggled to create new coalitions of support after its defeat in 1979. There was a growing recognition that individuals construct their identities in relation to each other. The theorization of identity politics was an outgrowth of the NSM politics of the 1960s and 1970s of which feminism was a part. Jonathan Rutherford[43] described NSM politics as a left-wing phenomenon that shifted the parameters of politics to include personal and private life, undermining the Left's narrow conception of equality and exposing Marxism's inability to account for the politics of the subject. Affinity groups, consciousness-raising therapy groups, and other forms of personal politics moved on to the terrain of class politics, challenging the privileged place of class in explanation. There was a dissonance between discourse and practice that recalled 'That troika of Women, Blacks and Gays who featured prominently in the political literature, but whose absence from the practical business of the left suggested a deeper malaise in Marxist praxis . . .'.[44]

If we use the language of political identity, equality, and difference, we can regard the WLM as the articulation of an alternative identity, that of the feminist. This assertion was accompanied by demands for equality through a liberation of women from the power of men. This implied a rethinking and expansion of the idea of equality (see Chapter 6). In the course of the exploration of the politics of equality, similar assertions of black, lesbian, working-class, Irish, and Jewish feminisms—that is, particularizations and (potentially competing) articulations of the original feminist identity—were made. The logic of such assertions or identifications of difference was straightforward enough. An individual's politics, as Stuart Hall wrote, consisted of competing and shifting identities. Describing the specificity of these identities was the political work to which political scientists refer as political

[43] Jonathan Rutherford 'A Place Called Home: Identity and the Cultural Politics of Difference', in *Identity, Community, Cultural Difference* (Lawrence and Wishart, London, 1990).
[44] Ibid. 16.

articulation. Such articulation involved a struggle for a political voice which, logically and practically, led to an assault on the very language in which it was expressed. Rutherford refers to Raymond Williams's description of how emerging groups cannot find a discourse or language in the dominant culture which adequately expresses their experience. The struggle for voice, therefore, took place on the very edge of semantic availability.[45] In other words, oppressed groups are disadvantaged by the very language which, as the ideological instrument of the dominant group in society, impeded their own recognition of their interests. The articulation of the identity of an oppressed group is therefore a very difficult project. It is easy to see how, under such circumstances, the affirmation of identity may become an end in itself.

It is this capacity to become an end in itself that makes the expression of identities a political problem. The affirmation of individual identities is a process that risks fragmentation. Because each individual has numerous identities (black, working-class, trade-unionist, young, English), she cannot normally make each of these a basis for political action. Identity operates at the level of the individual, who, if she is to act politically, must prioritize one or perhaps two or three of her identities which become the basis of her political action. Such prioritization is crucial if political alliances are to be made, if winning coalitions are to be formed.

The tension between articulation and aggregation is one that besets all political organizations, but it is particularly acute in the liberatory organizations that are established by oppressed groups. By the end of the 1970s it was clear that the finely balanced tentative democracy of the WLM could not contain the identities that competed for attention.

## Feminism and Difference

Discussions of difference became a feature of feminist gatherings. There the pattern was to encourage women to describe their experiences and to affirm their different identities. The 'hierarchy of oppressions' that arose in this 'naming and claiming' process

---

[45] Rutherford, in *Identity, Community, Cultural Difference*, 23

also implied that the most oppressed had the most knowledge. In many groups, the idea that lived experience is an important foundation of knowledge and understanding often became the belief that it was the only basis for knowledge. Thus, only black women could understand the problems of black women: only lesbians could understand the oppression of lesbians: and so on. To disagree was to take part in the oppression. Disagreeing with a black woman was seen as racist, with a lesbian as homophobic, and so forth. On many occasions, discussion between equals became impossible. This kind of fragmentation was part of the political experience of the 1980s: it was not confined to the feminist movement. Arguably, it was a measure of the success of the Thatcher project to replace society with the individual, to privatize social life (see Chapter 2).

The recognition of competing political identities—the acknowledgement of difference—was a watershed for British feminism, marking clearly its fragmentation. It undermined the basic premiss of feminism, that all women share some common political interests. The basic idea of difference for feminists was simply that women's experience varies, and so it is impossible to generalize from the experience of one woman, or some women, to all women. The recognition that women's identities were diverse turned the affirmation that the lived experience of women is the basis of knowledge from a slogan into a problem. How can diverse experiences become the basis of a credible body of knowledge? How, without the connections and generalizations of sisterhood, can feminism exist at all?

Difference issues were widely debated in the feminist politics of the 1980s. Frequently, those debates seemed to be repeated. As we have shown, the issue of difference became a problem in some context or other—a matter of particular political struggle—the arguments were rehashed and then, when the issues proved unyielding, led to splits within the original groups. The questions to ask now are: Was progress made? Was anything learned? Did feminist politics become impossible?

## DISCUSSION: BRITISH FEMINIST THEORY IN THE 1990S

Our discussion of feminist discourses of difference illustrates the many competing pressures and tendencies in the British WLM. We are well aware that these pressures and tendencies are not categorized adequately by the commonly used labels of Liberal, Radical, and Socialist feminism. In the course of writing this book, however, we have found that these are terms that we cannot do without. The three labels signify some themes, continuities, and developments that enable us to make tentative generalizations about the development of feminist ideas. In theoretical terms, Radical feminism maintains some distinctiveness and coherence, whilst Socialist and Liberal feminism have become more fragmented and certainly less easily distinguished from each other. Radical feminism continues to be located near, but not at, the biological determinism pole of the sex difference continuum, and it continues with an uneasy essentialism, unable to explain 'universal' patterns of male behaviour, especially violent behaviour, but unwilling to label such behaviour as 'innate'. Its coherence is maintained by paying the high cost of sexual sectarianism, and until the beginning of the 1990s Radical feminists continued implicitly and sometimes explicitly to regard the identity of the political lesbian as the preferred (superior) feminist identity. Moreover, Radical feminism does not incorporate the insights offered by many kinds of enquiry. Psychoanalytic thought is dismissed as a 'heterosexist' ideology that legitimates and strengthens heterosexual and, therefore, masculine domination. The idea of the unconscious is rejected in what amounts to a denial of history and culture. If the past can offer only images of masculine domination, then its effects must be expunged from our psyche and our experience. It appears, then, that there was no substantial shift in Radical feminist analysis during the 1980s.

But shifts were apparent in Socialist feminist ideas. Socialist feminists continued to contest Radical feminism. Psychoanalytic thought was more widely used as theorizations of sexuality were sought. Political struggles and programmes were described and analysed in a continuing search for an adequate feminist politics. By the early 1990s there was a widespread impression among Socialist feminists that identity politics leads to despair—to fruitlessness. But although the importance of class analysis was asserted regularly, it became more and more difficult to favour class analysis in explanations that embraced theories of subjectivity and that included an increasingly sophisticated analysis of the construction of identity. By the end of the decade *Feminist Review* was showing signs of confusion about how to treat the political fragmentation that resulted from the splintering of the numerous identities which comprised the Left.

The problem of fragmentation continues. In part, it stems from a tendency by oppressed groups to idealize struggle itself—exacerbated in Britain, perhaps, by the attempt to come to terms with the political defeats of the Left during the 1980s. It is also, as we have described above, a product of the great difficulties experienced by members of oppressed groups wishing to assert particular identities. Once a new identity is affirmed, others become apparent and the former identity is fractured. This process can go on and on, its very fluidity is anti-political, and it has significant strategic disadvantages. The problem is located in the notion that the personal is political. Explaining political dimensions of personal experience is a constant problem for feminists. Although affirming an identity creates a refuge for marginalized women, a transformative politics is required if that refuge is not to become a ghetto.

This is both a strategic and a theoretical problem. Indeed, Kate Soper has written that the feminist discourses of difference pulled the rug from under feminism as politics. Once the diversity of women is recognized and privileged over their commonality, no appeal to collective action can be addressed to common womanhood, because definitionally, it cannot exist. Once it is agreed that the term 'woman' expresses nothing, the central aspiration of feminist politics collapses.[46] For Soper, the logic of difference is a denial of feminist politics, and it is difficult to refute her clear and careful argument. But logic at the level of abstract thought does not necessarily translate into the conduct of social life. New identities will continue to be asserted and to fragment political coalitions. Competing identities will not cease to plague political coalitions simply because we deny their existence. And accepting that difference and competing identities are endemic does not mean that politics cannot happen. If this were the case, we would have to deny that politics ever took place.

It is possible to find a balance here between the necessity to

---

[46] Kate Soper, 'Feminism, Humanism and Postmodernism', *Radical Philosophy*, 55 (Summer 1990).

acknowledge oppressed identities and the necessity to make political coalitions such as parties, movements, and groups. Pratibha Parmar[47] has expressed this well in her discussion of the work of June Jordan, a prominent black American feminist and theorist. Jordan believes that no one has a single identity, and that everyone is more than any of their identities. Some identities are important because they result in persecution. Politics arises here because it is necessary to challenge the oppressor. The raped woman needs a refuge and space to recover, but rape is not eliminated by protecting women. It is also necessary to change men; women do not rape themselves. The basis of Jordan's argument is her understanding of politics as a process that involves the achievement of a goal. Both process and goal have to be present. The necessary process of recognizing identity belongs to the first stage of the political process, which is acknowledging that there is a problem. It informs the next stages of the process, which are getting people to agree with you and getting rid of the problem. Struggle is not a goal, it is a process; victory is a goal. If the exploration of identity is not mediated by a desire to solve the problem, then there will be no dynamic, no politics.

[47] Parmar, 'Other Kinds of Dreams'.

# 4

# The Autonomous Women's Movement

THE theoretical divisions amongst feminists that we discussed in Chapter 3 were accompanied by tactical divisions. During the 1980s some feminists prioritized the kinds of WLM activities and campaigns that were so prevalent in the 1970s, whilst others prioritized work in mainstream political institutions. Often this difference of tactics represented a tacit division of labour in which all concerned agreed that both kinds of work were important. But significant disagreements did take place about the danger to feminism of too much reliance on the support of state institutions, political organizations, and charitable foundations. The apparent decline of the autonomous WLM during the 1980s has been linked by many observers to excessive reliance on state sponsorship, raising doubts about the capacity of mainstream institutions to adapt adequately to the challenges of feminist politics, and the capacity of feminists to resist incorporation by powerful established organizations. Such debates are recurrent features of NSM discourses, because they address the issues that are raised by the development of different kinds of activities and priorities, by the emergence of distinct branches of a once-singular movement.

One of the themes of this book is the contrasting fortunes of the two branches that now characterize the tactics of British feminism. The next two chapters discuss their development. First, we describe changes in the autonomous movement, then we look at several grass-roots campaigns that engaged feminists during the Thatcher years, and finally, in Chapter 5, we address the movement of feminists into political institutions.

Later chapters will trace feminist campaigns that continued throughout the decade and were focused on specific issues—reproductive rights, health, male violence, child care—but the object of this chapter is to consider broad features of the evolution of the autonomous movement as a whole. In many ways the movement *did* experience decline—in membership, in networking, in organizational bases—and that decline was exacerbated, certainly in the early 1980s, by conflicts mirroring those that dominated theoretical debate, especially those between Radical and Socialist feminists, and between white feminists and the black women's movement.

But throughout this period there were also new surges of activism. The black women's movement, emerging from the late 1970s, really took off in the early 1980s. This has, of course, continued, though losing some of its momentum, and it has addressed a whole range of issues. However, there have also been three campaigns in particular which, while shorter-lived and narrower in focus, mobilized large numbers of women and brought new energy into the movement. In the early 1980s women mobilized support for their sisters at Greenham Common; 1984 the actions of the miners' wives galvanized new activity; and since the late 1980s there has been widespread consolidation around the issue of pornography. We shall trace all these themes in turn.

### MOVEMENT DECLINE

The WLM was almost bound to experience difficulties of declining momentum. As Claus Offe has written; 'Socio-political movements are extremely ill-equipped to deal with the problems of time.' In particular, the spontaneous desire of the relevant population to engage in protest is likely to be of a 'highly perishable nature'. If small victories are achieved, this encourages the feeling that further protest is no longer needed, but if the movement wins no concessions, its members begin to feel that their action is hopeless.[1] As, in addition, the sense of discovery and adventure wears off and internal arguments over values and strategy intensify, there will inevitably be some ebbing of the movement tide.

In Britain in the 1980s the women's movement had also to

[1] See Claus Offe, 'Reflections on the Institutional Self-Transformation of Movement Politics: A Tentative Stage Model', in Russell Dalton and Manfred Kuechler (eds.), *Challenging the Political Order: New Social and Political Movements in Western Democracies* (Polity, Cambridge, 1990), 237.

contend with the generally harsher climate created by economic change and Thatcherism. In various ways this drove the movement into deeper dependence on state agencies. Paradoxically, the expansion of 'municipal feminism' under Labour-controlled councils in the early 1980s only encouraged this dependence. Although new opportunities were provided, they also left women's groups more vulnerable in the long term as funding was withdrawn or cut, or such cuts were anticipated.

Little wonder, then, that commentators regularly suggested during these years that the WLM was on its last legs. This was a generalization that we were hoping to be able to refute in this book. And, indeed, we are certainly convinced that implications that the movement is 'dead' are premature. However, there is no avoiding the evidence that there has been a decline. The numbers of women prepared to go out on to the streets to defend women's rights have fallen away from their peak levels in the mid-1970s. We were repeatedly told of the difficulties that activists faced in trying to mobilize mass support. At the same time, individual feminists were less willing to give their time and energies, even their money, to feminist groups and activities. By the late 1980s very few groups without some form of public subsidy appeared to have survived. By the end of the decade, everywhere we went, except Scotland, we encountered a sense that numbers of activists were falling, local women's newsletters were folding, old networks were breaking down.

One aspect of this decline was that there were fewer and fewer places where feminists could meet as feminists,—most obviously, fewer women's centres. In the 1970s, as we have seen, as women's liberation groups proliferated, gained in confidence, and developed beyond the consciousness-raising stage, they got involved in all kinds of campaigns. Out of these grew various projects. Feminists sought public funding for many of those projects. For instance, in an article in *Spare Rib* in 1985 women looked back over the last ten years in Newcastle. They identified the late 1970s and early 1980s as a 'high point'. They had women's refuges, a rape crisis centre, a women's centre, a lesbian line, and a women's theatre group.[2] Often, particular importance was attached to setting up a women's centre. Here they could

---

[2] 'A Decade for Feminism', *Spare Rib*, Jan. 1985.

meet, put together some kind of newsletter, provide a drop-in centre for women for the local area, and so on. By 1980 such centres existed in many cities. Generally, local councils helped, if only to the extent of letting out a room at very favourable rates. Usually, too, these centres were quite humble affairs, a couple of rooms, minimal reprographic equipment, often very unsuitably located. None the less, they did provide a centre, a space for women. Yet by the late 1980s many women's centres were in serious trouble and some had had to close down.

But decline was not uniform across the country. As a social movement ultimately reliant on 'grass-roots' activists, and with a strong ethos of decentralization and participation, the women's movement varies tremendously from one locality to another. While we might come away with a broad impression of decline, there were regions like Scotland, but also cities like Leeds, where the movement appeared to remain lively, confident, and inventive.

However, the broad national picture has been one of lessening energy and activity in the WLM. The factors underlying this trend, as we have already indicated, are complex. We attempt a fuller explanation in the concluding chapter. Although it cannot be attributed simply to internal conflicts, we would argue that, in the early 1980s at the very least, internal conflicts did play an important part. Perhaps most damaging of all was the conflict between Radical and Socialist feminism.

### Radical v. Socialist Feminism

As the Introduction noted, by 1980 the division between Radical and Socialist feminists had become so bitter that it was no longer possible, or no one was prepared to try, to organize a national conference. Chapter 3 has shown that, at the level of national public debate, this polarization persisted right through the 1980s, producing, in effect, two instead of one women's liberation movements. But how did it affect the movement 'on the ground'?

Our impression is that, frequently, the division between Radical and Socialist feminists that was played out at national conferences in the late 1970s *was* reproduced at local level. Indeed, as we have hinted, in some case the very availability of a women's centre may have helped to precipitate fierce divisions. Often, the centre was especially attractive to Radical feminists. It has been pointed out that Radical feminism cannot simply be equated with lesbianism, and Socialist feminism with heterosexuality; there are many lesbian Socialist feminists, while heterosexual women can be Radical feminists. However, by the late 1970s it would be fair to say that Radical feminism was increasingly identified with political lesbianism,—with the view that whatever your sexual orientation, all sexual relationships with men are inherently oppressive. For Radical feminists, the centre provided an opportunity to spend time with similar women, perhaps to get involved in relationships with them. Even unwittingly, but sometimes more deliberately, this could help to create an atmosphere in which feminists with male partners felt out of place and inferior. It is easy to see how this could happen. (As we shall see, Jean Freer, in *Raging Women*, contrasts this atmosphere in many women's centres with the more open, accepting ethos of Greenham.[3])

In many cities, women's centres provided a focus and space for Radical feminism. In the 1980s this seems to have been true for the women's centres in Bristol and in Liverpool, for instance. In Bristol we were told that the women's centre was increasingly dominated by separatist women, though we were unable to talk to the women themselves. According to *Spare Rib*, the Liverpool Women's Centre tended to be identified with Radical feminists.[4] Of course, not all women's centres conformed to this pattern, and Radical feminists engaged in many other activities and campaigns, including the women's refuge campaign, Women against Violence against Women, and, most recently, the campaign against pornography.

It is likely that the difficulties that many women's centres experienced in just keeping going may have had some effect on the morale and numbers of self-styled Radical feminists 'on the ground'. One reason for these difficulties was that they were not very successful in attracting women from the wider community. This may partly be explained by the sectarian atmosphere, but there were practical problems with the quality of the accommodation and, above all, with its location. It was not easy to obtain

---

[3] Jean Freer, *Raging Women: In Reply to Breaching the Peace* (privately published document), cited by Jill Liddington, *The Long Road to Greenham* (Virago, London, 1989).

[4] Barbara Norden, 'City of Splits', *Spare Rib*, May 1986.

or to maintain council support and funding for premises or workers. Thus, in Liverpool 'The centre itself was in an inaccessible location, in a basement: women gradually stopped using it, and although the County Council would probably have funded a new centre in 1985 . . . the women involved were unable to come to an agreement about the basis on which it was set up.'[5]

Certainly, our impression is that, by the latter years of the decade, many local Radical feminists felt themselves to be increasingly beleaguered. It is true that, nationally, Radical feminists have continued to argue their position with great assurance and eloquence. The launching of their journal, *Trouble and Strife*, in 1983 speaks of this confidence. Locally, however, the scene is generally different. In Bristol one very active (Socialist) feminist told us that the women in the women's centre seemed to be becoming increasingly self-contained. She had never met a woman from the centre in her many years of campaigning. In Leeds, where revolutionary feminism had originated and where there continued to be a lively group, with its own newsletter, well into the 1980s, we were told by a Radical feminist that, by 1988, the group was no longer meeting and the newsletter had been discontinued. Radical feminists were suffering from 'burn-out'. They felt that they were still under constant attack from other feminists, although many of the things for which they had argued were now widely accepted in the movement. Even though Clause 28 (see Chapter 2) stimulated a campaign of protest, its overall effect was probably to increase this sense of siege. Symbolically, it seemed to signal and legitimate public homophobia; practically, it could be cited by councils, often looking for ways to cut funding, as an excuse for withdrawing support for lesbian groups. Women in Birmingham told us about a Women and Violence conference sponsored by the council in 1988. Panel speakers were told not to mention the word 'lesbian'; the lesbian workshop was held in the basement and was told that it could not report back to the full conference at the end of the day. This was not the fault of the women's unit who had organized the event, but the result of the insistence of the Labour council leadership.

We are not trying to argue here that there was a major showdown between Radical and Socialist feminists in the 1980s, and

⁵ *Spare Rib*, May 1986, 37.

that, from an earlier position of dominance, Radical feminists are now emerging the losers. It is true that, as Chapters 5 and 6 in particular will describe, the 1980s saw many Socialist feminists becoming involved, or re-involved, in the labour movement and in Labour Party politics. They were bruised by the movement's internal battles, but they were also responding to the political dangers implied by Mrs Thatcher's electoral victory and to the new opportunities and receptiveness apparent in the Labour Party and the unions themselves. The expansion of 'municipal feminism', so largely concentrated in Labour authorities, was both a reflection of this and a further stimulus. All these developments undoubtedly constituted a boost for Socialist feminism.

As the 1980s progressed, however, the meaning of Socialist feminism was changing. It no longer connoted a single, identifiable political practice. We noted three important indications that the designation was losing its sharpness. First, the women engaged in municipal feminism probably covered a broad range of ideological positions that could only very loosely be summarized as Socialist feminism. And the wider community of women involved in the various projects and groups spawned or assisted by municipal feminism were, of course, much more varied in their outlook. Secondly, although the majority of feminists, if asked, would probably identify themselves as Socialist rather than Radical feminists, this is generally a Socialist feminism that has been massively influenced by Radical feminism. As Melissa Benn has written, arguing against the picture presented by Socialist feminists like Lynne Segal of a drastically polarized opposition of views, there 'has been a bleeding of the boundaries between radical and socialist feminism to the point where they often erode into non-significance'. Not only have Socialist feminists absorbed so much of Radical feminism, but Radical feminists have become more sensitive to issues of race and class.[6]

Thirdly, and related to this, women involved in local projects and different single-issue campaigns are often, and perhaps increasingly, anxious to avoid sectarian conflict and labelling. Following the publication of Lynne Segal's *Is the Future Female?* in 1987, Liz Kelly wrote a critical review in *Trouble and Strife*. One point that she made quite fairly was that Socialist feminists

---

[6] Melissa Benn, 'Sisters and Slogans', *Marxism Today*, Apr. 1987.

tended to caricature Radical feminism and not to acknowledge the variety of positions that it contains, although her own discussion made clear that this did not stretch to tolerating heterosexuality. But, most germane to the present argument, she suggested that the perception of a bitter division in the movement between Radical and Socialist feminists was, above all, a London one: 'For those of us in the provinces, political differences have seldom had the same hostility and divisiveness. Our communities are not large enough, our resources too limited, for us not to find ways of working together. Feminist activism outside London has always involved coalitions.'[7] We have come across this suggestion of a distorting London lens more than once. While we cannot accept that there have not been bitter fights in a number of places in the past—for instance, Leeds, Glasgow, Liverpool—it is also clear that in many smaller communities, where numbers of activists are low, everybody knows one another, and there are pressing practical problems, these divisions may always have been relatively muted. At local level, certainly, this polarization seemed largely to be a thing of the past, by the mid- to late 1980s.

One partial qualification to this observation might seem to be the emergence of divisions closely paralleling those between Radical and Socialist feminists within the recent mobilization around the issue of pornography (discussed below). But these divisions relate chiefly to national campaign organizers and less to rank-and-file activists, who tend to follow the Radical feminist, pro-censorship line, without necessarily identifying with, or even fully grasping, Radical feminism as an overall perspective.

## THE BLACK WOMEN'S MOVEMENT

Race was, as we have shown in Chapter 3, an important source of theoretical divisions in the women's movement. It was also the basis of organizational divisions that led to the emergence of the black women's movement which evolved and developed through the next decade. There is no doubt that the confrontations between white and black women at this time were extremely

---

[7] Liz Kelly, 'The New Defeatism', *Trouble and Strife*, 11 (Summer 1987), 27.

bruising and painful. Black women were very angry, probably quite rightly. There were clashes in so many different arenas: in existing women's groups and campaigns, in contests for funding from local authorities, on the editorial boards of *Spare Rib* and *Feminist Review*. We remember one particularly tense 'workshop' at a Women Alive conference in 1986, where white and black women met to talk about working together: the black women complained and the white women were generally silent. A proper, equal dialogue seemed impossible.

We must also acknowledge that many black women's groups wanted to dissociate themselves from feminism altogether, which they understand as 'white' feminism. For example, when, in 1987, Monique Griffiths of *Spare Rib* asked different women what feminism had achieved, Sylvett Collins, replied on behalf of Southall Black Women's Centre: 'As Black women we have experienced no change. To lots of black women feminism means only a platform where white middle-class women can play their games in the name of sisterhood.'[8] Even so, in the same article Sandra Agard, a black woman writer, while rejecting 'feminism', talked positively about sisterhood and 'womanism'. Pat Whitehorn, a black media worker, argued that although feminism had not been of much direct help to black women, it had 'shown them the importance of being organised'.[9] Without denying the ambivalence, at best, that black women have felt about 'white' feminism, we do perceive many common themes between the two movements: sisterhood, women asserting themselves, and organizing separately from men. The black women's movement has also generally adopted the characteristic forms and styles of organization of the WLM, with participatory decision-making, managerial collectives, and so on.

So, while in one sense the black women's movement has been a further source of decline for the autonomous women's movement, especially in the early to mid-1980s, we would argue that it must be considered in its own right as another form of autonomous feminist organization. It represented an important new surge of movement energy and creativity.

A black women's movement was already well launched by the

---

[8] See 'Hurray for Feminism!', *Spare Rib*, July 1987: 23.
[9] Ibid. 24–5.

1980s.[10] As we have seen, its inspiration was largely a reaction against the sexism of black men in anti-racist campaigns, but it was also a response to the racism of the overwhelmingly white women's movement. As noted in Chapter 3, the black women's movement, like the white women's movement, was extremely heterogenous. One major difference was between women of Afro-Caribbean and of Asian origin. But in its early years these potential divisions were not yet sources of serious political tension.

One of the earliest Afro-Caribbean women's organizations was the Brixton Black Women's Group formed in 1974. It was set up by women from the journal *Race Today* and from the black bookshop Sabarr as a study group to look at issues like colonialism, the nature of capitalist society, and African history. Initially, members met in each other's houses; later they used a room at the back of the bookshop. By 1980 they had their own black women's centre. They operated as a collective and had links with some white women's organizations, especially those concerned with fighting 'imperialism', including Irish women's organizations, but also in the sphere of reproductive rights.[11]

Asian women took a leading role in industrial action at Imperial Typewriters, Grunwick, and at the Chix factory in Slough in 1980. Immigration was also a vital issue. During her campaign to be allowed to bring her children to live in Britain, Anwar Ditta addressed more than 400 public meetings before she finally succeeded in attracting the attention and support of Granada Television. One of the earliest Asian women's groups, Awaz, which became active in the late 1970s, campaigned around this issue and the so-called 'virginity testing' of Asian women at airports.[12] Southall Black Sisters, which included Afro-Caribbean women, was formed in 1979, in the wake of the demonstration against a National Front meeting held at Southall (Ealing) Town Hall, during which Blair Peach was killed: 'The organisers felt that yes, they were very angry about what was happening to

[10] For an account of these early years, see Beverly Bryan *et al.* (eds.), *The Heart of the Race* (Virago, London, 1985). See also the chapter 'Black Women Organise', in Anna Coote and Polly Pattullo, *Power and Prejudice: Women and Politics* (Weidenfeld and Nicolson, London, 1990).

[11] See Agnes Quashie's interview with Gail Lewis *et al.* of the Brixton Black Women's Group, 'Talking Personal, Talking Political', *Trouble and Strife*, 19 (Summer 1990).

[12] See Amrit Wilson, *Finding a Voice* (Virago, London, 1985)

black people—increasing racial attacks, institutionalised racism and increasing fascist activity particularly in Ealing—yet there was no mention of women's oppression.'[13]

In 1978 OWAAD was launched at a conference that attracted 250 black women.[14] The women behind it had been involved in the African Students' Union, though they worked in consultation with groups like the Brixton Black Women's Group. Discussion themes at the conference included health education, the law, and immigration. For many of the participants, it was an inspiring experience simply to come together with so many other black women, and the conference stimulated the formation of numerous further black women's groups. For example, the women, who went on to form Camden Black Sisters first met there. The conference gave rise to a newsletter, *FOWAAD*, to maintain and extend the network of black women's groups and to facilitate joint action. For instance, OWAAD organized a protest and sit-in at Heathrow Airport against virginity testing.

Though OWAAD played a vital role in the emergence of the black women's movement, rather like the WLM conferences of the 1970s, its very mission to bring black women together was bound to bring out the differences between them. Although the conference that followed in 1980 drew an even larger gathering, emerging rifts clearly marred the third in 1981, and the fourth and final conference in 1982 was 'inevitably a débâcle'. One of the difficulties lay simply in seeking to represent both Afro-Caribbean and Asian women, particularly given that Afro-Caribbean women predominated in the organization. A second tension was between those concerned to emphasize links with Third World women and issues, and those whose focus was the problems of black women within Britain. Yet a further source of conflict, as in the WLM, was women's sexuality. Initially afraid to 'come out', black lesbians grew increasingly assertive. At the 1981 conference, black lesbian demands for the space to hold their own workshop caused an 'uproar'.[15]

[13] Mandana Hendessi, 'Mandana Hendessi in Conversation', in Southall Black Sisters, *Against the Grain: Southall Black Sisters 1979–1989* (Southall Black Sisters, Southall, 1990), 10.

[14] This account is taken mainly from Brixton Black Women's Group, 'Black Women Organising', *Feminist Review*, 17 (Autumn 1984).

[15] Carmen *et al.*, 'Becoming Visible: Black Lesbian Discussion', *Feminist Review*, 17 (Autumn 1984).

If divisions within the black women's movement were becoming more apparent by the early 1980s, this was none the less a time of great activity and ferment, with new groups and organizations appearing, and a lively theoretical debate. Although there may have been a brief lull as black women's energies were temporarily deflected in the 1981 riots and their aftermath, for many this raised anew the question of their relationship with the men in their own communities. Moreover, in the wake of the riots, Lord Scarman's inquiry recommended large injections of capital into the affected inner-city areas. 'Almost overnight, a spate of new ethnic welfare projects, self-help groups, black women's centres and police monitoring committees appeared on the scene.'[16]

But this was also the time when the new local council women's committees and units were beginning to mushroom. A few made a point of recruiting black women: by 1986, 50 per cent of the women employed by Camden Council Women's Unit were black. Other women's committees were particularly anxious to identify and to cater for the needs of black women in their area (the problems that this posed for the black women's movement are considered below), and funding and other kinds of support were available for a range of groups and activities such as women's centres, health and educational projects, training schemes, child care, and publishing. Nearly 300 of the 400 or so women's groups that received some funding from the GLC over the period 1982–5 belonged to black or 'ethnic minority' communities.[17]

As noted in Chapter 3, black women made increasing inroads into the world of publishing. While still forming a miniscule minority, individual black women began to acquire positions of political influence—Linda Bellos and Merle Amory, leaders of Lambeth and Brent Borough Councils respectively; Diane Abbott, elected to the House of Commons in 1987. In 1989 Valerie Amos was appointed chief executive officer of the Equal Opportunities Commission (EOC). Again, this kind of 'success' was not universally welcomed within the black women's movement. But before looking in more detail at the new problems faced by the movement, we should briefly trace the development of each of its two main component 'branches', the Afro-Caribbean and the Asian branch, beginning with the latter.

[16] Members of Brixton Black Women's Group, cited in Bryan et al. (eds.), The Heart of the Race.
[17] Loretta Loach, 'Is there Life after the GLC?', Spare Rib, Mar. 1986: 10–11.

The Asian women's groups, as we have seen, tended initially to focus on issues related to immigration and racial attacks. Southall Black Sisters, which, it must be noted, has always sought to include some Afro-Caribbean women, was primarily about campaigning. It did not emphasize consciousness-raising, although there were discussions about issues like sexuality. It held advice sessions for women at a local law centre, but it could not easily be a 'service' group—the service that it provided to other local black women was purely voluntary, with members meeting in each other's offices or houses—without institutional support or funding. It supported families who were facing racial attacks, and campaigned against the provision under existing immigration law whereby British men, but not women, were allowed to bring their spouses into the country, arguing that this was sexist as well as racist. The group also joined Asian women workers on the picket line at the Chix factory in Slough.

However, increasingly, as Chapters 3 and 9 describe, Southall Black Sisters turned its attention to issues of domestic violence within its own community. As early as 1980 the group protested when Mrs Dhillon and her children were burned to death in their house by her husband. It began to work more closely with women's refuges in Ealing and Acton, arguing that black women there needed other black women's support. In 1984 it took to the streets again, when Krishna Sharma was found hanged after repeated assaults from her husband.[18]

In taking up this issue, Southall Black Sisters reflected a growing trend amongst Asian women's groups. But their willingness to campaign so publicly perhaps set them apart, drawing criticism not only from the leaders of their own community, but from other activist Asian women, who warned against the danger of reinforcing 'liberal racist . . . ideas of Asian men being more sexist than white men and Asian families being particularly barbaric and tyrannical'.[19] Although several other Asian women's groups were now concentrating on setting up Asian women's refuges, they were reluctant to bring issues of domestic violence within the Asian community to the attention of a racist public. Thus

[18] Here we rely on the account in Southall Black Sisters, *Against the Grain*.

[19] Pratibha Parmar, 'Gender, Race and Class: Asian Women in Resistance', in Centre for Contemporary Cultural Studies (Race and Politics Group), *The Empire Strikes Back* (Hutchinson, London, 1982).

Birmingham Black Sisters' defence of Iqbal Begum, who had been gaoled for the murder of her husband, concentrated on the racism of the state (which had convicted her without providing adequate translation facilities, so that her single utterance 'galti', Urdu for 'mistake', was taken as a confession of guilt), but made no reference to the issue of domestic violence.

Like a number of other Asian women's groups, Southall Black Sisters eventually received funding. In 1983 financial support from the GLC enabled it to set up Southall Black Women's Centre and to employ three paid workers. This apparent victory, however, brought new problems. Now that there was a real possibility of providing a service for women, there were disagreements over the extent to which the group should modify its former emphasis on campaigning. There were also the usual strains associated with reliance upon an uncertain source of funding: all funding temporarily dried up in 1986, in the period between the demise of the GLC and the election of a new Labour council in Ealing. Unfortunately, these disagreements culminated in a split along racial lines, with the Afro-Caribbean women continuing to run the service-oriented Southall Black Women's Centre, while Asian women set up Southall Black Sisters in new premises.

Although Southall Black Sisters took the decision to retain a high campaigning profile, some other Asian women's groups were more inclined to see themselves primarily as providing a service. For instance, the Asian Women's Resource Centre in Harlsden was set up in the early 1980s, with GLC funding, by a group of young Asian women who were critical of the way in which both statutory and voluntary organizations tended simultaneously to marginalize and to stereotype Asian women. They also believed that since the local Asian community organizations refused to acknowledge such issues as domestic violence, it was important for Asian women to have their own organization. The Asian Women's Resource Centre offered information, advice, and more extended counselling on a range of issues including welfare benefits, housing, immigration, and domestic violence. By 1991 they had five full-time paid workers—though they were expecting this to be reduced to three—each with a specialist area. In addition, they ran various activities for women: sessions on the poll tax, yoga, massage,

Our strong impression is that, by the end of the 1980s, the number of Asian women's groups—that is, groups which could in any sense be considered feminist—had declined from its early 1980s peak to around nine or ten. Many were struggling with acute resourcing problems and a preoccupation with day-to-day survival. However, one further development added to their difficulties in one sense, but also prompted some women to come out in favour of a less equivocally feminist position: the upsurge of fundamentalism, especially Muslim fundamentalism, in the wake of the Salman Rushdie affair.

As we have seen, Asian women's demands for their own organization and for action on issues like domestic violence within their communities were swiftly condemned by community leaders, including young militant leaders campaigning against racism, as divisive and as providing ammunition for 'liberal' racism. Earlier in the 1980s many young male Sikhs, versed 'in the language of black consciousness', took up the cause and symbols of a separate Khalistan (an independent Sikh state that would secede from India). As one Southall Black Sister observed: 'It's often these young men, not just their conservative elders, who harness religious revivalism in an attempt to control women's sexuality and limit their freedoms.'[20] At the same time, the process of Islamization in Britain, encouraged by its international resurgence, was gaining momentum. The seemingly liberal response of the national government and local authorities had been to continue the policy of 'multiculturalism' which had been adopted from the late 1970s onwards. As expressed in the 1977 ILEA document, *Multi-Ethnic Education*, this meant ensuring that 'within a society that is cohesive though not uniform, cultures are respected, differences recognised, and individual identities are secure'.[21] Such an approach could often be detected in the reluctance of social work departments to interfere in Asian family matters such as conflict over an arranged marriage.

It was the publication of Salman Rushdie's *Satanic Verses* in 1989 which triggered a more militant expression of Islamic

---

[20] Gita Sahgal, 'Fundamentalism and the Multi-Cultural Fallacy', in Southall Black Sisters, *Against the Grain*, 22.

[21] See Clara Connolly's thoughtful article, 'Splintered Sisterhood: Anti-Racism in a Young Women's Project', *Feminist Review*, 36 (Autumn 1990). The quotation is from p. 53.

fundamentalism. Even then, Gita Sahgal suggests that the real issue was Islam versus secularism: the book's publication crystallized fundamentalist leaders' fears that they would be unable to maintain people's faith in a secular society. Anti-racist arguments were then imported into the campaign, partly through the agency of socialist allies like the black Labour MP Bernie Grant. Women against Fundamentalism, a group set up in May 1989, saw that it was essential to separate the two issues, and that, for women's rights, resurgent fundamentalism marked a step backwards. It defended Salman Rushdie's right to freedom of expression, and, instead of demanding, with Muslim community leaders, the extension of the blasphemy laws presently applying only to the Church of England, it demanded their abolition.[22] While the Rushdie affair may have strengthened the resolve of some Asian women to pursue and openly to espouse a broadly secular feminism, it cannot have made life easier for most Muslim women involved in women's organizations, whose own ambivalence would now be reinforced by community suspicion and pressure.

We turn now to women's groups in the Afro-Caribbean community. The first interesting difference between these groups and those for Asian women is that they seemed much less concerned about direct oppression by men. Men were more likely to be seen as unreliable or simply absent than figures of suffocating patriarchal authority. They might be violent—and domestic violence was an issue for Afro-Caribbean women as well as for Asian women, rape perhaps more so—but, generally, women were under less pressure to keep quiet about it. Perhaps that should be qualified: they would be under less pressure from their own immediate family, even women folk, although, like Asian women, there would be pressure from the wider black community not to provide fuel for racism.[23]

By the same token, Afro-Caribbean women tended to express their feminism or 'womanism' in terms of helping themselves and other women to believe in themselves and to make the best of their lives, rather than asserting themselves against men. As one told us:

[22] Sahgal, 'Fundamentalism'.
[23] For one angry protest against the refusal to acknowledge that black women were raped during the Brixton and Tottenham riots, see Anna J. Hearne, 'Racism, Rape and Riots', Trouble and Strife, 9 (Summer 1986).

I see white women out there trying to get equality with white men. Whereas black women were trying to establish themselves as black women. So we weren't looking to go one step ahead and be equal. We were just trying to establish ourselves and go out there, into the workplace, finding the jobs, just to be able to survive. No way that we could take on the feminist movement.

While accepting the need, underlined by numerous black women writers, not to indulge in cultural stereotyping, it is difficult not to connect this observation with differences in family structure and values in the two communities, and, in particular, with the relatively high proportion of single mothers in the Afro-Caribbean community.

Like Asian women's groups, many Afro-Caribbean women's groups acquired some public funding by the early 1980s. They often had a centre and became increasingly involved in providing services to their community, most of all to its women. The emphasis of their service work varied. For instance, the London Black Women's Health Project was originally a voluntary organization centrally concerned with the issue of female circumcision. By 1983 it had succeeded in obtaining public funding, and thereafter its work widened out into general health care (we discuss it further in Chapter 7).

Another East London group, the East London Black Women's Organization (ELBWO), in Newham, has focused on education. Its founding members were involved in OWAAD, and initially met as a support group at one another's houses. Around 1982 they acquired GLC funding and were able to rent two rooms in the local community centre. In time they acquired their own centre, funded, after the demise of the GLC, by Newham Council and the London Borough Grants Scheme. By 1991 the centre had an elected management committee, made up exclusively— and as a matter of policy—of Afro-Caribbean women, and employed five full-time and three part-time paid workers. Though it deals with all kinds of enquiries, most notably about housing and mental illness, the initial impetus was to do with education, and this is still the focus of most of its activities. This partly reflects the well-known shortcomings of general school education in Newham, but also, more specifically, the founders' objective, 'to highlight the lack of educational provision in the borough for

Black people'.[24] Activities such as provision for the under-5s and an after-school project are clearly designed to support working mothers, but they also have an educational thrust. The centre also runs a Saturday school for children and parents, in which black cultural themes are emphasized.

The emphasis of Camden Black Sisters is different again. Its six founding members came together at OWAAD, and for a time they met in each other's homes. Around 1984 they got some funding from Camden Council and accommodation in Camden Women's Centre at Wesley House. In the mean time, the GLC purchased a derelict warehouse for their eventual use as a centre, but it was not until 1991 that the group had got together sufficient funds, including money that they raised themselves through dances, bazaars, coffee mornings, and such like, to have it refurbished. By the time one of us went to see it, it was quite a splendid building, but we were informed that the group had only a five-year lease. Camden Black Sisters, who presently have two paid workers but also rely heavily on voluntary efforts, see 'empowering' black women as their overriding objective. With that in mind, they organized an exhibition around the life and work of Claudia Jones, who lived for many years in this part of London and was prominent in the international communist movement. But there has been a wide range of activities: a mother and toddlers support group; surgeries offering practical help in areas such as housing, health, and welfare; a continuous advice service on housing, job applications, training opportunities, and the like; recreational workshops; and a library. The most frequent inquiries are about housing, a symptom of the desparate shortage of available and affordable accommodation in the borough.

The groups mentioned so far share a common focus—to offer practical help to black women in the local community. And this seems to be largely representative of groups outside London. For instance, in 1986 Liverpool Black Sisters described themselves as running a series of courses for black women on health, history, and trade unions. They collaborated with a local women's film and video co-operative in the black women's media project; they advised on issues such as deportation and harassment of black families.[25]

[24] Quoted from the organization's leaflet about itself, *East London Black Women's Organization*     [25] Liz Drysdale, 'Black Resister', *Spare Rib*, May 1986.

In order to show that this emphasis on assistance is not quite universal, we should note the contrasting approach of the Black Women for Wages for Housework group (BWWH), based at King's Cross Women's Centre. The centre itself was set up in the 1970s and includes black and white women, both in the collective which runs it and in the women who use its 'drop in' advisory service. Since 1988 it has had no funding at all for workers, but has relied entirely on volunteers. BWWH is part of the International Wages for Housework campaign founded in 1972. Within the British women's movement in general, support for this campaign, which demanded that women should be paid by the state for domestic labour, had largely disappeared by the 1980s. One reason for this was that feminists feared that it would reinforce assumptions about women's domestic role within the sexual division of labour. However, from the early 1980s the issue was revived internationally with a more Third World focus. Beginning from the premiss that women do two-thirds of the world's work and receive only 5 per cent of its income, the campaign aims in the first instance to persuade governments to take account of women's unpaid work in the Gross National Product (a recommendation taken up in the 'Forward-Looking Strategies for the Advancement of Women' formulated at the 1985 Nairobi women's conference and subsequently ratified by the UN), but ultimately to persuade them to compensate women for their unpaid work, using money released as a result of dismantling the military-industrial complex. Thus their analysis makes links across a very wide range of issues, but it tends to involve campaigns rather than more immediately practical activities.[26]

The 1980s, then, saw a proliferation of black women's groups. But there has been some decline lately. The recent demise of the Brixton Black Women's Group seems in many ways symptomatic, although we have been unable to discover the precise reasons for it. Another sign was the shutting-down of *Outwrite*, whose last issue came out in December 1988. This picture is not universal: most strikingly, growing activism in Scotland was marked in 1987 by the first Scottish Black Women's conference. None the less, by 1988, four years after *Feminist Review*'s special issue on black women, Pratibha Parmar was writing: 'Reading

[26] This account was built up from an interview with, and literature produced by, the group.

112 THE AUTONOMOUS WOMEN'S MOVEMENT

that issue now . . . it seems difficult to fathom where the optimism and stridency which many of us had who were active in the
black women's movement has gone, and why. Where are the
diverse black feminist perspectives which we felt were in the
process of growth? And where indeed is the movement itself?'[27]

Parmar herself appears to lay much of the blame for the
decline on conflicts both within the black women's movement
and with the white women's movement, and their manifestation
in 'identity politics'. As noted in Chapter 3, while it was important—indeed, indispensable—for black women to challenge the
implicit racism of the women's movement and to explore the
meaning of being 'black' and 'black women', after a while this
tended to become counter-productive. As with other forms of
identity politics, it could encourage women to retreat into a
lifestyle 'ghetto'. It made alliances with white women's organizations difficult. And it also tended to impose in turn a questionable unity on 'black women' which was bound to generate
further assertions of difference from Asian and Afro-Caribbean
women, lesbian black women, and so forth.

Other dimensions of identity politics are also present in the
black women's movement, but they seem less salient. Although
sexuality has been a divisive issue, as far as we can judge, it has
not generated the bitterness that it aroused in the (white)
women's movement. Often the issue remains subterranean, and
the real problem is to get women to confront it. As one activist
told us: 'It's an underlying issue. It's like a hidden agenda and
we have tried to bring it out into the open, but the people who
object don't turn up for the discussions.' But it also seems to us
that hostility towards white women has diminished as black
women have acquired their own organizations, forums of expressions, and new confidence. The very fact that Parmar and others
have expressed their fears about the dangers of identity politics
may imply that the worst is passed. There does seem to be a
greater willingness to work with white women in the last few
years. This is partly, of course, a consequence of the greater willingness of white feminists, and especially of Socialist feminists, to
take black women's arguments seriously.

[27] Pratibha Parmar, 'Other Kinds of Dreams', *Feminist Review*, 31 (Spring
1989), 55.

There are, doubtless, exceptions to this generalization. Liverpool Black Sisters, for instance, wrote in 1986:

The Liverpool Black Sisters has over the years established contact with many black and white women's organisations. We are able to draw support from some of our white sisters through the work of campaigns although the limitations of this support become more evident when clear cut demands are made by black women for recognition of the racism we face from white women. Often black women will find great difficulty with having to tolerate the tears and guilt and listen to the self-recrimination that some white women feel is appropriate when they are challenged about their racism.[28]

They subsequently boycotted (see Chapter 7) the Women's Health Network conference held in 1989, because, they argued, it had been planned without taking sufficient account of black women's health needs. On the other hand, black and white women came together to organize the Network of Women demonstration against male violence in 1986 (see Chapter 9). In 1991 black women joined pickets in support of Sarah Thornton, who was given a long goal sentence for killing her husband, although she claimed that he had been physically abusing her for years.

In 1986 *Spare Rib* carried a lengthy article about black and white women working together, amply demonstrating the difficulties, but also indicating a range of examples.[29] On balance, the possibilities for co-operation between black and white women look better now, in the early 1990s, than they did in the early 1980s. It is our firm impression that the difficulties faced by the black women's movement in more recent years have been more to do with the negative consequences of increasing involvement with state agencies, which has been a problem for the movement as a whole. This is a theme that runs through this whole book; it is taken up in the Conclusion.


## GREENHAM WOMEN

While the burgeoning of the black women's movement in the early 1980s coincided with, and may have hastened, the waning

---

[28] Drysdale, 'Black Resister', 40.
[29] 'Can Black and White Women Work Together?', *Spare Rib*, July 1986.

of the surviving WLM, it was a new form of autonomous feminist activity, for a time vibrant and confident. In a different way,
the mobilization around the women of Greenham Common was
also a fresh, vital shoot from the ailing parent plant.

The peace camp at Greenham Common was one of the most
sustained and controversial instances of the feminist politics of
the 1980s. It mobilized large numbers of women, attracted enormous press coverage, and generated a nationwide structure of
support groups. It caused controversies in the peace movement,
the labour movement, and the feminist movement, too. At the
outset, however, it was not an especially feminist initiative, and it
never gained the unequivocal support of the whole of the
women's movement (or, indeed, of the peace movement). To
develop these points, it is necessary briefly to narrate the events
of Greenham, and then to assess their significance for British
feminist politics.

The Women's Peace Camp began as a 'Walk for Life' organized by Women for Life on Earth. The immediate cause was the
decision by the British government to allow the United States to
install cruise missiles in Britain. Nuclear dumping was already an
issue in many rural areas, and there were a number of indicators
that the peace movement, in decline during the late 1970s, was
picking up. Jill Liddington[30] cites a number of women's peace
initiatives that took place at the end of the 1970s and the early
1980s. The peace movement had always mobilized women in
groups that were internationally linked. The idea of the Walk for
Life march was inspired by a march from Copenhagen to Paris
that was reported in *Peace News*. Anne Pettit, the organizer, told
Jill Liddington that once she agreed to take charge, there was
widespread interest and support. The initiative was rooted in the
home-grown experience of running anti-nuclear groups in rural
communities. There is little evidence that the organizers had
much interest in feminist theory. Their aim was to give a voice to
a wide range of women, without excluding men.

The march (of 36 women, 4 men, and 3 children) left Cardiff
for Greenham on 27 August 1981. Accommodation and support
were organized at different stages on the route; the march was
planned as a mobilization of local opinion and action. The press

[30] Liddington, *The Long Road to Greenham*.

was informed, but proved disappointingly immune. So, as they marched and handed out leaflets, the participants discussed more confrontational tactics. Gradually the decision was taken that four women should chain themselves to the fence once they reached Greenham. Supported by a large group of women from Newbury Campaign against Cruise, the march arrived on 5 September. The four women chained themselves to the main gate. The press did report it, but in a minimal way. The marchers began to feel that they could not just go home, so they established a peace camp. Gradually, the news that this had happened spread—by word of mouth, via *Spare Rib*—throughout the peace and women's movements generally.

For several months the camp continued quietly while support gradually built up, but at the end of 1981 there was a change of gear as the camp became a focus of widespread popular and movement attention. There were several related reasons for the shift. Perhaps the most important of these was the decision, in February 1982, that the camp should become a women-only endeavour. Liddington[31] draws attention to the importance of the events that precipitated the decision. Isolated women's peace groups had begun to link up and Greenham had become a focus for them; supporting Greenham was one of their activities. At the camp, confrontation between the authorities and the women had escalated. It was felt that tactics of non-violent direct action would be both more effective and easier to sustain if the camp became women only as well as women-led. Feminist influences were also apparent by this time, and it was no longer considered appropriate for a women's peace camp to include men.

The shift to a women-only camp sharpened the focus of Greenham, giving it a central place both in peace politics and in feminist politics. In terms of its impact on the public mind, the amount of immediate support that it was able to generate, and its weight in the feminist movement, the heyday of Greenham was between 1982 and 1984. During that time a whole series of unusual and imaginative political actions took place at the base. The scale of support amongst women for the campers became clear in December 1982, when the Embrace the Base demonstration attracted 30,000 women, who linked hands around the nine-

---

[31] Ibid. 235–56.

mile perimeter of the base. Personal effects were brought by demonstrators and attached to the chain-link fence; these included everything from photographs to a full scale tea service. The organization that this required was innovative and on a large scale. For example, chain-letters were sent to initial network mailing lists as a means of spreading information. On the night of the demonstration, 12 December, the national television news showed aerial shots of the Greenham base encircled by candles glowing in the dark. It was an inspiring demonstration. One participant described it vividly:

The fence around the airport has a nine mile perimeter. Not a yard was left untouched. It looked incredible. Wens of wool, a woman's diary, doves, recipes, women's and peace symbols made from ferns, fruits, records, an empty Bacardi bottle, thousands of balloons, vegetables, statements from the UN Declaration of Human Rights and the International Code of Nursing Ethics, a never ending stream of family albums, photographs, children's toys, pictures and clothes, an inexplicable postcard of the Royal Family and hundreds of tampons dipped in red.[32]

The next day, 2,000 women stayed on to blockade the base. Many of the women who took part in the demonstration returned to their communities to organize Greenham support groups. Visits to the camp became regular activities, as did collecting food, clothing, bedding, and money for the campers. These networks of support groups ensured the camp a presence in communities all over the country. By 1983 there were peace camps at most of the gates to the base (named according to the colours of the rainbow), and a national support network. Innovative demonstrations received press attention and captured the public imagination. On New Year's Day 1983 forty-four women climbed over the fence and danced in a ring on top of a cruise missile silo. On 1 April that year CND organized a human chain of 77,000 people to link Greenham to Aldermaston as 200 women staged a teddy bear's picnic at the base. Later, Greenham women padlocked all four gates with 'indestructible' locks. In June they sewed a 4½-mile dragon to weave in and out of the base. Meanwhile, court cases of earlier actions resulted in women being sent to Holloway Prison, which was where the suffragists

[32] Quoted in Roisin Boyd et al., 'Greenham Common', Spare Rib, Feb. 1983: 12.

were gaoled earlier this century. General police attention to the camp escalated, as did the resulting legal battles in which growing numbers of women were prepared to face the courts. The camp was seldom out of the news, and its centrality continued until the missiles arrived and were installed in November 1983. After that the impact of the camp gradually declined. But the protest continued over the decade, with a few women still there in 1991, and court battles over the various Greenham convictions a continuing reminder of its purpose.

The feminism of the Greenham movement was apparent from a very early stage, but it is important to note that Greenham never had the complete support of either the feminist movement or the wider women's peace movement. Support and admiration were tempered by ambivalence about the Greenham message and, most specifically, about the connections between women, nurturance, and peace which it seemed to many to signify.

To understand this ambivalence, it is necessary to remind ourselves of some of the theoretical debates that were current at the beginning of the 1980s. (These are dealt with more fully in the preceding chapter as well as in Chapter 9, which explores the issue of male violence.) By the time that the peace marchers set off from Cardiff, many feminists were influenced by more or less essentialist, pro-woman theories which rejected as male (and therefore bad) science, high technology, rationalism, hierarchy, and centralization, and embraced as female (and therefore good) nature, low technology, nurturing, spirituality, ancient mythologies, and the oppressed. The influential 'ecofeminism' of United States feminist Susan Griffin, for example, saw maleness as so destructive that women were advised against desiring any share of its power.[33] These ideas were in the air when the anti-nuclear discussion was spreading in British women's groups, and before long they gave rise to numerous debates about whether peace was a feminist issue. Meanwhile, within the women's movement, arguments also raged over how to understand violence. Over the course of the 1970s, for many women, violence had become identified with maleness. The focus of the debate on the Left also shifted, and arguments about the meaning of male violence left little space for discussions of military violence or of non-violence

---

[33] Liddington, *The Long Road to Greenham*, 215.

as an empowering feminist strategy.[34] Shifts in ideas about motherhood were also taking place. While some feminists reacted strongly against the stereotyping of women as naturally more caring or peaceful, others emphasized and extolled their maternal and nurturing virtues.

Greenham highlighted these divisions and difficulties in the feminist movement, notably the problem of how to assert the positive aspects of women's capacities whilst insisting that women should not be primarily defined by these capacities. As we have seen, disagreements amongst feminists were especially acute in the first half of the 1980s. Greenham, in mobilizing a new generation of women and in setting an example to the earlier generations, both reflected and contributed to those divisions. Thus, in May 1984 *Spare Rib* featured a set of interviews about Greenham which began: 'With Greenham support groups springing up everywhere, it would seem at first glance that feminism is once again spreading like wildfire. But can we assume that it has anything to do with women's liberation? Who is being reached, who is being active?'

The gender and peace debate was a complicated one that ranged from minimalist, tactical positions to fully blown theories of life and knowledge. The minimalist (and fairly common) line was that women-only action made for a more effective symbol of non-violence. The maximalist position was a form of the essentialism described above in which women's culture was celebrated, and at Greenham itself there was talk of witches and goddesses and being nice to trees.[35] A range of responses came from within the peace and women's movement. Sometimes the responses were quite bitter. Annie Tunnicliffe, writing in the peace movement journal *Sanity*, commented: 'I have sometimes felt that there was more sisterhood in a bus queue than in the women's peace movement.'[36] Nor were things all that sisterly in the women's movement. In 1983 Onlywoman Press, a feminist publishing collective, published *Breaching the Peace*, a set of conference papers in which Radical feminists criticized the peace camp as a diversion from the real struggle against patriarchy, a way of ending the WLM. In the inevitable response, *Raging Women: In Reply to Breaching the Peace*, Jean Freer, a woman from the Green Gate

[34] Liddington, *The Long Road to Greenham*, 202.    [35] Ibid.    [36] Ibid, 257.

camp, asserted the inherent feminism of the peace camp with the much-quoted observation: 'More wimmin [*sic*] pass through Greenham than any women's centre I've ever known.'

The reality is that Greenham included all kinds of feminism. Over time, the feminism that saw the arms race as a direct reflection of patriarchy gave way to more diverse strands of Socialist and Radical feminism.[37] The many conflicting images that were to be found in both the commercial media and the women's press were a reflection of the wide range of women involved. Greenham's mobilizing capacities were enormous. It involved women with no previous organizing experience, as well as attracting those who were disillusioned with other forms of organization. Some were refugees from the more rigid feminist politics of the early 1980s, bringing with them many of the early feminist ideas about organization and consensus. Jean Freer remarked in *Raging Women* that many women's centres at the time exuded bitterness and rigidity; they made new women feel uncomfortable, guilty, and confused. Greenham offered another approach, an open-handed way of doing things, which was both effective and empowering for the women involved. Growing out of the NSMs, it had their characteristic modes of operating. The local Greenham groups were as much a part of the movement as the peace camp. An emphasis was placed on democratic decision-making: from the beginning, Greenham decision-making followed the democratic conventions of consciousness-raising group politics. In 1981, when the marchers took the decision to chain themselves to the fence, they recognized that this would mean a reassessment of what they were all doing. There was concern that no one should feel compelled to do so, but that everyone should agree with the decision. The discussion rule that evolved was that comments would not be allowed until everyone had spoken. Such practices continued as the movement spread. As one woman from one of the eight Hackney Greenham groups said in 1986:

This has been a very different experience for those of us used to organizing within the traditional left. We have not had to leave our emotional lives behind at actions or meetings; we have been able to bring our fears and anxieties with us and deal with them. Many groups start their meeting with a 'go-round' of how each woman is feeling; there is an

[37] Barbara Norden, 'Many Visions—Many Hands', *Spare Rib*, Sept. 1985: 6–8, 32–4.

acceptance of women being able to offer different levels of commitment at different times or in different ways.

She goes on to point out that she believes this kind of organization is prefigurative: 'it's important that our way of doing things is consistent with the future that we'd like to build.'[38] Practices like this made for long meetings, but women felt empowered and supported by them. One woman told *Spare Rib* in June 1982 that it was common now to 'insist on organising our local mixed CND group so that it does not reflect the patriarchal values and structures we are rejecting. We have tried to create the sort of atmosphere in which everyone can speak and help to make policy . . . we all take a turn at chairing the meeting so that we gain confidence in our abilities to speak in public.'[39]

Not all women experienced the open and empowering atmosphere described by Jean Freer when they went to Greenham. Norden[40] recounts how members of the Manchester support group felt that it seemed like a closed shop to some women, who asked if it would be all right to go down there. Moreover, class and race differences were important. To be free for a total bestowal of time, to choose whether or not to go to prison, implies a position of privilege that many women do not have. Race was also an issue. Amanda Hassan, the co-ordinator of the black and Asian working group of CND, recalled how she

was holding on to the fence along with some other women (all white) and from nowhere a big burly policeman gave me a chop on my arm and sent me reeling into the mud. None of the other women who were also holding onto the fence got this treatment. When I commented on this a woman said 'Well, you're only picked on because you're so short' (I'm under five foot). *Couldn't they see it was because I was black?*[41]

Greenham issues and organizational principles were discussed throughout the peace movement, where some of its ideas were rejected, others were absorbed and used. There was considerable discussion in CND about the divisiveness of the women-only camp, and its separatist politics were sometimes severely criticized. But there was also a respect for the Greenham women,

---

[38] See Sue Finch *et al.*, 'Socialist Feminists and Greenham', *Feminist Review*, 23 (Spring 1986), 94.
[39] Sheila Riddell, 'Hell No—We Won't Glow', *Spare Rib*, June 1982: 23.
[40] Norden 'Many Visions, Many Hands',                    [41] Cited in ibid. 32.

who were treated as movement heroines and regarded almost with awe when they spoke at peace conferences. As we have seen, the organizational methods of feminism were adopted by some CND branches. Nevertheless, it is important to remember that the women's peace movement is wider than Greenham and includes many organizations that predate the camp by several decades.

There was also cross-fertilization between Greenham and other social movements. During the miners' strike, Greenham women spoke around the country, addressed rallies, picketed, raised money for Women against Pit Closures, and generally supported the women in the mining communities. The link between the nuclear power issue and the future of the coal industry made it possible for Greenham women to make interventions where other feminists might have been resented (see below).

The main reason why the Greenham movement declined was, of course, the installation of the cruise missiles in late 1983. Once that happened, although there was a long tail of activity (vigils, cruise-watches, etc.), there was a feeling that the action was largely symbolic. Participants and supporters became increasingly uncertain about the reason for their actions; media coverage diminished, and policing increased. The peace movement, too, was in decline, and once the agreement was signed, it became difficult to sustain Greenham as a movement, although a small camp was still there in 1991.

The impact of Greenham is the impact of an oppositional social movement, more politically significant for its effect on the participants than its effect on policy. Opinion poll evidence over the years of the camp gives little indication that Greenham changed women's opinions about cruise missiles.[42] It is impossible to tell what effect it had on government policy. Certainly, the Conservative government went all out to generate favourable publicity for its defence policy between 1983 and 1984; the spectacle of the Heseltine stump around the country is well documented.[43] Attention to public opinion could also have been why the government never used the full panoply of its powers against the Greenham women.

[42] Alice Henry et al., 'Greenham Inside and Out', Spare Rib, May 1984.
[43] See Paul Byrne, The Campaign for Nuclear Disarmament (Croom-Helm, London, 1988).

Greenham's capacity to mobilize was its most remarkable characteristic. This was largely a mobilization of existing opposition and fear; its strength came from the fact that it empowered women both by its forms of organization and by the sense that it gave them that their capacity to act enable them to take responsibility for their political views. The connections that this afforded were first and foremost feminist connections. The movement was one of women acting as women. But other connections were also present; the movement was influenced by previous non-violent, direct-action-based campaigns, by environmental concerns, and by the other feminist campaigns of the decade.

## WOMEN AGAINST PIT CLOSURES

Another prominent campaign of the 1980s that was built around women's action and came to have feminist implications was the mobilization of women in the mining communities during the 1984–5 miners' strike. This did not begin as a feminist intervention, nor did it ever become a wholeheartedly feminist movement. Women against Pit Closures (WAPC) was a rare instance of working-class women participating in high-profile political action. Its motivation was the desire of women in the mining communities to defend the jobs of their male relatives and thereby to defend their communities. It began as an effort to provide community-level kitchens, food for strikers, and to bring people out of their homes and into contact with the community, thus building solidarity for the strike. Jean McCrindle, who was involved in WAPC from its beginnings, believes that the strike revealed the natural political talents and capacities of women who were unaware of their abilities. This also enabled them to make feminist connections. Betty Heathfield, one of the women prominent in the strike was, says McCrindle, really a feminist of some kind all her life; the strike gave her the space to make the connections.[44]

The success of the miners' wives' initiative came as a surprise to practically everyone. A rally planned in Barnsley in May 1984

[44] See interview of Jean McCrindle by Sheila Rowbotham, 'More than Just a Memory: Some Political Implications of Women's Involvement in the Miners' Strike, 1984–1985', *Feminist Review*, 23 (Spring 1986).

was expected to be a modest affair, but 10,000 women turned out. The response of the striking men was mixed; some were hostile, some encouraging. The anti-hierarchical organizational forms that the women adopted to plan their activities did not sit well next to the bureaucratized hierarchical structures of the NUM. Feminist connections often come instinctively to militant organizations, and women in the WAPC felt that they formed their feminist ideas spontaneously. But each area of the strike probably contained two or three groups with contacts with the women's groups in the Labour Party or the CND. These were also sources of feminism. Initial fear and caution about feminist ideas soon turned to interest and, in many cases, support. Contact with Greenham began at a very early stage; there were regular toings and froings between the mining communities and the peace camp. The strike was heavily policed and often extremely violent, another politicizing experience for the women, who were often victims of enthusiastic policing. Those participating in the pickets and speaking at rallies supplied powerful images of women's political action. WAPC activists toured the country, speaking to socialist and feminist gatherings not only during the strike, but for some time afterwards. Support groups were established in different parts of the country, and a widespread network soon came into being. In Nottingham town centre, WAPC and Greenham women set up collection points side by side which survived the strike by some years. This vibrant symbol of feminist action and connections was replicated in many parts of the country.

But it was difficult to keep the mass action going once the strike was over. The miners lost badly, which meant a rapid reduction in the size of the mining community, and huge changes for the strikers and their families. WAPC tried—and failed—to gain associate membership of the National Union of Mineworkers (NUM) after the strike. The exception was in Scotland, where associate membership was granted in recognition of a widespread perception that, in many places, it was women's support that had kept the strike going.[45] The WAPC also organized activities such as raising money for sacked strikers, running

[45] Esther Breitenbach, 'Sisters Are Doing it for Themselves', in A. Brown and R. Parry (eds.), *The Scottish Government Yearbook (1990)* (Unit for the Study of Government in Scotland, Edinburgh University, Edinburgh, 1990).

campaigns against the imprisonment of strikers, and supporting other strikes.[46] But even though the campaign inevitably ran out of steam after a while, many of those involved have testified to the lasting difference that it has made to their lives and to their view of themselves. In Wales we were told: 'Even though the battle was lost and the women returned to their kitchens—these were new women. Poems, songs and stories written by miners' wives and daughters as a result of the fearful events of the previous 12 months bear witness to their permanent politicisation'.[47] North Staffordshire Miners' Wives were still going strong in 1990. Although many were critical of the middle-class character of women's liberation politics and uneasy with some of its assumptions, they also knew themselves to be changed women. One of them, formerly a housewife, now a Labour councillor, recalled: 'When the strike finished, it was obvious there was no going back. A lot of women who hadn't been politically involved before the strike were now completely involved. We knew we just couldn't go back to the way we'd been living before'.[48]

Greenham and, in a different way, the activities of the WAPC were important elements within the evolving WLM. They incorporated its notion of women's separate organization and participatory decision-making—indeed, for many, they may have provided a welcome return to the old, more tolerant decision-making styles which sectarian strife within the movement had tended to squeeze out. They brought new women to feminism, but they also spawned support groups amongst feminists all over the country. When we interviewed feminist activists—in different cities and involved in different issues (health, women's refuges, and so forth)—we regularly found that they had played some active part in supporting Greenham or the miners' wives, in some cases both, and that this had affected them quite deeply.

It is a moot point, therefore, whether either campaign could be seen as a damaging diversion and drain on feminist energy, as is sometimes suggested. For one thing, feminist activism is not necessarily a fixed quantity, nor is it simply transferable from one

[46] Vicky Seddon (ed.), *The Cutting Edge: Woman and the Pit Strike* (Lawrence and Wishart, London, 1986).

[47] See Rosanne Reeves, 'A Welsh Patchwork', in Amanda Sebestyen (ed)., *'68, '78, '88: From Women's Liberation to Feminism* (Prism, Bridport, 1988).

[48] *Guardian*, 7 Mar, 1990.

area to another. If feminist energies were not focused on Greenham, it does not follow that they would be available to defend abortion rights, for instance. But, more than this, we would argue that these campaigns were extremely valuable in regenerating the movement, allowing women to discover anew the exhilarating power of 'sisterhood', even if they, too, would inevitably learn how difficult it is to maintain.


### THE CAMPAIGN AGAINST PORNOGRAPHY

The WLM seems to have hit something of a low point in 1986–7. Greenham and the WAPC were petering out; old women's liberation networks were running down; and the black women's movement had probably peaked. Some activists identified this as a particularly difficult time to mobilize women for their campaigns. Factors already cited—the generally harsher employment and welfare climate of the 1980s, perhaps also the growing realization that Thatcherism was not just a passing phase (bad dream)—played their part. One of our interviewees suggested that this encouraged a kind of 'victim' mentality amongst feminists, a sense that everything was hopeless. The exhaustion and disillusion of in-fighting also took their toll. Another activist, thinking about what had happened to a number of her feminist friends, sensed 'a feeling that a lot of women plough their own furrows'. Many, for instance, looked to feminist-influenced forms of therapy to provide the meaning and support no longer to be found in women's groups. But there was one more specific and directly impinging development—the abolition of the GLC. The GLC under Ken Livingstone had provided a symbolic focus for socialist feminism, and a major source of funding and other forms of sponsorship for all kinds of feminist activity. Although this funding did not dry up immediately and completely, and although women's committees and units persisted, and have survived, in a number of other, primarily Labour-controlled, local councils (see Chapter 6), this was a major practical and psychological blow.

In September 1987 David Alton announced that he would be submitting a private member's bill to reduce the time-limit for abortion, and in December 1987 the Conservative MP

David Wilshire introduced an amendment to the new Local Government Bill (which subsequently became Clause 28), the aim of which was to prevent local councils from 'promoting' homosexuality. Both of these threats to established rights triggered considerable mobilization amongst existing feminists. They also helped to politicize young women, especially students, who had hitherto tended to take such rights for granted. We describe the anti-Alton campaign in some detail in Chapter 7.

But the issue that, seemed to strike a chord with an extraordinarily diverse range of women by the last two years of the decade is pornography. Chapter 9 explores the context of theoretical debate within which the issue came to assume such a central position. Rather than helping to bring together existing Radical and Socialist feminist camps, the question of pornography tended to accentuate their differences. Two broad stances are identified: the 'pornography as male violence' position primarily elaborated by Radical feminists; and the 'pornography as representation' position taken up by Socialist and also Liberal feminists.

In fact, the issue generated not two but three campaigning groups. These are the Campaign against Pornography (CAP), the Campaign against Pornography and Censorship (CAPC), and Feminists against Censorship (FAC). By the end of 1991 all three groups were well established. Between them they employed the full repertoire of tactics—direct action, mass demonstrations, parliamentary initiatives, and argument in academic and feminist journals—and together they comprised the largest feminist mobilization since the pro-choice campaigns of the late 1970s and the early 1980s.

Let us sketch out the concerns and characteristics of each group. CAP (in Scotland this is Scottish Women against Pornography, or SWAP) is the largest of the three groups. It was started by Labour MP Clare Short, who impulsively produced her 'Page 3' bill during a parliamentary debate about banning violence on television in 1986. Short's Indecent Displays Bill touched a nerve; the *Sun* newspaper launched a continuing campaign against her, but thousands of women who hated the newspaper pin-ups which the bill sought to ban wrote to her to express their support. By mid-1992 CAP had a widespread national campaigning network, built around strong local groups in most of Britain's cities. It is supported by many trade unions, by the National Union of Students, and by a number of local authority women's committees.

The campaign draws on, and highlights, the feminist ideas that are present in the general population of British women. Melissa Benn[49] has noted how many of the letters use feminist rhetoric to describe their hatred of the Page 3 image. Clare Short has said in many interviews that she chose this image because it is so pervasive, a strategy of striking near to home. One of CAP's most successful ventures is its Off the Shelf campaign, in which women picket newsagents who sell pornography. The campaign is directed against W. H. Smith, the largest 'family' newsagent in Britain. During 1991 CAP compiled a directory of 'porn-free' newsagents; members are kept informed of campaign progress and about the fate of parliamentary initiatives via occasional mailings and regional conferences. Interestingly, the campaign literature had to be adapted for Scotland, where there are only two W. H. Smith outlets. The active and successful Scottish campaign is directed at John Menzies stores. CAP also supports legislative efforts by Dawn Primarola, the Labour MP from Bristol, who seeks to restrict the sale of pornography to licensed premises only. In addition to parliamentary work, CAP engages in lobbying and tries to get as much press and media publicity for its views as possible. Its grass-roots activities mainly consist of local campaigns, and conferences.

CAP had its first national conference in Nottingham, in the autumn of 1990. The conference was heavily oversubscribed. The main speakers were prominent Radical feminists (Suzanne Kappeler, Liz Kelly) with a long-standing interest in issues of sexual violence, and Clare Short. The organizers were accused of preventing FAC members from participating in the conference workshops.[50] It was made clear at the conference that, on the issue of pornography, CAP is prepared to work with the moral Right, and believes that the law must be strengthened to permit the censorship of pornography.

Members of CAP argue that there is a direct link between

---

[49] Melissa Benn, 'Page Three and the Campaign against it', in Gail Chester and Julienne Dickey (eds.), *Feminism and Censorship* (Prism, Bridport, 1988).

[50] Barbara Norden, 'Campaign against Pornography', *Feminist Review*, 35 (1990).

pornography and crimes of sexual violence—that is, they regard pornography as dangerous because of its literal effects as well as offensive in its depictions of women as submissive, available, and enjoying abuse. Supporters of legislation contend that it is unrealistic to oppose legislation on the grounds that laws will be imperfect. Rape law is imperfect, but feminists are unlikely to give it up. Legislation restricting pornography is useful because it gives official state backing to women's fight to improve the way in which we are portrayed, because campaigns to achieve it bring about changes in society's attitude towards women, because it provides campaigners with additional weapons to use against degrading images of women, and because it gives new confidence to women who have suffered from the effects of degrading images.[51]

It is difficult to asses the size of CAPC, but it is clearly much smaller than CAP. CAPC differs from CAP in that it seeks to adapt the MacKinnon/Dworkin ordinance (or Minneapolis ordinance) to British circumstances. As explained in Chapter 9, this ordinance is a law designed by feminists in the United States which enables women to take pornographers to court on the grounds that pornography discriminates against women. However, it is not hostile to CAP and has supported the Off the Shelf campaign. CAPC was formed by a group of lawyers, journalists, women's rights campaigners, and trade-unionists. It is co-ordinated by Elizabeth Carolo, who classifies herself as a Radical feminist lesbian and who has considerable experience of campaigns against male violence, but its central actor is Catherine Itzin. Itzin believes that pornography is itself a form of censorship of women; that it is violence, both through the manner of its production and through the fear that it instils in 'all women'. Pornography, for Itzin, is a record of sexual violence, often a record of violent crime. When the Home Office published the Cumberbatch Report, which indicated that there was no causal connection between pornography and violent crime, the CAPC submitted evidence which, it claimed, demonstrated the contrary.

CAPC aims to provide information on every aspect of

[51] Wendy Moore, 'There Should Be a Law against it, Shouldn't there?', in Chester and Dickey (eds.), *Feminism and Censorship*

pornography, to publish research on the harm that pornography does to women, to pursue legislation against pornography on the grounds of sex discrimination and incitement to sexual hatred and violence, and to promote actions such as boycotts against the pornography industry. The legal precedent that Itzin has found is the ban on 'incitement to racial hatred', which is part of British public order law rather than equal opportunities law. (It is worth noting at this point that black feminists resent the way in which Itzin uses the race analogy to strengthen her arguments.) CAPC is supported by *Everywoman* magazine, which published the records of the Minneapolis hearings in Britain and which campaigns in support of CAPC positions. Itzin is specifically interested in pornography that depicts violence, and she believes that the Minneapolis ordinance definitions have the merit of distinguishing between violent and other pornography. She contends that sexually explicit material for use in sex education would not be proscribed by such legislation. A member of the Women's Rights Committee of Liberty (formerly the National Council of Civil Liberties), Itzin succeeded in 1988 in persuading that organization to agree to devise legislation to adapt the United States ordinance to the context of the British legal system; this decision, however, was reversed the following year. The CAPC argument was that because pornography itself censors women, and, as such, interferes with their civil liberties, *ergo* legislation to prohibit pornography was in keeping with NCCL principles. CAPC has also lobbied and campaigned on the issues of sex tourism and the exploitation of those who work in the sex industry.

Both CAP and CAPC are led mainly by people whose work focused on sexual violence and who campaign chiefly on the basis of information and evidence about sexual violence. The leaders of FAC, on the other hand, tend to be intellectuals and artists, some of whom are themselves directly involved in the production of feminist erotica. The first meeting of the group that formed Feminists against Censorship took place on 24 May 1989. It was called by Socialist feminists who wished to discuss how best to combat the pro-censorship forces in both the larger political sphere and in the feminist movement. There was also an interest in supporting those people trying to produce alternative sexually explicit material which was neither sexist, racist, nor coercive. FAC is strongly against state censorship. It also fears that the guilt and secrecy surrounding questions of sexuality could be aggravated by new censorship campaigns and new imperatives of secrecy. It points out the dangers in increasing government powers to ban books and magazines, and notes that it is often gay, lesbian, and feminist material that suffers from such policies.

FAC has a small core of activists and several dozen supporters. These are well-positioned women with access to informed opinion. In 1990 they were instrumental, in alliance with the Campaign against Censorship and the Stonewall Group, in reversing the CAPC-inspired Women's Rights Committee of Liberty decision to draft British anti-pornography legislation. FAC has also attended launch meetings and conferences of CAP, in order to persuade their supporters of the dangers of state censorship. Both implicitly and explicitly, FAC supports the production of a non-sexist erotica and the open exploration of sex and sexuality.

In terms of the evolution of the autonomous women's movement, perhaps the chief significance of the campaigns on pornography is that they have demonstrated its continuing capacity for revitalization. The autonomous women's movement may have been in decline, but it is not dead and it is constantly and unpredictably changing. Although the issue of pornography has been divisive within the women's movement, in many respects reactivating the long-standing Radical–Socialist opposition, this would seem to have been more at the level of nationally articulated debates than at grass roots. Those women, existing feminists or newly politicized, who have been active on the pornography issue have tended to support CAP, one of the two national campaigns adopting a more Radical feminist perspective. This does not mean that they are Radical feminists. On the contrary, we have been struck by the breadth of this campaign's appeal. For instance, in 1990 one of the authors was invited to a socialist students' conference at Cambridge, where it was clear that the only issue that the women undergraduates really wanted to discuss was pornography, and that they were not particularly sympathetic to arguments against censorship. When we sometimes suggested to interviewees that the pornography campaigns were a bit of a distraction from the 'real' issues, we rarely met with agree-

ment. For example, two women running a publicly funded training scheme for women informed us that pornographic materials
and the tendency to regard women as 'sex objects' were rife in
the trades in which they were involved, and were a major obstacle to getting women workers taken seriously. One said: 'on the
manual skills side . . . often a lot of the workplaces are plastered
with pornography. I've put a lot of energy into trying to get this
offensive material removed but it goes hand in glove in the building industry.' The other dealt with computing and electronics
skills. She told us:

Yesterday we sent some of our women out to have a go at CAD
CAM—computer aided design, computer aided manufacturing—at the—
—Science Park . . . and the man that was doing the . . . supposed to be
doing the stuff and showing them and letting them have a go or whatever . . . all afternoon he kept prodding them and asking them 'Well,
don't you want to take a look at these boobs that I've got on this computer screen?'

Pornography, in short, was widely perceived as an urgent issue
with a bearing not only on male violence, but on sexual harassment and male attitudes at work more generally. The dangers of
censorship appeared, by comparison, an almost pedantic foot-
note.

This chapter has not aimed to provide a comprehensive account
of the autonomous women's movement, its activities and concerns. That is, after all, a theme that runs through most of this
book. Rather, we have wanted to focus on some broad tendencies within this part of the women's movement. There has been
decline, and that decline will be documented further in later
chapters—in the successively weaker mobilizations around
defence of the 1967 Abortion Act for instance, or the problems
faced by child care campaigners in the mid-1980s. Yet, even if we
define the WLM in the narrowest sense, its decline has not been
terminal or uniform. Indeed, there has been considerable resurgence. The pornography campaigns have demonstrated the continuing vitality and responsiveness of feminism, and if we adopt a
more generous understanding and recognize the essential feminist
impulse within the black women's movement, the Greenham
movement, and the miners' wives' campaign, then the 1980s were
not an anticlimax after the 1970s, but a second exciting and

dynamic decade, one in which there was a continuing feminist mobilization. Moreover, there were promising examples of alliance-making and networking in political structures and institutions that put some feminist ideas into play in the mainstream of British politics. These are the subject of our next chapter.

# 5

# Feminism and Political Institutions

AFTER 1979 many British feminists became active in the traditional institutions of political competition—parties, unions, and local government, all were influenced by a new influx of women who had been politicized by the WLM. The reason for this was that feminists wanted to defend and extend women's social and political rights. Inevitably, some of the social movement strategies and styles of the WLM were adapted to the imperatives of political competition. With this came modifications in feminist thinking and developments of feminist ideas as efforts were made, first, to describe and understand the masculinity of traditional politics, and, later, to transform political institutions and practices so as to make them more hospitable to women. Although that project is far from complete, some shifts in political institutions are apparent. Political parties, trade unions, and other powerful institutions began to accommodate women's demands for a political voice. Such changes varied in scope and kind according to the particular institution and to the part of the country in which it was located. Some were slow and reluctant; others were more hospitable. All were responding not only to feminism, but also to other important pressures that were part of British political life after 1979. Those pressures were outlined in Chapter 2. Here we concentrate on the interaction between the changing feminist movement described in Chapters 3 and 4, and changing political institutions. As far as possible, we try to show how each influenced the other. We emphasize that the changes that characterized British politics during four successive Conservative governments brought advantages and disadvantages for women. Inevitably, feminism responded to that, and was shaped and changed by its increased involvement in established political institutions.

We have already described how the second wave of feminism
began as a grass-roots political movement that mobilized women's
creative energies and illuminated their skills and concerns. New
ways of organizing were developed which enhanced individual
confidence and created space for feminist political identities to
emerge. This has continued. But other concerns have grown in
importance. The decade of Thatcher government was one of
viciously fought sectional and class politics in which many of the
rights that had been taken for granted during the 1970s were
attacked. Women mobilized and organized in defence of these
rights, often drawing on the empowering techniques of the NSM
politics of the WLM years. Inevitably, some of the democratic,
anti-hierarchical ethos and practices that were so important during
the 1970s were sacrificed in the development of strategies to win
political competitions for resources, power, and autonomy.

Throughout the decade, feminists were divided over issues of
political power, representation, and participation. Feminist
debates found their way into the political mainstream and
became especially apparent in the labour movement, as well as
gaining at least some influence in the civil service, the judiciary,
local government, and, arguably, in the governing Conservative
Party. Obviously, the degree of that influence varied with both
the kind of feminism and the kind of institution involved. Some
feminisms are more easily accommodated than others. In each
case, the particular culture and traditions of the political arena
influenced the feminist politics that developed.

Here we must digress for a moment to announce an analytical
'health' warning. It is extremely difficult to draw a line between
feminist political participation and the participation of women.
Not all women's political participation is sympathetic to feminist
values, and some women participants are explicitly anti-feminist.
This chapter is mainly concerned to describe feminist influences
on mainstream politics. To do this, it is necessary to describe the
general patterns of women's political participation, but it is
important, although sometimes difficult, to maintain a distinction
between the two, obviously related, phenomena. Our distinction
is drawn from the definition that we offer in the Introduction,
where we describe as feminist any ideology, activity, or policy
whose goal is to remove discrimination against women and to
break down the male domination of society. Our definition will

create a number of very reluctant feminists, but it enables us to trace important changes in the political landscape.

In this chapter we describe the feminist infiltration of British political institutions and assess the extent to which those institutions have become carriers of feminist ideas and values. To do this, we offer three different kinds of evidence, reflecting different understandings of politics. We include accounts of how women influenced by feminist ideas have acted collectively within mainstream political organizations. To this we add assessments and accounts of how women are represented in acknowledged positions of power. Finally, we assess how feminist thinking has influenced the political agenda. Our observations are offered in conjunction with a discussion of the way in which feminists have understood power and politics; our examples and evidence are chosen to illustrate that understanding, in an attempt to do justice to its shifts and complexities. We show that the relationship is neither simple nor straightforward, and that neither conventional political analysis nor feminist concepts can, by themselves, capture the complexity of developments since the end of the 1970s. The scope and range of feminist political intervention is much larger than conventional wisdom would have it; its influence has been greater than many feminists have acknowledged. Feminists have gained important positions in state institutions and in participatory structures, widespread campaigns have mobilized new groups and generations of activists, and feminist ideas have found a place on policy agendas.

## LABOUR MOVEMENT INTERVENTIONS: THE CHANGING CONTEXT

Our account of collective feminist action inevitably concentrates on the labour movement. This is partly a response to the shape of political events, and partly a result of feminist preoccupations. British feminist writing and research about political structures and institutions has mainly consisted of Socialist feminists writing about the labour movement and women's relation to it. Its motivation is the desire to develop strategies for feminist interventions in the Labour Party and the trade unions. Very little research and writing has been done on other power networks, including the dominant Conservative Party.[1] Sustained feminist political practice during the 1980s took place on three sites: there was a continued intervention in labour movement politics; a set of feminist 'institutions' was developed in the form of the local authority women's committees; and, as we have described in Chapter 4, there were a number of long-running campaigns.

Both the Labour Party and the trade unions were under political attack from 1979 onwards. Constraints on union power and autonomy in combination with successive Labour electoral defeats were an incentive to a major reorganization of labour politics. In 1981 the new Social Democratic Party was formed, dividing the opposition and probably keeping the Conservatives in power. The Social Democrats, at first singly, later in alliance with the Liberal Party, made a direct appeal to women voters in their search for new constituencies, offering equal opportunities policies, positive action in respect of candidate selection, and so forth. This began a process of competitive bidding for women's votes that the Labour Party, in the throes of constitutional and political reform, was required to join.

For the unions, too, the 1980s were a period of decline. Systematic and effective Conservative attacks on union power led to the exclusion of the TUC from the established tripartite bodies that had been so powerful during the 1970s. Unemployment was also a pressure as union membership declined dramatically. Where new jobs developed, they were in the service sector, part-time, and often women's jobs. The unions, looking for new members, had to think about recruiting the women workers. Meanwhile the TUC, deprived of its traditional roles, was required to come up with new ways of justifying its existence. Here campaigns by feminists in the union movement bore fruit. Influential women trade-unionists were successful in committing the TUC to sex equality policies. At the same time, the decline of manufacturing and extractive industry employment weakened the powers of the traditional unions in the movement as a whole. There was a shift of emphasis to the more 'women-friendly'

---

[1] The exception is Bea Campbell's work on women in the Conservative Party. See Bea Campbell, *The Iron Ladies: Why Do Women Vote Tory?* (Virago, London, 1987); see also Joni Lovenduski, Pippa Norris, and Catriona Levy, 'The Conservatives and Women', in A. Seldon and D. Butler (eds.), *The Conservative Party 1900–1990* (Oxford University Press, Oxford, forthcoming).

unions. Each of these deve
nist intervention.

Political patterns were (
behaviour as members of the
appearance of the long-obser
likely than men to vote for th
more towards centre parties
there were both pressures and
way in which it took accoun
opened for feminists, who were
were heard in the debates that en

FEMINISM AND ...

138   is best established is in
traditional unions.
branches had litt
elaborate and
familiar w
zation
to

## THE LABOUR MOVEMEN ... cMINISM

### The Labour Party

Many feminist scholars believe that the sustained interaction
between the WLM and the labour movement in Britain is one of
its distinguishing features. It is this particular experience that has
shaped British feminism and that differentiates it from the
American and Continental European movements. Sheila
Rowbotham draws attention to the significant roots of British
feminism in the high levels of working-class action during the late
1960s and early 1970s. Feminists absorbed political and organizational traditions from this experience.[2]

To understand this dimension of feminist politics, it is necessary to know something of the politics of the Labour Party. The
Labour Party is a federation of trade unions, Co-operative
Societies, and party branches based on individual membership.
There has always been a split between Labour's Left and Right,
but, during the 1970s, divisions became more complicated. The
'old guard' Right continued, but the Left split into two distinctive tendencies: the 'soft' Left and the 'hard' Left. Traditionally,
the unions have been the party's paymasters, and have dominated party politics and decision-making. Historically, the large
manufacturing unions were a significant force on the Right of the
party. The dominant ethos in the areas of Britain where the party

[2] Sheila Rowbotham, *The Past Is before us: Feminism in Action* (Penguin;
London, 1990), 223.

formed by the patriarchal culture of the
In the past, individual members in party
c power in a highly formalized politics that was
ritualized. To be effective, individuals needed to be
th the 'rule-book' that was the basis of branch organi-
A long apprenticeship was required to learn the rules and
be able to use them. The party culture was a barrier to the
exercise of influence by all new members, and it proved especially
unpleasant for women, who had little other experience of organized politics.

Ideological divisions in the party were also an incentive to
reform. During the late 1970s and 1980s the hard Left, in the
form of 'Militant Tendency', became important in many party
constituency associations, notably on Merseyside, but also in
London and other parts of the country. At the same time, the
soft Left gathered support from the influx of new members who
had been politicized in the social movement politics of the 1960s
and 1970s. The overall growth of the Left was a major incentive
to the founders of the Social Democratic Party, which was begun
by four senior Labour politicians (all former Cabinet Ministers in
Labour governments) in 1981.

Within the Labour Party, the tendencies on the Left gradually
began a reform process that gave party constituency associations
the power to dominate aspects of party politics. For example, the
compulsory reselection of MPs was introduced. This reform was
granted a particularly poor reception in the press, as was much
of the programme of both wings of the Left. Nor did the traditional Right enhance party credibility with voters. Electoral
humiliation in 1983 brought Neil Kinnock to power in the party.
His leadership team believed that the general election defeat was
a result of the party image of being in thrall both to union
demands and to sectarian extremism. As a result, the Kinnock
leadership, which had been associated with the soft Left, began
its own process of reform. From the mid-1980s onwards a series
of changes were introduced that were designed to alter the
party's unpopular image by reducing the influence of both the
unions and the hard Left. The battles that ensued were conducted over issues of democracy and accountability. All sides
claimed that they were motivated by the desire for greater party
democracy, and the leadership was able to draw on soft Left sup-

port as it expelled the hard Left and amended the party constitution. The Kinnock reforms were designed to appeal to voters and
to make the party more attractive to individual members by giving them more power, but the 'rule-book' rituals have proved
difficult to shift in a politics that favours those with experience of
playing the game.

Thus the labour movement that feminists sought to influence
was inhospitable, but it was in the process of making reforms
that offered opportunities to increase women's power in the
party. From 1979 onwards women from the WLM went into the
Labour Party and became active in their unions. Sarah Perrigo
has written that the new Labour Party feminists found a party
that had scarcely changed in its attitudes to women since the
1920s.[3] Party women's organizations lacked power and could not
easily be used to press issues that were of interest to women. The
Labour Party Women's Organization consisted then, as now, of a
structure that parallels key party committees and councils. This
included local and regional women's sections and councils, the
National Conference of Labour Women, and the National
Labour Women's Committee. The annual three-day National
Conference of Labour Women was convened by the party's
National Executive Committee (NEC). It was a gathering of representatives from women's sections, constituency associations,
national affiliates, and women MPs. The National Labour
Women's Advisory Committee was composed of two women
from each of the Labour Party's regional areas, together with
women on the NEC. There was also a chief women's officer and
eleven regional women's officers. The structure depended upon
the, discretion of the NEC for its influence: it had no statutory
power.

As the decade progressed, however, the party was pressured
externally and internally to adopt a more positive policy to
women and to empower the women's organization. In part, this
was the result of internal direction by feminists. From the early
to the late 1980s a strong feminist campaign, in the form of the
Labour Women's Action Committee (LWAC), had pressed for
various special measures for women, including the automatic

---

[3] Sarah Perrigo, 'The Labour Party and the Promotion of Women', paper presented to the ECPR workshop on 'Party Responses to Women's Demands for
Political Entry', held at Essex University, Mar. 1991.

right of the National Conference of Labour Women to send five resolutions to the decision-making body, the annual Labour Party conference, each year, a scheduled debate on the report from the National Conference of Labour Women at the annual conference, provision for the National Conference of Labour Women to elect the five women's seats on the NEC, and the inclusion of women on all shortlists for parliamentary selection. From 1982 onwards the National Conference of Labour Women voted in support of these demands.

The LWAC campaign gave focus to, and united, a large number of women, but by 1990 it had succeeded in translating only one demand, the compulsory shortlisting of women, if nominated, into party policy. The success of the campaign was impeded by its place in party politics. LWAC was London-based and closely associated with the Left of the party, including both hard and soft Left supporters. Its image was that of the 'loony Left', from which the leadership was trying to dissociate itself. Feminists in other parts of the country resented being told what to do by what they perceived as London feminists. The party leadership was able to argue that the National Conference of Labour Women was not representative of the party's women members and that it preferred to avoid the precedent of giving so much say to a 'sectional' interest. Real change came only at the end of the 1980s, when the party's internal reform was well under way, when the leadership was more confident that the remaining Left was under control. By this time, many senior party women were prepared to identify themselves as feminists, and the party had considerable evidence that its appeal to women voters was being damaged by its masculine image. Also important was the weakened position of the industrial trade unions, the bastion of the party's traditionalist Right. Their decline diluted an important source of opposition to feminism.

In some respects, the shift seems rather sudden. The policy review group set up by the NEC to produce the 1989 policy document, *Meet the Challenge, Make the Change*, included no representation or direct involvement (despite repeated requests to be included in the process) from the National Labour Women's Committee, because the NEC considered the latter to be unrepresentative and dominated by members of Militant Tendency and by uncompromising LWAC feminists.[4] But by the end of the 1980s it was clear that LWAC was only one of a number of feminist voices in the party. This greater range of feminist voices made it possible to separate feminism from the Left, inclining the leadership towards greater accommodation. It is clear that the fate of feminist issues and politics in the Labour Party (or in any other organization, for that matter) cannot be assessed in isolation from the other preoccupations, allegiances, and tendencies of party feminists. In 1990 the monitoring group established by Jo Richardson, Shadow Minister for Women's Rights, was consistently involved in policy discussions. The 1991 policy document, *Looking to the Future*, had a considerable input from the National Labour Women's Advisory Committee. The issue of upgrading the National Conference of Labour Women continues to be on the party agenda, and it is likely that a more co-operative, harmonious relationship between the National Labour Women's Committee and the NEC will lead eventually to direct representation.[5]

At the level of internal party policy, the scale of the change in attitudes to women's representation is remarkable. The 1990 Labour Party conference passed a resolution calling on the NEC to establish a programme whereby, in ten years' time, at least 40 per cent of the members of all party decision-making committees must be women. The conference then gave the party three general elections to bring the proportion of women in the parliamentary Labour Party up to 50 per cent. It also called for the quota of women members on the NEC to be 40 per cent. In 1990 a quota was introduced in the Shadow Cabinet whereby ballot papers had to include votes for three women in order to be valid. Four women were elected. The 1991 conference amended the party constitution to establish quotas of women on most party councils. The significant exception to this widespread acceptance of quotas was in the selection of parliamentary candidates. NEC recommendations that, within the period of the next three general elections, 50 per cent of the parliamentary Labour Party should be women were not taken to the party Congress.

The NEC has accepted the radical principle that a quota place will remain vacant if no woman comes forward for it. Quotas are

---

[4] Interview with Sarah Perrigo, Spring 1990.
[5] Perrigo, 'Labour and the Promotion of Women'.

controversial, and it is likely that their acceptance by party decision-makers was made possible partly by other elements of the
process of party constitutional reform.[6] Many of the quotas are
envisaged either for wholly new councils and committees, such as
the new party policy forums, or for expanded existing councils
and committees. It is easier to establish quotas in new and
enlarged structures, because there are no incumbents to be considered: men will not have to be removed to make way for
women. But incumbency and patronage continue to be important
barriers to women who seek entry to established party committees.

It is interesting to note other changes brought about by feminist intervention in the Labour Party. Party women's organizations became revitalized: the National Conference of Labour
Women became less of a social, more of a political event during
the 1980s. The accompanying revival of women's sections
brought a new mood of militancy and activism into moribund
organizations. Each successive conference saw an influx of
younger delegates who had prior experience of women's groups.
Some old-time feminist campaigners were taken aback by the
urgency of the demands to extend women's rights in the party:
'. . . these young women are very impatient. It's not that I disagree with them. I've never discriminated against Lesbians, and I
agree with childcare, but they want crèches at conferences not
only during the day, but in the evening too!'[7] Labour feminists
put forward arguments about issues of concern to women, pres-
suring the party to consider more flexible working arrangements,
and to adopt policies that would alter gender relations within the
party. More general arguments were also made. Women
influenced by feminism debated not simply about access to the
structures of formal participation, but also about their inclusion
and exclusion across the range of modern social and cultural life.
Statements were made about the ways in which images and language may empower or diminish people, about organizing meetings to ensure that different voices are heard and considered. In
other words, feminists pressured the party to return to some of
the democratic principles that had been so important in its past,

[6] Perrigo, 'Labour and the Promotion of Women'.
[7] Rowbotham, *The Past Is before us*, 197.

to operate in practice the principles of inclusion and redistribution that were so prominent in its discourse.

The influence of feminism on the Labour Party was far from uniform. It was greater in the urban areas, where large numbers of white-collar workers and the soft Left are dominant. There is also evidence that feminist feelings about Labour's commitment to women has been mixed. Many feminists were unhappy with the party's response, and many disagreed with what they regarded as a recycling of feminist rhetoric to capture the support of women. After the 1983 general election, Sarah Roelofs argued in *Spare Rib* that Labour had lost because it was not inspirational enough to mobilize its supporters. Its address to women was not something in which women could believe. Although the manifesto included a string of commitments to women's rights, the party did not campaign on those commitments. In some localities, however, its women's section did. Special women's canvasses were organized as a form of local women's (or women's section) activity. Women's leaflets based on the manifesto policies were drafted and printed in some constituencies.[8] Throughout the country, special teams of prominent party and trade-union women fronted campaign activities in an effort to target women voters.

In the same article Roelofs expressed a real distaste for the 'liberal feminists' who sat on the platform at the party conference. They were perceived as, at best, politically mistaken in their view that feminist politics might be served by an accretion of particular material reforms; at worst, they were regarded as using feminism to further their own ambitions. Like many feminists, Roelofs has major reservations about the political ambitions of some party feminists, who are criticized for being interested only in 'jobs for the girls'. This is part of a more general and somewhat debilitating feminist distaste for competition and possibly also of a fear of success, heritages of the anti-hierarchical ethos of the 1970s. Ambivalence about the mobilization of feminists to support women's ascent to powerful political positions is a common theme in contemporary feminism. Indeed, in the course of conducting the research for this book, we became aware of a considerable bitterness on the part of women who prioritized

---

[8] Sarah Roelofs, 'Can Feminism Win?', *Spare Rib*, Sep. 1983: 28–30.

extra-parliamentary activism and alternative working styles at the expense of their careers. Their bitterness is directed against women who were less active then, but who are in more comfortable employment today.

Such discourses are an additional constraint on feminist participation in party politics. And there is no agreed set of strategies amongst those who do participate. There is disagreement about whether to support all women candidates, whether to support only feminist candidates, whether to support only feminist candidates of a particular political complexion, and whether to support male feminist candidates against anti-feminist women candidates. All of this inhibits the capacities of feminists to place women in powerful positions. Even with decisive, unified strategies, it is difficult to break down the barriers to political office. Division and hesitancy make it harder still. The obstacles are formidable. Many of the powerful party positions are occupied by male incumbents who are skilful at choosing their (usually male) successors. The result is that the progress of women into prized political positions is slow. At the time of writing, therefore, it is difficult to envisage the reforms that could produce a parliamentary Labour Party evenly divided between men and women.

Labour Party feminists have been more successful in influencing the policy agenda and in politicizing issues of concern to women. A growing acceptance of the need to take account of the gendered issues of policies may be traced from the early 1980s. The Shadow Ministry for Women, established in 1989, is an acknowledgement of the political significance of gender, and since 1983 party policy documents and manifestos have contained specific policy proposals for women. Moreover, in at least some elements of the party, there is space for women who join as a result of their own political interests and anger. They are not expected simply to adopt the traditional and masculine preoccupations that were once the party's only agenda. But when we look at feminist responses to Labour social policy, we find that there are still significant disagreements. Questioned about the party's appeal to women during the 1987 general election campaign, black feminist MP Diane Abbot was scornful of its unthinking racist and familial basis. One leaflet, she said,

. . . had on the front a family, a white family obviously, and there was a husband and a wife and two children and a granny . . . and inside it has individual photographs of these people and it detailed their worries. . . . it was so stereotyped . . . the women didn't have jobs, nor were they worried about jobs or unemployment or social security. They were worried about very narrowly defined 'female issues' and that leaflet sums up what was wrong with the campaign. . . . The problem with the campaign is it didn't use women enough and didn't really direct its energies to the reality of women's lives because it was so hung up on appealing to the mythical white skilled working-class families.[9]

After defeat in the 1992 general election, Neil Kinnock resigned from the Labour leadership. Although his successor, John Smith, and the deputy leader, Margaret Beckett, are committed to continued reform of the party organization, it remains to be seen whether reforms designed to empower women will be as prominent as they were under Kinnock.

## The Trade Unions

The story of British trade-union feminism in the 1980s has many parallels with Labour Party feminism. Not that 1979 marked the beginning of trade-union feminism. Sarah Boston recalls the optimism among women trade-unionists during the 1970s, after a decade of steady progress on improving women's conditions at work. But by the middle of the 1980s there were many signs that feminism in the trade unions was losing its momentum. The gap between men's and women's wages began to widen again in 1978, after narrowing steadily between 1970 and 1977. The first half of the 1980s saw a reversal in women's overall employment. The widely reported 'firsts' (fire-fighter, Prime Minister, etc.) obscured a lack of meaningful change in the areas in which women worked. But even under such adverse circumstances, progress was made. Throughout the period, women increased their power and presence in the unions (see Table 1), which published more on women's demands, took up more issues, and gradually began to address the needs of their women workers.[10] Issues of concern

[9] Lynne Segal, 'Lynne Segal Interviews Diane Abbot', *Feminist Review*, 27 (1987).
[10] Sarah Boston, *Women Workers and the Trade Unions* (Lawrence and Wishart, London, 1987).

TABLE 1. *Women members and decision-making positions in selected British trade unions in 1988 (%)*

|  | Members | Conference delegates | Executive committee | Full-time officials |
|---|---|---|---|---|
| AEU | 10 | 7 | 0 | 0.6 |
| BIFU | 54 | 19 | 23 | n/a |
| COHSE | 79 | 28 | 19 | 27 |
| CPSA | 71 | 34 | 41 | 18 |
| GMB | 30 | 14 | 30 | 5 |
| MSF | 20 | 11 | 8 | 9 |
| NALGO | 49 | n/a | 41 | 10 |
| NAS/UWT | 39 | 40 | 16 | 22 |
| NCU | 20 | 12 | 0 | 20 |
| NGA | 8 | 3 | 0 | 4 |
| NUPE | 77 | 36 | 50 | 11 |
| NUR | 5 | 4 | 0 | 0 |
| NUT | 70 | n/a | 24 | 27 |
| TGWU | 18 | n/a | 5 | 4 |
| UCATT | 1 | 1 | 0 | 0 |
| UCW | 26 | 20 | 14 | 23 |
| USDAW | 61 | 38 | 25 | 17 |

*Note:* n/a = data not available.
*Source:* Compiled from SERTUC Women's Committee, *Still Moving towards Equality: A Survey of Progress towards Equality in Trade Unions* (South East Regional TUC, London, 1989).

to women dominated the agenda of the unions' peak organization, the Trades Union Congress (TUC), during the 1980s and continued to establish themselves in the policies of the TUC's members.

Feminists became skilled at getting issues discussed in the local, regional, and national union hierarchies. The process of establishing their concerns on the negotiating agenda was one in which women in a particular union took up an issue, worked for it in their union, and then brought it to the TUC Women's Conference. There the issue was picked up by women from other unions, who took it back to their branches; such issues increasingly found their way to the TUC annual conference, from which it also went back to other unions. In this way, support was steadily gained for issues such as abortion, sexual harassment, and, specifically, for a TUC Equal Rights Unit. During the 1980s the TUC drafted model equal opportunities clauses for negotiators, as well as terms for workplace nurseries. By 1982 the TUC was persuaded of the need for positive action for women, and by 1985 this was linked to issues about women's status in the member unions. From the middle of the 1980s the TUC supported a campaign to raise awareness of the needs of black and Asian women workers as the union movement generally became more mindful of issues of race and difference. In 1987 a report on 'Black and Ethnic Minority Women in Employment and Trade Unions' was presented to the TUC Women's Conference and was accepted unanimously (see Chapter 6).[11]

During the 1980s the inequality experienced by women as trade-unionists became an issue, and policies to increase the representation of women on union councils and committees appeared. As with the process in the Labour Party, gathering support for women's rights and representation paralleled the increased significance of the TUC Women's Conference. In the early 1980s this was a bland conference with little debate, a 'permitted occasion' of no real political significance. After making the opening address to the 1983 conference, Len Murray, the General Secretary, had departed by 11.30 a.m., showing how much importance he attached to the occasion. It is unlikely that TUC General Secretaries will behave like that during the 1990s. Women's membership of the movement was taken seriously by 1990, and so was their representation on TUC controlling organizations. For example, the TUC made provision for a substantial increase in the proportion of women on its ruling General Council. This came about in the course of implementing a set of rule changes designed to redress an imbalance in the numbers of seats held by the larger and smaller unions. The proposed reform actually reduced the number of reserved places for women. However, in enlarging the size of the representation allocated to the larger unions, Congress ruled that these delegations must include at least one woman. As a result, 15 (28 per cent) of the 53 General Council places went to women in 1990.[12]

The TUC is a federation of national unions which are themselves often federations. For a policy to be effective, it must

[11] Sarah Boston, *Women Workers and the Trade Unions* (Lawrence and Wishart, London, 1987).
[12] Hansard Society, *The Report of the Hansard Society Commission on Women at the Top* (HMSO, London, 1990).

become the policy of the member unions, which must then implement it at the level of the workplace. The national executive councils of many unions took initiatives to prioritize women, including USDAW, ASTMS(MSF), CPSA, NUPE, NATFHE, COHSE, and SOGAT. Union initiatives included surveys of membership to obtain information about women members, the adoption of official sex equality policies such as equality charters, national and regional equality committees, rule-book amendments to reserve places for women on policy committees, the construction of women-only activities such as training weekends and, most difficult of all, some evidence of shifts in the priorities of the collective bargaining agenda to take account of women's needs.

That shift was an unintended consequence of the Conservatives' attack on the unions. During the Thatcher years, many of the traditional prerogatives of wage negotiation were removed, perhaps making it easier for union negotiators to take up new issues related to employment conditions rather than pay. New issues included maternity rights and child care, provision for parents to attend to their family responsibilities, health issues such as cervical cancer screening, sexual harassment at work, positive action in the form of training for women, and, most controversially, job evaluation. But it was particularly difficult for women to convince men in the union movement that women's jobs were unfairly evaluated and, therefore, unfairly paid.[13]

The establishment of the TUC Equal Rights Department in 1988 was a major victory for women trade-unionists. The decision upgraded the existing equality unit to a full-scale department, giving the head of department a decision-making role in TUC management. In short, the status of equality issues was enhanced. This proved fortuitous in 1990, when the TUC spared this sphere of activity from its 1990 budget cuts, retaining the status and budget of the new department despite swingeing cuts in the rest of its establishment.

TUC politics are a reflection of the politics of the member unions. The establishment of the equal rights department was, in a large measure, the result of work by MSF Women's Officer,

[13] Cynthia Cockburn, *Women, Trade Unions and Political Parties* (Fabian Research Series 349; The Fabian Society, London, 1987).

Anne Gibson, a long-time agitator for women's rights in the union movement. The crucial breakthrough came with the support of the TGWU, which was Britain's largest trade union during the 1980s and which dominated TUC politics. The TGWU has a mixed record on women's rights. It has appointed a national women's officer since 1919, but it only really started to take up women's issues in a serious way in the 1980s. Even today, the representation of women amongst its paid officials and on its ruling bodies is relatively poor. Nevertheless, since the mid-1980s the TGWU has had a structure of regional and national women's committees and it pursues strategies of equality negotiation in wage-bargaining. This is obviously in part a response to the changes in the structure of employment that many unions are experiencing, and the TGWU is not nearly as assiduous in this regard as NUPE, NALGO, or the MSF (which was created by a merger of ASTMS and TASS in 1988).

Although there have been considerable improvements in the unions' records on women, much remains to be done. A recent report from the SERTUC Women's Committee has criticized TUC unions for failing to take women's union organizations seriously enough. The report points out that unions continue to put resolutions to the TUC Women's Conference and then fail to send them on to the subsequent Congress. For example, five unions sent resolutions to the 1988 TUC Women's Conference suggesting priorities for the equal rights department, but then did not carry them forward to the annual conference. In fact, a sixth union put forward a conference resolution on these priorities, and a further three unions amended the resolution. The resulting motion bore very little resemblance to the composite that was carried at the TUC Women's Conference. The report goes on to observe that 'of course, the resolution of the Women's Conference "requests" the department to . . . whereas the Congress resolution "instructs" the General Council . . .'.[14]

Improvement at the national level of the unions was uneven, but, slowly, progress was made. Developments at the levels of the shop-floor and the union branch, however, lagged behind those at the centre. Cynthia Cockburn's important study of equality

[14] SERTUC Women's Committee, *Still Moving towards Equality: A Survey of Progress towards Equality in Trade Unions* (South East Regional TUC, London, 1989).

policy in four organizations is instructive here. It shows how local practices must alter if women's position in both the unions and the workforce is to improve. It also serves as an illustration of the importance of appropriate democratic institutions. One of Cockburn's organizations was a large national trade union, with a comparatively good record on equal opportunities issues. Reasoning that the level of democracy in an organization will have significant influence on how women fare, Cockburn anticipated that democratizing the union's structure would enhance women's representation, because such procedures would both prompt a realization that the membership was largely female and empower ordinary members. But the new system, based on elected lay representatives (branch secretaries and shop stewards) did not empower the membership so much as the lay representatives. A system of indirect representation delegated decision-taking from one tier to another and transformed the group of branch secretaries into a clique, a power bloc of individuals who nominated each other for important positions. Women were said to find it difficult to stand for elections. They were less fluent in the jargon of 'quorate', 'refer it back', etc. Such skills made the men seem like 'natural' leaders. And men were unwilling to give up their positions to incoming women. Lay representatives received commissions on membership subscriptions that brought in relatively large income supplements, as much as £500 per month. Rewards of status, authority, and income made it worth while hanging on to such posts. Often the male lay representatives did not represent women's interests. Many of those whom Cockburn interviewed believed that part-time workers should get only half a vote, that pay-claims should be based on the male breadwinner and the family that he supports, and that men's jobs should be supported and protected at the expense of women's.[15]

The effect of this interplay between the women's movement and the institutions on the trade unions is very important where the representation of women is concerned. Unions got better at representing women, because women struggled collectively and continuously to make them better, to press their interests, and to defeat specifically 'male' interests. But there is a long way to go

[15] Cynthia Cockburn, *In the Way of Women* (Macmillan, London and Basingstoke, 1991), 113–17.

before this struggle is won. The link between women's unionization, their representation in the union hierarchy, the kind of
work that women do, and the way in which that work is valued
are all part and parcel of a union ethos in which the hierarchy of
power in the unions reflects the hierarchy of power of occupations. Women are 'unimportant' employees, hence they are
'unimportant' union members, and at the beginning of the 1990s
women trade-unionists "still look forward to the day when they
are listened to at the TUC conference by a full and silent hall.'[16]

## LOCAL GOVERNMENT AND THE LABOUR MOVEMENT

Before summarizing and assessing the political patterns of labour
movement feminism, it is necessary to consider the experience of
the women's committees that first appeared in the 1980s. It was
in local authority politics that feminist interventions in the labour
movement were most concerned with state policy-making and
implementation. Beginning with the establishment of the Greater
London Council Women's Committee in 1981, women's committees spread to a number of other authorities during the 1980s.
Their initiatives were widely publicized and seemed at the time to
be widespread, but in fact, only a maximum of about 25 per cent
of Labour-controlled authorities had women's or equality committees or subcommittees of some kind. A few of the committees
sometimes had large budgets: the GLC Women's Committee, for
example, started with an annual budget of £7m., and they were
able to be very innovative in the programmes that they devised
for local women. From the outset, explicit connections were
made between the committees, feminism, and democratic local
politics. The GLC began its work with a series of mass meetings,
open conferences, co-options, and other consultation exercises
that were designed to bring the local community of women into
decision-making. This strategy of representation constituted a
political challenge to established patterns in both local authorities
and labout movement politics. Judy Watson observed in 1983.
that Tory councillors were worried that the extent of consultation would set precedents that would make life difficult for

---

[16] Boston, *Women Workers and Trade Unions*, 350.

elected representatives who were not accustomed to taking such account of the demands of their electors.[17] The local Labour Party establishment was often hostile to their development, a response that was still in evidence when the committees spread to Scotland at the end of the 1980s.

The problems that the committees encountered were political ones. They were partly a function of internal Labour politics and partly a function of the customary practices of local authority politics. As we explain in more detail in Chapter 6, the manifesto commitment to the committees was often a product of the local party membership; it might not actually have the support of more than one or two councillors. Thus the necessary political backing for it to be effective was usually absent. There were also problems with the support units of employees who serviced the committees. Feminists committed to democratic, anti-hierarchical, and consultative ways of working were employed in the equality units. A preference for collective responsibility meant that, frequently, no one had overall managerial responsibility in the unit. For example, Edinburgh's three women officers were appointed simultaneously and worked as a collective. This made for time-consuming decision-making. When members of the collective disagreed, conflict was highly exposed.[18] Such phenomena are not respected in local authority employment, which tends to be hierarchical and managerial and where power and respect are measured by pay and seniority. The combined impact of the absence of both senior personnel and high levels of councillor support meant that the committees risked marginalization. There were other political problems as well. Sarah Perrigo has observed that those who served on women's committees were not necessarily representative of the local community of women. Indeed, she argues that the pattern of co-option from certain groups made for a kind of corporatism that excluded most women.[19]

In the first years of their existence, too, the women's committees addressed themselves too often to white women, but this changed as experience was gained and as links were made

[17] Judy Watson, *Spare Rib*, 129 (1983).

[18] See Sue Lieberman, 'Women's Committees in Scotland', in Alice Brown and David McCrone (eds.), *The Scottish Government Yearbook (1989)* (Unit for the Study of Government in Scotland, Edinburgh University; Edinburgh, 1989).

[19] Sarah Perrigo, 'Feminist Politics in the 1980s', paper for the annual conference of the Political Studies Association, held at Warwick University, Apr. 1989.

between the committees and the black and Asian communities. A further problem for the committees was that their very existence tended to raise expectations. They were somehow expected both to service and to please a diverse feminist community and, at the same time, to struggle with feminist ways of working that were far from efficient. In addition, they had to prove their worth to the sponsoring political party.

In almost all cases, the sponsoring political party was the Labour Party, whose politics were, as we have seen, in crisis during the 1980s. The women's committees were largely the product of the rising WLM and the Labour soft Left, with its roots in community politics and its traditions of social movement and protest politics.[20] The committees were necessarily caught up in the power struggle between the old-guard Right, the hard Left, and the centre or soft Left that was waged in the Labour Party throughout the 1980s.

The Right was heavily dominated by male working-class trade-unionists and traditional worker politicians such as James Callaghan who were so prominent in the party's politics during the 1970s. These were not politicians who had progressive views on women. Callaghan's sexism was as notorious as his anti-feminism, and his strategy to help women was to secure their place at the centre of family life.[21]

In its way, the hard Left offered more of the same. Its old-fashioned Marxism makes the traditional class struggle paramount, and sees positive action and other feminist strategies as diversions from the main tasks of socialism. The dominant hard Left leadership in Liverpool after 1982 opposed any call for the establishment of a women's committee.[22] In this politics, the largely middle-class origins of Labour feminists were a matter for criticism, often made by men who were equally middle class. The party's traditional focus on class emancipation was used opportunistically against the women's committees. The strategy was effective. Some 75 per cent of Labour authorities never established women's committees or subcommittees of any kind.

The committees also fell foul of constitutional developments.

[20] Lieberman, 'Women's Committees in Scotland'.
[21] Elizabeth Wilson, 'Thatcherism and Women: After Seven Years', in R. Miliband et al. (eds.), *Socialist Register, 1987* (Merlin, London, 1987), 204.
[22] Lieberman, 'Women's Committees in Scotland', 257.

Many of the democratizing initiatives of the 1980s were part of a general Labour strategy to use local government as a way of resisting the impact of policy from Westminster. During the first part of the decade, local authorities were widely seen as forums in which socialist policies and strategies might be developed. Much was made of the capacities of the 'local state', as authority after authority defied Thatcher's policies. On balance, the popular and participatory element to these politics was often hospitable to feminism, which, in turn, was promoted by the soft left. Much Socialist feminist energy at this time was taken up with local political action in the Labour Party. For example, feminists were prominent in the debates on the alternative economic strategy in the early 1980s. And prominent Socialist feminists were employed by the new women's committees. But reliance on the 'local state' proved to be a hazardous strategy. The response of the Thatcher government to Labour's local government challenge was to abolish the GLC and to remove a range of powers, especially spending powers, from the local authorities. Under pressure, some authorities abolished their women's committees, while others subsumed them into small units within equal opportunities committees. Some carried on. Indeed, a number of new committees appeared in Scotland at the end of the decade, perhaps reflecting the success of Scotland's strong oppositional political culture. By this time Scotland was practically a one-party state. But Labour dominance was not proof against a growing militancy amongst Scottish women, who increasingly demanded a political voice from the old-guard traditionalist right that dominated the Scottish Labour Party.

Despite their Scottish revival, there are many signs that the immediate potential of women's committees has been exhausted, and that their routinized future will be in straightforward equal opportunities work for local councils and in servicing local women's groups. Nevertheless, their continued existence marks more than the high tide of municipal feminism. Setting up women's committees affirmed a commitment to feminist values and created the nucleus of a class of professional feminists, 'femocrats', who became important components of the sex equality networks that continue to promote the interests of women (see Chapter 6).

## LABOUR MOVEMENT 'MASCULINITY' AND THE
## POLITICAL PARTICIPATION OF WOMEN

Across the country, feminist involvement in labour movement politics continued and developed, and women's support for Labour Party initiatives increased. But their participation continued to be both on a smaller scale and to a lesser extent than men's. Traditionally, this phenomenon of a 'gender gap' in political participation has been explained by political scientists as a function of women's innate distaste for politics. Feminists have always contested such essentialist explanations, and in the second half of the 1980s accounts began to appear that attributed women's lower participation rates to strategies of exclusion operated by men. Such accounts owe an intellectual debt to earlier Socialist feminist explorations of patriarchy, identifying a 'masculinity' in political institutions that makes them inhospitable to women.

The analysis of the masculinity of the British labour movement has been most fully developed by Cynthia Cockburn. She describes the way in which the valuation of differences between men and women in the labour movement undervalues women, and argues that this is a critical factor in explaining the less enthusiastic support that working-class women voters give to the Labour Party.[23] Patricia Hewitt and Deborah Mattinson make a similar point about the Labour Party itself, arguing that although Labour has the policies and attitudes that women increasingly tell the pollsters they prefer, the party too often regards women as an odd 'minority'; it has not really digested the fact that women constitute the majority of the population. Labour's own research indicates that the party suffers from its masculine image, and that the few high-profile Tory women MPs give a public impression that it is the Conservatives rather than Labour who have the most women MPs (see Table 2).[24]

Similar arguments are offered about the trade unions. At the end of the 1980s employed women were about 60 per cent as likely as men to be unionized. These lower unionization rates are

[23] Cockburn, *Women, Unions and Parties.*
[24] Patricia Hewitt and Deborah Mattinson, *Women's Votes: The Key to Winning* (Fabian Research Series 353; Fabian Society, London 1989).

TABLE 2. *Conservative and Labour women voters, candidates and MPs, 1979, 1983, 1987, and 1992 (%)*

|  | Voters | Candidates | MPs |
|---|---|---|---|
| Conservative |  |  |  |
| 1979 | 48 | 5.0 | 2.3 |
| 1983 | 45 | 6.3 | 3.3 |
| 1987 | 44 | 7.3 | 4.5 |
| 1992 | 43 | 9.8 | 6.0 |
| Labour |  |  |  |
| 1979 | 38 | 8.3 | 4.1 |
| 1983 | 28 | 12.3 | 4.8 |
| 1987 | 31 | 14.5 | 9.2 |
| 1992 | 38 | 21.3 | 13.0 |

*Sources:* Joni Lovenduski and Pippa Norris, 'Party Rules and Women's Representation: Reforming the British Labour Party', in I. Crewe *et al.* (eds.), *British Parties and Elections Yearbook*, and 'British Conservative Parliamentary Recruitment: Patronage, Liberal-Rational, Radical and Feminist Models', paper presented to the annual meeting of the American Political Science Association, Washington, DC, 29 Aug.–1 Sept. 1991; I. Crewe, N. Day, and A. Fox, *The British Electorate 1963–1987* (Cambridge University Press, Cambridge, 1991); Harris Exit Poll, 9 Apr. 1992.

often read as an indicator that women are less political than men, but other factors may account for this difference. For example, women are employed in sectors of employment where there is a low propensity both to unionization and to industrial action by either sex. Women are also often employed in caring jobs, where industrial action punishes the client rather than the employer, a situation that inevitably reduces their willingness to be involved in it. Unions continue to project a male image, and many have built in structural barriers which ensure (possibly unintentionally) that women are less likely than men to achieve positions of influence. For example, many union rule-books limit access to official positions to those who have five or more years of current and continuous membership, a barrier to those with discontinuous work patterns. Often, the low-paid, low-grade posts where women predominate do not allow time to be given to union work. Shift-working and part-time hours may mean that women are simply not available when meetings are called, hence women's visibility in union affairs is low.

The diagnosis of labour movement masculinity is more than a statement about images, important though these are. It is something that is perceived as growing from the very heart of union-ism. Cynthia Cockburn's argument is predicated on her view that although the gender gap in support for the Conservatives reversed itself during the 1980s, and although working-class women became more likely than working-class men to vote Labour, the change was not one on which Labour could rely. In a detailed investigation of the components of women's political attitudes at the end of the 1980s, she writes that to understand women's political potential, one has to start with questions about which issues motivate women to participate. She finds women on school boards, in tenants' associations, on anti-deportation cam-paigns, in the environmental movement, and in the peace move-ment. She points to a variety of indicators which suggest that women are more concerned about social issues than men are. She avers strongly that, too often, party policy-makers ignore the well-documented preferences of women for consensual political styles, policies, and activity. For Cockburn, this all adds up to an argument that women are not accommodated within the cate-gories by which politics are understood. What is often taken as a sign of their naïvety is in fact a rejection by women of the terms of political debate. These, she writes, are the tendencies that underlay women's transfer of support to the Alliance parties dur-ing the 1980s. That transfer represented a rejection of the two major parties. Moreover, her argument continues, Labour will not retain the majority support that it has begun to attract from working-class women unless it heeds these lessons, projects a more feminine image, and promotes women and a consensual style.[25] She was proved right in 1992, when the gender gap re-emerged among women over 35, who voted Conservative in significantly greater proportions than men.[26]

Cockburn pushes her notion of labour movement masculinity to its limits, and argues that because women's political attitudes are expressed in terms of their differences from men, it tends to be assumed that it is women's ambivalence that requires explana-tion. But it is men's certainty that is more remarkable, she reas-ons, because it depends upon the possibility 'to inhabit a culture

[25] Cockburn, *Women, Unions and Parties*.
[26] The polls vary on the strength of the gender gap in favour of the Conservatives in 1992, but all agree that it was there; so, too, did Labour's post-mortem on the election results.

that brings together the umbrella of masculine identity, of male fraternity: work, working class allegiance, trade union membership and Labour party affiliation' [27] Women do not inhabit such a culture; they do not prefer the ties between the union movement and the Labour Party, and they object strongly to the hierarchy and bureaucratic conventions and practices that typify the labour movement.

Cynthia Cockburn's work on the masculinity of labour movement organizations, and her direct attack on their 'macho' culture, is part of an emerging strand of Socialist feminist theory that has not been entirely accepted in the feminist movement. Elizabeth Wilson has gone so far as to say that such feminism is no more than a critique of socialism, and that the critics should not refer to themselves as socialists.[28] Sheila Rowbotham is more sympathetic to the increased importance allocated to gender in this line of argument, but she, too, draws the line at an outright attack on trade-unionism, arguing that the union movement has been a resource for feminism, and implying that feminists and unionists are natural allies.[29]

Both views have their strengths. In practice, men are often no more unitary a group than women. Thus Elizabeth Wilson can cite the many instances of trade-unionists who have been supportive of women's rights as evidence of her case. Cockburn herself makes it plain that attitudes are mixed, and our exploration of feminist politics in the trade unions reveals instances of both opposition to, and support of, feminism by men. It is possible to accept that a masculine culture prevails in the labour movement, but that differences between men enable feminist interventions of various kinds. These interventions initiate a negotiation in which an alternative culture and practice is being produced as party structures are shifted and the discourse alters. The line between the public and private is moved as the policy agenda expands and the party seeks new kinds of supporters.

Such developments have important implications. In particular, the feminist democratic forms that have suited so many women are not well suited to labour movement politics. A consensual ethos in which all voices are heard, in which doubts are explored, does not suit the authoritarianism and demagogueries that char-

[27] Wilson, 'Thatcherism and Women'.    [28] Ibid.
[29] Rowbotham, *The Past Is before us*, ch. 13.

acterized the Labour Party of the 1960s and 1970s, and continue to be a feature of its traditional right today. But the forms of democratic organization that feminists have evolved may serve the modernizing Labour Party of the 1990s well.[30]

## FEMINISM AND THE POLITICAL CENTRE

The fact that the most sustained and direct feminist interventions in party politics took place in the labour movement should not obscure the extent to which other political parties and institutions became carriers of feminist ideas. In the electoral realignment of the 1980s, women were strong supporters of the centre parties.

That support was assiduously courted. During most of the 1980s the Liberals and Social Democrats, and, since 1988, the Liberal Democrats, directed special attention to women. They devised women's rights policies and they also implemented special measures to secure the selection of women candidates for Parliament. They were the first to make the compulsory shortlisting of women a feature of their candidate selection rules, with the result that their records of selecting women candidates compared favourably with those of the Conservatives and were on a par with—indeed, were slightly better than—Labour's.

But their effect was limited. The problem is that Britain's 'first past the post' electoral system means that 'third' parties have little hope of obtaining the election of more than a tiny fraction of their candidates. One effect that this centre party challenge had on women MPs during the 1980s was to ensure that the party that put forward the fewest women, the Conservatives, won repeated elections. So the contribution of the centre has been to generate ideas and to raise issues which may then be taken up by the dominant parties. But electoral weakness prevents it from demonstrating a commitment to establishing women in positions of political power.

The other minor parties represented in the House of Commons in the 1980s, the Scottish Nationalist Party and Plaid Cymru, have not really been active on behalf of women. But the Green Party, which began to show some vote-winning capacity in the

---

[30] Joni Lovenduski and Pippa Norris, 'The Conservatives and Women'.

elections to the European Parliament in 1989, has not only been keen to promote women candidates, but has been particularly hospitable to feminist ideas and ways of working. Greens take gender issues seriously, and on occasion their initiatives have been very influential. For example, A Woman's Claim of Right, the campaign to ensure that the proposed Scottish Assembly represents women adequately, was a Green Party initiative. A Women's Claim of Right has meant that the issue of women's representation has been on the agenda throughout the discussions leading to the Scottish Constitutional Convention. Moreover, it had some influence in ensuring that proportional representation is also on the agenda in Scotland, because of an increasingly popular view that such a system will guarantee a more satisfactory representation of women.

## WOMEN AND THE CONSERVATIVE PARTY

No British political party has benefited more consistently from women's political and electoral support than the Conservatives. Women constitute 60 per cent of the members of the Conservative Party, and, during the years for which systematic records are available, women were regularly and significantly more likely than men to vote Conservative (see Table 3). Without the women's vote, the Conservatives would have remained in opposition for all the years between 1945 and 1979. After 1955 the gender gap in voting which meant that British women were more likely than men to vote Conservative gradually diminished until, in 1983 and again in 1987, the Tories lost their advantage

TABLE 3. *Distribution of women's votes in the 1979, 1983, 1987, and 1992 general elections (%)*

|                        | 1979 | 1983 | 1987 | 1992 |
|------------------------|------|------|------|------|
| Conservative           | 48.3 | 44.9 | 44.2 | 43.0 |
| Labour                 | 37.5 | 27.7 | 30.9 | 39   |
| Liberal/SDP, Lib. Dem. | 13.0 | 26.0 | 23.4 | 18   |
| Other                  | 1.0  | 1.4  | 1.4  | 5.0  |

Sources: British Election Studies, 1979, 1983, 1987; Harris Exit Poll, 9 Apr. 1992.

in attracting women's votes.[31] In 1992, however, they regained the support of women over the age of 35.

Women continue to be the majority of Conservative Party members and the mainstay of constituency parties. The Conservatives are, at their grass roots, a party of women. But the hierarchies and leadership remain resolutely male. Margaret Thatcher's leadership was remarkable for the absence of other women MPs from her Cabinet. John Major's first Cabinet, appointed in December 1990, contained no women. In 1987 only seventeen Conservative women MPs were elected. In 1992, the Conservatives returned twenty women MPs, and John Major's new Cabinet included two women.

As we have noted above, the Labour Party's private research at the end of the 1980s revealed that the general public was under the impression that the Conservatives had more women MPs than Labour did. In fact, 17 Conservative and 21 Labour women MPs were returned in the 1987 Parliament (the period for which the research was conducted). Proportionately, the parliamentary Labour Party, with 9.2 per cent of women MPs, was well ahead of the Tory Party, with 4.5 per cent of woman MPs.

Conservative Central Office has publicly affirmed a desire for more women MPs and has exhorted constituency parties to give serious consideration to the selection of women candidates. Lady Seccombe, the party vice-president in charge of women in the early 1990s, became well known for her efforts to encourage women to become candidates, and her predecessor, Emma Nicholson, now herself a Conservative MP, was particularly industrious during the 1980s in increasing the number of women on the candidate lists, organizing widely publicized 'high fliers' conferences to draw successful women into Conservative politics. But candidate selection rules and a party ethos that eschews positive action mean that there is little more that can be done apart from exhortation and the inclusion of suitable women on the party's approved list of candidates.[32]

At the level of policy, the party has been more assiduous.

[31] Joni Lovenduski and Pippa Norris, 'The Conservatives and Women'.

[32] Joni Lovenduski and Pippa Norris, 'British Conservative Parliamentary Recruitment: Patronage, Liberal-Rational, Radical and Feminist Models', paper presented to the annual meeting of the American Political Science Association, Washington, DC, 29 Aug.–1 Sept. 1991.

Since 1986 a ministerial group on women's issues has met under the auspices of the Home Office to consider the effect of legislation on women. Until the 1992 election, this was not a Cabinet committee, and its powers were those of persuasion. Moreover, the scarcity of women ministers means that few women ever belonged to the group; certainly, no one reported that Mrs Thatcher attended its three or four meetings a year. Nevertheless, its very existence is one of a few signs that the Conservative leadership became more sensitive to issues of women's equality and representation during the 1980s. The fact that it was upgraded to Cabinet status by John Major in 1992 is an indication of a greater commitment to such issues. In 1988 the Thatcher government declared that the civil service was now required to scrutinize new policies and legislation to ensure that they did not adversely affect women. However, this policy was not to be retrospective. In 1988 the Home Secretary, John Patten, appointed Joanna Foster to head the Equal Opportunities Commission. Foster's competence and commitment to equal opportunities are such that this was widely seen as a boost for these policies. At around the same time, Mrs Thatcher was rumoured to be taking an interest in the appointment of women to the different quangos and public bodies to which government departments appoint directors and members. In 1990, when Angela Rumbold was appointed Minister of State at the Home Office, her responsibilities included 'women's issues'. Rumbold was not happy about that. Asked by journalist Philippa Brardewood to explain her new job as 'Minister for Women', she replied: 'Your profession has dumped that name on me. My major responsibility is Prisons.'[33]

Rumbold's unhappiness with the 'Women's Ministry' tag was a reflection of the Conservative Party's ambivalence about gender issues. Nevertheless, these developments were all indicators that, even during the Thatcher years, the Conservative Party leadership was well aware of the need to cultivate its woman-friendly image and of the fact that it could no longer take the support of women voters for granted. The dilemma that the party faced was partly due to its strong support for traditional family roles and to its current distaste for social intervention in the form of wel-

[33] The *Observer*, 29 July 1990.

fare support, positive action, and even much of the rhetoric of equality. Underlying changes in the position of women, including an irreversible overall increase in fertility control, an increase in educational opportunities and, with it, women's aspirations, the growing importance to the economy of women's employment, and the crucial role of systems of state support, all combined to pressure the party to promote women.[34] But the party also had—and has—a large natural constituency of loyal women workers and members who must be satisfied. Add to this the changes in the patterns of women's voting, and the dilemma began to be acute. Allowing women the promotions that they 'deserve' was an obvious Tory response to feminism. Although it would be denied by Conservatives, all of this suggests that 'common-sense' feminist ideas about equality of opportunity were becoming more influential, if only for the pragmatic purposes of recovering women's votes.

It is more difficult to determine whether there is a rising feminist tendency in the party itself. The British Conservative and Unionist Party has a tradition of unity and loyalty that makes it much more difficult to assess the influence of feminism on its policies and practices. Feminism is a form of dissidence, and, interesting though Tory dissidents are, they are not well studied by social scientists. In *The Iron Ladies* Bea Campbell attempts to assess the impact of feminism on Conservative women. She observes a duality in the party culture that on the one hand publicizes support for traditional women's roles and, on the other, acknowledges its reliance upon powerful and independent women, not least, of course, on Margaret Thatcher.[35] That duality operated at the level of policy and of custom, sometimes acknowledged, sometimes implicit. For example, Lady Joan Seccombe told us in 1991 that local Conservative associations organize two different kinds of women's meetings, one for the traditional Conservative woman, and one for the modern career woman who may be trying to juggle home, work, and party. By contrast, Tory rhetoric under Margaret Thatcher held that the Welfare State, on which so many women depended, eroded the

[34] Jean Gardiner, 'Women, Recession and the Tories', in Stuart Hall and Martin Jacques (eds.), *The Politics of Thatcherism* (Lawrence and Wishart, London, 1983).

[35] Campbell, *Iron Ladies.*

family. Government cuts in services such as school meals had the practical effect of tying women closer to the home. Such duality was sustainable because of the very nature of British Conservatism. The party's tradition is one that absorbs and mutes conflict, one that does not pursue and expose contradiction. We do not mean to imply that there was no conflict; rather, that it was managed internally.

To summarize: for most of the years of British second-wave feminism, the Conservative Party leadership appeared to take the representation of women for granted. But at the beginning of the 1990s there were signs that this was shifting. In the autumn of 1991 John Major declared his support for Opportunity 2000, a programme designed to place more women in top jobs. Party managers announced their efforts to recruit more women candidates, and a number of conspicuous public appointments of women to prominent positions were made.[36] It was emphasized that these were women of merit, that they were the best persons available for the job, but the intent to be seen to be promoting women was obvious. Gillian Shepherd, who was appointed Employment Secretary in John Major's government in 1992, was given responsibility for women's issues, and, in striking contrast to Angela Rumbold a few years previously, showed considerable enthusiasm for the task.

But we should be mindful of the contrast between policy and image, between substance and rhetoric. A new Tory willingness to acknowledge the importance of women's issues should not be equated with a conversion to feminism. We are witnessing a characteristic Conservative response, in which formal equality, such as the reform of taxation to allow independent assessment for married women, is on the policy agenda. There is a willingness to treat women as equals, but not to get at the sources of inequality that mean that such treatment risks institutionalizing inequality. For example, tax independence for married women implies that families might reverse roles, making women the breadwinners, and men take the major share of domestic responsibility. However, the realities of the job market, with its lower pay and opportunities for women, mean that the apparent free-

---

[36] e.g. the prominent feminist barrister Helena Kennedy took silk (was made a QC) and the first woman head of MI5 was appointed during 1991.

dom to choose is rarely a practical possibility. Similarly, the changes in the candidate selection procedure have made every effort to encourage constituencies to select women with the same qualifications to be MPs as men have. No effort has been made to address the fact that, through no fault of their own, significantly fewer women have such qualifications in the first place.


POLITICAL PARTIES AND ELECTED OFFICE

None of the British political parties has been successful in getting significant numbers of women into Parliament (see, for example, Table 2). The Liberal Democrats and the Greens do better at nominating women candidates, but with little realistic hope of getting them elected. Both the Labour and Conservative Parties reformed their candidate selection procedures during the 1980s, and both now express a wish to increase the parliamentary representation of women. The Labour Party has announced a target of having 50 per cent women MPs by the end of the century, whilst the Conservative Party wishes aloud (and quietly manœuvres) to nominate more women candidates. Under the present electoral system, both parties have difficulty in doing much to change the outcome of nomination decisions. Such decisions are taken at constituency level, and party centres have only a limited impact on them.[37] Constituency parties are naturally reluctant to take electoral risks, and they will generally opt for a candidate who closely resembles the 'normal' MP—who is white, male, and middle class. It is difficult to see how, in Britain's 'first past the post' electoral system, where only one candidate per constituency is chosen, local selectors will be persuaded to nominate candidates who do not conform to the stereotype of the normal male politician.[38]

[37] For extensive discussions of gender and party selection procedures in Britain, see Joni Lovenduski and Pippa Norris, 'Selecting Women Candidates: Obstacles to the Feminisation of the House of Commons', *European Journal of Political Research*, 17 (Autumn 1989), 533–62, and 'The Conservatives and Women'.

[38] Interestingly, by the beginning of 1992 the debate about electoral reform in the Labour Party had not been expanded to take account of the likely effect of reform on women's representation. Labour women were at a fairly early stage of organizing over this issue.

Currently, neither the Labour Party nor the Conservatives support the changes in the method of electing MPs that might make it easier to increase women's representation, although Labour did indicate by the end of the 1992 election campaign that it was at least willing to discuss the issue of electoral reform.

Women have done better at getting elected to local government, where their proportion of seats rose steadily, reaching 30 per cent on some London councils by 1990.[39] There is more political competition, as the minor parties are more successful at obtaining political representation. The powers of local authorities have declined during the 1980s, so the meaning of women's growing presence on local councils is open to some interpretation. The fact that the minor parties are more electable at a local level implies the kind of increased political competition that may bring more women into elected office.[40] But local office has become both more demanding, in that councillors now bear financial responsibility for council decisions and are hard pressed to deliver services in the light of increased financial control by the central government, and less powerful, in that many of its responsibilities have been removed by successive reforms during the 1980s, making such posts less attractive. There is therefore a sense in which competition has decreased as parties struggle to find suitable candidates for many offices.

### The Judiciary and the Civil Service

Electoral channels are not the only routes to British political élites. There are a number of important appointed positions in which crucial political decisions are made. The most significant of these are in the judiciary and the senior civil service, but there are also many public bodies of various kinds to which the government makes appointments. These tribunals, boards, and commissions exercise considerable discretionary power. About 20 per cent of these positions were held by women in 1988.

Over the 1980s, the civil service, under pressure from its unions and, it was rumoured, from the Prime Minister, introduced a

[39] Jim Barry, *The Women's Movement and Local Politics* (Avebury, Aldershot, 1991), 68, table 4.3.
[40] Jill Hills, 'Britain', in Joni Lovenduski and Jill Hills (eds.), *The Politics of the Second Electorate* (Routledge and Kegan Paul, London, 1981).

series of reforms in its promotion and recruitment strategies that were designed to improve the position of women and ethnic minorities in the service. A series of reports led to changes at all levels of the service. The structure of the civil service resembles a pyramid, a hierarchy with a small élite corps at the top, and a numerous base of clerical workers at the bottom. In between, are a number of intermediate 'professional' grades that may also form a career path for those who enter the service with a degree. Women predominate at the bottom of this structure and are rare at the top. The position of women in the civil service hierarchy has been a matter of frequent and continued political struggle, and there has been a long battle for the implementation of equal opportunities policies since the early 1970s.[41] As a result, women have made considerable advances within the clerical grades, but success in the senior grades has been more elusive. Our interest here is in the changes that occurred at the senior and most directly political levels of the service. By the end of the 1980s, one in twenty of the civil servants in the senior grades was a woman, a figure which represented a sudden improvement on previous years. Some senior civil servants believe that a real change occurred in attitudes towards women in the civil service in the second half of the 1980s. According to Treasury projections, it is expected that women will constitute about one-third of all senior civil servants by 2016.[42] This change is the result of a number of reforms of civil service employment practice, changes which the Hansard Society is careful to point out were not designed with women in mind. This is odd, given the considerable amount of equal opportunities activity in the civil service, which has had an equality action programme since 1984. The programme was amended and sharpened in 1987, after investigations showed that line-managers tended to judge women's suitability for promotion more harshly than men's. Whilst outstanding women were assessed as such, those on the borderline were not given the same benefit of the doubt as borderline men received. Other investigations showed that recruitment to the fast stream, the source of most senior civil servants, also favoured men.[43] These procedures were changed and made more

---

[41] Cockburn, *In the Way of Women*, 50–2.
[42] Hansard Society, *Women at the Top*.
[43] Ibid.

open, with a resulting increase in women's recruitment and chances of promotion. Child care schemes, career-break schemes, part-time working provision, job-share schemes, and the raising of the training age-limit to 52 have all been introduced, also with resulting improvements in women's recruitment, the retention of women civil servants, and their chances of promotion.

Long-standing barriers to women in the judiciary also began to be eroded during the 1980s. The publicity given to the nine women barristers who were made QCs in April 1991 is testimony to the scarcity of women in the senior ranks of the legal profession. For many years, entry to the British judiciary has involved a virtually secret process whereby the Lord Chancellor sought advice from senior judges about suitable individuals. So little was known about the process that the only way to identify the relevant qualifications was to audit the characteristics of those who were appointed. After reforms were introduced in 1972, it was possible for solicitors to be appointed as judges, but the reality of the typical judicial apprenticeship was long continuous service as a barrister, taking silk (which means being made a QC, and there is no 'taking' about it, it is given), and approval by the judicial establishment. These are characteristics that men are more likely to have than women. Progress to the bench is a natural step for British barristers. About half of those who were called to the bar in the 1960s were sitting as judges by 1991. But although 10 per cent of all barristers are QCs, only 3 per cent of women barristers are (there are about 1,170 women barristers). Britain's 1,200 assistant recorders (part-time judges) have, on average, between seventeen and twenty-one years of experience as lawyers. Between 1986 and 1991, 439 barristers were made recorders, of whom 413 were men and 26 were women. There were only 2 women among the 51 recorders who were made full-time judges in those years, and of the 176 circuit court judges appointed, only 8 were women. Moreover, those women who were appointed were better qualified than the men. For example, they had twenty-three years of experience, compared to twenty-one years for the men. A significant number of men had only twelve to fifteen years of experience on appointment as recorders, but no woman had less than sixteen years.[44]

[44] The *Independent*, 17 May 1991.

Both supply and demand factors are at work here. A look at the number of potential women judges shows that the pool of eligible women is smaller than the pool of men, and it is only recently that significant proportions of women have begun to qualify as barristers and solicitors. On the demand side, there has been direct and indirect prejudice against women. Indirect prejudice has resulted from a method of appointment in which a closed oligarchic élite is allowed to reproduce itself. An inner circle of male judges, unused to scrutinizing its prejudices—indeed, unused to much scrutiny of any kind—is unlikely to be struck by the maleness of the recruitment criteria. Lord Hailsham, who was Lord Chancellor between 1979 and 1987, when he was replaced by Lord McKay, was known for his reluctance to consider women for judicial office. Lord McKay, who began his term of office with a reform of the appointments procedure, is more even-handed, and more women have been appointed and promoted since 1987.

Nevertheless, it is clear that male gatekeepers to the appointed offices of the civil service and the judiciary have been able, wittingly and unwittingly, to keep in place criteria of selection that are essentially male. Only when their procedures were reformed and particularly obstructive gatekeepers were removed, was change possible.

## FEMINISM, MASCULINITY, AND THE STATE

Amongst British Socialist feminists, growing practical activity in political institutions has been accompanied by increased theoretical interest in the nature of those institutions. One of the most striking features of the second decade of the WLM is the way in which feminist ideas of the state have changed and developed. Nowhere is this more true than in Britain, where conceptualizations of the state in the 1970s were often stark and simple. There were several reasons why the state was important to feminist theorizing. First, the socialist beginnings of the second wave of British feminism brought with them habits of political thought that centred on the state as a kind of master concept which, once correctly understood, would illuminate the strategies for empowerment that the movement needed and sought. Secondly, a significant amount of the post-war rise in women's paid employment outside the home was employment by the 'state', notably by the Health Service, the local authorities, and the civil service. Thirdly, the question of whether women should seek political office was important to many feminists. Fourthly, the 'state' is an elusive concept, difficult to get a grip on; intriguing in its multiplicity and flexibility, it invites attention from theorists of all persuasions.

At first, however, the nuances and complexities of the state were rarely perceived or discussed. Indeed, the main divisions of the movement were often characterized in terms of highly simplified understandings of the state. For many Socialist feminists, it was an oppressive entity that acted in the interests of capital, supporting a class politics that was particularly harmful to women, who were to be found in the least privileged class positions. For Radical and revolutionary feminists, the state was a patriarchal construction that underpinned male power. Liberal feminists regarded the state as neutral, a resource that could be used to achieve feminist aims simply by removing the legal barriers to women's participation.

None of these characterizations proved itself to be capable of sustaining a political practice. One problem was that the nature of the state changed. Another was that its effects on women varied considerably. Rowbotham has commented that the anti-state proclivities of feminists were formed in an era in which the Welfare State could be taken for granted. The breakdown in the post-war settlement, the political theme of British public policy in the 1980s, made it clear that the impact of the state on women, and its importance to feminist politics, is differentiated, ambiguous, and contradictory. Pressure to 're-theorize' the state came from many areas of feminist experience. Black, white, middle-class, and working-class women were affected differently by state policy, and Irish women fared differently to English, Welsh, and Scottish women.[45] These different experiences became apparent in the campaigns about abortion, domestic violence, and rape which precipitated arguments in the movement about the specificity of the experiences of different groups of women. The arguments about difference ran on throughout the 1980s and

[45] Rowbotham, *The Past Is before Us.*

underlined the variation in the ways in which par
affected different groups of women. The women's s
ment was instrumental in altering perceptions. Fem
ians and social scientists produced studies that showe
state was sometimes a resource, sometimes a ba.
significance of which was often apparent only at the leve          ...ar-
ticular experiences. Such insights correspond to a drift in feminist
analysis away from top-down power theories and towards formulations that stress the omnipresence of power as something that is
produced in every social relationship. They lead away from a
functionalist concentration upon state institutions such as the
judiciary, the legislature, the government, etc., and towards a
concern with understanding the techniques and apparatus of regulation.[46]

Practical politics were an equally important influence. The
1980s saw an extension of police powers which was most evident
in their implementation in the black communities, at Greenham
Common, in the miners' strike of 1984–5, and in the policing of
the Irish in Britain. Social security protection was decreased,
hard-won women's rights to employment protection and maternity leave were rolled back. From the second half of the decade,
cuts in the public sector threatened the major source of women's
jobs, particularly their employment by local authorities.
Gradually, many feminists began to conclude that the protection
offered by legislation, and the resources offered by the Welfare
State were essential to the improvement of women's condition,
that the state provided both protection and control, and that
women's relation to the state was not easy to generalize.

It is no longer really possible to categorize feminists as
Radical, Liberal, or Socialist in terms of their understanding of
the state. The early ideas have grown and burst their boundaries
to produce thinking that takes elements from all the strands of
feminist thought. This has happened in the context of a crisis in
socialist thinking as the British Left came to terms, first, with the
popularity of the Thatcher agenda, and, later, with the collapse
of state socialism in Europe. As we have shown, the space that
was opened up by a rethinking of the socialist project freed

[46] See the collection edited by Sylvia Benhabib and Drucilla Cornell, *Feminism
as Critique* (Polity, Oxford, 1987), which contains essays by many of the theorists
who are concerned with these issues.

feminists to rethink the relations of class and gender and to draw on a variety of sources to construct sophisticated understandings of power and domination. Incvitably, established ideas about the state were scrutinized and found wanting.

Thus, in 1990 Sophie Watson noted that care should be taken not to over-theorize the state, arguing that it is no longer possible to conceptualise it as a contradictory complex entity (but, nevertheless, one entity, one single institution).[47] It is much more useful to see the state as a set of arenas, a by-product of political struggles, whose coherence is as much established in discourse as it is in temporarily apparent, but shifting, connections of individuals, policies, and institutions.[48] This set of arenas is one in which there are opportunities for feminists. Interests are not 'given', and there is no such entity as a unitary controlling state in complete control of its interests. Nor is there any abstraction capable of capturing and communicating the incoherence of the state. Feminist interests and women's interests, like those of any group, do not somehow arrive at the state for representation fully formed; rather, they are defined, refined, and articulated as they are put into play in the various arenas of the state. It is there that they become fully constituted.

Sophie Watson and Ros Pringle are at pains to stress that they are not implying a pluralist analysis.[49] Although power is diffused throughout society, it operates as a network, but a network that has dominant characteristics. One of these is fraternity. In an argument that has much in common with Cynthia Cockburn's exposition of labour movement masculinity, they draw on Carole Pateman's work on the fraternal nature of the social contract which describes how men have been able to consolidate and defend their power, to regroup as a fraternity, through discourses that deny the relevance of gender. Men's interests are also constructed and constituted in the various arenas of the state. In men's construction, the discourse of fraternity (the dominant discourse) presumes and evokes the notion that men alone are the political actors, that state and civil society have been established

[47] Sophie Watson, 'The State of Play', in *Playing the State: Australian Feminist Interventions* (Virago, London, 1990).
[48] Sophie Watson and Rosemary Pringle, 'Fathers, Brothers, Mates: The Fraternal State in Australia', in Watson (ed.), *Playing the State.*
[49] Ibid.

by men who act on behalf of the population as a whole. In patriarchal politics, women are constructed as political actors only in
terms of how they differ from men; that is, women are constructed in relation to men, but men are constructed in relation
to each other.[50]

This exploration of the dominant networks of state power
explains why politics is understood as it is, how it has been 'masculinized'. The dominant discourse, whether political commentary
or political science, basically accepts the formulation of politics
that is negotiated within the dominant group, it sees this as the
only significant politics, a perception that is sometimes signified
by designations like 'high politics' or 'real politics'. Such conceptualizations rule out consideration of much of what women do
that is political. Feminist theorists contest such biases. The
significance of Carole Pateman's deconstruction of politics is that
it both recognizes differences between men and shows how it is
that women's constructions of political interests are separate and
disadvantaged. It also facilitates an understanding of how the differences between men's interests provide opportunities for feminist political interventions.

The way in which politics is masculinized excludes women
from political institutions and structures. It underwrites a culture
in which common sense decrees that politicians are naturally
male. The power of this barrier is enormous, and it is incorporated into a whole range of formal rules and informal practices
and customs that make it difficult for women to gain entry to, or
function in, the arenas and institutions of political decision-making. This is as true in the elected as it is in the appointed élites.

Feminist attempts to modify and influence political institutions
are a characteristic of contemporary British politics. Their interventions are conditioned and shaped both by the imperatives of
the relevant political arena and by feminist notions of appropriate political style and action. That the rules of the political game
inevitably mediate the intervention has been one of the most
important obstacles for feminists. On the one hand, the hierarchical, class-driven reality of British politics is welcoming only to
upper-class men and to those prepared to play by their rules. On

[50] Carole Pateman, *The Sexual Contract* (Polity, Cambridge, 1988), 'The
Fraternal Social Contract' in her *The Disorder of Women* (Polity, Cambridge,
1989).

the other hand, many feminists are unwilling to sacrifice the collective ways of working that have been forged in the women's movement: they are, at best, ambivalent about demanding inclusion. Nevertheless, where feminists have attempted entry on their own terms, they have sometimes been able to affect the rules of the game, normally where those rules are being contested (for example, in the Labour Party, in the GLC, in the discussions leading to the Scottish Constitutional Convention). These are instances where differences in the dominant networks of (male) power enable feminists to intervene, to modify the relationship between different state arenas.

# 6

# The Women's Movement and the Politics of Equality at Work

THE issue of equality at work has, at one time or another, engaged almost the whole of the women's movement. It has been a preoccupation for women in the political parties, professional associations, and trade unions, and it was important in the social movement politics of both the first and second waves of feminism. Equal opportunities issues potentially underpin alliances across gender, class, and racial lines. Demands for equality at work became so significant during the 1970s and 1980s that Cynthia Cockburn refers to an equal opportunities movement that includes feminists, trade-unionists, and organizations to empower disabled people.[1] Equal pay and equal opportunities were two of the seven demands adopted by the WLM conferences of the 1970s, but they are not exclusively feminist demands. Feminist attitudes to equal opportunities strategies are often similar to their attitudes about political institutions. Some are ambivalent or hostile, the result of a belief that such strategies incorporate women within male power structures where they must either become like the men already there or fail in their objectives. Moreover, equality at work is a demand that is often made by women who would not regard themselves as feminists, and some feminists regard it as an impossible goal.

Such ambivalence does not prevent considerable feminist support for sex equality policies. The argument for support is straightforward. Employment rights are the fundamental condition of women's liberation. In a society that is organized around work, those who do not have paid employment lack status and power. The relationship we suggest is not a simple one. Women's subordination is not

---

[1] Cynthia Cockburn, 'Equal Opportunities: The Short and Long Agenda', *Industrial Relations Journal* (1989), 213–25.

reducible to economic dependence upon men. Rather, it is a function of many components of male strength and social dominance which, historically, have produced structures, norms, and patterns that are effective at controlling women, particularly women who are mothers. Cultural norms about the family empower male breadwinners (whether or not they are actually breadwinners), and support a power structure that may be violent and impoverished. Although there are many good marriages, and although the family may provide protection for many women, for others, its habits and obligations may be demeaning and dangerous, but still, for a variety of reasons, inescapable. Many women feel that they have no choice but to tolerate a subordinate role in the family. Power in the family is in part a function of the male wage and its cultural and actual importance to family incomes. For women to escape or alter these conditions, they need the financial independence which only adequately paid work can provide in a society such as ours. The issues raised by demands for equality at work are too important for too many women for feminists to avoid them.

In this chapter we discuss the politics of equal opportunities. We consider what they have meant to organized women, and how the issues have altered and expanded since they first appeared on the agenda. The decision to allocate a chapter to equality at work places us in the position of drawing some arbitrary boundaries. The ambit of equal employment issues is, in practice, extensive. Although the starting-place is paid work, the issue spreads out from there and overlaps with issues of violence to women (sexual harassment), family roles (child care provision), and issues about citizenship and participation (women decision-making positions). It is not possible to draw precise boundaries. Equality of opportunity is clearly more than a matter of pay and conditions at work, important though these are. It is also about access to state benefits, to housing, to education and training.

The development of sex equality issues during the 1980s represented an expansion from original demands which were workplace- and employment-focused to a wide-ranging critique of the gendered division of labour and its role in the subordination of women. This has been described as an expansion from a short to a long agenda.[2] In the course of this development, a policy com-

---

[2] Cynthia Cockburn, 'Equal Opportunities: The Short and Long Agenda', *Industrial Relations Journal* (1989), 213–25

munity was created that includes national and international state agencies, trade unions, firms, political parties, traditional women's organizations, and feminist activists.

The political agenda has expanded to include feminist preoccupations with sexuality. During the 1980s, important political links between economic and sexual power were made. For example, the politicization of the issue of sexual harassment at work is a coming-together of traditional workplace demands with the preoccupations of contemporary feminism. The way in which it emerged and developed, and its treatment by established structures like the trade unions, links several sets of political fragments, and the struggle to get rid of the practice may mark a feminization of the workplace, the first steps in a pluralization of the workplace culture as a result of feminist efforts to transform masculine institutions.

To demonstrate our case, it is necessary to describe the way in which women have organized and been active around the issue of equality at work. This is a natural extension of our discussion of gender and political institutions. The setting for the politics of equal opportunities has tended to be the established political structures, and the actors have been the traditional political actors of parties, unions, employers' organizations, local authorities, state agencies, and established pressure groups. In the course of seeking to influence those institutions, feminists joined—and sometimes transformed—a structured policy process for which the rules had long since been agreed.

The discussion that follows is not comprehensive. Because we stress feminist engagement of employment equality, we do not treat all of the actors in detail. Instead, we focus on feminist initiatives, in order to demonstrate the shape and style of the relevant politics, offering examples of how women have engaged political structures, coped with them, and occasionally transformed them, if only temporarily. Accordingly, we will begin with a discussion of sex equality in employment as an issue, and the role of women in placing it on the agenda. We follow with a discussion of the legislation and the agencies that it brought into being, an investigation of the role of the politics of the local authority women's committees which were so prominent in the 1980s and early 1990s, and, finally, we will examine the role of the trade unions as agents and resisters of equal opportunities at work. In the course of this, we outline the networks of the new equal opportunities policy communities that have developed since 1979.

## SEX EQUALITY AS A MOBILIZING ISSUE

Remembering the 1980s, one does not get a sense that employment equality was a burning issue for the women's movement. In the course of our interviews with feminists in different parts of Britain, only those who were actually employed in equality agencies of one kind or another made unprompted mention of employment rights as an issue of concern. When we asked about it directly, the response was a sort of interested surprise. The 1980s were a time when, according to one feminist in Edinburgh, 'interest in issues about women's employment was quite low. I think it was the time when women were . . . I suppose it's issues about violence and images, I mean, things that seem to be more directly linked to male power than employment.' One explanation may be that the notion of equal opportunities does not have much resonance for ordinary women, who see it as a more privileged level of problem than they are likely to have. In Manchester we were told that it had little to do with the issues that women faced there. The interviews that we conducted with women's officers and equality officers in various women's units about their consultations with local women (described below, in our discussion of women's committees) confirmed that local women were most concerned about child care provision, male violence, and housing rather than employment issues.

The pattern was not uniform, however, and we were also told of instances where women were drawn into feminist politics through working on an equal opportunities issue. A young Edinburgh woman recalled the exhilaration that she experienced as a result of organizing a campaign to support a woman who was taking Burton's to an industrial tribunal for unfair dismissal after they had sacked her on learning of her pregnancy. A picket was mounted outside Burton's on Princes Street every week from January 1988 until the tribunal in July: 'Every week at least one picket all the time . . . we really organised it, there was a lot of publicity a lot of support, we had benefits, we did all the stuff you have to do for a campaign and then we won. It was really brilliant . . . I still get a good feeling when I walk past Burton's . . . the day we found out she'd won we went with a bottle of champagne . . .'. This was her first involvement in feminist politics, and it was compulsive: 'all the time through all these things you know you're making contacts, you're meeting people and it was really good after such a struggle of standing out in freezing February picketing . . . to win in the end, its just great when you do, you have wins as well, you know, it's not all just like constant battling and getting hammered into the ground . . .'.

Work in the local authority equality committees and units was also politicizing. Women who had been commandeered to chair local council women's committees or recruited to posts as union women's officers, a feature of the issue's development in the 1980s, spoke of how their work made them think of themselves as feminists. For some, it was not a matter of changing their views, it was rather a realization that the term 'feminist' described them. For others, a job that required them to think about the differences between men and women at work converted them to feminism. In this sense, the 1980s were a time of consolidation, of extending the ideas and of building on the achievements of feminist campaigns of previous decades.

### Equal Employment and the Women's Movement before 1979

Feminists were closely involved in the campaigns to put equal rights at work on the statute-books. Equal pay and opportunities campaigns had their roots in the first wave of feminism, and were in evidence during the 1950s. But it was during the 1960s that women in a variety of organizations began to take up the issue of equality at work in a sustained way. Initiatives came from within the labour movement, from parliamentary women, from women's organizations, and from women who had not previously been organized. The formation of Working Women's Charter in 1964 produced a manifesto for women's employment rights in the trade-union movement. The first private member's bill to outlaw discrimination against women was introduced by Labour MP Joyce Butler in 1967, and was followed by a succession of bills over the next few years. Meanwhile, a women's rights group was formed in Hull in the spring of 1968 around the campaign led by

Lil Bilocca and the fishermen's wives to improve the safety of trawlers after two ships had been lost in bad weather in January 1968. The move encountered hostility, and Mrs Bilocca received threatening letters and could not get a job.[3] A highly publicized equal pay strike by women workers at Ford's Dagenham factory put the issue of equal pay on the agenda of the British Left, and, according to contemporary activists, made it possible for discussions of women's specific oppression to take place in left-wing political groups.[4]

The rising WLM in Britain and in the United States helped to create a widespread momentum behind these campaigns. In 1970 the first national WLM conference at Ruskin College, Oxford, adopted demands for equal pay and equal opportunities. But, for many feminists, 1968 was the crucial year. Labour MP Audrey Wise, who was at the Ruskin conference, recalls that the beginnings were really in 1968:

This is very important because it predates the American Influence . . . the first demonstration was in 1969, arising from the National Joint Action Campaign Committee for Women's Equal Rights (NJAC-CWER). Every word was pondered in the title. I remember discussions when we fixed the title. You could actually say NJACCWER, so you didn't have to remember each one. That was initiated by the Ford Women.

There are two things that were crucial about 1968. One is, it was the fiftieth anniversary of women getting the vote for the first time . . . and that sparked off no end of articles . . . this sounds trivial but it wasn't . . . there were times when you couldn't open a paper without articles like 'Well, women have had the vote for fifty years, what difference had it made?' . . . there was a kind of consciousness.[5]

The Ford strike and the formation of NJACCWER are important, both because they were symptomatic of the times and they were instances of women organizing for women's rights. Audrey Wise recalls that:

. . . the Ford's strike was extraordinarily important because it was the first strike since the match girls, eighty years before, which was identified as a women's strike. You had a Labour government which was supposed

[3] Sheila Rowbotham, *The Past Is before us* (Penguin, London, 1990), 17.
[4] Ibid.
[5] Audrey Wise, 1988, quoted in Michelene Wandor, *Once a Feminist: Stories of a Generation* (Virago, London, 1990), 120.

to be interested in equal pay and that heightened consciousness as well.

NJACCWER is remembered by quite a lot of trade union workers. It organised a rally in Trafalgar Square in May 1969, two years before what is normally referred to as the first post-suffrage women's liberation demonstration. It is important because it shows that there was a working class women's liberation movement.[6]

The pressure generated by the Ford strike was one of the important factors in assuring the passage of the Equal Pay Act in 1970. Another pressure was the activities of the Equal Pay Campaign Committee, which linked at least thirty women's groups and professional organizations to the parliamentary campaign. By this time there was considerable women's activity on issues of sex equality, and there was widespread national debate about the issue. Links were made between the WLM and more traditional women's groups. During the winter of 1971–2, feminists in Women's Lobby began to co-operate with the Fawcett Society, providing a bridge between the two wings of British feminism. There was extensive lobbying and campaigning around William Hamilton's private member's bill against sex discrimination, which was due for parliamentary debate. The Home Office's rejection of the bill, and its filibustering by Ronald Bell were criticized on the women's pages of the national newspapers. A national newsletter was established to keep women informed of the activities of the government, the parties, the unions, and a variety of groups on the matter.[7] All the usual techniques of political lobbying were used to keep up the pressure. The Conservative consultative document 'Equal Opportunities for Men and Women', published in 1973, provoked responses from over 300 groups. The change in government during 1974 saw a growth in activity. A major campaign in Parliament that involved women from both sides of the House was linked to campaigns by a variety of interest groups including union women's sections, the NCCL, the Fawcett Society, Women in the Media, the National Joint Council of Working Women's Organisations, and a range of other similar bodies.[8]

Women's liberation groups were prominent amongst those

[6] Ibid.

[7] Elizabeth Meehan *Women's Rights at Work* (Macmillan, Basingstoke, 1985).

[8] Ibid., *passim*.

engaged in the campaigns to get equal rights at work on the statute-books. Indeed, several of these groups began as equal pay groups. Even at this stage, however, there were ambiguities in feminist attitudes towards the issue. The Socialist feminist historian Sheila Rowbotham is certain that an emphasis on class and a need for connection with the labour movement was an important feature of the emerging women's movement. There was, she writes, a commitment to equal pay and better conditions at work.[9] But accounts from other tendencies in the WLM suggest a different emphasis. According to Elizabeth Meehan, the Ruskin College conference adopted the equal employment demands by only a very narrow margin.[10] And many descriptions of the Oxford meeting never mention the debate over the issue.[11] Feminists of all tendencies have reservations about what statute law might deliver in the way of rights. Writing in the *Guardian* in October 1974, Anna Coote argued: 'New laws and regulations don't bring social change. The most they do is to create a climate more favourable to change and make life more tolerable for some in the meantime. If the Equal Pay Act achieves nothing else it will have taught us a valuable lesson: women will get nowhere unless they organise and fight for themselves.'[12]

In general, women on the Left during the 1970s were wary of using the state and the law as a means to liberation. But members of the WLM gave practical support to equal pay strikes and to women such as the night cleaners who were organizing for better conditions of work. Ambivalence about the means to liberation did not prevent women of all shades of opinion from recognizing the significance of equal employment policy.

## THE LEGISLATION AND THE EQUAL OPPORTUNITIES COMMISSION

The equality legislation of the 1970s that first established the Equal Opportunities Commission was enacted with the active

---

[9] Rowbotham, *The Past Is before us*, 169
[10] Meehan, *Women's Rights at Work*.
[11] See e.g. Wandor, *Once a feminist*; Amanda Sebestyen (ed.) *'68, '78, '88: From Women's Liberation to Feminism* (Prism, Bridport, 1988).
[12] Anna Coote, 'Putting Britain to Rights', the *Guardian*, 24 Oct. 1974.

support and direct engagement of organized women. But that did not mean that the involvement of women was welcomed by the EOC when it opened for business in 1976. Under the leadership of Betty Lockwood, formerly women's officer of the Labour Party and an active campaigner for the Equal Pay Act and the Sex Discrimination Act, the EOC distanced itself from involvement with feminist and other women's organizations.

The EOC was set up as a standard 1970s British quango established on tripartite principles. The TUC and the Confederation of British Industry (CBI) had nominating rights to the commission, which also contained regional, political, and family planning representatives. The caution of the TUC and CBI commissioners dominated EOC strategy, and for many years groups with feminist connections had no input into EOC policy-making. The EOC disappointed many of its supporters and well-wishers by concentrating its networking efforts on high-level lobbying and negotiation, avoiding work at the grass roots. This was partly due to near paranoia in its Manchester headquarters about the commission's image. Press ridicule alarmed commissioners and many of the EOC's senior employees. Defensively, they cultivated a cautious, professional, and old-fashioned civil service style of working which promised and delivered little in the way of radical change. Disappointed staff sought other employment, and employers and trade-unionists got a clear message that they might proceed more or less as before. But early interest in the EOC was huge. There were 3,000 enquiries in its first five weeks of operation, 10,000 during its first year of business. There is little doubt that, at the time, employers, unions, and individuals expected change.

So, partly for institutional reasons, partly because of the caution of the original commissioners, feminism was excluded from the EOC. It was only through conventional pressure-group activity or as clients that feminists could become involved in EOC policy-making. The notable exception was the contribution of feminist scholarship and research in studies commissioned by Christine Jackson, who was the EOC's first director of research. By the end of the 1970s the WLM had written off the EOC, leaving the frustrating task of influencing its policies to established, traditional groups. The WLM had little to do with policy about equality at work; and women seeking rights at work were not likely to seek feminist assistance. For example, Jeanne Gregory's study of eighty-two women who dropped their equal pay and sex discrimination claims before the tribunal hearings found that women trying to use the new acts did not seek the help of women's liberation groups. The exceptional one who did was exploited by the local group, which, she believed, sought only the publicity value that offering support might bring them. Gregory regarded this incident as unfortunate and atypical, and drew attention to the important work of the NCCL in publicizing the acts and in providing legal representation and backing.[13]

During the 1980s, attitudes changed on both sides. Feminist groups began to regard the EOC as a resource, and the EOC became more inclined to take feminists into account. This was partly a result of the emergence of the coalitions of feminists, women's auxiliaries, and traditional women's organizations that we term the women's movement In other words, changes occurred in the ways in which second-wave feminist groups worked and were organized. There was also an evident shift in the politics of the EOC as expertise was gained and as staff attitudes altered.

The early aloofness of the EOC did not prevent women's organizations from continuing to campaign about employment equality. Here we find early evidence of the existence of the women's movement. In 1980 Women in the Media, the Equal Pay and Opportunities Campaign, the National Women's Farm and Garden Association, and the Fawcett Society all recommended wide-ranging improvements in the enforcement of the sex equality legislation, and on 27 November 1980 a day of action was organized by Women in the Media and the Fawcett Society which was attended by sixty-seven other groups. An important phenomenon of the 1980s was the growing influence of new feminist ideas on traditional women's groups such as the Women's Institute, the Townswomen's Guild, the British Federation of University Women, who gradually became involved in equal opportunity politics. By the early 1980s the EOC was beginning to recognize the importance of networking and to cultivate links with women's organizations. Slowly, contacts were established, conferences were organized, and meetings between commission

[13] Jeanne Gregory, 'Equal Pay and Sex Discrimination: Why Women Are Giving up the Fight', *Feminist Review*, 10 (1982), 87.

staff and women's organizations were held, until, by the end of the decade, such meetings were an integral part of the EOC's work. In 1990 The EOC recognized that it had a role to play in constructing a strong women's lobby, and sought to bring together traditional and more radical women's groups: 'Self-starting women's groups and other voluntary organisations committed to equal opportunity goals are important partners working with the EOC for equality.'[14]. In 1989 the EOC ran seminars and meetings with groups as diverse as the National Child-Minders' Association, the Working Mothers' Association, the Women's National Commission, Asian Women's Network, UK Business and Professional Women, the Fawcett Society, and Child Care Now! The EOC has become part of the universe of groups and agencies which we may think of as women's pressure groups.

## State Feminism: The Women's Movement and the EOC

The initial timidity of the EOC seemed at the time—and seems in retrospect—to have been a lost opportunity for British feminism, which did not become integrated into equal opportunities policies until the appearance of local government women's committees during the 1980s. There were several problems. First, the law itself made for difficulties. The legislation was wide-ranging and innovative, but it was flawed in a variety of ways. Secondly, the first commissioners were selected according to inappropriate criteria, and no structure of accountability to the community of women was envisaged or established. Thirdly, the political climate changed.

The fact that the law was innovative was as much of a problem as the fact that it was flawed. The equality legislation of the 1970s—Equal Pay Act 1970, the Sex Discrimination Act 1975, and the Race Relations Act 1976—were a radical departure from previous British equal opportunities legislation. The coverage of the sex equality law extended to employment, training, and related matters, but also to housing and the provision of goods, facilities, and services. Borrowing from legislation in the United States, two kinds of discrimination were defined and prohibited: direct discrimination, which was defined as less

---

[14] EOC, *Annual Report, 1989* (HMSO, London, 1989), 26.

favourable treatment in these areas on grounds of sex; and indirect discrimination, which took the form of applying conditions that would favour one sex more than the other, but which could not be justified on grounds other than sex. Enforcement was divided between industrial tribunals, county courts, and a new law-enforcement agency, the EOC, which was also given the responsibility to monitor the legislation and to recommend changes as necessary. There were a large number of exemptions and special procedures which complicated law enforcement. This was a new body of law and a new agency in an area of civil rights which had very little British legal tradition behind it. Few lawyers were trained in equality law of any kind, judges and tribunal heads had little relevant experience on which to draw. In short, the EOC was empowered to undertake a task of considerable complexity in an area in which there was little in the way of relevant experience to use as guidance. Moreover, as Elizabeth Meehan[15] has pointed out, in guaranteeing specific forms of equality for some groups identifiable by innate characteristics, the legislation made a move away from the principles of universalism and anonymity underlying some of the intentions of the Welfare State. In short, the law was both obscure and controversial. Even a confident and able leadership would have had difficulty.

But the leadership was far from confident. The location of the EOC in Manchester rather than in London was an early signal that the government was not going to take it seriously. The first commission appointments followed the style of Westminster politics which prioritized the inclusion of party, regional, and industrial divisions that were established long before the re-emergence of the women's movement. Between them, the first commissioners had some of the skills, but almost none of the representativeness, which might have made them more willing to act quickly and effectively.

The change in the political climate was also important. The change in the Labour government from Harold Wilson, who was sympathetic to issues of sex equality, to James Callaghan, who was not, did little to encourage an early high profile. The Conservatives never favoured an activist EOC. At the time of the first discussion of an anti-discrimination bill in the early 1970s,

---

[15] Meehan, *Women's Rights at Work*, 4.

the current Conservative government was reluctant to creat a single body with 'extensive power', to investigate discrimination on its own initiative. In evidence to the Commons select committee, the Home Secretary argued that it would be undesirable to combine enforcement functions with the role of enquiring, reporting, and generally educating public opinion. Consequently, the Conservative consultative document[16] did not envisage enforcement powers for the EOC, which it saw as a campaigning organization, with functions limited to educating and persuading the public. The election of a Conservative government in 1979 did not encourage the EOC to take an activist stance. Thus, the EOC's law-enforcement powers were first exercised under a government known to oppose its possession of those powers. This, combined with economic recession, rising unemployment, public expenditure cuts, and the emergence of the Conservative New Right, did nothing to enhance the EOC's confidence.

It is not surprising, therefore, that the first three or four years of the EOC's operation were disappointing. The commission was widely criticized for outcomes which were the result of weaknesses in the founding legislation and for failures of administration and imagination. It failed to achieve an effective decision-making strategy, it failed to make adequate use of its law-enforcement powers, and it failed to establish itself as a presenter of equal opportunities.[17] In the early 1980s, however, the pattern began to change. Although progress was hesitant and, particularly under the chairmanship (*sic*) of Thatcher-appointee Baroness Platt, there were instances when it seemed that its law-enforcement powers were more of an embarrassment than a strength, by the end of the decade the EOC was able to play a central role as an actor in the equality policy community.

There are many reasons for the transformation of the EOC. They include the accumulation of experience, skill, and ability by commission staff, the appointment of women with women's movement experience and strong feminist commitments to positions of responsibility, and a growing ability to utilize the rules of the political game. The laws have been variously amended, and sex equality has been the subject of European Community law

[16] Cmnd. 5724, *Equality for Men and Women* (HMSO, London, 1974).
[17] Vera Sacks, 'The Equal Opportunities Commission: Ten Years On', *Modern Law Review*, 19 (1986).

which compels member states to legislate for sex equality in accordance with five directives on equal pay and equal treatment. Resources have been made available to those charged with the promotion of sex equality, and, by and large, those resources have been used. The EOC now, although far from perfect, looks more as its original supporters intended it to look. It has changed, and the story of this change is in its way, a story about feminism and public policy.

Legal developments during the 1980s are at the centre of the story. There were at least two dimensions to those developments: (1) the role of the EOC changed from being mainly an advice and information agency to that of an active legal protagonist; and (2) the law was greatly strengthened by amendments and court decisions. Needless to say, these two dimensions are closely related. Policy in the agency is made by the commissioners in conjunction with senior staff. Opportunities were spotted and cases were selected by staff in the legal department who wanted to make use of the courts. Gradually, the commission was per- suaded that using the law and the courts would be faster and more effective at bringing change than chipping away at govern- ment opinion. The persuasion strategy was described by one staff member as 'ten years of writing great screeds, putting every pos- sible argument in response to consultative documents with gov- ernment taking no notice whatsoever. But when a court says that a piece of legislation means $x$ or $y$ there is no way of avoiding it, the government has to do what the court requires.' The aim was to wear the government down. An important breakthrough was the use of judicial review whereby the commission may sue the government. This has revolutionized judicial proceedings.

Change in the law was made possible by equality policy in the European Community. This happened in two ways: the EC took judicial proceedings against the United Kingdom government in respect of certain defects and exclusions in its domestic legisla- tion; and the EOC supported a series of cases brought to the European Court of Justice which clarified the rights guaranteed by European law. The changes from both sources became part of the 1983 Equal Value (Amendment) Regulations and of the Sex Discrimination Act 1986, which removed many of the exceptions and loopholes from the original legislation and established the principle of pay parity whereby men's and women's different work was judged according to criteria of comparable value.[18] EOC staff were both active and imaginative in this process, which was not simply a matter of waiting for EC rulings to trickle through. Legal staff were innovative and became more strategic in their thinking as they looked out for cases which would clarify the law and establish the precedents that they regarded as important.

Women seeking help and resources for feminist causes found that support from the commission was easier to get and that EOC leadership generally improved. It became both more skilled and more feminist. When Joanna Foster was appointed to the commission in 1988, the EOC was headed for the first time by someone with a background in improving women's rights at work. Within a very short period of time, Valerie Amos was appointed as chief executive of the EOC. Amos, a black feminist whose immediate employment experience was women's rights work for a London local authority, emphasized the importance of strategic thinking and of the law-enforcement roles of the commission, confirming much of the philosophy of the legal section.

Under Foster and Amos, the structure of the EOC has been streamlined to enable a balance between development and law-enforcement work. Some of this may have happened anyway as experience of the legislation was gained, and relations between commission and staff improved. The EOC won some major cases at the end of the 1980s, and judicial review proceedings now enable it to take on a public interest role. These strategic gains were possible because of research and development work completed earlier in the decade. But the previous absence of an active effective leadership, and its presence now, would seem to imply that recent gains are likely to be consolidated and extended. Valerie Amos does not believe that the legislation is being fully exploited. Her view in 1991 was that the Home Office wanted the EOC to use its power, wanted the EOC to do its job.[19]

The unique role of the EOC is that of law enforcement, and

---

[18] See Peggy Kahn, 'Introduction: Equal Pay for Work of Equal Value in Britain and the USA', in Peggy Kahn and Elizabeth Meehan (eds.), *Equal Value/Comparable Worth in the UK and the USA* (Macmillan, Basingstoke, 1992).

[19] After the 1992 general election, ministerial responsibility for equal opportunities moved to the Department of Employment under Gillian Shepherd.

now, for the first time, it has a law-enforcement strategy. Five
judicial review proceedings against the government were under
way at the end of 1990. Evidence suggests that the EOC's more
aggressive stance has won it many more friends than did the
timidity of its early years. Networking with other equality agencies is an important new part of the development role of the
EOC. There are now high-level staff meetings with the
Commission for Racial Equality, the Northern Ireland Equal
Opportunities Commission, and the Fair Employment Commission. There was an inaugural meeting between the NIEOC,
the EOC, and the CRE joint group in July 1990. Legal advisers
from each agency met in January 1991. Otherwise, the policy network is rather segmented; for example, the TUC Women's Unit
lobbies through the TUC. Alliances and groups are made over
particular issues, they form and re-form. Firms approach the
EOC for assistance in developing equal opportunities recruitment
and employment policies, and personnel officers are key members
of any potential policy network.

There are still problems with the legislation. Taking an equal
opportunities case to the tribunals or courts is extremely hard on
the complainant, who may find herself isolated at work, unsupported by her union, and, at the end, in receipt of inadequate
compensation and victimized at work. There are real difficulties
with the equal value legislation which entitles women to equal
pay for work of equal value (Equal Value (Amendment)
Regulation). This legislation was introduced as a result of EC
action against the United Kingdom in 1983 in the European
Court of Justice, which ruled that Britain was not fulfilling its sex
equality obligations under the Treaty of Rome. A reluctant and
uncooperative Conservative government complied, but was determined to meet no more than the letter of European law.[20]

Arguably, the government simply aggravated problems in an
already difficult legal area. The equal value legislation addresses
a complicated area. The meaning of 'equal value' may well not
have been clearly made by a supportive government. However,
most observers believe that the government deliberately made the
legislation less usable than it might have been. If so, that was a

---

[20] For a full account, see Jeanne Gregory, 'Equal Value/Comparable Worth:
National Statute and Case Law in Britain and the USA', in Kahn and Meehan
(eds.), *Equal Value/Comparable Worth*.

very effective response. The law had barely been implemented by the end of the decade. In 1990 the equal value law had been in place for six years, but no codes of practice or guidelines for employers had been drafted, and none was in preparation. Moreover, procedures were so lengthy that it could be argued that applicants' right of access to judicial proceedings was denied and that the substantive issue of equal value had not been addressed by the courts. The EOC has offered formal proposals to amend the legislation,[21] and will press the government on this during the early 1990s.

Despite flaws in the employment equality legislation, it has had a measurable impact on women's lives. Industrial tribunal statistics, which record only the small number of equal pay and sex discrimination cases that are heard by tribunals, give no idea of the vast number of out-of-court settlements, almost all of which are in favour of women applicants. Collective bargaining practices have been modified as trade unions have taken on the requirements and implications of the legislation (see below). Above all, attitudes are beginning to change. Women increasingly expect to have equal rights at work, and take action when such rights are not forthcoming.

To summarize: when the EOC failed to link with the women's movement in the 1970s, it lost an opportunity to legitimize its work, an opportunity which has been clawed back by the skill and tenacity of its staff, who have struggled against an inhospitable political climate and a litigation-shy culture. Its legal achievements and official status are an impressive achievement under the circumstances. Moreover, they give the EOC a central position in the sex equality policy community of the 1990s.

## MUNICIPAL FEMINISM: LOCAL AUTHORITY WOMEN'S COMMITTEES

Early failures by the EOC did not mean that feminists suspended the politics of employment equality. On the contrary, they took it up at local level and devised structures in local authorities that

---

[21] See EOC, *Equal Treatment for Men and Women* (EOC, Manchester, 1988), and *Equal Pay for Men and Women* (EOC, Manchester, 1991).

were designed both to promote women's rights and to bring a women's perspective to the policies and practices of local government. In 1978 a group of women councillors and other women in Lewisham formed a women's rights working group, which was one of the first of these initiatives.[22] By 1986, about 40 per cent of local authorities had some kind of equal opportunities policy covering sex equality. These were mainly Labour-led authorities, although a few Conservative-controlled authorities also had them. About one-third of Labour councils had no such committees. As noted in Chapter 4, some councils had full women's committees, others had women's units within equal opportunities units which also covered racial equality and the rights of disabled people. The very appearance of the first full committee, the Greater London Council Women's Committee, in 1982 led to immediate calls by feminists for similar committees in the London boroughs. Some of these were the Socialist feminists who were just becoming involved in local politics, but others were women who had been struggling for years to get women's issues on to the agenda of their local authority.

There are several reasons why the pursuit of equal employment rights for women is a matter of local authority concern. The local authorities are large-scale employers; together they represent the largest employer of women in Britain. Local authorities are major providers of community services, and women are major consumers. Thus, although there is no legal requirement that local authorities take responsibility for the provision of equal rights for women,[23] there are obvious political reasons why a council might involve itself in sex equality policy.

The establishment of women's committees and the more narrowly constructed equal opportunities committees was one of the most conspicuous concessions that politicians made to feminism in the 1980s. Broadly speaking, the work of women's committees covers three main areas, reflecting the political purchase that women have on local authorities: (1) direct service and/or support to/for women; (2) working with other committees and council departments to modify existing practices in favour of women; and (3) tackling council employment practices and conditions of

[22] Julia Edwards, 'Local Government Women's Committees', *Local Government Studies*, July/Aug. 1988: 39.

[23] The Race Relations Acts do place such a requirement on local authorities in respect of race.

service. As the committees have developed, direct services have often moved to the forefront of their concerns, with a predominance of attention given to child care provision, health, and protection from violence. These are concerns that are consumer-led; that is, these are the issues that women have raised in the consultation processes which women's committees have established. Working with other council committees is slower work, as structures and practices must change to make this effective. Local authorities have well-established internal pecking orders and bureaucratic procedures which must be learned, negotiated, and, finally, altered if the women's committee is to prevail. Employment policies are direct local authority responsibilities, and often the women's unit is no more than an office in a council's personnel department. Council equal employment policies are generally innovative and are much researched, described, and discussed. It is in local authority employment that many new recruitment, promotion, and training initiatives are launched in special projects or pilot schemes.

The politics of the women's committees were mix a of Labour Party and women's movement practices and concerns. Each was the product of local circumstances, but when we examine the way in which they were established and worked, a number of common themes become apparent. To illustrates this, we will describe and discuss the experience of several committees.

## The GLC Women's Committee

The Greater London Council Women's Committee was a product of the Labour victory in the May 1981 local elections which returned a Left-dominated Labour majority led by Ken Livingstone. It differed in important respects from the provincial women's committees that were established later, in that the victorious Labour group did not have a manifesto commitment to setting up a women's committee. According to one account, the idea originated in discussions between feminist Labour councillors and women's groups already funded by the administration which began at the end of 1981.[24] Labour councillor Valerie Wise was a key actor in these developments. Irene Breugel, a Socialist

---

[24] Kate Flannery and Sara Roelofs, 'Local Government Women's Committees', in Joy Holland (ed.), *Feminist Action* (Battleaxe Books, London, 1984).

feminist who was involved with the committee and who was also employed by the GLC, recounted to us how several people were consulted by Valerie Wise when she was elected secretary to the Industry and Employment Committee. 'This was not a representative group at first, just people who knew people . . . Later younger women came in. But that first group said we should have a women's committee. Valerie then took it up with enormous energy.'

All accounts agree that mass involvement was sought from the start. A public meeting was held in May 1982 that was advertised in women's movement, labour movement, and other London publications. The meeting was well attended by women representing over sixty organizations and a spread of political opinion. It set up working groups to cover about fifteen different issue areas, including employment, transport, violence, lesbians, and child care. The working groups were to operate independently of the council and to be open to all women. Their task was to formulate policy ideas for inclusion in a programme of action for women in London. A co-ordinating committee was soon established to monitor policy and the implementation of the proposals. Open meetings continued on a three-monthly basis to hear and ratify the proposals for recommendation. Some of these meetings were attended by 500 people.[25] It was an unprecedented experiment in local democracy.

The women's committee was chaired by Valerie Wise, who was convinced of the need to extend democracy in local government. She had been influenced by a trade-union group, the Lucas Aerospace Shop Stewards, whose spokesman, Mike Cooley, espoused a form of organization that was grounded in the expertise of its worker members. Wise translated this into the working principle that women are the experts on what women want.[26] The committee treated women as members rather than as clients, a striking contrast to accepted local authority procedures at that time. The women's committee was innovatory in that it elected a significant group of women with full decision-making powers to a full council committee; eight co-opted women went on to a council committee of three Tories, one Social Democrat, and seven

[25] Flannery and Roelofs, in *Feminist Action* (Battleaxe Books, London, 1984).
[26] Hilary Wainwright, *Labour: A Tale of Two Parties* (Hogarth, London, 1987), 100–1.

Labour members. The councillors had no say at all about how the co-opted members were elected. People who attended the meetings recall the concern to ensure that the co-opted members were representative. The Labour group caused resentment by insisting that two places were allocated to trade-union women chosen by the South-East Regional TUC (SERTUC).

The ensuing argument was typical of feminist debates at the time. The problem was that if the co-opted places on the women's committee were made representative, then some structure had to ensure that representativeness. But this raised questions about the kind of women who might be chosen. For example, those who were chosen by the labour movement would have had to work their way through a set of Labour Party or union structures. Who would be able to do that? Many of the younger feminists at the consultation meetings thought that those women with the skills and toughness to fight their way through what were essentially male structures could not really represent women. The process raised all the usual questions about representation. The debate reflected the different political experiences of the women who took part. The GLC Women's Committee mobilized women who had not previously engaged in party or union activities. It sought the support and ideas of feminists from as wide a range of groups as it could contact. Many of the women involved were young and had no previous political experience.

An early task of the consultation was to establish the categories of representation. The principle of including women trade-unionists as a category was widely agreed, but this raised the issue of SERTUC nomination. Older feminists with backgrounds in the union movement and in left-wing political organizations recognized the disadvantages of representation backed by male-designed political organizations, but believed that it would be worse just to take anyone who called themselves a trade-unionist. In the absence of feminist trade-union structures, they preferred women trade-union representatives to be nominated by SERTUC. The younger women who came in straight from the women's movement disagreed; they could not understand this preference for left-wing feminists, and were utterly horrified when it turned out that some of the left-wing feminists were men.[27]

---

[27] On this, see Flannery and Roelofs, 'Local Government Women's Communittees'.

The GLC prioritized the promotion of equal opportunities for women in council employment, and set up an equal opportunities committee to devise employment equality policies in conjunction with the women's committee. The problem that the women's committees were supposed to solve was a pattern of institutional sexism and racism whereby women and employees from the ethnic minorities were concentrated in the worst-paid, low status jobs. Both committees had the services of paid administrative and clerical staff. The equal opportunities unit worked with the women's committee support unit to devise a strategy to remedy the employment sectorialization. This followed what were to become the ideal procedures of anti-discrimination policy implementation. First, the employment structure was analysed, and then a programme was produced that not only dismantled discriminatory practices, but instituted a programme of positive discrimination. The programme was necessarily comprehensive. It involved child care provision, training programmes, and a programme of contract compliance whereby local authority contracts were awarded only to firms with effective equal opportunities hiring and promotion practices and with a representative gender and racial mix of employers. The firms were also required to subcontract according to these guidelines. The idea of contract compliance was borrowed from equal opportunities practice in the United States. Its rationale is that local firms anxious to retain lucrative council contracts will modify their management structures and hiring and promotion practices. In addition, the cascade effect of the policy will create a favourable economic environment for new firms whose managers come from groups that have previously suffered from unfair discrimination. EOC staff formed a natural part of the network of equality workers that was being established at this time. But the policy community could not rely on the EOC leadership for support. For example, when local authority power to use contract compliance to implement gender equality was lost in the 1989 Local Government Act, it was widely believed that a forceful intervention from Baroness Platt would have saved it. The CRE was able to defeat a similar threat in respect of racial equality, and we were told in our interviews with equality officers that Baroness Platt had informed the government privately that she would not mind if the gender restriction went ahead. Now local authorities may use contract compliance strategies in respect of race, but not gender.

The employment policies that were devised at the GLC were widely copied; they are relevant not only because of the high level of women's employment in local authorities, but also because of the large number of problems that were encountered and then solved. A key problem here is that the structure of local authority employment is cumbersome and rigidly hierarchical. There are formidable boundaries between management, professionals, administration, and clerical workers. There are few opportunities to cross these boundaries, and no employee is expected to advance very far in any one move. This is a structure with huge disadvantages for women, whose pay and status will reflect the history of the labour market rather than the value of their job. Indeed, many of the skills that women bring to the job are not integrated into the job descriptions.[28]

In short, local authority employment presents many of the classic structural problems of equal pay and equal treatment for women employees. It also presents many of the political difficulties. Divisions between women made policies difficult to devise. The concerns of women manual workers, for example, are the exploitation of low pay and part-time working. It is difficult for them to share the preoccupations of women in higher grades, who appear to be better off. Black women and white women also experience disadvantage differently. Equal opportunity initiatives for women tended at first to be white initiatives. Job-share schemes were regarded as institutionally racist by some black women, who could not afford to have half of a job.[29]

Training proved to be another vital part of equality strategy. The GLC Equal Opportunities Group found that it was important for the women themselves to be trained as trainers, a strategy which provided continuous feedback, upward mobility for the trainers, and successful role models. This was repeated in other local authority training projects. Employment and training schemes were monitored by the EOC, which recognized that the local authorities were important examples of good practice in equal employment policies.

[28] Angela Coyle, 'The Limits of Change: Local Government and Equal Opportunities for Women', *Public Administration* 67 (1989), 42.
[29] M. Mackintosh and Hilary Wainwright, (eds.), *A Taste of Power* (Verso, London, 1987), 107–8.

The GLC example was very quickly copied in Camden, where a women's committee was set up about a week later. Camden generally followed the GLC model of widespread consultation via public meetings, and it also took special note of local issues. The Camden committee became very involved in activity to prevent police harassment of Kings Cross prostitutes, directing police attention to the kerb-crawlers who, rather than the prostitutes, were causing a local nuisance. They also set up the 'women's bus' to carry information, advisers, and committee members to the community. The idea of the bus was to take the committee to women, bypassing the press and ensuring that local women would see for themselves what the committee offered. Southwark also established a much less well-funded committee. A model of consultation was established there which was widely used later by provincial women's committees. Southwark committee members believed that mass meetings were inappropriate to its residents, and wrote instead to 750 community groups, seeking women's views about what its priorities should be.[30]

Women's committees in London were greeted with enormous enthusiasm by organized white women's groups, but soon ran into trouble with black women's groups over the issue of race. This was symptomatic of a frequent gap between the promoters of women's committees and the communities that they serve. In London the general absence of black women from the Labour Party and the women's movement meant that racial differences between women were overlooked at first. The London women's committees were some of the first public places where the issue of racial difference was confronted by feminists.

### Women's Committees in the Provinces

Women's committees in the provinces came later, were less well funded, and were often less radical than those in London. But they had the benefit of the London experience and were able to learn from the mistakes of the London committees. The abolition of the GLC in 1986 brought its women's committee to a close, although those in London boroughs continued until after 1990. In other parts of the country, however, new women's committees

[30] Flannary and Roelofs 'Local Government Women's Committees'

were established right through the 1980s, and in Scotland a number of new committees were set up in 1990 and 1991.

In provincial cities and towns, pressure for the committees normally came from outside the council, often from feminist activists in the local and district Labour Parties. Thus the initiative was often imposed on hostile councils, which meant that support had to be sought directly from the local communities. In this respect, the consultation model pioneered by the GLC became a political resource for the new committees.

The local history of the committees varies. Trade unions, especially those which represent council employees, were often important supporters, as were Labour Party women's sections. In Leeds NALGO approached the Trade Union Community and Resource Information Centre (a national research centre which was based in Leeds) for help in formulating an equal opportunities policy for women in the area. TUCRIC, as it was called, convened a group of interested women, including Labour Party women, women from the city council trade unions, and representatives of Leeds' women's groups. This established itself as the Women's Equal Opportunities Group in September 1982. The group formulated a number of proposals that were sent to the council, and called for a city-wide conference in November. The conference was successful, attended by 17 women's groups, 17 trade unions, 7 local Labour Party branch representatives, various community groups, and a member of the Leeds SDP. Twelve pages of demands were formulated at the conference and were added to later by black women's groups.

In April 1983 the Leeds City Council formally established a women's subcommittee of its Policy and Resources Committee. The subcommittee included co-opted representatives of women's groups. Locally, the council's responsiveness to the proposal for a women's committee is attributed to their consideration of a race relations policy following the large and prolonged race riots in the Chapeltown area during 1981. Once race is on the agenda, the reasoning goes, it is fairly easy to get gender and disabled persons on the agenda as well. At the end of 1988 the women's unit in Leeds had five established posts plus about twelve employees or seconded employees on two projects, one on women's training and one on cancer screening. The committee's agenda has been devised in response to issues raised by local women, who are consulted via co-optees and regular open meetings with the committee.

The Birmingham Women's Committee was established after Labour regained power in the city in 1984. In response to sustained activity in the women's sections of the Birmingham Labour Party, a resolution was moved at a policy conference, asking for a women's committee to be set up. The policy conference is a local party forum established to develop the policies on which to fight local elections. The resulting resolution called for the city council to establish a women's committee and a race relations committee and was very much inspired by the GLC experience.

In both Birmingham and Leeds, women councillors were pressured into chairing the women's committee (Trudy Livingstone and Jill Page). Both women felt obliged to take on this task, despite preferences for other areas of council work. This may be a common dilemma for feminist politicians, who must choose between a direct responsibility for gender issues and bringing their perspectives into other areas of political work. The Birmingham Women's Committee was not very well received on the council itself, but it soon established networks of support. Many supporters were gained among women council employees, who flocked to the training courses that the women's unit developed.

The women's committee and the race relations committee were blamed for Labour's losses in Birmingham in the May 1987 local elections. On the day after the election, senior Labour and Tory councillors on the nominations subcommittee (an important committee overseeing other groups) decided that both committees should go. Trudy Livingstone learned that her committee had been abolished when the press telephoned her to ask her what she thought of the decision. Equality policy in Birmingham became the remit of a Personnel and Equal Opportunities Committee with a subcommittee on women. Two units established to serve the original committees now work to the new combined committee. The women's subcommittee has four women and four men on it. Trudy Livingstone, who continues to chair the women's subcommittee, believes that the abolition of the women's committee was politically unnecessary and that the decision was in part an effort to exclude feminists from channels of influence in the Labour Party. Members left the Labour Party in Birmingham in 1987 because of the abolition of the women's committee. Particularly affected were those Socialist feminists who came into the party at the end of the 1970s.

The work of the committee continues. The thrust of the Birmingham unit's work is equal employment opportunities, and the council has funded innovative and popular women's training projects. It also does the kind of outreach work that is common to all women's committees. But it does not offer grant aid to local women's groups, a constraint which inevitably limits its contacts with women's movement activists. The unit had nine staff in October 1990; it was criticized in the past for being an all-white operation, but this has now changed.

Bristol Women's Committee has similar origins to the Birmingham committee, but it has been able to maintain its status. It is a full committee of six elected members, two co-opted members, and rotating advisers representing Asian, Afro-Caribbean, disabled, and lesbian groups. The elected committee members are white; the two co-optees are of Asian and Afro-Caribbean origin. As in Leeds and Birmingham, the Bristol initiative came from outside the city council. Women in the district Labour Party worked together to secure a manifesto commitment to a women's committee. As in Birmingham, there was powerful opposition to the committee. One of its early chairwomen told us that reactions amongst Labour councillors were often hostile, and that it was a struggle to get a hearing from the more powerful spending committees whose co-operation was needed if women's policy needs were to be taken into account. The Bristol committee has responsibilities to the city council and to the local communities of women. It has a remit to work through other council committees to ensure that the gendered dimensions of local policy-making are accommodated. Support unit officers meet with the council's management team, which consists of the chief officers of the big council departments. This team has weekly policy meetings, hence the women's officers are engaged in corporate-level decision-making as well as in working with individual departments.

Consultation with the community of women is ensured via open meetings and the use of co-optees who represent sections of the women's movement. Grant aid is made available to these groups, who often make contact initially in order to secure funding for their activities. Considerable care has been taken to ensure that different communities of women can be involved with the unit, which publishes a newsletter and various advice and information documents. Bristol was late to establish a women's committee, but it has made sure that its structure and terms of reference avoid some of the constraints that earlier committees experienced.

In Scotland, where several new women's committees were appearing as we conducted our research, only one, in Stirling, had come about as a result of a decision by the Labour majority on the council. The others were the product of manifesto commitments after political battles at the level of the party membership.[31] Much of the initiative came from within the Labour Party, where feminist ideas and demands for women's representation are widespread amongst women members. The Edinburgh story is a typical one. The women's committee there was first established in 1984, when Labour took over Edinburgh District Council. The party manifesto carried a commitment to a women's committee. However, staff in the women's unit were not in post until towards the end of 1985, reflecting the fact that council support for the initiative was fairly minimal, at least at first. Much of the energy to get it going came from one committed woman Labour councillor. Conservative opposition to the idea was initially very vocal. A call was made at at least six consecutive council meetings for the women's officer to be sacked on the spot, the committee to be disbanded, etc. Gradually, the Tories moved their ground and began to suggest that the work of the women's committee should be switched to an equal opportunities subcommittee, a victory of sorts, one of the officers told us.

The Edinburgh committee's brief covers the usual employment, service, and community activities, and its way of working involves a considerable attention to consultation. Its links to the women's movement often begin with its grant aid budgets, which, in common with other women's committees, it uses to support a variety of activities. Groups come forward initially to get a grant, but then the contact is maintained, the group is put on a mailing

---

[31] Esther Breitenbach, 'Sisters Are Doing it for themselves: The Women's Movement in Scotland', in Alice Brown and R. Parry (eds.), *The Scottish Government Yearbook (1990)* (Unit for the Study of Government in Scotland, Edinburgh University, Edinburgh, 1990), 250.

list and kept in touch with other projects. The Edinburgh mailing list included seventy-two groups in 1990. As well as contact through groups and meetings, the Edinburgh Women's Committee paid for a survey of the needs and attitudes of Edinburgh women, in an effort to find out what women wanted from the council. The exercise revealed how utterly unaccustomed the women were to thinking that their opinion mattered, to being consulted, and, as a result, they maybe had less to suggest than they might otherwise have done. The survey team think that women will be more forthcoming as they become more accustomed to consultation.

In 1990 there were women's committees or women's sub committees of equal opportunities committees[32] in twelve of Scotland's local authorities. There is a flourishing network of Scottish women's and equality officers, some fifty people who meet quarterly to exchange ideas. Throughout the country the diffusion of innovation was an early priority. There is a long tradition of networking amongst British local authorities, and women's committees are no exception. One important legacy of the GLC is the National Association of Local Government Women's Committees (NALGWC), which was first established at the GLC as the standing conference of local government women's committees. Soon after the GLC closed, it moved to Manchester, where it initially received clerical support at Manchester Town Hall. Later NALGWC moved to the Pankhurst Centre in South Manchester, where it now services forty-three women's committees. Networking has been very important to the women's committee movement, providing considerable support to women's officers who have difficulties fitting into local authority employment structures. Typically, they walk a tightrope between officer initiative and councillor hostility.

Much of the work of local government women's units involves direct contact with women in the community under the protective eye of a women's committee or subcommittee chairwoman, who may be stretched almost to breaking-point. Employees of such units have been called 'femocrats' in some societies, a term whose élitist connotations do not really encompass the outreach nature of much of the grass-roots work of women's officers. The women's officers are normally feminists and often have considerable experience in the women's movement. They tend to be committed to their job and imaginative in the way in which they undertake their work and ensure that their units are relevant to the local community. But there is a tension involved in trying both to maintain a good relationship with feminists in the community and to satisfy the local authorities. Generally, the position of the committee in local authority politics is not secure. A large number of women's committees and sub-committees exist on the sufferance of the majority of councillors, who did not campaign for the committee to be established. The typical pattern is for local Labour Party women to secure a manifesto commitment prior to a local election, rather for the women's committee initiative to be councillor-led. And many Labour councils strongly resisted the establishment of women's committees. This means that women's committees are often in a weak position politically, precarious outcrops of an otherwise integrated political structure.

### The Politics of the Women's Committees

Although parties in the centre were sometimes sympathetic to the idea of women's committees, they rarely had the political power to demonstrate the genuineness of these sympathies. The Conservative Party almost invariably opposed such initiatives. Thus it is in internal Labour Party politics that we find much of the explanation for the political strengths and weaknesses of women's committees. The majority of authorities did not have a committee, and Glasgow, with its huge population, was one of these. The same pattern obtains in England and Wales, but the difference is that Scotland is almost entirely Labour-controlled. Women's committees grew from the local socialism movement on the Left of the Labour Party. They are not the product of the traditional labour politics of the industrial unions; they are a manifestation of the impact of the women's movement on labour politics. Traditional Labour Party politics is not congenial to such initiatives, and the women's movement cannot rely on the party's support in its heartlands in the north and in Scotland.[33]

[32] Aberdeen District Council, Dundee District Council, Dumfermline District Council, East Kilbride District Council, Edinburgh District Council, Fife Regional Council, Kirklees Metropolitan District Council, Kyle and Carrick District Council, Stirling District Council, Tayside Regional Council, West Lothian District Council, and Strathclyde Regional Council.

[33] Sue Lieberman, 'Women's Committees in Scotland', in Brown and McCrone (eds.) Scottish Government Yearbook (1989)

Over and over again, our interviews offered evidence of this. In Manchester we were told that the women's committee resulted from the growing influence of the Labour Left, particularly the soft Left, in the city. The Left campaigned on a promise to implement the party's manifesto, which by 1983 included a pledge to establish a women's committee. In 1984 the Left did well in the council elections. Previously, the aspects of manifesto policy to be implemented were those which reflected the interests and ambitions of councillors. The 1984 generation of councillors brought a new set of ambitions and interests into the council. The manifesto commitment meant that the women's committee was established, and the other preoccupations and interests of the councillors meant that those interested in gender politics were left to get on with it. This proved to be a mixed blessing. At first the political going seemed easy. Often, it was not necessary to rehearse the political arguments for strategic and policy decisions. When the political going got harder, however, 'people didn't come with us because they had not been through the arguments'. Because real support from councillors and senior administrators had not been won, there was a tendency for old habits to be re-established.

Local government in Britain is very hierarchical, and council politics are not exempt from the rituals and hierarchies of parliamentary politics. They have hegemonic routines and cultures that make them capable of neutralizing most initiatives. For example, councils have absorbed requirements that committee policy reports should describe and accommodate gendered issues almost without faltering. On the first, and maybe the second, occasion that committees had to demonstrate that such a consideration was made, real thought probably did go into it. But soon everyone became familiar with the necessary forms of words to satisfy the requirements. At this point, the exercise becomes nothing more than a ritual as a return to habitual priorities and procedures takes place. The bottom line for the women's committees is political—without political support at the level of the council, they cannot continue to deliver the policies and services that local· feminists demand.

The most hospitable councils are those where a new Left is working with a new party membership. Where the old-style, industrial, union-led politics predominate, it is difficult for women to win sex equality policy and for women's committees and units to gain a toe-hold. The battles about women's committee power are battles that have been fought almost entirely in the Labour Party. Most of them have been fought between men and some women on the traditional wing of the party, sometimes in alliance with its hard Left to oppose women and men on the soft Left of the party.

It is hard to escape the conclusion that opposition to feminism in the Labour Party comes from the hard Left and the old-guard Right. Liverpool is an example of a council where the hard Left, in conjunction with the traditional Right, prevented a women's committee from being established. The fate of the Birmingham committee was very much a reflection of the fortunes of the Labour Party in the city, and, in particular, of the balance of power between its traditional Right and soft Left. The women's committee was established when the Left was ascendant, and its abolition came at a time when soft Left councillors had lost seats, leaving the traditional Right-wing Labour councillors in control of the group. In early 1992, when the soft Left was once again gaining strength, plans were made to re-establish the two committees. Glasgow provides an example of the effects of the masculine dominance of the old-guard Right. The proposal for a women's unit was being discussed there in the spring of 1990 as a result of a Labour election manifesto commitment that the need for such a unit would be investigated. The local prediction was that it would have a hard time. Once elected, Labour councillors did not want a women's unit at all. So, we were told,

what they did was they kept the investigation of what was needed internal to the council, so that . . . they were sending letters to the Roads Department and all this saying 'Do you think a women's unit is appropriate?' and the reply was no. One woman who works for the region was particularly angry about this, highlighted this, what they were doing and argued that feminist groups had to be consulted. So they set up this particularly awful way of consulting people . . . invited people like women's aid groups and that, to go down to the council meetings. And people were not given any information in advance, they were just asked to attend, for an appointment. They went along and representatives from women's groups were taken in, one at a time, and interviewed. So there was no way you could actually organise it or coordinate it or anything. . . . out of that they did decide to have a Women's Officer appointed along with a research worker and a clerical assistant. And that their task would be to set up a Women's Unit.

Of course, much can be done once a unit is in place. The women's movement in Scotland was on the rise in the early 1990s, so Glasgow's grudging concession to sex equality policy might well lead to demands for a full council women's committee.

The political line-up that we describe is symptomatic of Labour Party politics of the 1980s. The party is looking for new constituencies, but trying to retain its traditional support. This process simultaneously created the space for the women's committee movement to emerge and the conditions under which it would struggle for survival. The fact that many women's committees do not have councillor support is a real problem. Women's officers are enormously resourceful in discovering the needs and in gaining the support of the community of women, but once hostility to the women's committee is entrenched, officer-led initiatives are easily defeated in local councils. The rules of the political game decree that decisive support is councillor support. Thus it is vital for the debates about gender equality to be brought into the council chamber and kept there until converts are made and political support is won.

But without the energizing support of a grass-roots movement, the experiment may be run down. At the time of writing, the indicators are that momentum is slowing. Marilyn Taylor at NALGWC in Manchester has observed that the enthusiasts of the early 1980s who were prepared to push through the policies and to work the system are not there any more. Many of the councillors who now chair women's committees have come up through the Labour Party and have no direct commitment to feminism. A tendency to absorb women's committees into equality units risks a depoliticization of their activities, and may conceal staff losses and a decline in the already low levels of commitment to sex equality.

As the work of the committees becomes more routine, some feminists believe that the cost of participation in municipal politics has been too high for the women's movement. Lynne Harne, who worked for a GLC-funded lesbian custody project before joining the GLC Equal Opportunities Unit in 1985, feels that the effects of municipal funding for feminism were

contradictory and the implications are still being worked out today. On the one hand there seemed to be a watering down of autonomous and radical women's liberation politics in order to meet grant conditions set by a male dominated bureaucracy. On the other hand, local government funding gave groups a stability they could not have had while they depended solely on the political commitment of volunteer women who would get burnt out. But one problem with having a core of paid workers was that it tended to reduce the involvement of a wider group of women who had been active precisely because they were politically committed.[34]

The fact that the survival of women's committees is not assured, that some have disappeared and others have been downgraded, does not mean that their accomplishments have been small. We can identify at least five important achievements. The committees have (1) allowed feminist ideas to be put to practical political use, and (2) demonstrated the wide scope needed for adequate equal employment policies. Despite considerable press hostility and sustained campaigns of ridicule, (3) the women's units are popular with local women, and (4) their patterns of consultation put pressure on councillors on other committees to take gendered issues seriously. (5) Precedents have been set, and the regular appearance of a few new women's committees each year suggests that there is considerable life yet in the movement.

There is reason for optimism. Women's committees in the south proliferated in the heyday of radical town hall politics. In the north their origins involve rather more of a political struggle, and their politics have been adjusted accordingly. Born under more difficult political conditions, these may prove long-lived. Nevertheless, what seemed like a victory at the beginning of the 1980s, as feminists were, for the first time, sought out, consulted, and later paid for their ideas and innovations, has come to look like the first step on a long and difficult journey.

BARGAINING FOR EQUALITY AT WORK:
THE TRADE UNIONS

The gradual inclusion of the trade unions in the equality policy network was a feature of the 1980s. Trade unions have several roles to play in promoting women. As representative organizations, they have positions of influence on councils, committees,

---

[34] Lynne Harne, 'Reinventing the Wheel', in Amanda Sebestyen (ed.), '68, '78, '88.

and executives in which women should be included. As federal components of the Labour Party, they have nominating rights and considerable other political influence over the choice of parliamentary candidates. As part of the tripartite arrangements that direct many of Britain's employment agencies, they engage directly in the making of equality policy; as agents of collective bargaining, they share legal responsibility for the negotiation of employer–employee agreements that are free of unfair discrimination on the basis of sex. Finally, as the recognized representatives of workers, they negotiate the conditions under which women work. The first two of these functions were discussed in Chapter 5. Here we are mainly concerned with the role of the unions in constructing equal employment policy in the workplace and in the public policy arena.

At the beginning of the 1980s there was considerable evidence that unions were resisting the implementation of equality policies. At the level of the TUC, an equal opportunities unit often had little to report on gender issues. At the level of the workplace, it appeared that familial ideologies remained dominant over egalitarian ideologies. Early in 1980 Nicola Charles conducted a study of 160 women involved in different shift patterns in different kinds of employment and their 11 union representatives and officials (4 of whom were women). The study showed that, at local level, unions had little idea of the aspirations and needs of women workers, who were regarded as less competent members than men.[35] At national level, although the TUC was persuaded to take up issues of reproductive rights and although many unions supported the aims of the National Abortion Campaign, it was difficult to find much evidence of union support for sex equality law. Part of the problem was that the unions saw such legislation as a threat to their traditional collective bargaining prerogatives. But many of them were also unwilling to negotiate for equality in wage-bargaining; nor would they provide support to women taking sex equality cases to industrial tribunals. In 1976, only about 22 per cent of the equal pay cases that came before tribunals did so with trade-union representation. The supposed improvement of this figure to 73 per cent by 1979 is based

---

[35] Nicola Charles, 'Women and Trade Unions in the Workplace', *Feminist Review*, 15 (1982), 3–22.

on a drop in the total number of cases—from 1,742 in 1976, to 91 in 1980—rather than on any statistically reliable improvement in the amount of backing that unions were providing for women litigants.[36]

In the first ten years after the sex equality legislation was enacted, there were few appreciable gains for women workers. Job segregation continued, pay differentials persisted. Despite press reports of occasional 'firsts', few women broke into male occupational preserves. But women were not silenced:

Throughout the period women trade unionists fought to achieve new rights and to defend those rights previously won. The period saw more women trade unionists being more active, more vocal and more in evidence than in any previous period. During those ten years more unions published more material relating to the demands of women than in any previous period. In ten years the TUC published more pamphlets, guidelines, charters, discussion papers and research papers on women and issues concerning women than it had published during the previous century. Women tried with some measure of success to make the movement aware of and understand the many and various forms of discrimination and oppression of women. . . . [by their arguments] women forced at least some sections . . . to realise that the oppression of women takes many forms.[37]

If tangible successes were few at first, women were gaining strength in the union movement during those years. There were a number of strikes over equal pay and equal treatment at the end of the 1970s, but there is little evidence that the TUC took its many declarations and resolutions on equal pay seriously before the early 1980s. The analogies between developments in the Labour Party and in the trade unions during the 1980s are very clear. By this time, the Thatcher government's attack on trade-union power was well under way, and union membership was in decline.

The unions, looking for new members, had to think seriously about recruiting these women workers. Meanwhile, the TUC, slowly being deprived of its tripartite role, had to seek new ways of justifying its existence. Influential women trade-unionists (most notably Anne Gibson, who is often credited with engineering

---

[36] Sarah Boston, *Women Workers and the Trade Unions* (Lawrence and Wishart, London, 1987), 314.
[37] Ibid. 312.

much of the new pro-woman line in the TUC) were finally successful in persuading the TUC to substantiate its paper commitment to sex equality at work.

The turning-point came in September 1988, when the TUC agreed to upgrade its equal rights unit (which had responsibility for race and gender equality) to a department at the annual conference. This change in status is crucial in the TUC. With departmental status, equal rights work gets an authority that it did not previously have. It has more resources and a say in policy. The conference decision followed strong pressure during the preceding year. Women delegates (unusually) dominated the debate, the terms of which were set by a successful resolution from the Health Service union, COHSE, and strengthened with an amendment from the National Union of Teachers. The *Guardian*'s report on the debate noted the passion of speeches in which the cause of employment equality for women was portrayed not only as morally just, but also as crucial to the long-term survival of a movement with a falling membership.[38] The resolution was passed 102 years after the first TUC equal pay resolution. Just over two years later, feminist observers were pleased—but somewhat surprised—when an internal review of TUC organization and structure resolved to keep the equal rights department and not to cut its funding, in spite of Draconian cuts for other parts of the organization. For the moment, it appears to be firmly established. In 1990 the department was well integrated into equality networks. It works closely with the EOC, with women's organizations, and with both women's officers and negotiators in member unions. At the end of 1990 its official priorities were equal pay, Europe, and child care. In conjunction with the EOC, close attention is paid to the equal value amendment and to the job evaluation schemes which are part of its implementation. A great deal of training is required in this area. The department runs seminar programmes for negotiators and full-time officials at regional level.

Perhaps the most important work is in the area of pay-bargaining. The EOC published a report in 1989[39] which showed that collective bargaining is conservative and narrow and almost

---

[38] The *Guardian*, 11 Sept. 1989.
[39] EOC, *Equality Bargaining: Why Not?* (EOC, Manchester, 1989).

entirely obsessed with pay. This leads to percentage rises which reproduce differentials—not least, differentials between men and women. An enormous amount of trade-union wage-negotiation strategies are built around differentials of one kind or another, a fact that institutionalizes and perpetuates gender, class, and racial inequalities. According to Kathy Porter in the TUC Equal Rights Department, much of the problem results from the way in which unions reflect the culture of the workplace and of the wider society. Equal pay negotiators will often have to spend time persuading the women concerned that they deserve equal pay. Women workers are often reluctant to embark upon the process of claiming equal pay, fearing that they will encounter opposition from male colleagues in their own union. The issue becomes more complicated if the case requires a comparator from another union. These are practical difficulties that are increasingly addressed and dealt with by union negotiators.

Support for equality bargaining by union officials is uneven, however. A growing consensus at national level is only slowly filtering down the union hierarchies to those involved in the bargaining. MSF Women's officer, Ann Gibson, says: 'the most helpful people are our national officers; regional officers are half and half and most of our male membership are still to be persuaded.'[40] The TUC strategy is to provide as much support and information as possible for equality bargaining, and many national unions operate the same strategy. A TUC pamphlet published in February 1990, *Trade Unions Working for Equality*, contains a twenty-two-page list of equal rights publications, meetings, research, and news published by individual unions, much of which is to do with gender issues. Topics include equal opportunities in employment, parental leave, adoptive leave, child care, sexual harassment, women returners, health screening, sexuality, and pensions and social security, amongst others. Twenty-nine unions are included on the list. A similar set of priorities is outlined in the TUC Charter for Women at Work. Other initiatives are 'equal value' and 'child care' negotiation packs which the TUC has prepared for local and regional officials.

The most important developments, though, are those that take place within the individual unions that are affiliated to the TUC.

[40] Quoted by Bea Campbell in 'Trading Places', the *Guardian*, 24 Oct. 1990.

Here the pattern is very mixed. Whatever the formal democratic arrangements of a particular union, it is the officers who hold the power. They support and advise branch secretaries and shop stewards and do much of the negotiating.[41] There are many examples of good practice, and many instances where negotiators, normally men, have taken on the tasks of equality bargaining. But there are also examples of unions refusing to address an issue which they see as contrary to their members' interests. The print compositors' union, the NGA, refused to press equal pay cases, a practice it attributed to its policy of refusing to use the courts. The real reason is that its members will lose out. NGA jobs changed fundamentally when the new printing technology was introduced during the 1980s. Hot metal became a thing of the past, and de-skilling was widespread as former compositors were retrained as computer typists. Another print union, SOGAT, led by Brenda Dean until 1991, became especially good at taking equal pay and equal value cases to the tribunals, and often used NGA members as comparators.[42]

A study of forty-five national unions conducted by SERTUC during the summer of 1988 reports a huge array of good practices on the part of individual unions. As well as a range of policies that are designed to get women into union decision-making, a variety of tactics are pursued to promote workplace equality and to represent the needs of women workers. But often the overwhelming majority of women officials in a union are the women's officers. By 1988 relatively few women had entered the mainstream of union policy-making (see Table 1, Chapter 5). In 1988 the EOC found that union and employer negotiators were usually men, that job segregation was accepted and often reinforced by collective bargainers who often regarded women's issues such as child care, flexible working, sexual harassment, and parental leave as minority interests which need not be raised at the bargaining table.[43] There is growing pressure on these men to change their practices, but, as Inez McCormack, the only woman divisional organizer in NUPE has remarked: 'We've now got good men who are trying to change their practices, but I don't know any who are prepared to give up their power.'[44]

[41] Cynthia Cockburn, *In the Way of Women* (Macmillan, London and Basingstoke, 1991), 122–5.     [42] NGA and SOGAT were due to merge in 1992.
[43] EOC, *Equality Bargaining*.          [44] Quoted in Campbell, 'Trading Places'.

Women's position in the workplace and, consequently, in the unions is not a simple function of gender. It is also mediated by race and class. Racial difference was an important input into TUC discussions during the 1980s. Angered that much of trade-union policy about gender was policy for white women, black women raised the issue of race at the 1985 TUC Women's Conference, when a motion was passed acknowledging that women from ethnic minority groups suffered greater discrimination than white women. The motion called on the TUC to take steps to promote women from ethnic minorities in the union movement, and called upon the women's committee to produce a report and recommendations on the issue for consideration by the conference. The report, 'Black and Ethnic Minority Women in Employment and Trade Unions', was unanimously accepted by the 1987 conference. The report made several recommendations to trade unions seeking to tackle discrimination in the workplace, including the negotiation of equal opportunity clauses, targets for the achievement of equality, and support for individual members taking cases of racial and/or sex discrimination to the tribunals.[45] These clauses have been taken up by many unions, but too often their commitment is merely a paper one.

Union policies have improved enormously during the 1980s, but they have a long way to go. As we have seen, many local unions were influential in the establishment of local authority women's committees. Often they set up local equal opportunities committees that became part of the local policy network. Similarly, women's officers are part of a growing national equality policy community. Most unions have appointed women's officers or equality officers in local authorities and trade unions to deal with equal employment issues. Some enormous victories were won during the 1980s. For example, local authorities undertook a major regrading project that raised basic pay rates for large numbers of women workers.[46] The pressure on unions to change their practices has come from the women's movement, and there are numerous examples of good practices drawn from feminist politics which have been adopted by unions. USDAW sometimes uses discussion groups to discover members' needs and

---

[45] Boston, *Women Workers and Trade Unions*, 322–4.
[46] By the end of the decade, however, this gain was being lost as local authority services were privatized.

interests. Other unions survey their members or hold workplace meetings to identify the needs of their women members. Slowly, the union movement is committing itself to different strategies of positive action to secure workplace equality for women. Women's status in the union is a reflection of their status at work. Where women are employed in low-status jobs, especially those that are lower than for most men in the same union, their representation at union conferences and on union executives is poor.[47] The problematical conclusion is that the difficulty that women have in raising their status at work is a product of their low status in their unions, which will only be properly dealt with when their status at work is raised. As we argued in Chapter 5, unions have hierarchical internal power structures that give their officers benefits of status, power, and sometimes income. Male power over women is part of the basis of such benefits. Most of the office-holders are white men who operate strategies of exclusion on the basis of both gender and race. Union resistance to equality policy is well established, and male power in these structures is not necessarily dying out with the retirement of traditionalist men.

## ACHIEVEMENTS SINCE 1979: A TALLY

During the 1990s, progress towards women's equality at work is likely to be a continuation of the processes that we have described above. These processes have produced some real achievements. Legal expertise has been gained, important victories have been won in the domestic and European courts, good practices have been established in the unions, the sex equality agenda has been expanded to fuse domestic and workplace issues in a way that enables decision-makers to take account of women's needs. A structure has been established that offers a basis for further progress and new developments.

One sign of progress is the large community of equality experts that has emerged who may take existing policy to its limits, who have moved from the short to the long agenda of equal opportunities. They make a number of recommendations for improvement. Lawyers believe that the ability to take class actions might

[47] SERTUC Women's Committee, '*Still Moving towards Equality*' (SERTUC, London, 1988).

vastly improve the situation for British women workers; political
scientists think that legislation obliging local authorities to promote equal opportunities for women would legitimate and secure
women's committees. The EOC argues that the time has come to
mainstream women's employment issues, and, in so doing, seeks
to generate widespread debate on women's equality.[48]

Other feminists argue that mainstreaming is dangerous, that it
risks incorporation by entering the male political world and by
doing the male political thing. They believe that institutions will
change women faster than women will change institutions. Ruth
Elliott argues that what is required is a dual strategy of organizing separately as women in order to work out needs and
demands and of trying to develop the confidence and skill to
mainstream those needs.[49] The experiences of the 1980s confirm
the necessity for such a dual strategy, but they also demonstrate
its costs. One cost may have been feminism's radical edge.
Loretta Loach has written, with evident regret, that one effect of
the Thatcher era on British feminism is that the possibility of
radical intervention has gone. The feminism that prospered in the
1980s was not the liberatory model of the previous decade.
Rather, it was an emancipationist feminism which succeeded in
making women feel that they belonged and which welcomed the
go-getting ambitious women about whom feminists are so
ambivalent.[50]

Concern about the loss of feminism's radical edge occurs over
and over again in the literature, and we met it repeatedly in our
interviews. Various arguments were made, but the general thrust
was that by joining the policy community, by pursuing the dual
strategy but, nevertheless, entering political institutions, 'femocrats' lost contact with the WLM. The feeling seemed to be that
many of the best people went into professional employment as
feminists and, in this new, state-funded employment, took over
the functions of the movement. As a result, feminism collapsed.
We think that this is an odd formulation, and note that there are
steps missing in the account. Did all the feminists turn into

[48] EOC, *From Policy to Practice: An Equal Opportunities Strategy for the 1990s*
(EOC, Manchester, 1988).
[49] Ruth Elliott, 'How Far Have we Come? Women's Organisations in the
Unions in the United Kingdom', *Feminist Review*, 16 (1984), 64–73.
[50] Loretta Loach, 'Can Feminism Survive a Third Term?', *Feminist Review*, 27
(1987) 24 36,

equality agents? Why is it that it is the equality officers who most often press the 'long agenda' of equal opportunities in their organizations? If feminism collapsed, where is the energy (much in evidence, as our account here shows) for new initiatives coming from? The more likely explanation is that some feminists took up positions in the new bureaucracies while others continued to work in grass-roots activities, and others went on to do other things. The development of the women's committee movement provides evidence both of the incorporation of feminists into existing structures and of the continuation of a grass-roots-based feminist politics. The fact that activities are often instituted and led by women's officers rather than by autonomous feminists or councillors suggests that the movement's future is not secure, but in no way does it indicate that its politics are not radical. Nor does it indicate that nothing has been accomplished, that no difference has been made. Even as she noted the wane of the aura of support for municipal equal opportunities policies in Manchester, Jo Somerset, a feminist women's training officer, remembered that 'ten years ago I would not have thought that women's groups would be meeting in work time, feeding our issues into official policies. I did not think that sexual harassment would become a disciplinary offence at work, or that applications for extended leave for women to visit families in Pakistan would be treated sympathetically . . .'[51]

To summarize: equal employment policy is an area in which women's movement politics have influenced practices, transformed the agenda, and populated the policy community. The skilled practitioners now in equality posts normally have backgrounds in the women's movement and pursue feminist agendas. This is a gain for feminists. The partial decline of the autonomous movement's mobilizing capacity is a set-back, but one which is partly offset by the rising presence of feminist structures within many of the organizations that are influential in policy-making. Whether sufficient balance has been achieved to secure the continuation of feminist politics by other means will become apparent over the next few years.

Equal opportunities politics are an example of the feminist

---

[51] Jo Somerset, 'I Was a Teenage *Jackie* Reader', in Sebestyen (ed.), *'68, '78, '88.*

intervention in significant state arenas that we discussed at the end of Chapter 5. If it is to be effective, such intervention must be undertaken at the level of the state, in public institutions Employment equality may not necessitate conflicts between particular men and women at a given workplace. But contemporary society is based upon a division of interest between men and women that will be transformed by the advent of equal pay and equal opportunities. The point is simple and obvious: men cannot both support women's demands for equal pay and equal opportunities and continue to organize their work around dependence upon women's unpaid work. Nor can they expect to go on earning more than women, or to have more free time than women, or to exercise greater economic power within the family than women. Equal rights for women will mean less for men, in relative terms.[52] Equal opportunities for women is a politically contested area. It raises issues about gender, class, and racial difference. There are also ideological disputes about the scope that such policy should have and whether it can be delivered by the state, at local or national level.

Our point is that the authoritative public decisions that are required to settle such issues are, of necessity, government decisions. But an important constraint on the development of sex equality policy is that strategic disagreements are rarely the subject of public debates. The lack of such debate does not augur well for the cause of sex equality at work. If important issues are not discussed, attitudes are unlikely to change. A good example here is the absence of controversy over positive action strategies. There is relatively little popular support in 1991 for the use of positive action or discrimination to bring about equality of opportunities. Often, the mere comment that a policy constitutes positive action is enough to ensure that it will not happen. The absence of public debate means that relatively little progress may be expected in this area, because the framework in which attitudes might be reconsidered and changed does not exist.

In the absence of relevant public debate, the sexist underpinning of popular discourse continues to be secure. It is still difficult to talk about the oppression in women's day-to-day lives. Such conversation is not taken seriously, it is not accepted.

[52] Anna Coote and Polly Pattullo, *Power and Prejudice* (Weidenfield and Nicholson, London, 1990), 24.

This is a feature of male hegemony. It protects the dominant sexist culture, reinforcing the masculinity of the political culture. So long as a problem cannot be openly named and discussed, it cannot be examined or solved. Substantial developments in equality policy therefore await the breaking of a public silence and the opening of a public debate on its meaning and importance.

# 7

# The Politics of Reproduction

Two of the original mandates of the WLM were free contraception and abortion on demand. Throughout the 1970s, abortion was almost the definitive issue of the movement, with tens of thousands of people supporting demonstrations against the anti-abortion bills of White in 1975 and Corrie in 1979. David Alton's anti-abortion bill, introduced in 1987, showed that abortion—or, more specifically, defence of the 1967 act—was still the feminist issue that could mobilize the most mass activity in the 1980s, although its place was taken by the issue of pornography by the end of the decade. Yet it is important to realize that abortion itself has increasingly been seen as raising just one in a range of questions about women's reproductive rights and health.

In examining the changing definition and politics of reproductive issues in the 1980s, we encounter many of the changes that have characterized the women's movement as a whole. There has been a continuing, if selective and not unchallenged, seepage of feminist concerns and perspectives into public debate. This reflects in part the growing influence of feminists or feminist-sympathizing women within the hierarchies of the Labour Party, the trade unions, the media, and the medical profession. But at the same time we find a further weakening of coherent national organization and identity within the movement itself, more narrowly conceived; further differentiation of women's groups and campaigns in terms of both their analysis and their practical focus; and considerable regional and even local variation in the extent and emphasis of feminist activities. These changes have partly been a response to specific government policies, the activities of pro-life groups, and the medical profession. But they have also come out of the internal dynamics of the women's movement.

## THE 1970S AND ABORTION

As one of us has written elsewhere: 'Abortion emerged in the early 1970s as almost the definitive issue of contemporary feminism.'[1] Virtually from the outset of the WLM, abortion was identified as a vital question for women. One of the movement's four original demands was for 'free contraception and abortion on demand'. Initially, however, this only gave rise to limited and local activities. A number of local women's liberation groups responded in different ways to a call for an abortion and contraception campaign—for instance, offering free pregnancy testing, investigating maternity hospitals, and family planning provision[2]—but it was difficult to mobilize larger numbers of women on the issue. Perhaps this was because the provision of both contraception and abortion was seen as relatively unproblematic. In Britain the contraceptive pill became commercially available by the 1960s, and in 1967 the National Health Services (Family Planning) Act authorized local authorities to provide contraceptive aids and advice to all who needed it, free of charge if necessary. At this stage, feminists, whether Socialist or Radical, tended to see contraception—and specifically the pill—as enormously liberating. As early as 1966 the Socialist feminist Juliet Mitchell wrote: 'what it means is that at last the mode of reproduction could potentially be transformed. Once childbearing becomes totally voluntary (how much so is it in the West even today?) its significance is fundamentally different. It need no longer be the sole or ultimate vocation of women: it becomes an option among others.'[3] The American Radical feminist Shulamith Firestone explained second-wave feminism as being 'the inevitable female response to the development of a technology capable of freeing women from the tyranny of their sexual-reproductive roles'.[4] Even she acknowledged some disquiet about side-effects of the pill, and subsequently, of course, Radical feminists

[1] Vicky Randall, *Women and Politics* (Macmillan, London, 1987), 263.
[2] From the *Women's Abortion and Contraceptive Campaign Newsletter*, Apr.–May 1973, cited by Sheila Rowbotham, *The Past Is before Us* (Penguin, Harmondsworth, 1990), 65.
[3] Juliet Mitchell, 'Women: The Longest Revolution', *New Left Review*, 40 (1966), also cited in Rowbotham, *The Past Is before Us*.
[4] Shulamith Firestone, *The Dialectic of Sex*, 2nd edn. (Paladin, London, 1973) 37.

came to criticize compulsory heterosexuality altogether. British feminists were voicing their doubts about new forms of contraception from the start, and these had become part of a more general feminist anxiety about the development of reproductive technology by the late 1970s. But, for the moment, contraception was not an urgent problem.

The same was true of abortion. Before the emergence of the WLM, Britain had already adopted a law which considerably liberalized abortion provision. Introduced as a private member's bill by David Steel, the Act, as it eventually emerged in 1967, represented a compromise. It provided for abortion up to twenty-eight weeks of pregnancy in cases where two registered doctors agreed that the mother's life or health was at risk or that the baby was likely to be handicapped. The bill's sponsors had to drop a further clause permitting abortion where doctors judged that a pregnant woman would be under excessive strain as a mother. And they had to accept an additional provision allowing doctors or nurses to refuse to take part in abortions on 'conscience' grounds. As such, the Act's terms sounded quite narrow. They certainly came nowhere near the subsequent WLM objective of 'abortion on demand'. None the less, in practice, the Act was implemented more liberally, although there have always been marked variations in the availability of abortions on the National Health from one region to another. By 1972, 14 per cent of recorded pregnancies were already being terminated. The number of legal abortions performed in England and Wales in that year was 160,000, of which roughly one-third were on non-resident women.

The other important consequence of the 1967 Act was that it stimulated a backlash. The same year saw the formation of the Society for the Protection of the Unborn Child (SPUC). This gave rise in turn to a splinter group, LIFE, formed in 1970. These groups claimed large memberships. By 1980, SPUC estimated its overall membership at 26,000, and LIFE stood at 20,000. They were always much better funded than the pro-choice organizations.

Almost immediately the Act was passed, there began a series of attempts to introduce restrictive amendments to it, which still continue. The first four met with no success. Moreover, a parliamentary committee appointed in 1971 to inquire into the working of the Act reported substantially in its favour, although recommending a reduction in the maximum time-limit for abortions from twenty-eight weeks to twenty-four. The committee was especially impressed by the favourable comments of the British Medical Association (BMA) and the Royal College of Obstetricians and Gynaecologists (RCOG). Initially resistant to Steel's bill in 1967, they had been won round to the legislation as a result of putting it into effect.

However, by the mid-1970s, SPUC's campaigns in the constituencies were beginning to have an impact. The 1974 publication of *Babies for Burning*, a highly sensationalized account of abuses under the Act, attracted sympathetic media attention. This was the background to the submission of Labour MP James White's private member's bill in 1975 which, if passed, would have seriously restricted access to legal abortion. Alarm increased when Parliament voted by 203 to 88 to give the bill a second reading.

It was in response to White's bill that the long-standing feminist organization promoting women's abortion rights, the Abortion Law Reform Association (ALRA), called a meeting. This resulted in the formation of the National Abortion Campaign (NAC). NAC rapidly mobilized a militant campaign throughout the country. The mid-1970s were, in any case, a time of soaring feminist emergies and activity, but the issue of abortion found a particular resonance with feminists of all hues. In July 1975 NAC managed to persuade around 20,000 demonstrators on to the streets to protest against White's bill, the 'biggest demonstration on a women's issue since the suffragettes'.[5]

NAC's call was for abortion on demand. It also adopted a non-hierarchical, decentralized structure. Locally, it consisted of a network of groups; nationally, co-ordination was supplied by annual conferences and six-weekly planning meetings. The latter were open to all, though in practice they tended to be dominated by the London group. This loose organization meant considerable diversity in local group activities. While Radical feminists might be more inclined to picket their MP's surgery, for instance, to counteract SPUC activities in the constituencies, Socialist feminists often worked through the trade unions or the Labour Party. (It must be remembered that women's share of total trade-union membership grew during the 1970s, and reached 30 per

[5] David Marsh and Joanna Chambers, *Abortion Politics* (Junction Books, London, 1981), 47.

cent by 1979.) NAC members were encouraged to submit motions calling on their trade-union branches to support abortion on demand and to affiliate to NAC. Though encountering considerable resistance, they made real progress in some white-collar unions such as NUPE and NALGO. A similar initiative, if more modest in its achievements, was launched by NAC/LARC (Labour Abortion Rights Campaign) in the Labour Party. Though the parliamentary Labour Party leadership refused to impose a three-line whip, the 1977 annual conference made it official party policy to support the 1967 Act.[6]

While NAC was the main pro-choice campaigning group, mention must also be made of the Co-ordinating Committee in Defence of the 1967 Act (Co-ord), formed in 1976. This had the more modest objective of protecting the existing Act, and took the form of an umbrella organization for a range of national groups. By 1980 it had fifty-six such member organizations, including groups representing doctors, lawyers, and the media.

In May 1979, four years after the White bill, fears were again aroused when John Corrie, the Conservative MP, drew first place in the private member's bill ballot. Although his bill proposing restrictive amendments to the Act was eventually defeated, many at the time were unsure what to expect of this new Conservative-dominated Parliament. A major pro-choice offensive was launched. NAC itself co-ordinated a broad coalition in an organization known as the Campaign against Corrie. Within a few months this had attracted sixty local groups. Perhaps its high point was a massive march, with some 100,000 participants, which took place in October and which was sponsored by the TUC. But Co-ord and individual MPs also played an important role in briefing MPs and deciding on strategy inside Parliament. However, probably the most fundamental reason for the failure of the bill was the ineptitude of its sponsors, together with the reluctance of the government to grant it extra time. In fact, it was becoming apparent that no such bill was likely to get through unless it had effective governmental support.

---

[6] This discussion draws extensively on Joni Lovenduski, 'Parliament, Pressure Groups, Networks and the Women's Movement: The Politics of Abortion Law Reform in Britain (1967–83)', in Joni Lovenduski and Joyce Outshoorn (eds.), *The New Politics of Abortion* (Sage, London, 1986)

## INTO THE 1980S: ABORTION NO LONGER THE DEFINITIVE ISSUE?

Even before Corrie's bill in 1979, tensions were apparent in NAC.[7] The most important area of disagreement concerned the main focus of the campaign. It had always been difficult to maintain NAC's momentum and appeal in between mobilizations to fight off attacks on the 1967 Act, as well as frustrating to try and move beyond this purely defensive activity to promote abortion and contraception on demand, in keeping with NAC's own stated goals. But criticisms of NAC's priorities were growing more specific. In 1980 speakers at a Socialist feminist conference on women's oppression and imperialism voiced their disapproval of what they saw as a Socialist feminist concentration on the practical concerns of middle-class white women. NAC was held up as an example.[8] Shortly before the organization's division in 1983, members of NAC who advocated a change of name and emphasis put their case in *Spare Rib*. NAC was supposed to be about 'women's right to choose'. It was right to concentrate on abortion rights in the 1970s, when they were most publicly under attack. But in the 1980s, they argued,

we are deluding ourselves if we believe that women in this society can make choices about having children or not, when there are over 4 million unemployed, when the wages most women earn (if at all) are still abysmally low, when being married or not makes such a difference, when there is such a lot of very often unchallenged racism on both an individual and institutionalised level and when we are faced with virulent anti-lesbianism.

The focus of the campaign needed to broaden out to cover reproductive rights generally and the way in which these were offered or denied to women in different situations.[9]

In expressing these concerns, NAC members were clearly reflecting the growing importance of 'identity politics' in the

[7] Discussion in the following section relies heavily on a series of interviews, together with NAC and WRRC newsletters and other relevant documentation.

[8] See the planning group for the 1980 national Socialist feminist conference, 'What's Imperialism Got to Do with Me?', *Spare Rib*, Jan. 1981.

[9] See Jane Marshall *et al.*, 'What Future for the National Abortion Campaign?' *Spare Rib*, Oct. 1983: 26.

women's movement. Though NAC itself did not include black women, their voices and distinctive demands were increasingly heard in the wider movement. Disabled women were just beginning to organize, with the formation, in 1982, of Sisters against Disablement. But some NAC members were also influenced by international developments. Marge Berer, one of NAC's three paid workers, was involved in the International Campaign for Abortion Rights (ICAR), set up following a conference in Paris in 1977. ICAR soon became ICASC, expanding its focus to take in the problem of forced sterilization and contraception. It was growing increasingly conscious of the distinctive concerns of Third World women, and moving towards a reconceptualization of the issues taken together as 'reproductive rights' (the actual term 'reproductive rights' originated in New York in the late 1970s, where it inspired the formation of a Reproductive Rights National Network). Later still, ICASC was to become the Women's Global Network for Reproductive Rights.

A second source of conflict was the inclusion of men in NAC: some branches, such as the one in Leeds, had been women-only for some time. A number of lesbian members of NAC complained of an oppressive heterosexism and of hostility towards their 'coming out'. Related to this, was the issue of the influence of left-wing groups on the campaign: some suspected that NAC's concentration on the issue of abortion reflected the preference of such groups for single-issue campaigns—ideally, ones that presented a sharp conflict between an oppressed group and the British state. A final exacerbating factor appears to have been the contractual position of NAC's paid employees. For the first few years, workers were only employed on short-term contracts, and so this did not really arise, but in 1981 NAC was faced with the dilemma of whether, as some of its critics urged, it should follow the GLC's example and be a model employer, or whether it should concentrate its very limited funds on the actual campaign. In the event, all three paid workers sided with NAC's critics in the split.

The arguments that led to the final division in the organization in October 1983 were real ones, though undoubtedly they were compounded by personality clashes and organizational tensions. However, it is not easy to identify the protagonists with particular strands of feminism. NAC's principal defenders tended to be 'aligned' or associated with left-wing groups or with the Labour Party. On the other hand, many of those most critical of NAC saw themselves as Socialist feminists—this was apparent at the 1980 conference cited above and it was exemplified by the Leeds group—but they were more likely to be 'non-aligned'. That is, those who split away were perhaps closer to a 'Radical feminist' position in their separatism than those who stayed with NAC, but they were still sufficiently 'Socialist' to be susceptible to arguments about the need to recognize class and racial oppression amongst women (though they themselves were predominantly white).

A further factor seems to have been regional. In particular, it should be noted that the entire Scottish Abortion Campaign stayed in NAC. A number of Scottish women told us that there was a feeling that, as far as Scotland was concerned, the move from a campaign on abortion to one with a broader reproductive rights focus was 'premature'. In Scotland, especially in the west, where one respondent referred to a 'Catholic mafia' of doctors, the first task was to get the 1967 Act implemented. On the other hand, it may be that apart from Edinburgh perhaps, certainly in the west of Scotland, traditional lifestyles and a patriarchal working-class movement still predominate, providing an inhospitable environment for a gay or lesbian subculture or for revolutionary feminism. The primary concern with abortion would reflect both the reality, or at least the perceived reality, of women's lives and feminists' relationship with the traditionalist labour movement.

Following the October 1983 conference, a meeting was held in Manchester in November to determine how the split was to be implemented. The new Women's Reproductive Rights Campaign (WRRC) was launched at a further conference in Cardiff in January 1984. It was immediately successful in its application to the GLC's Women's Committee for funding for an information centre, whereas NAC received no GLC funding. NAC maintained that this was because one of its paid workers had withdrawn NAC's original application and because Valerie Wise, the chairwoman of the women's committee, felt that it could not fund both organizations. On the other hand, NAC as a campaigning group had not received government or charitable funding hitherto.

In the event, both NAC and the WRRC persisted throughout

the 1980s (and to the time of writing), though it would be an exaggeration to say that either of them 'flourished', and, with time, the bitterness between them subsided sufficiently to allow them to work together, notably on the Alton bill. Following the split, NAC was left with around 100 individual members and a much reduced affiliated branch membership. It was desperately short of funds, but it eventually acquired a tiny office in Wesley House, the centre for a number of women's groups and activities, off Holborn, which it rented on favourable terms first from the London Residuary Body, which had taken it over from the GLC, and then from Camden Council. Its main achievement in this period was to put together a package of teaching materials for schools. Ironically, it was David Alton's announcement in September 1987 that he intended to submit an anti-abortion private member's bill in the new parliamentary session that gave NAC a real shot in the arm.

In the mean time, the Women's Reproductive Rights Information Centre (WRRIC) was now formally independent of the WRRC. In April 1988, at the suggestion of its main funding body, the London Borough Grants Scheme, it merged with the Women's Health Information Centre (WHIC) to form the Women's Health and Reproductive Rights Information Centre (WHRRIC), which has subsequently adopted the less intractable name, Women's Health. The ostensible rationale for the merger was that the two organizations were doing similar kinds of work. However, WHIC had been set up by a Women's Health group, itself a subgroup of the Politics of Health group, which was active in the late 1970s and early 1980s and offered a left-wing critique of the National Health Service. Its members tended to be women with a professional interest in health issues. As such, it had a rather different perspective from WRRIC, and the merger was not without its tensions. It also resulted in considerable organizational disruption. A recent article notes, moreover, that:

Unfortunately, the potentially increased strength of the organization has been somewhat undermined by financial insecurity . . . Each new project undertaken by the centre must be considered in terms of its financial potentials, and those that are not self-supporting must be balanced off against those that are. In addition, the increasing demands as a result of the closure of hundreds of voluntary organizations across Britain, the changes in the NHS and the ever-increasing numbers of health issues for consideration result in a heavy load for the centre's workers.[10]

At any rate, Women's Health now has a relatively large and well-appointed office in a building originally acquired by the GLC in Featherstone Street, near Old Street tube station. It has a number of paid workers (in 1987, before the merger with WHIC, WRRIC had three, and by November 1988 there were ten, or the equivalent of seven full-time employees), a comprehensive and well-organized library, and computing and photocopying facilities. Despite external pressures to adopt a more hierarchical organizational structure, it has resisted so far, and retains a collective process of decision-making as far as possible. As its name indicates and its charitable status requires, it does not directly engage in political campaigning, although it does articulate a consistently critical, feminist line. Instead it concentrates on providing information—directed at women rather than at feminists—researching new areas, producing a newsletter, and running various support groups (for instance, in 1986 it ran three, on abortion, infertility, and artificial insemination respectively).

WRRIC/WHRRIC, despite its formal independence, provided the campaign with a London institutional base. Featherstone Street has served as a correspondence address, individual women workers have also been members of the WRRC, and the campaign can draw on the centre's information resources. It sees the information work of the centre as being in keeping with its own emphasis on the broad range of reproductive issues and on practicality and constructiveness, in contrast with what it would characterize as NAC's primarily 'defensive' approach. The WRRC itself, however, has been an extremely loose-knit network of local women's groups whose numbers have probably never gone into double figures. One of its founding members, Marge Berer, goes so far as to say that the campaign 'never really got off the ground or defined itself'.[11] Following the campaign launch, it briefly produced a national newsletter from its London base, but this had lapsed by 1985. The Leeds and York groups were the most active, and also ran a newsletter for the northern regional network. The Leeds group made a submission to the Warnock

---

[10] Barbara James, 'Ten Years of Women's Health: 1982–92', *Feminist Review*, 41 (Summer 1992), 38.
[11] Ibid. 42.

Commission of Inquiry into the issue of embryo research; it campaigned locally on the question of Depo-Provera, and lobbied its local health authorities about providing better abortion facilities, while individual group members got involved in the work of the Community Health Council. Moves were afoot to organize a national WRRC conference in 1987, but were hastily suspended when Alton's announcement concentrated energies once more on defending the 1967 Abortion Act. The conference was finally held in May 1988 and was attended by over sixty women. It was agreed that the campaign should continue to be a network of local women-only groups and individuals, and that changes to its organization and philosophy should only be adopted following their discussion at a national conference or in the campaign newsletter. York Women's Centre was to act as the campaign's national address, and the Leeds group was to administer its finances.

So, though WRRC has been prepared, when the situation was judged urgent enough, to campaign on the abortion issue, it has concerned itself with a much broader range of reproductive issues. How has it come to identify these issues? All are a reflection of its basic commitment to full and meaningful reproductive rights for women, but, with the exception perhaps of the issue of adequate pregnancy testing, they are also a response to new policy developments, possibilities, or simply awareness. Campaigns to save local family planning clinics have been a response to government cuts (more than fifty clinics had been closed by the end of 1987). Victoria Gillick's attempt, through the courts, in 1984 to make it compulsory for doctors to inform parents if under-age daughters were receiving contraceptive aids prompted the organization of a counter-petition. WRRC's activities to highlight the misuse of injectable contraceptives like Depo-Provera and Net-Oen, IUDs like the Dalkon Shield, and sterilization are in large part a consequence of the greater awareness of these abuses abroad, an awareness that has come with the growth of the international network of women's groups concerned with reproductive issues, culminating in the Women's Global Network for Reproductive Rights, from the late 1970s. This has been reflected in the increasing scope and sophistication of WHRRIC's database. At the same time, the decision of the Leeds group to mount a local exhibition on Depo-Provera in

1989 was prompted by its discovery that the drug was being given to black and Asian women in Leeds.

But the 1980s have also seen developments in the technology of reproduction whose implications for women's reproductive rights are clearly far-reaching, though also, in some ways, disturbing. (As Arditti *et al.*[12] remind us, of course, technology is not autonomous: such developments do not 'fall from heaven', but are products of a particular social and political system.) Initially, there was a tendency to equate reproductive rights with the rights to prevent birth—abortion, contraception, sterilization—even though these included the rights to refuse such prevention. But developments in reproductive technology raised the inevitable question: Should not reproductive rights extend to the positive right to choose to give birth as well as to the negative right to choose not to? Eventually, this did indeed become the position formally adopted by the WRRHIC, but many feminists active in this field retained considerable reservations about it.

At face value, new techniques were giving more women the option to have a child. Louise Brown, the first test-tube baby, was born in 1978. By 1984 more than seventy clinics for *in vitro* fertilization had been established world-wide, and in Britain around eighty children had been produced in this way. Despite all the expense, problems, and disappointments entailed (the success rate is variously estimated at 10–20 per cent), there was an enormous waiting-list. In this period, too, surrogacy was becoming a major industry in the United States, although commercial surrogacy was still officially resisted in Britain. Finally, artificial insemination by donor had been practised for many years, before, in the mid-1970s, it became technically possible to freeze sperm, which enormously extended the procedure's application. In 1978 the British Pregnancy Advisory Service (BPAS) began to provide a non-profit-making donor insemination service. Feminists—many, but not all, of them lesbians—had been practising self-insemination of donated sperm earlier in England than elsewhere. By 1980 six women had formed the Feminist Self-Insemination Group, whose instructive pamphlet was widely circulated. However, as a result of the growing awareness of AIDS

[12] Rita Arditti, Renate Duelli Klein, and Shelley Minden (eds.), *Test-Tube Women: What Future for Motherhood?* (Pandora, London, 1984).

in the early 1980s and of the need to test to ensure that donated sperm was not HIV positive, women have become more dependent on official agencies. This is one of the issues addressed in the Human Fertilization and Embryology Act, discussed below.

Such medical 'advances' presented feminists with many difficult questions. Control over these processes remained largely in male hands and, indeed, seemed to inflate the authority of the male medical profession over women's bodies. Access to them required that women have the necessary resources and, except in the case of self-insemination, that they accord with the social norms of respectable motherhood (excluding single women, lesbians, the disabled). Surrogacy in particular could mean the exploitation of poorer women, the surrogates, by other women. Many feminists went on to suggest that it was social conditioning that made women so 'desperate' to be mothers. The WRRC's evidence to the Warnock Commission expressed many of these reservations.

Neither WRRC nor the WHRRIC has arrived at a clear position on these difficult issues. Nor, given their technical and ethical complexity, have they been widely taken up in the women's movement as a whole. However, there *is* a feminist debate, if largely confined to a circle of 'experts', which has developed and, indeed, polarized during the 1980s. The first national feminist conference on reproductive technology was held in Leeds in March 1984. In 1983 Naomi Pfeffer, herself a feminist and infertile, had published *The Experience of Infertility*,[13] in which she asked why other feminists, in their preoccupation with freeing women from the burden of unwanted children, ignored the plight of infertile women. She and several others went on to argue that it was inconsistent to depict infertile women who wanted children as the 'desperate' victims of social conditioning, but not to apply the same criticism to women with children. Though not necessarily free of doubts about the new technologies, they were asking for their reproductive preferences to be regarded more sympathetically. Other women, with medical backgrounds and seeing themselves as feminists, have maintained that developments in reproductive technology can give women more choice. As individual 'experts', a number of these have advised the government, most notably during consultation with the committee appointed

---

[13] Naomi Pfeffer, *The Experience of Infertility* (Virago, London, 1983).

in June 1988 to advise on legislation to implement the recommendations of the Warnock Commission, which eventuated in the
Human Fertilization and Embryology Bill. On the other hand,
some British Radical feminists have played a central role in setting up the network called FINRRAGE (Feminist International
Network of Resistance to Reproductive and Genetic Engineering), which has had its own journal, *RAGE*, since 1988. As its
name suggests, it is deeply opposed to the development of reproductive technology, which it sees as inspired by the male medical
profession's drive, in response to women's bid for greater reproductive autonomy, either as a means of extending its control over
women's bodies or of doing without them entirely.

WRRC, then, has sought to transcend NAC's original focus
on abortion and to campaign instead for the full range of
women's reproductive rights, although there have been continuing uncertainties as to how those rights are to be defined and
realized. Local groups have been flexible and pragmatic in their
selection and pursuit of campaigning issues, but this has
remained within the context of a highly critical feminist analysis.
In Women's Health, however, the reproductive rights campaign
has linked up with what is sometimes referred to as the 'women's
health movement'.

## THE 'WOMEN'S' HEALTH MOVEMENT

The 'women's health movement' is not simply a product of the
1980s; it was already emerging in the late 1970s. A major
influence was the example of the women's movement in the
United States, where publications like *Our Bodies Ourselves*,
aimed at helping women to understand their own health needs,
had gone hand in hand with the proliferation of women's health
centres founded on the principle of self-help. In Britain, too, the
abortion issue in particular had brought home how subject
women were to the control of the predominantly male medical
profession. As early as 1974 the Essex Road Women's Centre in
Islington set up a health group which 'produced literature on
women's health, did pregnancy testing, provided a woman doctor
for advice sessions, learned self-examination, took health classes
with schoolchildren, collected information on doctors and their

treatment of women, provided information on abortion facilities, and more generally, argued for the importance of preventive health care rather than simply curative medicine'.[14] As this quotation illustrates, there is no clear dividing line, either in theory or in practice, between women's health and reproductive rights issues. Indeed, the women in Women's Health have come to believe that it is impossible to divide them. 'How can infertility as a reproductive rights issue be separated from the health issue of endometriosis, a frequent cause of infertility?[15] In practice, too, women's health groups have been substantially, though not exclusively, taken up with reproduction-related problems.

Women's health initiatives proliferated during the Thatcher years. As Peggy Foster writes: 'The British women's health movement is a heterogeneous, unstructured organization with no clearly agreed, publicly stated goals other than the long term objective of increasing women's autonomy and improving their total sum of health and well-being.'[16] But she suggests that there are 'some key guiding principles': that feminist health-care providers should work together in non-hierarchical, co-operative teams; that they should not just consider a woman's physical health, but adopt a 'holistic' approach that takes psychological and emotional factors into account; that they should share their knowledge with their patients and encourage them to play an active role in their own health care; and that feminist health care should not discriminate against women on grounds of race, class, or sexual orientation.

Women's health initiatives have taken a great variety of forms. Amongst the most important are local and national campaigning groups and self-help or support groups with varying degrees of dependence on the state sector, well-woman centres and also some well-women clinics, and professional women's networks. Many of these are clearly feminist in outlook and mode of operation, but others have a much more tenuous connection with feminism, although they have undoubtedly benefited from the changed climate of women's expectations. More than one respon-

[14] Ruth Petrie and Anne Livingstone, 'Out of the Back Streets', *Red Rag*, 11 (Autumn 1976), cited in Rowbotham, *The Past Is before us*.
[15] James, 'Ten Years of Women's Health',
[16] Peggy Foster, 'Well Women Clinics: A Serious Challenge to Mainstream Healthcare?', in Mavis Maclean and Dulcie Groves (eds.), *Women's Issues in Social Policy* (Routledge and Kegan Paul, London, 1991), 82.

dent suggested to us that there had been a coming-together of feminist ideas about understanding and controlling our own bodies and 'Thatcherite' values of consumer choice.

Both the variety and the prevalent informality of organizational forms or contexts within this 'movement' cannot be overemphasized. First, there are the well-women centres. These should not be confused with well-women clinics run more directly by local health authorities. These often have a very different philosophy, and are generally criticized by the well-woman centres. There are presently estimated to be around thirty-six well-woman centres. Though originally inspired by well-woman initiatives in the United States, and sharing a broadly feminist perspective and emphasis on taking practical steps to help women gain control over their own bodies, the centres do not conform to a single model or outlook, nor do they participate in a common, national umbrella organization. Usually, they have a management or steering committee and rely on voluntary workers, all of them women. Some are explicitly opposed to using the services of any professional doctor, male or female, because they would inevitably introduce an element of hierarchy into the proceedings. According to Foster, however, this has made them less attractive to women at large, since 'Most women—for whatever reason—still wish to consult a doctor when they believe they have a medical problem.'[17] Most centres rent what may be very modest premises and receive some kind of support, in the form of a grant or accommodation, from a range of sources such as their local council, the district health council, or a charitable body, though the centre in Blackpool has a deliberate policy of doing without any support from statutory bodies, and relies entirely on voluntary subscriptions. Well-woman centres also vary in their activities. Almost all will provide pregnancy testing and a general information service, including appropriate literature. Often, they allow women's support groups—for instance, for women experiencing premenstrual tension—to hold their meetings there. Some arrange for women doctors and nurses from the district health authority to run counselling sessions and to conduct vaginal and breast examinations.

Bristol's Well-Woman Centre was formally established in 1983. The women in its management collective had got to know each

---

[17] Ibid.

other in the 1970s in a self-help health group. Some had been involved in abortion campaigns, some were perhaps closer to the WRRC's outlook, but this was on an individual basis. Initially, they were hoping to use the local women's centre, but this was dominated at the time by Radical Lesbians who were hostile to the heterosexist assumptions of the initiative. However, the Health Education Council in Bristol was prepared to offer a room in which to establish a well-woman information service. In 1987 the council's new women's committee provided sufficient funding for one year for the centre to acquire its own premises, in St Thomas Street, where it could provide a wider range of services. Avon County Council also funded a community worker to assist them. The information function of the centre multiplied; indeed, by the autumn of 1988 its workers were feeling overwhelmed by the volume of enquiries, and were reluctant to advertise more extensively. In addition, women's self-help groups on the menopause and eating and body image met regularly at the centre, it held day events on issues of women's health, and it worked with Asian women's groups.

At Bristol Well-Woman Centre, as in so many women-centred projects, we got the impression of women workers who were dedicated but overstretched, struggling to cope with a seemingly endless and growing flood of demands, exacerbated by the spread of poverty under Thatcher. They were worried about future resourcing, and had even begun to explore the possibility of funding from private business. They also felt somewhat isolated working with a local medical profession whose outlook was quite conservative, and they were even at odds on some issues with the women's committee. However, they regarded proposals by the Women's Health Network (discussed further below) for a national conference of well-woman workers with some suspicion, as London-based.

But, in addition to the well-woman centres proper, there are over 100 well-women clinics within the National Health Service itself. While the great majority of these probably have very little feminist input, something like one-fifth are more explicitly run on feminist principles. Some of these are community-based: Foster cites the example of Wythenshawe Well-Women's Clinic in South Manchester, set up in 1981 by a group of feminist health-care providers together with some volunteers. Alternatively, they may be set up by feminist GPs. Both kinds face considerable problems in reaching their intended customers and in staying true to feminist values, but they certainly deserve to be included within the women's health movement.

The second—most numerous and probably most important— category of women's health projects comprises local self-help and campaigning groups. Again, the fluidity of these organizational forms cannot be overstated. Some groups are entirely spontaneous and self-resourcing, but most have some kind of relationship with one or more voluntary or public sector bodies.

Many campaigning groups are short-lived and extremely *ad hoc*. They are influenced by national events and preoccupations, but they also respond to specific local developments. Some local campaigns have been concerned with the impact of cuts—for instance, proposals to close a family planning clinic or a maternity ward. Others have demanded improved cervical screening provision. However, some related issues—natural childbirth, breast screening, reproductive technology, and, more recently, AIDS—have not really been taken up locally, although they are the subject of considerable national and feminist debate. Some of those taking part in local campaigns are often professionally involved, and can make use of their access to institutional resources—a room to meet in, a photocopier—and contacts.

Self-help or support groups, as we have seen, form around a variety of issues or shared experiences—PMT, the menopause, eating and body image, hysterectomy, abortion, miscarriage, cystitis, infertility, artificial insemination, cancer. In so far as they consist of women coming together to discuss common problems, they hark back to the consciousness-raising tradition, and chime well with present feminist emphases on 'empowering' women. However, their assumptions and analysis will not always be explicitly feminist, and sometimes they will hardly be feminist at all. A self-help or support group could be set up purely on the initiative of the women who need it, and meet in one of their houses. More typically, though, it would be a body like the local Community Health Council, a well-woman centre, or WRRHIC which began the group, offering premises and the assistance of one of its workers.

What does become clear, as we consider the range of these local activities, their vitality but also their protean nature, forming and re-forming, is the importance and complexity of their relationship with more formal and enduring institutions in the voluntary and, especially, the state sector. Such activities burgeon wherever they can find a toe hold. It could be a local council women's committee that officially adopts and funds favourable policies at one extreme, but, at the other, it could just be a sympathetic official or free access to a room for a couple of hours a week. Some groups 'piggy-back' on feminist bodies that are themselves largely dependent on state or charitable funding, like the well-woman centres and WRRHIC. There is an admirable flexibility and ingenuity in the way in which groups seize such opportunities.

Even so, most of them are ultimately dependent on what turns out to be a rather precarious institutional base. As the chapter on equal opportunities has described, local government women's committees proliferated in the early and middle years of the 1980s, but many of them have come under increasing financial and political pressure, and some have been dismantled. The Community Health Councils, (CHCs) first established following the reorganization of the National Health Service in 1974, have provided another valuable organizational matrix. Their broad brief is to represent the public's interests to the local health authority. The council itself is elected, with one-third of its members nominated by local authorities. A number of Labour feminists have acquired seats on councils in this way. The councils also usually employ a couple of full-time staff, the key position being that of secretary. What a CHC actually does tends in practice to be determined by its membership and its secretary, leading to a great diversity between CHCs, but those concerned with women's issues can prove a tremendous resource. In addition, during the 1980s, at the hazy intersection of local government, local health authorities, and charities, the 'community health movement' appeared, centred on 'community health projects'. Beginning with considerable government approval because of their 'cost-effectiveness', community health projects have been located firmly in the voluntary sector, but have drawn on funding from local government and health authorities. As in the 'community development projects' a decade or so earlier, the job of the key actor, the community health worker, has been to help local people define their own health needs. The ultimate object is for the resulting local health projects to become self-sustaining, wher outside funding and the paid worker are withdrawn. At this point, it is important to remind readers that a great majority of the community health workers are women. Still more encouraging, many have feminist leanings. On the other hand, however, the very radicalism of the community health movement as a whole may give the government second thoughts about this particular approach to health policy.

It is also regularly suggested that such a relationship with government institutions may create a dangerous culture of dependence. Interestingly enough, a number of older feminists (that is, of our own generation) expressed misgivings about these developments. One comment, for instance, was that 'in our day' we would never have waited for government funding before embarking on a project. We would have tried to raise the money ourselves—for example, by organizing a benefit.

Despite these organizational uncertainties, local campaigning and, especially, self-help women's health groups proliferate. By and large, however, they remain local initiatives, with little contact with similar groups in other localities or at a national level (exceptions here are the formation of a national network of hysterectomy support groups and a Miscarriage Assocation). At a national level, on the other hand, there are a number of associations that in one way or another promote women's health, though there are relatively few that are explicitly feminist in their thinking and that are only concerned with women's health questions. For instance, the National Childbirth Trust argues for a woman's right to choose how she gives birth, but otherwise it is not obviously identified with a feminist position or primarily concerned with women's health. The Women's National Cancer Control Campaign has campaigned for improved breast and cervical screening, and also runs an information and support helpline, but it has a relatively conservative social philosophy. More controversially still, the Amarant Trust, whose patrons include the Conservative MP Teresa Gorman, is an enthusiastic proponent of hormone replacement therapy (HRT), though feminists themselves are divided over its advantages and risks.

Finally, there are associations or less formal networks of professional women involved in women's health issues, such as Radical Midwives, Radical Health Visitors, and Women in Medicine. Women in Medicine (WIM) was formed as a breakaway from the much older and more traditional Medical Women's Federation. (Significantly enough, it is the Medical Women's Federation which has continued to be consulted by the government, through the eminently respectable and toothless National Women's Commission.) A group of women doctors began to meet after two of them placed an advertisement in *Spare Rib* in 1979. In 1981 they organized a conference of women doctors and medical students, and out of this emerged WIM. By the late 1980s it had local groups in seven cities, including London, and plans for three more. In 1989 membership was around 350. Originally, membership was confined simply to women doctors and medical students, with others being offered the associate membership only. Following quite a heated argument, it was eventually agreed to open the membership to all women who supported the association's aims.

WIM has a formal constitution which, perhaps paradoxically, commits it to attempting 'to function on a non-hierarchical, collective basis as evolved by the Women's Movement'.[18] The association organizes annual conferences and produces a lively newsletter. Besides taking up the issue of the career progress of women doctors—particularly following the publication of Isobel Allen's *Doctors and their Careers*—WIM has been concerned with a very wide range of women's health questions, including women doctors' relationship with other health workers and patients, defending the National Health Service, the experience of lesbian doctors, the diagnosis and treatment of breast and cervical cancer, premenstrual tension, and female circumcision. It campaigned in support of the Wendy Savage Appeal Fund set up when one of its founder members, Wendy Savage, was suspended from her clinical and teaching duties in the medical college in Tower Hamlets. On the basis of five obstetric cases, she was accused of professional incompetence by the district health authority. The case raised procedural questions, but it also reflected more political differences about the proper way to care for women's health. Wendy Savage identified herself with 'progressive, woman-centred, community-based maternity and women's health care'.[19]

[18] We are grateful here for access to past Women in Medicine minutes and newsletters.
[19] Women in Medicine minutes and newsletters; see also Wendy Savage, *The Savage Inquiry* (Virago, London, 1986).

The Association of Radical Midwives (ARM) was founded in 1976 by two student midwives who were particularly concerned about the increasing incidence of obstetric intervention to induce births. As the association grew, its central philosophy was to maximize women's choice in the process of childbirth. Its origins and approach clearly owe much to the women's movement, although many of those subscribing to its views might not see themselves as feminists. Its organization similarly reveals the imprint of feminism. Its membership (presently standing at 1,300) is distributed between forty or so local centres. There is an elected steering group, and a part-time secretary, who provides the contact address. There are national quarterly meetings, with a rotating venue, and biennial conferences. But apart from campaigning in support of Wendy Savage, and, more recently, successfully demanding the reinstatement of a midwife who had been struck off the register for pursuing the association's aims, activity has centred on the largely autonomous local groups. In contrast to many feminist organizations, the ARM has actually grown in membership and momentum over the last few years.

The 'women's health movement', it is apparent, consists of enormously diverse groupings and individuals, and displays great organizational flexibility, fluidity, and vitality, especially at local level. In any given locality, networking and overlapping membership help to bring different activities into contact with one another. But there is much less co-ordination amongst different localities, or between them and a national centre. Recently, two bodies have emerged that are designed to promote greater dialogue of this kind. The Women's Health Network was set up by its parent organization, the Community Health Initiatives Resource Unit (CHIRU), in 1987. In 1988 CHIRU merged with another similar body to form the National Community Health Resource (NCHR). The brief of the NCHR is to promote the work of the community health movement, and it receives funding from the Department of Health, the Health Education Authority (HEA), and charitable foundations. From the start, the Women's Health Network has been directed by a steering group of about ten women, and initially it had only one part-time worker, who produced the newsletter. In 1989, however, funding was obtained for a full-time post, and this made it possible to organize a conference in July of that year. As we have seen, the network is also hoping to mount a conference of women involved in well-woman centres. The network has around 430 groups and individuals on its circulation list, some two-thirds of whom are based in the voluntary sector.[20]

The other body is the Women's Health Forum. Set up in 1988 by the Health Education Authority to widen the HEA's contacts with women's health organizations and networks, it tends to cater for the more 'respectable' or formalized side of the movement, but, on the other hand, it may have somewhat greater input into government thinking.

Paradoxically, these recent steps in the direction of more systematic and cross-national networking have served to highlight a further development in the women's health movement which we need to note and which again finds parallels in other areas of the women's movement: the emergence of separate black women's health projects and initiatives. The Women's Health Network conference, 'Feeling Strong, Growing Stronger', held in Liverpool in July 1989 and designed to bring women health workers and activists closer together, also revealed the extent to which many black and ethnic minority women felt that the women's health movement ignored *their* health concerns. One group, Liverpool Black Sisters, withdrew at the planning stage, and a number of other black women who attended the conference criticized the fact that the issue of health care in a multiracial and multicultural society was not on the initial agenda, and that there was an underrepresentation of black women on the panel of speakers.

Without claiming that it is in some way 'typical', it may still be useful to describe one black women's health initiative, the London Black Women's Health Action Project (LBWHAP). The moving spirit behind this project has been Shamis Dirir Shur, a woman of Somalian origin, though she was born in what was then Aden, who came to Britain in 1967. In 1979 she was instrumental in forming a Somalian women's association in Tower Hamlets, where there is a sizeable Somalian community. The aim was to help to break down the isolation of these women, many of whom were without education or any knowledge of the English language, and whose menfolk were usually sailors and

---

[20] This and the subsequent discussion of the Women's Health Network draws on interviews and issues of the newsletter of the NCHR.

away at sea. Then, in 1981, Lord Kennet introduced a bill prohibiting female circumcision. Though not in favour of female circumcision herself, Shamis feared the consequences for her community if this legislation went through (in the event, Kennet's bill fell, but a similar measure became law in 1985). Amongst Somalians, female circumcision is taken for granted; it is not a contentious or public issue. But now mothers who practised it on their daughters could find themselves criminalized, and, without an accompanying change of attitudes, banning the practice could simply drive it underground. So, in 1982 Shamis helped to found LBWHAP, which initially was entirely voluntary, without any outside funding, in order to 'educate' Somalian women—and thus men—about circumcision and other health issues. By 1984 the project had succeeded in attracting some funding from the GLC Women's Unit, and subsequently its funding sources have included the London Borough Grants Scheme, Tower Hamlets Borough Council, and the district health authority. In the process, it has acquired a more formal management structure, and presently employs four full-time workers and a number of other helpers on a more provisional basis. In principle, these should all be women, though they have had to allow one man to be involved as part of a reciprocal arrangement with the British Council for Refugees. Although the project, which is open to all black women, is linked into the state welfare system, it is clear that it sees a major component of its role as 'consciousness raising', and that its values are in many respects 'feminist'. At the same time, although it has not been hostile to the white women's movement—it participated enthusiastically in the July 1989 conference, for instance—it has also clearly viewed itself as fulfilling an essential role for black women and as being part of a wider black women's movement.[21]

Despite divisions and fragmentation, there was little sign by the end of the 1980s that the women's health movement was abating. The Women's Health Network emerged towards the end of the decade, bringing many groups into closer contact; two of the professional associations, Women in Medicine and the Association of Radical Midwives, were experiencing a relative

---

[21] This account of the LBWHAP draws on an interview and various LBWHAP reports.

upsurge in membership and activities. The health movement had largely originated in issues focused on reproductive rights, but, while never losing that area of central concern, it had spread out to encompass the whole gamut of questions surrounding women's health problems and the way in which these have been understood and treated by a 'patriarchal' medical profession.

## RALLYING TO FIGHT THE ALTON BILL

Yet, despite all that has been said so far about the changed status of abortion on the movement agenda in the 1980s—the fact that it ceased to be a definitive issue and became one in a spectrum of reproductive rights—and, more broadly still, of women's health concerns, it is still abortion, or, more accurately, threats to existing legislation governing its provision, that galvanizes the different reproductive rights and more radical of the women's health groups into collective action. This was demonstrated from late 1987, in the campaign to fight the Alton bill, and again, most recently, in the Stop the Amendment Campaign.

We have seen that despite its seemingly restrictive features, the 1967 Abortion Act allowed a surge in the rate of legal abortions. During the 1970s the abortion rate stayed fairly steady, but in the 1980s it began to climb again, modestly but perceptibly, and, given the fall in the numbers of non-resident women having abortions, this meant a more significant rise for resident women. It is also the case that, by the 1980s, the twenty-eight-week limit was one of the highest in Europe, but, on the other hand, several European countries had abortion on demand in the first twelve weeks.

Following the Corrie bill, some believed for a while that the anti-abortion lobby had been finally routed. Marge Berer [22] cites opinion polls commissioned by ALRA in 1980 which found that more than 80 per cent of respondents supported a woman's right to decide on an abortion in consultation with her doctor. But such optimism soon proved unfounded. One of the striking features of the anti-Corrie campaign within Parliament had been the effectiveness with which Co-ord, the umbrella body co-ordinating

[22] Marge Berer, 'Whatever Happened to "A Woman's Right to Choose"?' *Feminist Review*, 29 (1988).

defence of the 1967 Act, briefed pro-abortionists in the committee set up to consider the bill, and with which its supporters in
Parliament made use of parliamentary procedure. The Act's
defenders had been learning from experience. But the anti-abortion or pro-life campaigners had not stood still either. By 1980,
as we have seen, SPUC estimated its overall membership at
26,000, and LIFE's at 20,000. Both received considerable financial support, and SPUC alone had five full-time officers. By 1988
SPUC had 30,000 members, twelve full-time workers in London,
and five regional organizers. Though retaining their separate
identities and priorities, the two organizations were now much
more aware of the need to work closely together, and had been
able to reflect on the lessons of the Corrie failure. They had
become increasingly expert in handling the media, especially giving stories to the local press, and they had acquired a significant
following amongst schoolchildren, through their educational
work, and amongst college students.

The anti-abortion lobby appeared to find further encouragement from scientific developments and related shifts in medical
and governmental opinion. Both the Warnock Report, published
in 1985, and Enoch Powell's private member's Unborn Child
(Protection) Bill, although it was filibustered out, reflected and
fostered a growing public concern about medical research using
human embryos. Many feminists agreed with Julia South's comment that the very title of Powell's bill 'gave away its anti-abortion intentions',[23] although some FINRRAGE members
supported the bill. At the same time, technological advances
meant that it was theoretically possible for a human foetus to be
'viable', or capable of sustaining independent life, at twenty-four
weeks. Both the BMA and the RCOG put increasing pressure on
the government to reduce the legal limit for abortions to twenty-
four weeks. As a consequence, it is widely believed that the government entered into a 'gentlemen's agreement' with NHS
doctors in 1984 not to perform abortions over this limit, and it is
absolutely certain that since 1986 no new private abortion clinic
has been granted a licence unless it accepts the twenty-four-week
restriction.

[23] Julia South, 'And at the End of the Day who Is Left Holding the Baby?',
*New Statesman*, 15 Nov. 1985: 11.

In December 1982 Lord Robertson submitted a further amending bill in the House of Lords, but it made little progress. Pro-abortionists were more concerned when, in the same year, the DHSS under Gerard Vaughan altered the form that doctors had to sign to authorize an abortion so that only medical grounds could be cited, but, in the event, it made little difference to the way in which doctors behaved. As we have seen, Powell's bill in 1985 was interpreted by many feminists as an indirect attack on abortion, because it wanted to give the embryo the legal status of a person from conception, but it failed. In February 1987 SPUC turned to the courts, and one of its members sought an injunction to prevent his former girlfriend from having an abortion, on the grounds that at eighteen to twenty-one weeks the foetus would be potentially 'viable'. This injunction, too, was refused.

All these developments were worrying for pro-abortionists, but not sufficiently dramatic to mobilize mass action. As we have seen, NAC itself was in something of a doldrums. It was David Alton's announcement, when he came third in the private member's bill ballot, that he intended to launch another amending bill that finally provided a focus for such a mass campaign. He made clear that, learning from previous experience, the bill would be kept simple. It would consist of a single clause, concerned only with the issue of the time-limit, which it would bring right down to eighteen weeks for *all* cases, except if the foetus had an abnormality which made it incapable of independently sustainable life, or if the mother's life was threatened. The announcement was made at LIFE's annual conference in September 1987. Obviously, a major reason for the timing of the announcement was Alton's success in the ballot and his long-standing commitment to the anti-abortion cause. But there is also some case for arguing that SPUC and LIFE were anxious not to let the twentieth anniversary of the 1967 Act go by without some decisive action. And although in retrospect it is easy to understand how the bill was defeated, it is important to realize that many seasoned pro-abortion, or rather pro-choice, campaigners thought that this time the pro-life lobby might win.

Almost immediately following Alton's announcement, Leonora Lloyd of NAC contacted Cerys Williams of Co-ord and others at ALRA and WRRC, and it was agreed to call a meeting.[24] The

---

[24] The following account of FAB draws on several interviews and NAC and

meeting, held in October, was relatively well attended, and resolved to launch a Fight the Alton Bill (FAB) campaign. Making use of NAC's networks in particular, FAB got off the ground quickly, and by Christmas it had raised enough money to pay two part-time workers and, for a brief interlude, to have its own office in Wesley House. At its height, FAB claimed supporters in 42 areas of London, 8 in Scotland, 4 in Wales, and over 100 in other areas of England, though not all of these were proper 'branches' as such. Although the numbers of those involved in FAB never reached the levels attained during the Corrie bill, their geographical spread was much greater. The branches themselves were variously constituted. Some were set up by local NAC or WRRC groups. In some cases, like Bristol, the council's women's committee took the initiative. In Scotland it appears to have been a joint venture by the Scottish Abortion Campaign (linked with NAC) and the women's committee of the Scottish TUC. Many were based in local student unions, but in these cases, as well as in a number of others, they were often initiated by far Left groups, notably the Socialist Workers' Party (SWP) and the Revolutionary Communist Party (RCP). In Leeds, for instance, women in WRRC were intending to set up a local FAB group, but found that the RCP had beaten them to it. They did manage to arrive at a working arrangement, however, and to persuade the RCP women that men should not be included as members.

Between the bill's formal introduction in the House on 16 December and its second reading on 22 January, activities on both sides intensified. FAB produced bulletins with information and campaigning suggestions for its local branches, but they tended to do their own thing. In Bristol, for instance, where Labour Party women and members of left-wing groups were prominent, the campaigners leafleted council estates and tried to get local union branches involved. Nationally, though NAC and WRRC worked together in FAB, NAC put a lot of its energies into contacting sympathetic women trade-union officers and the Labour Party to mobilize support, while WRRC was unhappy about the inclusion of men and left-wing groups in the campaign. WRRC soon called a meeting for women's groups only; it was well attended and subsequently took a number of independent steps, including inviting Frances Kissling, from the American group Catholics for Free Choice, to address a public meeting which attracted considerable media coverage. Much of FAB's energy was devoted to organizing a major demonstration in London on 21 January, the eve of the second reading of the bill. The demonstration was well attended, with coachloads of FAB supporters coming from all over the country, but, none the less, . it was not on the same scale as those for White or Corrie.

Perhaps one of the reasons why the campaign, even at this stage, was comparatively subdued, was that, however clear-cut FAB tried to make them, the issues were already beginning to appear less straightforward than they had at the outset. So long as it was simply a question of whether the time-limit should be reduced to eighteen weeks or not, the pro-abortion lobby could assume that a sizeable chunk of both public and parliamentary opinion, and virtually all feminist-inclined thinking would be behind them. But by December, if not sooner, there were signs of an emerging national consensus for the imposition of a time-limit at twenty-four weeks. In October a Marplan poll for the *Guardian* had found that more than half of its female respondents did not approve of abortions after twenty-four weeks; only 15 per cent were in favour of retaining the twenty-eight-week limit.[25] Mrs Thatcher and her Health Minister, John Moore, also stated their support for a reduction to twenty-four weeks. In November David Steel, the 'father' of the 1967 Act, said that he would accept such a reduction, while a BBC Panorama survey of 409 MPs found that only 126 preferred the eighteen-week limit and that the most popular option (161 MPs) was twenty-four weeks. Finally, in December, the BMA and RCOG issued a joint report advocating a twenty-four-week limit while condemning the Alton bill as 'inhumane'.

In the event, the bill passed its second reading by 296 votes to 251. This vote, incidentally, does not necessarily indicate support for the bill, but simply a desire to have the issues debated further. The composition of the examining committee accordingly gave the supporters of the second reading a majority of nine to eight. While FAB sought to mobilize the grass roots, Co-ord was concentrating on the campaign inside Parliament. It now had the equivalent of 1½ full-time workers, based in the office of the

[25] See the *Guardian*, 16 Oct. 1987.

Birth Control Trust. Though nominally acting as an umbrella group for more than fifty member organizations, Co-ord found that, in practice, some groups attended meetings more regularly than others and were more active during the campaign. Besides NAC and FAB, these included the Pregnancy Advisory Service, Doctors for a Woman's Choice on Abortion (DWCA), Liberals for Choice (some Liberals were particularly dismayed that the bill was being promoted by one of their colleagues), and Tories for the Abortion Act of 1967 (TACT). Sharon Spiers of TACT had cut her campaigning teeth on the Benyon bill while still at school, and again on Corrie. Though her relations with NAC and FAB were guarded, she 'did her own thing', giving every spare moment to the campaign, sending between 1,500 and 2,000 letters to MPs, and working with four Conservative MPs, and especially with Andrew McKay, to keep a record of MPs' opinions and voting patterns on the issue. Doctors for a Woman's Choice on Abortion was formed in the 1970s. By the end of the decade it had a national membership of around 600, including male as well as female doctors, though since this was widely dispersed, most central decision-making resided with a small committee which met four or five times a year or when there was urgent business. Other DWCA members supported the campaign by, for instance, writing to MPs or speaking at public meetings.

Co-ord got a briefing to every MP before the second reading in January. Once the parliamentary committee to review the bill had been established, its prime concern was to brief committee members opposed to the bill, led by Jo Richardson. Members of the public are entitled to attend committee meetings, and committee members can leave the meeting to consult them, but Co-ord's briefing was generally in written form. However, Jo Richardson initiated her own briefing meetings, which representatives of Co-ord and NAC attended. Although Jo Richardson herself was already a veteran of parliamentary struggles over abortion, most of her supporters on the committee were relatively inexperienced. At these briefing meetings it was agreed not to table amendments about time-limits in committee, since the composition of the committee, weighted in favour of the bill, meant that they would be defeated and would not then be admissible at the report stage. Instead, opponents of the bill concentrated on exceptions to its provisions. The bill as it stood would have proscribed early screening procedures and abortion on the ground of foetal disability. The campaign by Alton and his colleagues had placed great emphasis on the perspective of disabled people, but Co-ord was able to enlist and to make effective use of the support of SATFA (Support after Termination for Abnormality) and of Mencap. They were also helped by the fact that a select committee in the Lords, chaired by Lord Brightman, had been reviewing the same issues in relation to a bill submitted by the Bishop of Birmingham; its unanimous report at the end of January called for stiffer conditions to be imposed before allowing abortions between twenty-four and twenty-eight weeks, but otherwise opposed lowering the limit and favoured measures to give women easier access to an early abortion. Alton's opponents tabled twenty-seven amendments, only two of which got through. One allowed abortions after eighteen weeks in cases of severe disability as well as rape or child abuse. The other made a further exception in cases where the mother's life was endangered.

Unlike the Corrie bill, Alton's effectively had only one day to get through the report stage. It had also become clear (and was confirmed by a survey by Alton's own supporters) that, as it stood, his bill was unlikely to get a parliamentary majority. But Alton and, behind him, SPUC and LIFE were unwilling to accept twenty-four weeks as a temporary compromise. That being so, it was relatively easy for their opponents to spin out the preliminary parliamentary procedures and debate on further amendments until the time was up.

In retrospect, it is not too surprising that Alton's bill was defeated. The main body of medical opinion was against it. Nor should the influence of the feminist pro-choice lobby, and especially of Co-ord, be entirely discounted. Individual women MPs on both sides of the House played their part, though there was no systematic cross-party collaboration of the kind that Vallance[26] records on abortion and other issues amongst women parliamentarians in the 1970s. But, as usual, the crucial consideration was the attitude of the government. Although the bill's advocates claimed that, at the report stage, the Speaker of the House exercised his discretion in the opposition's favour, members of that opposition argued to the contrary, that the Speaker helped

[26] See Elizabeth Vallance, *Women in the House* (Athlone Press, London, 1979).

Alton. Whereas for Corrie's bill the Speaker had rearranged amendments to the time-limit in descending order, beginning with those nearest the status quo, this time he intended to begin with Jo Richardson's twenty-six-week amendment, and then take Alton's for twenty weeks and work upwards, though in fact they never got that far. But, whatever the truth of this claim, the more decisive factor was the government's refusal to grant extra time.

## THE HUMAN FERTILIZATION AND EMBRYOLOGY ACT

But the significance of Alton's bill extends beyond the fact of its defeat, for it helped to harden the government's resolve that, abandoning precedent, it *would* intervene in the parliamentary determination of abortion policy. The growth of a new public consensus around the twenty-four-week limit had been apparent as the bill proceeded. The government was already planning legislation to regulate the use for research of human embryos created in the course of new fertility treatments, as recommended in the 1985 Warnock Report. And by March 1989,[27] if not sooner, it was rumoured that an amendment would be attached to the ensuing bill, proposing a twenty-four-week limit.

It is still not entirely clear why the government did decide to intervene in this way. Did the growing criticisms of Mrs Thatcher's leadership inside the Conservative Party persuade her of the need to appease the moral fundamentalists in her ranks? After Alton's defeat, anti-abortion groups protested vehemently against their dependence on the private member's bill procedure, which, they claimed, would never allow sufficient time for the issues to be properly debated and thus for a considered vote on their amendment. Following the failure of Ann Widdecombe's bill, shortly after and virtually identical with Alton's, in January 1989, Mrs Thatcher wrote to her personally, saying that the government would find time to debate a reduction in the abortion time-limit, though without indicating what form this would take. The government's stated reason for intervening was that the issue needed to be resolved before the next general election. Certainly, it had taken up an inordinate amount of parliamentary time in

---

[27] The *Guardian*, 10 Mar. 1989.

exclusively on the amendment or should consider issues arising in the main body of the bill. STAC itself did stick with the one issue. But some NAC members were also extremely concerned about possible restrictions on access to donor insemination. There had already been an early day motion in the House of Lords deploring the finding of the Pregnancy Advisory Service, published in its annual report, that around 700 lesbian couples had been helped to have a child through donor insemination, and it seemed likely that the issue would be taken up again in the course of debate on the embryology bill. Even so, and interestingly enough, it was not NAC or WRRC but women in the Rights of Women's subgroup working on lesbian custody who took the initiative. They held a well-attended meeting in December, as a result of which a Campaign for Access to Donor Insemination (CADI) was formed. Working closely with NAC, this held regular meetings in London, and a few groups met outside London, for instance, in Newcastle. Members of CADI concentrated on persuading parliamentary opinion (its convener, Gill Butler, was a lawyer) and on presenting access to donor insemination as a civil liberties issue. They got valuable support from the NCCL, but they were criticized by many women who were concerned about donor insemination for what they saw as the narrowness of their campaign, its parliamentary focus, and its low chance of success.

A further group of NAC members, notably those associated with the RCP, wanted to campaign against the bill as a whole, arguing that there was no need to monitor or regulate embryo research. This was the position adopted by the Nottingham NAC, for instance, but, nationally, NAC was careful not to commit itself publicly on the question of embryo research, for fear of dividing the campaign.

In practice, the national co-ordination of STAC proceeded from NAC's office. At national level, STAC included NAC and groups on the Left, but, unlike FAB, it did not include WRRC or ALRA. Although a number of local STAC groups were formed, there were fewer of them than there had been for FAB. As in the Alton campaign, there was considerable support from women in trade unions—women's officers in the NGA, SOGAT, and NALGO were particularly helpful—and amongst students. There are a number of likely reasons for STAC's low profile that are connected with the immediate circumstances of the campaign: although it was fairly certain that there would be an amendment, nobody knew when it would be or the form that it would take; the issues raised by the embryology bill were very complex from a feminist standpoint; the twenty-four-week limit commanded such widespread support, including from such prominent Labour women MPs as Clare Short and Joan Ruddock. But it probably also reflected the continuing decline in the women's movement's grass-roots campaigning activity.

Following publication of the embryology bill (without any reference to the abortion amendment) in November, Co-ord met to discuss its response to any move to tack an amendment on to it. Though members were generally agreed that a reduction of the abortion time-limit to twenty-four weeks would make only a minimal difference in practice, there was some disagreement on tactics. Some members wanted Co-ord openly to support such a limit, but the organization had been set up to defend the 1967 Act as it stood, and it was decided that, initially at least, Co-ord, like STAC, should fight any attempt to alter the Act.

STAC aimed to mobilize constituents to put pressure on their MPs by writing letters or even by going to see them at the House of Commons, while Co-ord concentrated on briefing MPs, as with the Alton bill. A Week of Action, was held early in March, with around 400 attending a rally in London to launch the campaign. In the House of Lords, which voted in favour of embryo research at the second reading, of the bill, Lord Houghton had succeeded in preventing the attachment of an abortion amendment. On the eve of its second reading in the House of Commons, Co-ord's briefing to MPs reiterated its opposition to any change in the Act, but argued that if, as expected, an amendment was introduced, the limit should go no lower than twenty-four weeks and that there should be exceptions, to this.

At the second reading, on 2 April, Sir Geoffrey Howe, the Leader of the House, finally did move that amendments on abortion should be allowed. Given the strength of feeling on both sides, the government also ruled that before going into committee, Clause 11 of the embryology bill, the controversial clause about embryo research, and any abortion amendments should be debated by a committee of the whole House on 23 and 24 April respectively. On 24 April, beginning with Sir Geoffrey's proposed amendment for a twenty-four-week limit, MPs debated a series of possible time-limits, but Howe's amendment was eventually passed by 409 votes to 152. Towards the end of the debate, which lasted over eight hours, the House also passed amendments removing *any* time-limit for abortions where there was risk of grave harm to the mother's health or of serious foetal abnormality. This meant that obstetricians who occasionally had to perform abortions after twenty-eight weeks need no longer fear prosecution under the 1929 Infant Life Preservation Act.

The vote on 24 April settled the issue for the time being. Pro-choice MPs claimed to be delighted at the outcome, though, in the longer run, NAC and Co-ord have tended to see it largely as a confirmation of the status quo. Pro-life groups declared themselves appalled, and argued that the voting procedure had been so complicated and confusing that, by the end of the session, many MPs were no longer clear what they were voting for. As a consequence, when the bill came out of committee, and went into the report stage in June, they were allowed to table new amendments. At this point, pro-abortionists also submitted two further amendments: one for abortion on request up to twelve weeks, and one for abortion requiring only one doctor's signature up to twelve weeks. Though both were defeated, the second was only by a narrow margin. The main debate, however, centred once more on time-limits, but the anti-abortion MPs were unable to secure a revision. Attendance was low, suggesting that MPs were tired of the issue and felt that it had been resolved in April. Finally, in October, the bill, with attached abortion amendments, went to the Lords, where a move led by the Duke of Norfolk failed to revoke the exceptions that had been introduced to the twenty-four-week limit in the Lower House.

Once more, the attitudes of the government and the medical profession were probably the most decisive factors in the outcome. The BMA and RCOG reaffirmed their preference for the twenty-four-week limit in September and December 1989 respectively. But Co-ord and NAC's cumulative campaign of educating parliamentary and public opinion also contributed to the result. On the other hand, it was widely suggested that the pro-life lobby miscalculated and caused offence when, just before the 24 April debate, it sent each MP a life-size model of a foetus at twenty weeks. These were actually paid for by the 'philanthropist' property speculator, Godfrey Bradman, who has long been one of SPUC's most generous supporters.[30]

If the outcome is, in the main, reassuring for those concerned with abortion rights, the bill's provisions for artificial insemination are more worrying. The Act stipulated that a licensing agency was to be established to regulate infertility treatment, including insemination, as well as embryo research. Attempts in the House of Lords to add amendments restricting access to artificial insemination to married couples, or insisting that only a husband's sperm were to be used for such procedures were soundly defeated, but another amendment restricting such treatment to women living with a male partner was defeated more narrowly. The amendments were moved by Lady Abernathie of Saltoon, but they were inspired by the Conservative Family Group, a group of Tory parliamentarians committed, as they saw it, to defending family life. In the end, the bill that emerged from the Lords did require that the welfare of the child be considered, and this was strengthened in the Commons to include the child's need for a father. However, these amendments only amount to guidelines which infertility clinics licensed by the central agency would be expected to follow, so much will depend on the attitudes both of the central agency and of the clinics themselves in applying them: there is an understandable fear that they could be the grounds for denying artificial insemination to lesbian women and even to single mothers.

It is very difficult to arrive at an overall assessment of the achievements or failures of the women's movement in the field of abortion, reproductive rights, and health since the late 1970s. The picture, in so far as we have been able to piece it together, is complex and contradictory. One consistent theme has been the decline, though not the disappearance, of grass-roots campaigning on the 'classical' WLM model. On the other hand, long-established campaigning groups like NAC and Co-ord have survived and have compensated for continuing shortages of funds and staff with growing expertise and skill in pursuing their political objectives. (The immediate sequel of the campaign for NAC was a gratifying increase in membership and funding, but this

[30] See the *Guardian*, 22 July 1991, for a 'profile' of Godfrey Bradman.

proved short-lived.) The movement has been weakened by dissent over the relative importance of abortion and other reproductive rights issues, over the definition of reproductive rights and responses to the new reproductive technology, over the insensitivity of white women to black women's concerns, even over perceived attempts by London or a national centre to dictate to the regions. And yet, women have found ways of coming together when it really mattered, notably to defend the 1967 act. Although the membership of NAC and, still more, of WRRC has been low in the 1980s, large numbers of women have been involved in the 'women's health movement' based in the voluntary sector: in women's centres, health projects, and self-help groups. The numbers of women in relevant professions—doctors, biotechnicians, community health officers, local government officers—has continued to rise, and some, though not all, of these have contributed to what Mary Fainsod Katzenstein has described, in an American context, as 'unobtrusive feminist mobilization'[31] within their employing institutions, or have at least used their expertise, status, or resources to help other women. At the same time, many feminist assumptions have increasingly permeated public expectations and even the mind-set of male policy-makers.

One area in which feminism has arguably had relatively little impact on policy today is reproductive technology. We have suggested that this is partly because of the technical complexity of the issues involved. But it also reflects feminists' considerable ambivalence towards motherhood itself, which has become more apparent and explicit in the 1980s and which is the subject of the following chapter.

[31] See Mary Fainsod Katzenstein, 'Feminism within American Institutions: Unobtrusive Mobilization in the 1980s', *Signs*, 16/1 (Autumn 1990).

# 8

# The Family, Motherhood, and Child Care

THE central questions to be addressed in this chapter are, first, the changes in feminist thinking about motherhood, and, secondly, the way in which these changes relate to mobilization around the specific issue of child care. But, to set these properly in context, it is also necessary to discuss feminist attitudes to the 'family' and the nature of family policy under Mrs Thatcher.

It might be supposed that both motherhood and the issues surrounding it—in practical terms, child care especially—would be of passionate concern to feminists. They have played such a crucial part in social definitions of women's nature and role within the family and outside it. In the early years of women's liberation, there was a tendency for motherhood to be viewed negatively and in fairly simplified terms. From the late 1970s, feminists have come to pay increasing attention to the meaning of motherhood and to value it more highly. And yet the 'pro-woman' perspective within which this reassessment has taken place has significantly limited any spillover into campaigns of practical assistance to mothers.

The chapter begins with a 'case-study' of the debate over child sexual abuse arising out of the events in Cleveland in 1987. This highlights, first, some of the 'contradictions' in government family policy, and secondly, the complexity of feminist attitudes towards the family and mothering. Subsequent sections examine more systematically the Conservative government family policy in the context of which feminist attitudes have developed, and the feminist attitudes themselves, still largely negative towards the family, though less so towards motherhood. Finally, we trace how these attitudes have fed into specific feminist campaigns around maternity rights and, most of all, child care, and what their policy impact has been.

CHILD SEXUAL ABUSE: THE CLEVELAND AFFAIR

In June 1987 the national media highlighted reports of an unprecedented number of children being taken into care in Cleveland on suspicion that they were victims of sexual abuse. The issue of child sex abuse suddenly became the focus of enormous public concern. Events in Cleveland called for a response both from government and from feminists, but in both cases that response was less wholehearted than their stereotypes might lead one to expect. Such drastic intervention by state agencies into the lives of individual families could not but clash with the 'Thatcherite' view of the family and its relation to the state. But the government's response was to devolve responsibility for assessing the actions of local agencies to a judicial inquiry, rapidly convened in October of the same year, and to refrain from a direct judgement itself. Individual feminist writers, including many involved in social work, were mostly very clear that child sex abuse was a feminist issue, though not all of them saw it as essentially about fathers' power over their daughters, but no major new organizations or campaigns emerged around their analysis. Before attempting to describe and explain these responses more fully, a brief account of the way in which the issue emerged, the political conflicts it generated, and its presentation by the media will be necessary.

Within the women's movement, there had been a growing awareness of the prevalence of child sexual abuse since the late 1970s. In the context of consciousness-raising, women had gained the confidence to speak out about their own childhood experience. Following the conference organized by Women against Violence against Women in London in 1981, a number of women set up Incest Survivors to campaign for the recognition of incestuous abuse (incest was widely defined to include abuse by older people in positions of authority or trust) as a feminist issue, organize workshops, and encourage the formation of self-help groups.[1] A number of Incest Survivors groups were subsequently set up in different parts of the country.

Newly established rape crisis centres and women's refuges

[1] See letter to *Spare Rib* from Emily Driver, 'The Incest Survivors', Mar. 1982: 8.

found themselves dealing with survivors of past abuse. As the scale of the problem became clearer, specific initiatives were taken in response. For instance, from 1981 Strathclyde Rape Crisis Centre in Glasgow was increasingly approached by women who needed to talk about their own sexual abuse as children. With the help of Urban Aid funding, it established a women's support project in 1983. Initially, the project workers planned to encourage such women to make greater use of appropriate local services, but they soon realized that there were none. They knew that if they took on counselling work themselves, they would be swamped, and so they concentrated on 'development' work instead—that is, on developing awareness in the social services, by, for instance, offering training.[2]

The experience of the Glasgow Women's Support Project illustrates the way in which feminist activists found that they had not only to turn to government agencies for support, but to seek to change the attitudes and practice of those agencies themselves. Another illustration, particularly relevant to the Cleveland case, is provided in Tyneside, where, in 1983, Tyneside Rape Crisis Centre finally got agreement from the Northumbria police to set up a women police doctors' group specifically to deal with instances of rape. According to Bea Campbell,[3] it was almost immediately deluged with sexually abused children.

But there was also growing awareness of child sexual abuse within the social work profession. Back in 1973, the tragic case of Maria Colwell, beaten to death by her stepfather, had 'marked the beginning of child abuse . . . as a major object of social welfare mobilization'.[4] But resources had not been correspondingly expanded, and public concern grew with a succession of scandals, of which the latest were the cases of Jasmine Beckford and Tyra Henry in 1985. A focus on child abuse increasingly meant on child sexual abuse also. According to Parton, an important contributory factor was the growth of national concern about child sexual abuse in the United States in the late 1970s.[5] And this awareness was further facilitated by

[2] Patricia Bell and Jan Macleod, 'Bridging the Gap: Glasgow Women's Support Project', *Feminist Review*, 28 (1988).
[3] See Bea Campbell, *Unofficial Secrets* (Virago, London, 1988).
[4] Mary McIntosh, 'Introduction to an Issue: Family Secrets as Public Drama', *Feminist Review*, 28 (1988).
[5] Nigel Parton, *Governing the Family* (Macmillan, London, 1991), ch. 4.

the small but growing numbers of feminists going into social work by the early 1980s.[6] Then, in October 1986, BBC 1 broadcast its Childwatch programme, presented by Esther Rantzen, and ChildLine was launched.

So, the issue of child sexual abuse was inexorably emerging from the shadows by the 1980s, and in that sense, as Bea Campbell writes, what happened at Cleveland 'could have happened anywhere'.[7] What is more, even though it was not feminists who were directly responsible for bringing the issue on to the public agenda so dramatically in 1987, its emergence *was*, in a number of ways, due to the influence of the women's movement.

In 1986 Cleveland County declared child abuse to be a priority, and appointed Sue Richardson to direct work in this field. In January 1987 Dr Marietta Higgs was appointed consultant paediatrician at Middlesborough General Hospital. When examining specifically for sexual abuse, she employed a relatively new and controversial anal dilatation diagnosis of buggery. By June she had referred 110 cases of suspected child abuse.

This does seem a disturbingly high figure. Campbell tends to defend it, while Parton cites the finding of the subsequent report of inquiry, namely that the paediatricians' 'belief in the validity of the conclusions from the physical signs led them to overconfidence in the diagnosis' at a time when medical opinion was in fact acutely divided on this question.[8] There is also some question as to what forced the issue into public view. Campbell maintains that it was not the scale of referrals, but the conflict between the agencies involved—notably, between council child abuse officers and the police—over procedure.[9] But what is perhaps most significant for the present discussion is the way in which the issue was taken up and represented in the national press. Although it was not feminists who had brought the issue of child sex abuse on to the national political agenda in 1987, and although a feminist perspective was largely absent from the ensuing public debate, the more popular press tended neverthe-

---

[6] Mary MacLeod and Esther Saraga, 'Challenging the Orthodoxy: Towards a Feminist Theory and Practice', *Feminist Review*, 28 (1988).

[7] Campbell, *Unofficial Secrets*, 1.

[8] Cited by Parton, *Governing the Family*, 102.

[9] Campbell, *Unofficial Secrets*.

less to portray the Cleveland affair as a clash between obsessive, power-crazed feminists and defenders of normal family life.

Mica Nava[10] attributes this in part to a sense of 'moral panic', the need to make sense of this disturbing series of events. Two main contending teams were identified: the women, including most notably Dr Marietta Higgs and Sue Richardson; and the men, in particular the parents' 'champion', the Labour MP Stuart Bell, and the Cleveland police surgeon Alastair Irvine. Journalists went to great lengths to find details in support of their interpretation in Dr Higgs's background: the fact that she was foreign, that her parents separated when she was 2, that she was a working mother of five whose husband stayed at home to look after the children. She and Sue Richardson (who, from Bea Campbell's account, *does* appear to have been a feminist, having 'a long-time connection with socialist-feminism along the North-East coast'[11]) were associated, through their council-related work, with left-wing empire-building in local government. It was even discovered that Sue Richardson was married to a humanities lecturer at Teesside Polytechnic![12]

How did feminists respond to Cleveland? As Campbell notes, one question that seemed largely to be overlooked in the furore over Cleveland was why child sexual abuse occurs. A week before the report of the inquiry by Lord Justice Butler-Sloss was released, a feminist coalition of individual women and groups from different parts of the country (Feminists against Child Sexual Abuse) issued a press statement and briefing document deploring the absence of a feminist perspective from the public debate, which was itself in turn largely ignored.[13] Feminists, certainly Radical feminists, were clear that child sexual abuse was one aspect of male violence towards women and children. They emphasized that the great majority of perpetrators were men. Indeed, there was some tendency—and this was a general feature of public debate over Cleveland—to associate child sexual abuse with incest—that is, abuse within the family. Campbell herself referred to Cleveland as constituting the 'ultimate crisis of

[10] Mica Nava, 'Cleveland and the Press: Outrage and Anxiety in the Reporting of Abuse', *Feminist Review*, 28 (1988), 119.
[11] Campbell, *Unofficial Secrets*, 165.      [12] Nava, 'Cleveland and the Press'.
[13] See article by Liz Kelly, 'Talking about a Revolution', *Spare Rib*, Aug. 1988: 8–11.

patriarchy', when children blew the whistle on their abusing fathers. In a thoughtful article in *Feminist Review*, Liz Kelly, a Radical feminist employed in a child abuse research unit, pointed out the dangers of failing to distinguish carefully between child sex abuse and incest, as well as the need to recognize the different forms and degrees of abuse,[14] but such caution was rare.

Although, therefore, feminists did not generally query the high number of child sexual abuse diagnoses, they were critical of the way in which such abuse was explained and of the consequences of this for the form of state intervention. Some criticism was directed at the way in which social workers had been trained to understand child sexual abuse, focusing on the family as a system of relations rather than as a collection of individuals. Within this perspective, it was said, the mother came in for much of the blame. She encouraged abuse by being insufficiently receptive to her husband's sexual advances, by going out to work and leaving him at home, or by colluding more subtly, perhaps even through a psychological compulsion to see the re-enaction of her own sexual abuse as a child. The father (assuming again that child sexual abuse was essentially about incest) was thus somehow cleared of responsibility.[15] Some feminists critized the conduct of the social workers involved specifically in the Cleveland case, notably for separating children from their parents (and thus their homes) instead of simply removing their fathers.

But while these critiques were telling, not only was there no major national feminist campaign around the issue, but, as Campbell notes, there was little active local feminist support for Dr Higgs and her allies, or even intervention into the debate. Even women involved in Cleveland Rape Crisis Centre and the Cleveland Refuge and Aid for Women and Children felt unable to participate. One reason for this was that the arguments seemed to be dominated by the professional protagonists and to centre on procedural questions. Although the media presented both Higgs and Richardson as demented feminists, Dr Higgs certainly did not perceive herself as a feminist, and neither appears to have made any attempt to mobilize feminist opinion or

[14] Liz Kelly, 'What's in a Name? Defining Child Sexual Abuse', *Feminist Review*, 28 (1988).
[15] See Carol Ann Hooper, 'Getting him off the Hook', *Trouble and Strife*, 12 (Winter 1987); also MacLeod and Saraga, 'Challenging the Orthodoxy', 32.

support. But many local feminists also felt torn: some had friends directly affected by the referrals, others were concerned by the lack of support offered to mothers. In many cases, mothers themselves protested against the removal of their children and would not accept that there had been abuse. Should feminists deny what they were saying? Feminists who were also mothers wondered if it could happen to their children. In fact, one criticism that emerged more widely amongst feminists was that the children were separated from both their parents, rather than simply from their fathers.

Finally, compounding these misgivings, was feminists' traditional ambivalence, at best, towards the state. Could they really support social workers snatching children away from their mothers? Even those who urged the need for state intervention criticized its form and insensitivity.

Cleveland, then, brought out the contradictions in feminist approaches to the family and the state. It also demonstrated the strength and complexity of feelings centred around the issue of motherhood. Before we explore these questions further, we need to ask what it revealed about family policy under Mrs Thatcher.

According to Campbell, the Cleveland affair represented 'nothing less than a fundamental challenge to the familial politics of Thatcherism, which sought to restore the absolute autonomy and authority of the patriarchal family'.[16] We have already tried to argue—and, indeed, Campbell herself at other times suggests[17]—that familial politics under Thatcher cannot be defined so easily. Although it might seem that local state officials were ruthlessly invading family privacy and integrity in Cleveland, and despite Stuart Bell's appeal to the Health Minister, Tony Newton, the government's response was cautious, deferring judgement to the inquiry. The government had been made increasingly aware of the prevalence and seriousness of child abuse, and it was already committed to a systematic reappraisal of child care procedure, the roots of which went back to the previous administration. The White Paper that it issued at the beginning of 1987, *The Law on Child Care and Family Service*, which was to pave the way for the 1989 Children Act, actually urged on local

---

[16] Campbell, *Unofficial Secrets*, 162.
[17] See Bea Campbell, *The Iron Ladies* (Virago, London, 1987).

authorities a more active duty to investigate and intervene on suspicion of child abuse.

## FAMILY POLICY UNDER MRS THATCHER

As Chapter 2 has suggested, one needs to approach the characterization of family policy during these years with some caution. Many left-wing or feminist critics of Thatcherism have claimed that an emphasis on the 'traditional' family and its values has been central to its ideology and influential in social policy. 'Traditional' generally meant 'a nuclear family where the parents are married and *stay* married. The parents are clearly and firmly in control of their children: they exert strong discipline over their children when they get into trouble; they inculcate traditional moral values in their children—respect for elders, hard work, thrift and chastity.'[18] Thus, for instance, Coote et al.[19] maintain that, from the mid-1970s, the Conservative Party's approach to the family was based on three assumptions: that there was one true and natural family type, that the family was 'the main defence of individual freedom' against the menace of collectivism, and that it was the site of social, especially paternal, control. But as we have noted, until recently, the Labour Party leadership was not conspicuously more 'realistic' in its assumptions about the family. On the other hand, a considerable section of the Conservative Party did not entertain such illusions and were less concerned about paternal authority. In practice, moreover, policies—whether directly geared to the family or indirectly affecting it through economic measures, for instance—did little to shore up the traditional, patriarchal family. Indeed, it could be argued that by reducing state support, they made family life more difficult, although they also threw vulnerable individuals back on their families.

As we have seen, the importance of the family was a central Conservative Party theme in the run-up to the 1979 general election. Periodically thereafter, Mrs Thatcher and certain Cabinet

[18] Gillian Douglas, 'Family Law under the Thatcher Government', *Journal of Law and Society*, 17/4 (Winter 1990), 412.
[19] Anna Coote, Harriet Harman, and Patricia Hewitt, *The Family Way* (Institute for Public Policy Research, London, 1990).

members deplored the breakdown of traditional family values. More concretely, the Family Policy Group was set up in 1982 to advise the Cabinet, but its recommendations of measures to reinforce the traditional family form were not taken up after the 1983 general election. Concern about the growth of single-parent families was mounting by the end of the decade, eventuating in the 1991 Child Support Act, which sought to compel absent fathers to contribute to the upkeep of their children, but this legislation actually postdated Mrs Thatcher's 'abdication'. Moreover, as we have suggested, the decision to act seems to have reflected an unusual convergence between the moral conservatives and the neo-liberals. More precisely, the latter were becoming increasingly worried by the symptoms of urban disorder, most of all by the sheer cost to the Exchequer of supporting the 'non-traditional' family. A telling sign was when the notoriously free-market group, No Turning Back, argued in *The Next Ten Years* that the government should *not* be morally neutral towards the family. The authors declared themselves 'dismayed at the strain placed on the social services by the notion that voluntary single parenthood provides automatic entitlement to state support'.[20]

On the other hand, when the government actually formulated policies explicitly concerning the family, a much less dogmatic approach was generally evident. For instance, the Matrimonial and Family Proceedings Act of 1984 reduced the time-limit for a divorce from three years to one, a step widely criticized by Conservative back-benchers as weakening the marriage bond. The 1987 Family Law Reform Act aimed to eliminate the legal disadvantage associated with illegitimacy, again, as Gillian Douglas notes, 'hardly a return to Victorian values'.[21] But the outstanding example is the 1989 Children Act, which, of course, came in the wake of the Cleveland affair.

The very fact that this was a major piece of legislation in the area of family law appears to contradict the Thatcher government's supposed 'hands-off' approach to the family. But it was also widely recognized—not simply by the government's supporters, but by its ideological opponents, as well as by the various professional groups concerned, as being 'a major achievement,

---

[20] See Martin Durham, *Sex and Politics: The Family and Morality in the Thatcher Years* (Macmillan, London, 1991), 137.

[21] Douglas, 'Family Law', 418.

bringing together both the private law affecting the relationship between parents or other carers and children and the public law concerned with their welfare and protection, for the first time in one statute'.[22] While the Act's provisions ranged over many different aspects of the care of children and sought to satisfy a number of different criteria, a central concern was to strike the right balance between the rights and responsibilities of parents and those of the state. With memories of Cleveland still fresh, the debate in Parliament and the coverage by the popular press tended to focus on the need to protect the family from the interventions of overzealous social workers. But the legislation itself was more even-handed: it did strengthen the rights of parents in a context in which earlier legislation had left them very unclear, but at the same time it allowed state intervention, when deemed necessary, to be much more decisive. In arriving at this formulation, the government was guided not by 'Thatcherite' family rhetoric, but by the findings of successive committees of inquiry. The first of these was the inquiry set up in 1982 by the All-Party Social Services Committee of the House of Commons and chaired by Renee Short, but that reflected concerns and drew on findings from the mid-1970s onwards. In sum the government was guided by the recommendations of those professionally involved—the social workers, lawyers, police, and others. This is why, despite reservations about the likelihood of there being adequate resources to implement it properly, the legislation was so well received. Indeed, Parton[23] suggests that the government may have welcomed such a rare opportunity to pass legislation likely to command such widespread support.

The point here, then, is that, under Mrs Thatcher, 'family policy' was by no means as blindly concerned with shoring up the 'traditional' family and protecting it from state interference as some of its own rhetoric or the accusations of some of its critics might suggest. But, on the other hand, a whole battery of policies stemming from economic neo-liberalism *did* have considerable, and mainly adverse, implications for the family, or at least the working-class family. As Chapter 2 has described, policies associated with deregulation and attempts to reduce public bureaucracy and state expenditure meant less job security, reduced benefits,

---

[22] Douglas, 'Family Law', 418.
[23] This discussion draws heavily on Parton, *Governing the Family*.

increased homelessness, and cutbacks in various public services—all placing strains on family life. At the same time, the family became more essential for many, providing care, succour, or just a roof that could not be found elsewhere.

## FEMINISM AND AUTHORITY

Having outlined the perspective that informed family policy under the Thatcher governments, and so helped to shape the context of feminist perceptions and activities, we can turn now to a consideration of the change, or lack of change, in feminist attitudes to the family during those years. Feminism, almost by definition, implies some criticism of the family, at least in its present form. Though to differing degrees, feminists have always recognized the role of the 'private' family in the construction of the sexual division of labour and the perpetuation of unequal relations between men and women. They have pointed to the importance of 'conditioning', of childhood socialization, within the male-dominated family in teaching women their 'place'.

From the start, WLM feminists looked on the family as an oppressive, patriarchal institution. As Lynne Segal has pointed out,[24] this feminist critique of the family was influenced and preceded by a more general attack on the family by the radical Left in the 1960s. Marriage was denounced as 'bourgeois', and the prevalent nuclear family was depicted as repressive, stifling all spontaneity and fostering neuroses. 'Liberation' itself was, to a large extent, defined in terms of emancipation from this kind of family form. This gave rise simultaneously to a new kind of individualism and to the search for new forms of collective living. In the United States by the end of the 1960s, 10,000 communal households were listed in the census. Feminists absorbed many of these assumptions about the 'typical' nuclear family, although clearly, in so far as blame was to be apportioned for the tyranny of familial relations, feminists were less inclined to lay it on the all-controlling mother to be found in the influential work of R. D. Laing, and more inclined to look to the father.

---

[24] Lynne Segal, 'Smash the Family? Recalling the 1960s', in Lynne Segal (ed.), *What Is to Be Done about the Family?* (Penguin, Harmondsworth, 1983).

Though the general perception of the family was negative, therefore, one can detect some differences in the way in which this negative evaluation was expressed. The sociologist David Morgan, writing a decade ago, constructed a simple matrix of family policy orientations using two dimensions, attitudes to the family and attitudes to the state. He saw all feminists as opposed to the family, but he distinguished between those who opposed the state, whom he called 'libertarian' feminists, but amongst whom we should probably include Radical feminists, and the Socialist and Marxist feminists who supported state intervention in the family.[25] Drawing on this suggestion, we shall make a rough and ready distinction between Radical feminists, feminists emerging out of a 'libertarian' Left tradition, and feminists associated with the more organized Left.

In their personal lives—and there were exceptions—Radical feminists tended to reject the male–female partnership altogether. Their analysis concentrated on patriarchal power relations within the family, and especially, as time went by, on male violence within the family form. Initially suspicious of state intervention, they were eventually driven to seek it by the logic of their analysis of male violence. Amongst Socialist feminists, many of those on the libertarian wing became involved in experiments in communal forms of living, as an alternative to the conventional nuclear family. They looked primarily to collective, self-help solutions to problems like child care, rather than to the state.

Other Socialist feminists were more interested in analysing the relationship between women's domestic role and the economic system. This gave rise to the voluminous 'domestic labour debate', within which women sought to demonstrate, in increasingly ingenious ways, that this domestic labour, understood not simply as physical labour but as less tangible 'caring' services, was necessary for the reproduction of capitalism. By the early 1980s this line of argument was largely exhausted, however, and there was a growing acknowledgement that women's domestic role could not be accounted for satisfactorily in this way. But many of these Socialist feminists—and, of course, more 'liberal' feminists in general—while still critical of the traditional family, recognized that most women lived within one for at least some

[25] David Morgan, *The Family, Politics and Social Theory* (Routledge and Kegan Paul, London, 1985).

part of their lives, and were also concerned with the policy implications. One response was the Wages for Housework campaign,
but many Socialist feminists regarded this as a dangerous argument which could seem to condone the existing sexual division of
labour in the home and which also ignored the growth of
women's paid employment. A different tack was to campaign to
change taxation and social security arrangements so as to
increase the financial independence of married or co-habiting
women. This was the objective of the London Women's
Liberation Campaign for Legal and Financial Independence,
established in 1975 to pursue the 'fifth' demand of the movement,
legal and financial independence for women. It gave rise to the
YBA Wife? campaign launched in 1977. Another group, Rights
of Women, which still exists today, was formed by legal workers
and took up other aspects of matrimonial law.[26]

However, the point here is not to detail all the different campaigns centred around women's position within the family, but to
demonstrate that, while they drew differing consequences from it,
Radical and Socialist feminists in the 1970s were largely united in
their rejection of the traditional nuclear family. By the end of the
decade, this rejection often seemed to be virtually unthinking. An
important exception is the particularly eloquent and powerful
rendering of the feminist critique of the family to be found in
*The Anti-Social Family*, written by two Marxist feminists,
Michèle Barrett and Mary McIntosh, and first published in
1982.[27] As sociologists, the authors do recognize that the stereotype of the 'traditional' nuclear family conforms less and less to
reality. As such, their target is as much the ideology of the family,
or 'familism', as it is the family itself. None the less, they subject
the family to a series of devastating charges: it helps to perpetuate social inequalities by facilitating the transmission of material
and cultural advantages: it encourages individualism by focusing
loyalty on the family unit rather than on a wider collective: it
permits all kinds of physical and psychic abuse of the weaker
family members by the stronger under cover of privacy: and,

[26] See e.g. London Women's Liberation Campaign for Legal and Financial
Independence and Rights of Women, 'Disaggregation Now! Another Battle for
Women's Independence', *Feminist Review*, 2 (1979).
[27] Michèle Barrett and Mary McIntosh, *The Anti-Social Family* (Verso,
London, 1982).

finally, it embodies and maintains the sexual division of labour. The strong influence of the New Left critique is evident here. Although the final chapter does acknowledge that the existing family meets, or fails to meet, *real* needs for 'affection, security, intimacy, sexual love, parenthood', the conclusion is that alternative, more social means must be sought to satisfy these needs. Communal living is one option considered, but only one amongst others.

How have feminist attitudes towards the family changed subsequently? The bottom line must be that this very negative appraisal has not substantially shifted. By the late 1970s, the 'libertarian' feminist approach to the family was much less audible. Amongst Socialist feminists, there was less publicly voiced interest in reconstructing some kind of alternative or communal family which included adult males. But the negative overall approach persisted. And yet, since that time, feminist thinking about the family may have changed in more subtle ways. There is a greater awareness that feminism may not have got it quite right, that there is more to learn before arriving at a final verdict on the family, although the basic mistrust runs deep. Thus, despite its strong conclusions, *The Anti-Social Family* itself pointed to the need to acknowledge the diversity of family forms in the real contemporary world. But as it was coming into print, some Socialist feminists were expressing further reservations,[28] and these have grown. While the 'traditional' nuclear family is still perceived as a patriarchal institution, there has been greater recognition that it may have some positive features and that it is very difficult to devise a satisfactory substitute. This very cautious reassessment seems to reflect several developments.

One possible factor may be the growth, or revival, of feminist interest in motherhood, discussed below. Bound up with this, was the emergence of 'pro-woman' or 'cultural' feminism, originating in the United States but increasingly popularized over here, which emphasized women's special childbearing capacity and maternal, caring qualities.

In the United States, pro-woman thinking, although initially associated with Radical feminism, also fed into a more 'conservative', pro-family variant of feminism. According to Conover and

[28] See the contributions to Lynne Segal (ed.), *What Is to Be Done?*, esp. Wendy Clark, 'Home Thoughts from not so Far Away: A Personal Look at the Family'.

Gray,[29] this was in response to the strength of a New Christian Right, concerned above all to defend the traditional family against the threat of permissive values and of feminism. As the New Christian Right contributed to the defeat of the ERA, some feminists joined up with a section of the Left which was also anxious to refute the charge that it was out to destroy the family. Together they adopted a new pro-family position, standing for the family purged of its traditional objectionable features.[30] In the classic statement of this position, the 'revisionist' Betty Friedan urged her sisters to recognize in the family 'the symbol of that last area where one had any hope of control over one's destiny, of meeting one's most basic human needs, of nourishing that core of personhood threatened by the vast impersonal institutions and uncontrollable corporate and government bureaucracies'.[31]

In Britain, where the political forces championing the traditional family have been less threatening, no parallel pro-family feminism has emerged. None the less, it may be that a more positive image of motherhood and of the sheer experience of being a mother has brought greater awareness of the needs of children and of the parent–child unit. Perhaps one should say that it has made it easier for these to be discussed, since many feminists would protest that they have always known them to be important, but felt inhibited about talking about them.

And here we should remember that just because the moral ascendancy, as it were, of Radical feminism made it more difficult to raise questions, or at least to acknowledge and to talk constructively, about heterosexual relationships, this did not mean that all Socialist feminists (or even all Radical feminists) abandoned their existing male partners or failed to enter into new relationships with men. In practice, those who had children inevitably encountered questions about changing male attitudes, 'reforming' the family, and by remaining within these relationships, they implied in a sense that this was possible. It is in this context that feminist researchers Liz Stanley and Sue Wise

---

[29] Pamela Johnstone Conover and Virginia Gray, *Feminism and the New Right* (Praeger, New York, 1983).

[30] See the discussion of this question in Barbara Epstein and Kate Ellis, 'The Pro-Family Left', *Feminist Review*, 14 (1983).

[31] Betty Friedan, *The Second Stage* (Abacus, London, 1983), 229.

pointed to a growing gap between the oppressive 'family' in the abstract and 'my' family which was more acceptable.[32]

Another influence upon the reappraisal of the family may be growing disillusionment with the alternatives. We may speculate that some of those women who experimented with lesbian relationships for more or less political reasons found that, in the longer run, they needed relationships with men. Furthermore, by the early 1980s the commune movement was in decline. For their part, feminists had soon discovered the real difficulties in persuading men to share domestic and child caring responsibilities. Even more depressingly, some may have recognized their own ambivalence about surrendering control over young children. But it was not just that the commune was not necessarily the answer to the strains and isolation of motherhood. Wendy Clark pointed out how the very same feminists who 'loved to hate' the family trooped off to their parental homes at Christmas. What was it that these homes offered that their own communal or alternative arrangements could not? In a commune, there was a constant tension between the need for intimacy and security and the demand for personal freedom and 'open' relationships. But were these reconcilable? Was it possible, she asked, for these alternative households simultaneously to 'recreate "home" and leave behind "family"'[33]? For all its faults, the family may be psychologically and emotionally indispensable.

A further factor has been the growth of the black women's movement. Particularly in the early 1980s, black women were highly critical of white feminists' assumptions about the family. In one of the earliest formulations of this position, Hazel Carby[34] argued that white women failed to recognize the extent to which the family could provide black women with a shelter from, and a source of political resistance to, racism in British society. She also maintained that many of the features of black women's oppression that were attributed to their families were in fact the consequence of white racism—for instance, discouraging Asian girls from pursuing careers. Subsequent formulations have often

[32] Liz Stanley and Sue Wise, *Breaking Out* (Routledge and Kegan Paul, London, 1983).

[33] Clark, 'Home Thoughts', 175.

[34] Hazel Carby, 'White Woman Listen! Black Feminism and the Boundaries of Sisterhood', in Centre for Contemporary Cultural Studies, *The Empire Strikes Back* (Hutchinson, London, 1982).

been more cautious: for instance, Valerie Amos and Pratibha Parmar[35] conceded that 'many Black feminists would agree that the ideology of mother/wife roles is oppressive to women and that marriage only serves to reinforce and institutionalize that oppression.' But white women needed to recognize the extent to which they themselves had absorbed crude stereotypes—the passive Asian daughter and wife, the dominant Afro-Caribbean mother, exploited none the less in a sexist culture—and the ways in which these stereotypes supported racist practices. Again, there was the suggestion that, in certain situations, the family could be a source of strength for black women. In fact, black feminists themselves have not agreed on these matters: those involved in women's refuges and centres have been all too aware of how oppressive their own families can be, and of the dangers in allowing community leaders to silence women's protests in the name of denying fuel to racism.

Notwithstanding these internal disagreements, black women's criticisms may have had some impact on the wider women's movement. At the least, they have obliged white feminists, or the more honest ones, to admit that they had assumed, without actually investigating, black women's experience of the family. In so far as this implies a recognition that the family is not a single, unchanging institution, nor one whose significance stands divorced from its specific social and political context, it is another step towards a less dogmatic and dismissive approach.

But black women's arguments about the potentially positive aspects of the family may also have resonated with Socialist feminist concerns about the impact of Thatcherism in the 1980s, especially upon the lives of working-class women. Those Socialist feminists who recognized both that they were not faced with an imminent return to Victorian patriarchalism and that so many working-class women were struggling with the consequences of Thatcherite economic policies for their families must have felt increasingly uncomfortable with pat feminist accounts of the family, even if they were unclear about how to replace them.

Incidentally, the contrast between rhetoric and actual family policy under Thatcher also raised anew—for Socialist and

[35] In Valerie Amos and Pratibha Parmar, 'Challenging Imperial Feminism', *Feminist Review*, 17 (1984), 15.

Radical feminists alike—the thorny problem of the relationship between feminism and the 'state'. According to the crudest caricature, Thatcherism could have seemed to be synonymous with the ultimate, evil, patriarchal-capitalist state, but clearly things were not that simple. With the threat that Thatcherism posed to the 'Welfare State', Socialist feminists had, like the Left in general, increasingly registered the need to stop looking on the state as a monolithic structure dominated by a single, unified ruling interest, and to recognize the plurality of arenas and political forces that it contained (see Chapter 3). The fact that, even under Thatcher, family policy did not necessarily reinforce the traditional family seemed to confirm this perception.[36] But it also posed the question of what family policy Socialist feminists wanted. Radical feminists, on the other hand, were challenged to explain government policies that were not in the obvious interests of patriarchy and to decide their own position *vis-à-vis* those policies.

Going back, however, to the question of a feminist reappraisal of the family—that is to say, the family including an adult male—we must emphasize that its importance should not be exaggerated. Though there has been a growing theoretical interest in masculinity in its own right, not simply its consequences for women—for instance, Lynne Segal's new study, brought out in 1990, which suggests that men are redeemable, not beyond hope—this has not yet produced any major rehabilitation of men, either inside or outside the family.[37] And although there has been much talk about the 'new man', this has mostly been confined to newspapers and women's magazines, and we suspect that few women who consider themselves as feminists would give much credence to it. Despite the increased importance that feminists attach to motherhood and thus to the needs of children, in general, men's parenting potential continues to be viewed sceptically. Instead, feminists have continued to pin more hope on alternative family forms. In practice, this has largely meant support for single-mother families, a group whose size has grown steadily over the 1970s and 1980s.

[36] See Rosemary Pringle and Sophie Watson, 'Fathers, Brothers, Mates: The Fraternal State in Australia', in Sophie Watson (ed.), *Playing the State* (Verso, London, 1990).
[37] Lynne Segal, *Slow Motion: Changing Masculinities, Changing Men* (Virago, London, 1990).

Feminist support for lesbian families, it must be admitted, has tended to be more at the level of theory than of practice. In 1982 Rights of Women set up a lesbian custody subproject to advise in relevant cases. It received GLC funding for a room and a worker in the Featherstone Street building. As time went by, the number of cases increased, many of which were successful, although a favourable outcome is still by no means assured.[38] But although practical support was forthcoming from some feminist lawyers, by the late 1980s it was gay groups like OUTRAGE and Gay and Lesbian Rights Coalition which seemed to be most active on this issue. Not all feminists are prepared openly to champion the rights of lesbian families. Particularly where they are engaging with the state system, in local government or party politics, lesbian claims have often been sacrificed to other, more 'realistic' objectives. For instance, the discussion document *The Family Way*, drawn up by Anna Coote and others, was published just before the Labour Party conference in October 1990. It recognizes that 'Families are social, not natural, phenomena', and that the model of the middle-class Victorian family, with a breadwinning father married to a housewife mother with two or three children, is increasingly irrelevant.[39] However, Radical feminists have criticized this document for what it leaves out. While urging the need to work with families as they are rather than as some nostalgic ideal would have them, nowhere does it explicitly refer to the concerns of lesbian women as actual or potential parents.[40]

## MOTHERHOOD

It is sometimes suggested that feminists not only rejected the family in the 1970s, but motherhood itself. That view now seems to be mistaken: there have always been feminists for whom motherhood is one of the most central and potentially fulfilling of experiences. Even so, it was in the 1980s that motherhood really came into its own.

There is some disagreement about feminist attitudes to motherhood in the early days of the WLM. For many feminists, as the previous chapter has suggested in relation to the issue of

---

[38] See Helen Garlick, 'Sex and the Single Parent', the *Guardian*, 5 Dec. 1990.
[39] Coote *et al.*, *The Family Way*.
[40] See Jayne Egerton, 'The Family Way', *Trouble and Strife*, 20 (Spring 1991).

abortion, mothering was the quintessential experience of oppression. On the other hand, not only were young mothers a significant group amongst the founders of the movement, but many of them felt very positively about motherhood itself, if not about its social and political consequences.

At face value, it would certainly seem that the WLM as it emerged in the late 1960s and 1970s was centrally concerned with autonomy, and that, in this context, motherhood connoted the 'antithesis of liberation'.[41] The American Radical feminist Shulamith Firestone had written that 'the heart of women's oppression is her child bearing and child rearing role'. Being a mother meant losing control—specifically, of the conception, of the birth, and of the childrens' upbringing, but, in a broader sense, of oneself and of one's own life. The key mobilizing issue of the mid-1970s, abortion, was all about the right to choose not to have a child. One contributor to *Spare Rib*[42] noted that the reason why some women had children and others did not was almost a non-question in the women's movement. Sheila Rowbotham confirms this general picture when she describes many of the early members of the movement as young, housebound mothers who felt that they had been trapped by the popular fantasy of family love. But Rowbotham is keen to point out that 'It is not in fact true that in the early days of the women's liberation movement in Britain there was an outright rejection of motherhood.'[43] Although one of the sources of division in early women's groups was between women with children and those without, the mothers often acknowledged the pleasure that motherhood could bring. She cites an anonymous contributor to *Shrew* in 1970, who wrote: 'When I looked at the beautiful baby, so perfect, I thought very clearly, "This is the first time in my life when I've done something really *well*" . . . I felt the outside world could go and tie itself up in knots and I didn't care.'[44]

In similar vein, Lynne Segal writes: 'I know I was not alone in finding a new pride and pleasure in my own motherhood in those days.'[45]

[41] See Katherine Gieve, 'Rethinking Feminist Attitudes towards Mothering', *Feminist Review*, 25 (1987).
[42] See Anna Briggs, 'Why Children?', *Spare Rib*, Feb. 1981.
[43] Sheila Rowbotham, *The Past Is before us* (Penguin, Harmondsworth, 1990), 97.
[44] Ibid. 98–9.
[45] Lynne Segal, *Is the Future Female?* (Virago, London, 1987), 14.

Such an affirmation of the special joys of motherhood was still unusual—perhaps the general ethos of women's liberation inhibited its expression—until the 1980s. One reason for this change may be that many of the early WLM members, including some of the most articulate, who had not had children, began to feel more broody as they got older. Rowbotham herself cites Claire Duchen, writing of a similar development in France. 'Women have very different attitudes to motherhood when they are 20 and when they are 30.'[46] Liz Heron noted a 'latterday feminist baby boom' in which many feminists were 'melting into motherhood'.[47]

But this coincided with the growing influence of the 'pro-woman' perspective within Radical feminism, spilling over into other strands also. Originating largely in the United States, the pro-woman position, unlike earlier forms of Radical feminism, accepted that women were different from men, either essentially or because of their distinctive experiences, but it celebrated that difference and found within it an argument for women's *superiority*. Central to this pro-woman interpretation of women's nature was motherhood, not simply as an experience but as a capacity and an expectation, together with all the qualities associated with mothering—caring, empathy, intuition, creativity, affinity with nature and the earth. Such a view gave rise to a large and often highly romantic literature in the United States[48] which has been widely read and discussed amongst British feminists. It is actually quite difficult to find examples of an equivalent point of view in British feminist literature. One exception is the influential work of Dale Spender, an Australian, but one who has long been resident in this country and who tells us, for instance: 'for generation after generation women have tried to assert the feasibility of a human society in which procreation, nurturance, warmth, security and creativity are fostered.'[49] At the same time, similar ideas,

---

[46] Claire Duchen, *Feminism in France* (Routlege and Kegan Paul, London, 1986), 60.

[47] Elizabeth Heron, 'The Mystique of Motherhood', *Time Out*, 21–7 Nov. 1980.

[48] For a critical account, see Hester Eisenstein, *Contemporary Feminist Thought* (Unwin, London, 1984); Joan Cocks, 'Wordless Emotions: Some Critical Reflections on Radical Feminism', *Politics and Society*, 13 (1984); Segal, *Is the Future Female?*

[49] Cited by Segal, *Is the Future Female?*, 34.

but in a 'softened' form, were popularized through the 'women's pages' of newspapers, soap operas, and popular fiction.

They may have had an especial appeal not only because individual feminists were contemplating motherhood themselves, but because they emerged at a time when, as we have suggested, many feminists were turning away from public campaigning into a more private sphere and intimate relationships. Segal argues that this 'maternal revivalism' has in part come

from feminists' disappointment that our aspirations to engage in creative and rewarding work, to struggle for social change, to build warm and supporting communal spaces and friendship networks—as well as to choose to have children—have proved so often difficult, stressful or transitory. Decent work, committed politics and real community are not easy to find or sustain in the public world of a market economy.[50]

Chapter 7 has described how such changed attitudes to motherhood were reflected in developments in the feminist politics of health and reproductive rights. A major issue to emerge, for instance, was a woman's right to choose *how* to give birth. In 1986 a national campaign was mounted to support the London consultant, Wendy Savage, who insisted on this right when a disciplinary case was brought against her. Feminists involved in reproductive rights campaigning increasingly recognized a woman's right both to choose to *have* a baby and to choose *not to*. At the same time, many feminists feared that developments in reproductive technology would enable the male-dominated medical establishment to increase their control over women's reproductive capacities, while the women in FINRRAGE suspected a bid to exclude women entirely from the reproductive process.

The importance of women's special mothering and caring capacities was a theme that was taken up by women in the peace movement and in Green politics. It occurs, for instance, in two collections of writings by women who took part in the peace camp at Greenham. When they joined hands to surround the base, some believed that they could 'both contain the evil within the base and surround it with positive, healing energy . . . Our women's energy would make a difference to the military potency of the base.'[51] The recurrent use of the image of the web was

[50]  Cited by Segal, *Is the Future Female?*, 145.
[51]  Barbara Harford and Sarah Hopkins (eds.), *Greenham Common: Women at the Wire* (The Women's Press, London, 1984), 90.

meant to symbolize the ancient spider goddess, weaving together the web of life. One woman writes: 'I think that most women are really in touch with what life is about. You can't even contemplate having a child without considering the value of that life.'[52] (Having said this, it must be emphasized, contrary to what Segal tends to suggest, that what these collections really reveal is the tremendous range of views held by the women who took part in Greenham.)

It seems clear, then, that while feminists' attitude to the family changed only in subtle ways during the 1980s, a much more positive image of motherhood has emerged within feminist discourse. In many ways, this is to be welcomed. It must be a good thing that feminists have openly acknowledged the great happiness and love that motherhood can bring (one of the authors, who has only recently enjoyed this experience, feels this particularly strongly). It is also good that feminists have recognized the centrality of motherhood in a large part of most women's lives, if only so that analysis and strategy can take due account of this consideration. And yet, when we come to estimate the practical and political consequences of this reassessment for feminist activism, it is difficult to identify any significant contribution that it has made to the campaigns for maternity rights and, especially, child care. The irony is that the main thrust in these areas has come not from this pro-woman feminism, with its, on occasion, semi-mystical elevation of motherhood, but from feminists involved in the labour movement and in campaigns to secure equal employment opportunities.

It is difficult to be sure why this might be. One reason may simply be that this whole reappraisal of motherhood tended to be associated with a retreat from the public arena and from political campaigning. Some may also see a contradiction between asserting the importance of motherhood and simultaneously demanding the right to assistance with child care. And it is difficult to present child care as a 'radical' issue—in the sense of concerning women's fundamental physical and psychic integrity—in the way that, say, domestic violence or abortion could be perceived. Elevation of motherhood can fuel demands for women's right to

---

[52] Alice Cook and Gwyn Kirk (eds.), *Greenham Women Everywhere* (Pluto Press, London, 1983), 87.

choose how to give birth or a resistance to reproductive technology, and a sense of women's special mothering nature can feed
into campaigns about the survival of the planet, 'mother' earth,
but they do not translate so easily into the more mundane campaigns to make the lives of actual mothers more tolerable.

## FEMINISM AND MATERNITY RIGHTS

A consideration of campaigning in the area of maternity rights
will confirm this point. The only voluntary organization directly
concerned with the quality of the initial experience of motherhood as such, Maternity Alliance, was formed in 1980 not as a
result of any feminist initiative, but out of a campaign mounted
by the National Council for One-Parent Families, the Spastics
Society, and the Child Poverty Action Group to make the mater-
nity· grant, at that time only available to women with a national
insurance record, universal. When the policy was changed,
Maternity Alliance continued as an umbrella group focusing on
policies affecting maternal and child welfare from the period
prior to pregnancy to the end of the first year of life. As such, it
covered not only 'feminist' questions of maternity leave and pay
and women's right to return to work, but concerns like the
dietary requirements of pregnancy and ways of reducing infant
mortality. It could not, then, be described as an avowedly feminist organization, although many of both its presiding officers and
its paid workers have seen themselves as feminists.

  Otherwise, campaigns to defend and expand maternity rights
have mainly been part of the wider struggle for equal employment opportunities (see Chapter 6). In 1974 the Employment
Protection Act gave women a statutory right to paid maternity
leave, protection from unfair job dismissal during pregnancy, and
the right to return to their jobs up to twenty-nine weeks after the
birth. As Elizabeth Meehan describes,[53] there were various calls
in the late 1970s for improved maternity arrangements and provision of parental leave, and some modest achievements such as
the workplace agreements negotiated in Camden Borough
Council, Norfolk Capital Hotels, and *Time Out*. But the real

---

[53] Elizabeth Meehan, *Women's Rights at Work* (Macmillan, London, 1985).

stimulus came in the 1980s and was twofold. First, there were the new Conservative government's moves to cut back on existing employment protection. In 1980 the government had already limited the terms of the 1974 Act to women who had been in their present employment for the two years or more. Secondly, and perhaps more importantly, there was the growing realization that 'a sex equality policy which does not recognise that family and welfare are important components of women's opportunities is doomed to eventual failure.'[54]

Partly as a result of these pressures and, more recently, because of fears of future skills shortages (discussed below), there were some real gains in the area of maternity rights, though the government under Thatcher made no direct concessions. For instance, the civil service now provides maternity leave of up to fifty-two weeks to all women who have worked a minimum of fifteen hours a week for one year. This is with thirteen weeks' full pay, together with statutory maternity pay. It has also introduced the option of longer career breaks in a number of departments. Similar career-break schemes have been adopted in the private sector in the last couple of years, by Sainsbury's, the National Westminster Bank, British Petroleum, and Unilever.[55] Needless to say, these career-break schemes mainly apply to women in managerial positions.

## FEMINISM AND CHILD CARE

But we must now turn directly to the issue of child care. The emphasis that the following discussion places on various kinds of public provision is not intended to imply that, where relevant, fathers should not take on a fairer share of the care of their own children. Indeed, feminists have regularly made this point.

It was mainly in the context of communal forms of living that some early feminist articles envisaged the possibility of a new sexual division of domestic labour. Men would increasingly share in the housework and in child care. Mica Nava cites a feminist

[54] Joni Lovenduski, *Women and European Politics* (Harvester, Brighton, 1986), 259.
[55] The Hansard Society, *The Report of the Hansard Society Commission on Women at the Top* (HMSO, London, 1990).

critique of the influential writing of the child psychologist John Bowlby, famous for his theory of 'maternal deprivation', discussed below. The critique maintained that: 'If the undervaluation of women in society is to end, we must begin at the beginning, by a more equitable distribution of labour around the child-rearing function and the home.'[56] However, this point of view was criticized by other feminists, especially those associated with the more organized Left, as excessively 'personal' and, by implication, individualist and 'bourgeois'. How many women could afford these 'personal' solutions? What about working-class women who needed to go out to work to support their families? The state, or at least public institutions, should be made to take responsibility for child care provision.

As we have shown, a much greater emphasis on motherhood could be found in public feminist discourse in the 1980s, and yet this did not appear to feed significantly into child care campaigns. We suggested that this was because it was associated with the pro-woman perspective that grew out of Radical feminism. As Lynne Segal notes, many pro-woman feminists in the United States, as well as Luise Eichenbaum and Susie Orbach, who launched the feminist therapy movement in Britain in the 1970s, believe that the only way to overcome endemic male violence is to involve men more systematically in caring for children.[57] But again they seem to have in mind an essentially personal and private arrangement. At the same time, we have shown that, in this country at least, many feminists retain serious doubts about men as fathers, which could make this option unattractive. More fundamentally, how many women have an earning capacity high enough, and a partner obliging enough, to make this practical, delightful as it may sound?

We would argue that it is indeed vitally important to question the sexual division of labour within the home, and that, where relevant and feasible, men *should*, for both symbolic and practical reasons, share in child care. But the immense practical limitations to this option must be recognized, and it seems to us that any really serious examination of issues around motherhood must

[56] Mica Nava, 'From Utopian to Scientific Feminism? Early Feminist Critiques of the Family', in Segal (ed.), *What Is to Be Done?*
[57] See Luise Eichenbaum and Susie Orbach, *What Do Women Want?* (Fontana, Glasgow 1984)

point to the necessity for a massive quantitative and qualitative improvement in child care provision. Yet, as already emphasized, the pressures to improve child care provision have not emerged from a 'pro-woman' perspective, but from Socialist feminism and from women concerned with equality at work.

However, whilst maternity rights issues in the 1980s were mainly taken up within pre-existing equal opportunities net-works—trade unions, the EOC, local government women's com-mittees—the question of child care was not confined to these channels, but spawned its own campaigning organizations. It generated wide-ranging debate amongst feminist activists, though the terms of the debate shifted as the decade wore on. But, given all their efforts, and it must be said that their campaigns never really took off in a dramatic way or captured the public imagina-tion, feminists achieved disappointingly little in concrete terms over this period.

Child care provision in the United Kingdom has been scan-dalously inadequate. In 1985 there were 764 local authority and 999 voluntary and private nurseries, between them providing places for around 2 per cent of the under-5s. Comparisons with other European countries are complicated by the fact that the provision itself, the age-range to which it applies, and the age at which children begin school all vary, but the stark contrast is still apparent. In Denmark 44 per cent of children under 3 are in publicly funded child care services; in France and Belgium the figure is between 20 and 25 per cent; and even in Italy and Portugal it is 5 and 4 per cent respectively. Although the United Kingdom provides publicly funded child care services for around 44 per cent of children aged 3–4, that is, in the pre-school range, this is largely in the form of nursery education or primary school, for the under-5s, much of which is part-time. By contrast, the corresponding figure for Belgium and France is 95 per cent, and in Italy it is 88 per cent.[58]

Parents can, of course, make use of nannies, au pairs, or child-minders, if they can find them and afford them. By 1990 there were enough places for 5 per cent of the under-5s with registered child-minders. But child-minders are often exploited, isolated,

---

[58] These figures are mainly drawn from Coote et al., The Family Way.

and without support. Many local authorities felt compelled to save money in the 1980s by cutting back on training and support schemes. The new Children Act envisages closer regulation of child-minders—and nannies when they are looking after more than two lots of children—but it is unclear how the local authorities are to be expected to do this.

The implications for young mothers are demonstrated by employment statistics. Over the last decade, the rate of employment for women with children under 5 climbed steadily from 24 per cent in 1983 to 41 per cent by 1989. But the rate of full-time employment was only 12 per cent.[59] Within the EC, only The Netherlands has lower rates than these. Single mothers have suffered most from the inadequacy of child care provision. In 1988, only 6 per cent of single mothers with children under 5 were in full-time employment, the lowest rate in the EC.

Finally, provision for after-school and holiday care for children aged 5–9 is minimal. A survey conducted in 1989 by the Kids Club Network found that such schemes covered only 0.2 per cent of this age-range in term time and 0.3 per cent in the school holidays. Not surprisingly, rates of full-time employment for mothers of children in this age-range are the lowest in the EC after The Netherlands and Ireland.[60]

It is still not entirely clear to us why state child care provision should have been so grudging in this country. Although the Thatcher governments did very little of substance to rectify the situation, its roots go back a long way. Some accounts point to a British family policy tradition that exalts the family and seeks to protect it from interference. However, while this may be true in ideological terms, in practice it seems to us that the post-war state has increasingly, whether under Labour or Conservative administrations, been willing to intervene in the family on a whole series of grounds—social work, education, medicine. The EOC discussion paper *The Key to Real Choice*[61] argues that traditional assumptions about the family and the mother's role within it were powerfully reinforced by the publication in 1951 of John Bowlby's *Maternal Care and Mental Health*. In this book,

[59] OPCS figures cited in the *Guardian*, 31 Oct. 1990.
[60] Figures for the preceding discussion have been drawn from Bronwen Cohen, *Caring for Children* (Family Policy Studies Centre, Edinburgh, 1990).
[61] EOC, *The Key to Real Choice* (EOC, Manchester, 1990).

Bowlby insisted that it was essential for mental health that 'the infant and young child experience a warm, intimate and continuous relationship with his mother (or permanent mother substitute)'. Without it, the child would suffer from the crippling psychological effects of 'maternal deprivation'. According to Tizard,[62] Bowlby's thesis had a massive impact on the outlook of doctors, teachers, and social workers. But this cannot be the whole story. Bowlby's work is widely known on the Continent, but this has not resulted in the minimal provision of child care experienced in Britain. One further factor may be institutional: there is no government body to take an overview of child care. Nursery education is seen as an educational matter, but that means that no account is taken of the hours that children attend and of how these fit into working parents' schedules. Day care is the responsibility of social service departments, but, partly because provision is so limited, these have tended to confine access to those children with special needs. It is to overcome this kind of compartmentalization that the EOC has recently proposed the establishment of a national child care agency.

For their part, feminists in the movement's second wave have been aware of the importance of child care from the start. One of the four 'demands' formulated at the first WLM conference in Oxford in 1970 was for twenty-four-hour nurseries. Indeed, Rowbotham recalls that 'The contradictory situation of the mother with small children, expected to care and yet denied an environment in which this was possible was one of the factors that brought many women into the movement.'[63] But there have always been disagreements about the approach to follow. Although Radical feminists seem to have played little part, Socialist feminists were divided. One strand, which stemmed both from a more traditional, labour movement view of nurseries as a practical necessity for working-class women and, in some cases, from the urgent needs of young mothers themselves, looked to the state to expand day care provision. The other, with its roots in the libertarian Left, had a more 'prefigurative'—some might say Utopian—vision of collectively run, community-based nurseries, involving fathers as well as mothers and consciously

---

[62] Jack Tizard, *The Care of Young Children: Implications of Recent Research* (1986), cited by the EOC, *The Key to Real Choice*, 38.
[63] Rowbotham, *The Past Is before us*, 129.

instilling progressive values. One woman who identifies with this position suggested to us that many of these young mothers 'did not really want to think in terms of getting a job or pursuing a career'. They wanted to be full-time political activists, taking part-time work only as necessary. It was only towards the end of the decade, as economic survival became a more pressing concern, that they moved into regular occupations. Naturally, such women tended to mistrust state provision, fearing that these nurseries would be 'hotbeds of sexist ideology and authoritarian organisation'.[64]

Such disagreements were one reason why a sustained national campaign for child care failed to get off the ground in the 1970s. But there were a great number of more local initiatives, some of which fed into the developments of the 1980s. One of the earliest of these was the Dartmouth Park Children's Community Centre, opened by Camden Women's Group in 1972. Val Chorlton and the other women behind the scheme were 'exasperated by holding meetings for campaigns which never materialized and with a practical need for childcare'.[65] Others followed, like the one in Powis Square, and what became the Market Nursery in Hackney. At the same time, feminists associated with the Working Women's Charter set up a nursery action group as early as 1974 in anticipation of cuts in local authority provision. Out of this came the London Nursery Campaign, which in turn fed into the National Child Care Campaign of the 1980s. There were similar projects outside London, in such cities as Birmingham and Manchester.

So, one reason why child care campaigning became more conspicuous in the 1980s was that various developments of the late 1970s were coming together. There was also a greater sense of practical urgency. In its publicity, the National Child Care Campaign maintained that increasing pressure was being brought to make mothers stay at home. But, as Chapter 2 has suggested, there is little evidence for this. Rather, the effect of cut-backs in benefits and local authority services was to compel women to seek paid employment to supplement their income. At any rate, we have seen that the rate of employment of mothers with children under 5 grew during the 1980s. But these mothers were then

[64] Val Chorlton, quoted in Rowbotham, *The Past Is before us*, 132.
[65] Ibid. 134.

faced with the desperate scarcity of reasonably priced child care. Their concerns were slowly filtering through into the policy agendas of trade unions and, from the early 1980s, the new local women's committees.

The National Child Care Campaign (NCC) was launched in 1980.[66] Its declared object was 'to build a mass national child care campaign around the demand for comprehensive, flexible, free, democratically controlled child care facilities funded by the state'. The campaign saw itself as influencing government, particularly local government, and trade unions, and, as this statement indicates, it had inherited from the 1970s the assumption that child care services should be free, provided either directly by the state or through state-funded community schemes. Only reluctantly did the campaign include demands for workplace nurseries to supplement other provisions and for better conditions for child-minders.

Its policy statement, issued at the same time, also insisted that this was a feminist issue:

We believe that in the current political climate tremendous pressure is being exerted on women to make them feel they should remain at home and take the major responsibility for the care of their children. We would like to see a National Child Care Campaign that says loud and clear that women do work, need and want to work, and that child care facilities are absolutely necessary and central to women's equality.

Such a splendidly unequivocal declaration of women's rights is almost inconceivable twelve years on.

In formal constitutional terms at least, the campaign was governed by a steering committee, mostly women, but including one or two men, which was elected by local branches. The posts of chairperson and secretary were rotated. An attempt was made to avoid a London bias by holding meetings in different parts of the country. The campaign was established with the help of a launching grant from the EOC, which made it possible to employ one part-time worker. A further grant from the GLC in 1982 paid for another full-time worker. But the campaign was running short of funds. Latent tensions came to a head when the possibility of a huge, one-off grant arose (the original sum contemplated was

---

[66] The following discussion draws on several interviews and campaign documentation.

£500,000, though what finally came through was considerably less) as part of the 'Under-5s Initiative' launched in 1983 by Norman Fowler at the DHSS. As with the split in NAC (see Chapter 7), which occurred at about the same time and, still more bizarrely, in the same building, Wesley House, there were many different dimensions to this disagreement, some of which are difficult to unravel, but they were cumulative and eventually led to a fairly clean break.

One central problem seems to have been the different understandings that the two paid workers had of their jobs. One saw the NCC's role as developing awareness in government and unions through such means as conducting research, consultancy work, publicizing research findings, and holding conferences. The other saw her job more in terms of support for existing local campaigns. A second tension was organizational: how far the democratic structure needed to be modified in the interests of greater economy and effectiveness. A further conflict emerged over the short-lived employment of a further, black, paid worker. One side argued that she was grossly incompetent; the other replied with charges of racism. The last straw was the DHSS grant; to those who broke away, this represented a final commitment to the élitist, research-oriented, managerial path.

In 1985 the breakaways, who included half the NCC's founding members, formed the London Child Care Network, which was a much looser organization; it got some limited funding and persisted until 1988. Some of them also became involved in the Workplace Nurseries Campaign (discussed below). The DHSS grant meant that the NCC could expand, but it also changed considerably in character during the decade. In 1986 members of its collective constituted themselves as a charitable organization, the Day Care Trust, while the NCC persisted as a voluntary body. The Day Care Trust succeeded in obtaining funding, primarily from the London Borough Grants Scheme, and by 1990 it had three full-time workers. Their role has been to provide information and advice about child care provision to parents, employers, and other interested groups. At the same time, the outlook of the NCC/Day Care Trust has altered. As one of the women working there pointed out to us, they would never now present child care claims in terms of sex equality, or demand that it should be free, and they had long since shed misgivings about private provision by employers.

From the start, the NCC saw one of its central roles as advising local authorities. It developed many links with the new Labour administration under Ken Livingstone at the GLC, including, as we saw, receiving funding for a second paid worker. But the GLC was to become a major initiator in the field of child care itself. There were two main channels. The women's committee, set up in 1982 with a multimillion budget, saw child care as one of its most important concerns. It gave funding to existing child care centres. For instance, one of those involved in the Market Nursery in Hackney recalls that it meant that the nursery could employ a special needs worker. Pay and conditions for workers in the voluntary sector could be brought up to the level of the public sector. It also set up new child care centres. By 1984–5 the women's committee support unit was providing 140 grants to child care organizations, and funding over 11,000 full- and part-time child care places. It accounted for over 12 per cent of all full-time child care places in London.

This was a massive contribution, unrivalled before or since, but under the influence of feminists like Sheila Rowbotham, child care was also seen as an integral part of the new London industrial strategy. These Socialist feminists argued strongly that child care should not be seen purely in the context of the 'domestic economy', but as intrinsic to the local economy as a whole. This was part of an even more fundamental questioning of the *purpose* of the economy (Anna Coote was raising similar issues in relation to the national Labour Party's new 'Alternative Economic Strategy'). At the GLC, feminists found that even if their arguments were not always well understood, they were, as one of them said, 'pushing at an open door'. Child care questions were regularly addressed in popular surveys, exhibitions, and the newsletter of the Popular Planning Unit, *Jobs for a Change*. More tangibly, this unit was authorized to award grants of up to £750 to local child care campaigns.

In addition to all this, the GLC provided two day nurseries for its employees, with the alternative of financial assistance for child-minders.[67] Hearing about it now, this all sounds like a kind of paradise for women workers—and, indeed, for all mothers.

[67] These and preceding figures are taken from the GLC, *Annual Report, 1984/5* (GLC, London, 1985).

Those involved, whether in the women's committee support unit or the Popular Planning Unit, obviously found it a tremendously exciting time. All the projects that they had been discussing for so many years, whether in child care campaigns or as public sector workers, now seemed possible. As one interviewee put it: 'The bureaucracy was there to help not hinder.' Many worked incredibly long hours because there was so much to do. Now they look back nostalgically. Of course, all was not sweetness and light. There were inevitable tensions between the women's committee and the people in the industry and employment programme area. Doubtless, personalities and bureaucratic empire-building played their part. There were also arguments about quality versus quantity; in particular, child care planners in the women's committee support unit may not always have approved of the campaigns that the Popular Planning Unit was helping to finance.

But, much more distressing than any conflicts during the heyday of the GLC's child care initiatives was the sequel when the GLC was abolished. The London Strategic Policy Unit which was set up in its wake had only limited funding, and did not continue to include child care in strategic planning. Some existing schemes folded, but many were devolved either to the London Borough Grants Scheme or to individual London boroughs. In the long term, however while there does not seem to have been any systematic monitoring of these projects, it looks increasingly likely that they have had to compete with one another for scarce resources, and many have died out.

Although the GLC was the outstanding instance and pioneer of local government support for the expansion and improvement of child care provision in the early 1980s, some other local authorities followed its example, notably in Manchester, Leeds, and Newcastle. In Manchester, for instance, following the election of a left-wing Labour council in 1984, the new women's committee held several consultation meetings in different parts of the city to find out what local women really wanted. The three issues raised most regularly were education (women returning to further education or training), child care, and street lighting. Accordingly, the committee reviewed current child care provision. There had been no expansion of day nurseries for nearly ten years. Existing places, moreover, were allocated by social services to children in special need. The result of this review was a decision to build five (initially) new, strategically located, specially designed 'children's centres'. They were to provide not only day care, but care for children before and after school as well as rooms that could be used by the local child-minders' group and local playgroups. Access to child care was to be open to all residents in the relevant catchment area rather than being restricted to particular categories of children. Although funded and staffed entirely by the local authority, it was hoped that these centres would involve parents and other local community figures on their management committees.

Following the 1987 general election, capital programmes, including that for child care, were cut back. Although the existing centres have not been threatened so far, only one new centre has been completed since then. Moreover, while child care was initially provided free, it has gradually become necessary to adopt a sliding scale of fees, though most parents still do not have to pay. Another recently introduced scheme, one that not all those involved in the child care programme feel entirely happy about, allows local businesses to buy places for their employees. This has the advantage of bringing money into the centres, but obviously it reduces the number of places available for other children.

So, although there were some major achievements at a local level, the general climate of the mid-1980s was not conducive to campaigning for child care—indeed, for any campaigns of a 'redistributory' nature. As one activist told us: 'People now don't realise how tough it was in the mid-80s to campaign for child care. It was hard just to get a small item in the newspapers. There was a general resistance to public spending.' And yet, new campaigning bodies emerged, reflecting perhaps the continuing urgency of working mothers' needs.

The Workplace Nurseries Campaign (WNC) was formed in 1985. The immediate trigger was the announcement by the Inland Revenue in 1984 that employer subsidies to workplace nurseries would be taxed. This led some of those who were still in the NCC, but who were to form part of the breakaway group in 1985, to set up the WNC, informally at first and based in the NCC office. After the split, the campaign was set up officially as a separate organization. We have seen that while the NCC did include a reference to workplace nurseries in its initial statement of aims, many of its members accepted this reluctantly, believing instead in the need for *community* child care provision. Those who went on to found the WNC, however, argued for a *mixed economy* of child care. Many had close links with trade unions. They saw the WNC as primarily a lobbying body, one that should put pressure initially on those institutions, trade unions, and political parties most likely to be sympathetic. The specific campaign objective, the removal of the workplace nursery tax, was only achieved a long time later, in 1990. Increasingly, however, this objective was recognized as largely symbolic: the real purpose was to bring pressure on employers to establish workplace nurseries. That purpose has persisted, but, interestingly, in the last couple of years it has been modified once more. Now, partly in reaction to the government's continuing refusal to take on responsibility for child care itself, despite the demographic time bomb arguments, the WNC is emphasizing that employers will not, and cannot, make adequate provision without proper state support.

We have seen that one of the issues underlying the rift in the NCC was a debate about the way in which the campaign should be organized. There were tensions between the more participatory and decentralizing tendencies and the drive for economy and efficiency. This conflict reflected a more general problem for all feminist campaigning organizations: how to reconcile the participatory model which had been the hallmark of the early WLM with the practical requirements of working with, and persuading, more traditional and hierarchically structured political institutions such as parties, unions, and local authorities. These pressures were particularly acute in the 1980s as political lobbying became more 'professional' and business-like.

In contrast to the NCC, the WNC was, from its formal inception in 1985, much more conventionally and hierarchically organized. Although it had some individual members, its membership consisted chiefly of organizations, totalling around 200 by 1990, many of which were trade unions or local union branches. It was run by a management committee, large to begin with but smaller as time went on, with a chairperson. Initially, the GLC funded one paid worker, then the London Borough Grants Scheme paid for two. By 1990 it had the equivalent of four full-time workers, one of whom, Delyth Morgan, was designated chief executive, and two freelance consultants.

A rather different organization set up to campaign for child care at around the same time was the Working Mothers' Association. Significantly, this body did not originate with public sector workers or voluntary workers in the child care field, but with young mothers sharing experiences in a local branch of the National Childbirth Trust. The trust is a relatively old organization, and by the 1980s inevitable differences were emerging between older and younger members, most pertinently on the question of mothers going out to work. Members of the Clapham branch were generally receptive to the problems of working mothers, and one of their number, a social worker, used the national organization's newsletter to invite women facing these problems to come to a meeting. There was an enthusiastic response: some of those who came to the meeting helped to produce a handbook for working mothers, but other women responded by asking how to set up similar groups in their own area. At this point, one of the early members, Lucy Daniels, formerly employed in electronics until the birth of her second child, suggested a funding strategy that would enable them to set up a national organization.

After a lengthy process of research and consultation with local branches, this new organization put together a charter which covered a wide range of issues of relevance to working mothers, but the central issue remained child care. However, the question of childcare was approached primarily from the perspective of the mother as 'consumer'. The association wanted mothers, or parents, to have access to child care that was readily available and that provided a choice of services. It was not directly concerned about the possible exploitation of child-minders, and it certainly had no expectation that child care should be free. Not surprisingly, members of the NCC and even of the WNC have tended to perceive the Working Mothers' Association as élitist, catering for women who are already advantaged. As confirmation, they point to the association's campaign to have the cost of child care deducted before assessment of individual liability for income tax. This is only an issue, they maintain, for wealthier women; it has no relevance for the 5 million women whose income in 1988–9 fell below the tax threshold.

None the less, the emergence of the association represents an interesting development. Assisted by recent shifts in government and employers' attitudes (to be discussed shortly), it has mush-roomed, and by 1991 it had around 145 local branches or con-tacts and 120 corporate members. Initially, there were the familiar feminist reservations about 'male' organizational struc-tures, but gradually association members came round to more formal procedures, including decisions by majority vote. The association holds an annual general meeting, which is also a con-ference with workshop sessions, and is open to all members. This in turn elects an executive committee of about ten members. The association faces the perennial problem of all local membership organizations of balancing requirements of economy with the need not to seem too London-orientated. It employs one full-time and two part-time workers. Much of their work is answer-ing enquiries, estimated at around 7,000 a year, but the association also lobbies central and local governments.

As we have emphasized, the burgeoning child care campaigns of the 1980s were struggling against a most inhospitable political climate by the middle years of the decade. But in the last two or three years there has been a remarkable change. A report by the National Economic Development Council (NEDC), published in December 1988, referred to the anticipated impact of a falling number of school-leavers on the job market. The numbers of school-leavers are expected to drop by nearly one-third by 1993, and then to rise in the second half of the 1990s, though never to the level of the early 1980s. This was the so-called 'demographic time bomb'. The implications of this were that government and employers would have to take much more active steps to per-suade mothers of young children, especially those with badly needed skills, to come back into the paid workforce. Logically, this had to mean better child care provision. As John Patten, chairman of the ministerial group on women's issues, himself declared: 'The 1990s, unlike the 1960s, will be a decade in which childcare becomes a substantial part of the pay package.'[68] Employers also showed more interest. Early in 1988 the Midland Bank had approached the Workplace Nurseries Campaign for guidance in setting up nurseries for their employees' children, and, following the NEDC report, such enquiries multiplied.

One attempt to exploit this more favourable outlook met with

[68] The *Guardian*, 2 Jan. 1989.

only limited success. In 1988 Bronwen Cohen published a report for the Child Care Network of the European Commission, *Caring for Children*, which highlighted and detailed the woeful inadequacy of child care provision in Britain as compared with other European countries. Taken in conjunction with the NEDC report, this seemed to offer a valuable basis for an effective short-term campaign. Jenny Williams had worked as a project manager for the GLC Women's Committee. She was reponsible for purchasing and managing Wesley House, where the NCC, two other nurseries, and the Association of Under-Fives Advisers were all situated. Subsequently, she worked for Camden, which took on responsibility for Wesley House. She had therefore remained in touch with many of the child care campaigning bodies and issues, and saw a campaign around the Cohen report as a chance to overcome their divisions over principles and the competition for resources. The idea was to maximize publicity for the report's findings and recommendations. But although the campaign, which called itself Child Care Now!, produced a film and mounted a rally in October 1989, the overall impact was disappointing. In part, this simply reflected the way in which campaigning had changed over the decade. Now, as we have seen, much greater resources—professional skills, glossy presentations—had to be used to impress and interest the media; it was much harder to get grass-roots supporters out on to the streets, and there was no certainty that the media would cover the event in any case.

But if Child Care Now! failed to ignite, the established organizations, the NCC, WNC, and the Working Mothers' Association, have all flourished in the more propitious, post-NEDC environment. The issue of child care has also assumed a higher position on the agenda of both the trade unions and the EOC. Thus the TGWU, the largest of the unions, has a long tradition of local involvement in child care campaigns. Many public sector child care workers have been in the TGWU. In the 1980s the union launched its 'Link-Up' drive to recruit women workers and part-time workers (often the same). They were particularly affected by the inadequacy of child care provision, so this became one of the union's campaigning issues. However, it was not taken up in actual negotiations with local employers. Very recently, that has begun to change. The TGWU Equality Office produced a negotiator's guide, based on agreements that had already been concluded, and this has been widely circulated both within and outside the union.

The EOC produced its discussion paper, *The Key to Real Choice*, in 1990. This provides a very strong and informed argument in defence of expanded child care provision, within which employers, the voluntary sector, and local and central government must all play a role. Most specifically, it recommends the setting-up of an independent agency, the National Child Care Development Agency, under the Department of Education and Science, to develop national policy, administer a development fund, set standards and monitor child care services, run training programmes for child care workers, and promote relevant research. The various child care organizations, the EOC, and trade unions now consult one another more regularly. For instance, the TGWU organized a conference on equality and child care in 1989, which was attended by representatives of the EOC, the voluntary organizations, and local community groups. An increasingly well-informed, confident, and integrated network of child care activists seems to be emerging.

Such pressures seemed to have some effect in highlighting the issue of child care during the 1992 general election campaign. Indeed, a number of newspaper articles predicted that it would be crucial.[69] The Labour Party committed itself to nursery education for all under-5s, and £50m. towards an additional 50,000 child-care places. The Liberal Democrats declared that they would establish a national child care agency and a system of tax-free child care vouchers. Even the Conservatives pledged the provision of after-school and holiday schemes. It must be said, however, that these issues failed to acquire the pivotal position predicted for them in the last few weeks of the election. The outcome seems to have been determined by quite different concerns.

After the general election, Gillian Shepherd was appointed as Minister of Employment with special responsibility for women's issues. Unlike Angela Rumbold, nominally responsible for women's issues in the pre-election Home Office, she appears genuinely concerned to promote equal opportunities for women and,

---

[69] See e.g. the *Guardian*, 18 Jan. 1992: 'Childcare looks set to become one of the crucial election issues.'

in that context, to improve child care provision. She has rapidly moved forward proposals for a national network of after-school clubs and holiday schemes. These are to be run through the Training and Enterprise Councils (TECs), with funding provided by employers.

And yet it is difficult to be sanguine about the long-term prospects. The real obstacle here is not those continuing hostile Conservative voices warning that child care provision will damage children and destroy family life, but the government's extreme reluctance, not noticeably modified under John Major, to spend money. Even the new after-school and holiday schemes are to be largely dependent on private funding. However dramatic the predictions of the 'demographic time bomb', the fact is that we are bogged down in a serious economic recession, and employers' willingness to collaborate in such schemes is likely to be limited. As one employers' representative is reported as saying: 'The recession has knocked the teeth out of the less adventurous and committed companies.'[70]

Overall, then, the impact of feminist campaigning on child care in the 1980s has been disappointing. There have been several national campaigns which have persisted in some shape or form even through the bleak years of the mid-decade, but to little tangible effect. A principal reason for this failure must be the attitude of the government, and especially its resistance to any new claims on public expenditure. But can the women's movement itself be exonerated from all responsibility? Despite the central importance of the question of child care in any analysis of women's oppression and women's liberation, it has failed to arouse the movement-wide enthusiasm and energy of issues like abortion or rape. (Suzanne Franway's study of child care in Australia provides an interesting parallel. There also, 'child care has failed to arouse . . . passion or widespread attention. Child care is properly provided at feminist conferences but rarely features as a central topic on the agenda.'[71]) Radical feminism, even in its pro-woman form which emphasizes the importance of motherhood, has not really taken up the issue of child care. But there may also be apathy or inaction in other quarters. Women

[70] Ibid. 26 Feb. 1992.
[71] Suzanne Franzway, 'Childcare', in Suzanne Franzway, Dianne Court, and R. W. Connell (eds.), *Staking a Claim* (Polity Press, Cambridge, 1989), 59.

without children may not see it as an issue for all women. High-earning women with small children may have no difficulty in arriving at private solutions, while other women with small children may be too overwhelmed by domestic and work pressures to become involved in public campaigns.

In the 1970s, feminists, whether Radical or Socialist, viewed the conventional 'family', including an adult male, in largely negative terms, as a primary source of women's oppression. Those influenced by 'libertarian' thinking did explore alternative, communal ways of living with men, though the increasing moral ascendancy of Radical and, most specifically, of political lesbian feminism made this less and less ideologically acceptable. Though many individual feminists felt much more positive about motherhood, the growing influence of Radical feminism also came to inhibit acknowledgement of these feelings. Child care was always recognized in principle to be an important issue, constituting one of the four initial demands of the WLM, but though numerous local campaigns were mounted, there was no movement-wide sense of urgency. Disagreements were rife about the form that child care should take, and a national campaign was relatively slow to emerge.

The 1980s saw changes in feminist attitudes in all these areas. But the changes have not really resolved the confusions or inconsistencies in feminist approaches to motherhood, the family, and the state. For a complex of reasons, including the nature of governmental family policy, Socialist feminists began to reconsider their sweeping dismissal of the family as such, but this reappraisal never approached the scale of that taking place amongst feminists on the Left in the United States. There was also greater willingness within the WLM to contemplate working with, and within, the state. Yet the limits of both these developments were apparent in the feminist response to Cleveland. Cleveland also reflected the shift in feminist thinking about motherhood. As a feminist 'baby boom' coincided with pro-woman ideas infiltrating from the United States, it became much more acceptable to celebrate the joys of motherhood and women's special maternal qualities.

But while this 'maternal revival' fed into a number of policy areas—reproductive rights, peace, ecology—it did not extend into those areas most directly affecting mothers, that is, maternity rights and child care. Instead, these issues were taken up through other—union and equal employment rights—networks. At last a series of groups campaigning at a national level for child care provision emerged. Though their objectives were steadily 'toned down' over the decade, reflecting the political and economic climate, the discovery of the 'demographic time bomb' seemed to augur a much more favourable reception for their arguments. But still the child care issue failed to ignite mass feminist action, and, despite the advent of a new Conservative leadership, the government's continuing reluctance to spend money, together with prolonged economic recession, have served so far to inhibit any significant tangible results.

# 9

# Feminism, Violence, and Men

BRITISH women report a fear of violence three times as great as men, yet official statistics show that the risk of violent crime is higher for men.[1] This is often interpreted as evidence that women are oversensitive to crime and have unfounded fears; it contributes to women's vulnerable image. But if we take into account the spectrum of abuse that women receive and how often the violence is committed by people who are known to their victim, and thus goes unreported, women's fear may well be a legitimate response in a society in which male violence is often unchallenged and frequently condoned.

When the demand for freedom from male sexual violence split the British WLM in 1978, it was entangled with the debate about separatism. Arguments about women's right to determine their sexuality and about whether feminists should interact with established (male) power structures were conflated with arguments about the relationship between maleness and violence. At the heart of the split, was a division over whether violence is a universal attribute of men which is crucial to their domination of women, or whether that violence was, like the domination of women by men, an effect, albeit a complex and mediated one, of capitalist society. Feminist analyses of the significance of male violence to women range from Sheila Jeffreys's view that the former was the case, to those Socialist feminists who took the latter view. On issues of male violence, the strength of feeling that attends the split in feminism waxes and wanes, but the disagreement continues. Over the years, the arguments on each side have become more sophisticated, more nuanced, more knowing, and, at the level of theory, the positions have become more entrenched.

[1] NALGWC, *Responding with Authority: Local Authority Initiatives to Counter Violence against Women* (Pankhurst Press, Manchester, 1990).

At the level of practice, there was an apparent division of labour between feminists in the years immediately following the split. Revolutionary and Radical feminists concentrated an increasing amount of their energies on issues that were defined in terms of male sexual violence. Domestic violence and, later, rape and pornography were the focus of their activity and thought. Socialist feminists were preoccupied with other issues, namely, their work in the Labour Party, in the trade unions, and around the miners' strike of 1984–5. In some localities this amounted to no more than a difference of emphasis, whilst in others activities were quite sharply separated. Many feminists engaged in a range of campaigns that were determined as much by what was an issue in their locality as by theoretical disputes between feminist intellectuals. Despite a growing interest in psychoanalytic thought during the 1980s, which brought Socialist feminists into debates about sexuality and sexual difference and into a resulting coincidence of preoccupations, the two sides did not come any closer together. It is fair to say that, for most of the decade, Radical feminism had the political initiative in the task of theorizing male sexual violence. Only at the end of the 1980s, when large-scale campaigns to censor pornography began to gather strength and influence throughout the movement, did many Socialist feminists begin to think and argue and, most importantly, to organize politically about masculinity and its connections with sexual violence.[2]

To the extent that feminists wished to win the hearts and minds of ordinary British women, to the extent that the feminist project develops through a process of gaining political support for its definitions and issues, Socialist feminists were at a disadvantage. Policies to control violence were popular; issues about male sexual violence struck a responsive chord in the many women who have first-hand experience of it. Thus, the problem of male sexual violence was successfully maintained on the feminist agenda of the 1980s by Radical feminists. But Socialists were suspicious of these initiatives, not least because such policies were

[2] Accounts of the movement by Rowbotham and Coote and Pattullo which were published in 1990 barely mentioned the issue. Lynne Segal's books, *Is the Future Female?* (Virago, London, 1987), and *Slow Motion: Changing Masculinities, Changing Men* (Virago, London, 1990), were amongst the first in Britain to offer analyses and critiques of feminist preoccupations with male sexual violence.

easily hijacked by law and order lobbies, they could easily become part of the arsenal of the extreme Right. An important feature of debate at the beginning of the 1990s, therefore, is the extent to which co-operation with the political Right is possible or wise.

Understanding male sexual violence draws on key dimensions of feminist thought. It involves conceptualizing the relationship of sexuality to power. Because policy-making institutions and agencies of law enforcement are implicated, it raises issues about the state and how to relate to it. Because women experience violence in different circumstances and in different ways, it raises questions about the differences between women, and requires a thoroughgoing critique of tendencies towards universalism and essentialism in Radical feminist thought. In this chapter we shall look in detail at four of the issues which feminists have defined in terms of male sexual violence: wife battery or 'domestic' violence, rape, sexual harassment, and pornography. A fifth issue—child sexual abuse—was dealt with in Chapter 8. Of the five issues under scrutiny, four would not be on the political agenda had feminists not become interested in them.

We describe two different kinds of politics here. The first is an issue-based politics in which, although definitions were contested, basic agreement among feminists was rapidly established. The issues of domestic violence, rape, and sexual harassment have generated a politics that focuses on the practical work of institution-building, resource allocation, and networking as solutions were sought to important problems. But the politics of pornography continues to be a politics of contested definitions in which feminists compete with each other and with other established political actors to determine the nature of the issue. The accounts that follow are accounts of feminists identifying problems, struggling to establish feminist definitions of these problems, and devising solutions for them. The various demonstrations, campaigns, lobbies, organizations, arguments, strategies, theories, and other interventions that are included are examples of feminist practice at the grass roots of politics and in a number of state arenas.

## DOMESTIC VIOLENCE, FEMINISM, AND THE WOMEN'S REFUGE MOVEMENT

Women's Aid is unusual in contemporary feminism in that it has sustained an organization at national level since 1975. In virtually all other cases, autonomous feminist organization is local, community-based, with communication a matter of informal networking. Women's Aid's organizational continuity is possible because the federation is extremely loosely constructed, and local organizations have considerable autonomy. Members have identified clear advantages in having a national office which is able to act as an information exchange and to lobby national government.

The women's refuge movement was very much an initiative of the WLM of the 1970s. The problem of male violence to women in the home became an early concern of the second wave of feminism. The sheer scale of domestic assault shocked the women who became interested in the issue. Knowledge about male violence to their partners grew as women shared experiences in consciousness-raising groups, and the first refuges were established either in women's centres or by squatting in suitable property. Erin Pizzey's refuge at Chiswick (actually the second refuge to be set up in London) received widespread publicity in the national media, and the issue of 'wife abuse' found its way on to the political agenda. By 1977 there were nearly 200 refuges in the United Kingdom. In 1990 there were almost that many in England alone. After considerable discussion at the WLM conference in Manchester in 1975, a national co-ordinating body, the National Women's Aid Federation, was established. This was a federation of refuges which accepted five basic working principles and demands. These aims illustrate the dual concern of Women's Aid: to offer a service to battered women, and to campaign for policies to protect women. They also embody feminist principles of self-help, a 'woman-centred' understanding of domestic violence, and a feminist understanding of the social structure. The aims are:

1. To provide temporary refuge on request for battered women and their children.
2. To encourage these women to determine their own futures and to help them achieve this, whether it involves returning home or starting a new life elsewhere.

3. To recognize and care for the educational and emotional needs of the children involved.
4. To offer support and after-care to any women and children who have left the refuge.
5. To educate and inform the public, the police, the courts, the social services, and other authorities with respect to the battering of women, mindful of the fact that this is a result of the general position of women in our society.[3]

The title was deliberately chosen to avoid a reference to the domestic battery of women, a term that was disliked because it did not suggest the social construction of domestic violence to women. At the end of the 1970s the organization divided into Welsh, Scottish, English, and Irish federations, all of which maintain communication with each other.[4] The English federation (WAFE) was the most disunited of the national organizations, and its failure to agree on a constitution resulted in the loss of state funding for some years during the 1980s, although this was finally restored. The Welsh federation celebrated ten years of existence in 1988, by which time refuges were open in every Welsh valley. Scottish Women's Aid (SWA) established with funding from the Scottish Office in 1976 and the opening of its Edinburgh office. The Dundee office was opened in 1981. All the federations survive on a base of state funding, making up the shortfall with money from donations and charitable foundations. Not all women's refuges belong to Women's Aid; some are autonomous because they disagree with some of its aims and practices, others are local authority initiatives which do not run open-door policies. However, the majority of refuges in 1990 are affiliated to Women's Aid, and most of those which are not receive information mailings from the federations. In other words, they are a part of the network.

The political history of Women's Aid shows both the contradictions and the more general dilemmas of feminist politics. It illustrates the continuity and expansion of certain issues and net-

[3] Gail Stedward, 1987 'Entry into the System: A Case Study of Women in Scotland', in J. Richardson and Grant Jordan (ed.) *Government and Pressure Groups in Britain* (Clarendon, Oxford, 1987), 217–18.
[4] For lists of refuges and other information, see WAFE, *Women's Aid into the 1990s: Annual Report, 1989–90* (Bristol, 1990); SWA, *Scottish Women's Aid: Annual Report, 1989–90* (Edinburgh, 1990); WWA, *Welsh Women's Aid: Annual Report, 1989–90* (Cardiff, 1990).

works, the growing but always ambivalent engagement with the state, and the accompanying risks of 'incorporation'. On the one hand, there is evidence of the growth and establishment of feminist expertise and increased political dexterity. On the other hand, there are clear signs of the strains of providing a service that protects women, but is true to feminist principles; that insists that society take responsibility for the consequences of its gendered power structure, but empowers the women whom it seeks to help.

Initially, refuge workers concentrated on achieving recognition of the problem and on organizing provision for battered women according to feminist principles. A parliamentary select committee on violence in marriage reported in 1975 and firmly established violence against women at home as a social rather than an individual problem. Continued campaigning ensured that public knowledge of the issue grew. The 1977 Homeless Persons Act required local authorities to rehouse women at risk of violence. The need to rehouse the women who came to the refuge, and to make provision for their children, meant that women's refuge groups tended to focus their day-to-day political activity on local authorities, because they had the relevant statutory powers.

To find and develop feminist ways of working was a central concern of the refuge movement. Its feminist principles challenged common assumptions about domestic violence. Its ways of organization are drawn directly from the WLM. A high value is placed on non-hierarchical, democratic functioning in which conflict is dealt with collectively, and distinctions between helper and helped are overturned. Most refuges employ paid workers and rely on volunteers. As the years have passed, an increasing number of the paid workers and the volunteers are women who once lived in the refuge. Women who come to refuges are encouraged to take part in its collective management. This has been an important part of their empowerment. The 'management structure' of the refuges has been evolved to avoid hierarchy. An emphasis on co-counselling, discussion, and collective agreement underlines an interchangeability of helper and helped that is a very important part of feminist political practice. Such ways of working were developed as a challenge to the existing hierarchical structures of the contemporary Welfare State. Feminist refuges were formed with the explicit aim of providing an alternative political practice to that of the state. Although Women's Aid refuges are cheaper to run than local authority hostels and other homeless provision, the absence of 'client' status for refuge dwellers has often offended local authority professionals. Local authorities are challenged in other ways: refuges often begin as squats in local authority property. Open-door policies mean that refuges may violate council regulations about crowding and sanitation. Collective working principles mean that refuge administration is difficult for local officials to comprehend. There is therefore a predictable desire by local authorities to try to take more control over refuges. Such interference may range from insisting on particular kinds of administrative structure to the establishment of local authority hostels which run refuges on traditional welfare bureaucratic lines. These initiatives are on the increase. They amount to an effort by welfare professionals to neutralize the political challenge of Women's Aid feminism. Ultimately, they will probably fail, although they may destroy the refuge movement in the process. Women's Aid argues that it provides the best service for women, and that no alternative construction of service and empowerment will be effective.

Feminism is the key resource of the refuge movement. The participatory structures and therapeutic perspectives that it supplies foster confidence in women, and help them to lead the lives that they want to lead. Paying attention to the reality of women's lives has enabled feminist refuge workers to build up an expertise which involves social-structural explanations of domestic violence and is translatable into policies to protect women. This translation is an important part of the story of the women's movement in Britain. It is a significant instance of the impact of feminism on policy. But, before we can elaborate this point, we need to describe the changing nature of the feminism of the refuge movement.

### Difference: Race and the Refuge Movement

All recent feminist politics are in some measure conditioned by the debates about sexuality and violence that we have described above. Within that framework, two objects of feminist debate in the 1980s are important here: the first is the different experiences of different groups of women, and the second is the problem of engaging the state. As we recounted in Chapter 3, the meaning of difference has been most extensively explored around gender, race, class, and sexuality. Each of these has been important in the refuge movement, but race has probably been the most significant. The issue of race surfaced at about the same time as the divisions about the causes of sexual violence. Black women felt that their circumstances were not taken into account, that demands for women's protection and safety were white women's demands which took no account of the impact of racism on the black community. Black women coming to refuges were often met by racism. Racism also meant that black women were under considerable pressure not to accuse black men of violence; such charges were regarded as treacherous in the black communities. Women from Asian backgrounds were under additional pressure because of the threat of deportation if they sought state aid or if they did not stay with their spouses for at least one year after entering the country. Restrictive immigration laws result in women staying with abusive spouses in order to avoid deportation.

Amina Mama has described the perspective of black women who were involved in the black community struggles in the late 1970s. Those struggles focused on police violence, a perennial problem in the black communities. This experience meant that it took 'a long time to address a reality in which black women are more likely to be assaulted by their male partner than to be attacked by racists'.[5] The matter was brought to a head in Women's Aid as more black and working-class women used the refuges. Racism poisoned relations in many refuges, promoting guilt and irritation amongst white women and righteous anger on the part of black women. What was needed was open discussion, but this was not always easy or even possible.

Black women's groups established refuges during the 1980s, and several black women's groups developed strategies for working around the issue of domestic violence. Their initiatives appeared throughout the country, encountering different degrees of local authority support and different kinds of community response. In Scotland there were uproars in the black communities when aid for black women was started: 'It was seen as a shame to the community.' Amina Mama believed that neither feminist theories nor

[5] Amina Mama, 1989 'Violence against Black Women: Gender, Race and State Responses', *Feminist Review*, 28 (1989), 16–55, and 'A Hidden Struggle', *Spare Rib*, Feb. 1990: 11.

black rhetoric about women being traitors when they called in the police and divided up black families can capture the reality that she found in her research on women of Asian, African, and Caribbean backgrounds in London. She argues that 'the community should be challenging violent men not calling women who try to escape them traitors. The beating and maiming of women in the home is what is destroying black family life.'[6]

This point is well substantiated by the experience of Southall Black Sisters. Gita Sahgal has described the pressures on black women to keep silent about their experiences of male violence. The engagement of the issue of domestic violence by Southall Black Sisters broke an important silence in their community. Not only did they challenge the right of male leaders to speak for them, but black feminists also implicitly challenged the 'heroic' tradition of antiracism. These challenges took the form of a number of campaigns in support of justice for women murdered by their spouses and for women gaoled for fighting violence with violence. Speaking out in this manner raised acute dilemmas for women, who were pilloried as traitors to their communities' fights against racism.[7]

The pressure for silence is strong and deep-rooted. When the first Asian women's refuges were set up, they were often not intended as a challenge to community values. An account of the Brent Asian Women's Refuge showed how, in the first few months, workers saw their duty as helping women to go back to their husbands. They understood how the role of the woman in her community made her the moral mainstay of her family, the bearer of its honour, its *izzat*. Transgression would corrupt the honour of the family and, indeed, of the whole community. The wife and mother were responsible for the behaviour of husband and children; if they beat her, it was her fault for not changing them. All women found it difficult to leave home, but for Asian women there was the added burden of maintaining the *izzat* of the family. Feminists soon became established in the refuge at Brent, but their antiracism and sensitivity to local values prevented them from publicizing their experiences.[8]

[6] Mama, 'Violence against Black Women'.

[7] Gita Sahgal, 'Fundamentalism and the Multiculturalist Fallacy', in Southall Black Sisters, *Against the Grain: Southall Black Sisters, 1979–1989* (Southall Black Sisters, Southall, 1989).

[8] Muneeza Inam, 'Opening Doors', in Southall Black Sisters, *Against the Grain*.

The complexities of the problem of racism for feminists are apparent here. In everyday practice, feminists have to address both their own racism and the racism of the larger society. Antiracism has sometimes taken the form of forgiving instances of the sexual violence by black men by regarding it as an understandable effect of racism. Here is a situation in which the only way forward is a painful identification and exploration of the experiences of different women. That progression must be led by black women, and it has been. By the early 1990s considerable experience had been gained of addressing racism in the refuges. Discussion was more readily undertaken, black women numbered prominently amongst refuge volunteers and workers, and black women's groups were well established in Women's Aid. This does not mean that the problem was solved; rather, that it was acknowledged and was being worked on.

### The Refuge Movement and the State: Local Authority Policy

The reality for women who experience violence at home is that, if they are to escape it, they must be in a position to relinquish their dependence on men. In practice, it is the woman who must leave her home, and for most women this means poverty and homelessness. Although local authorities have statutory obligations to rehouse women with children who are at risk of violence, in practice they are often reluctant providers, and they make it extremely difficult for women to claim their entitlements. Refuges support women as they make their way through this process. To provide the relevant expertise, feminists in the refuge movement must engage the state. The same applies when refuge workers seek police protection, government funding and change in public policy.

This is another instance of the dilemma that feminists face when they encounter public institutions. Fear of incorporation or of the loss of autonomy is central to this dilemma. The range of feminist responses to it is wide. At one end of the spectrum is the liberal view that citizenship requires such activity; at the other is a radical separatist view that no such engagement is ever justified. The work of Women's Aid places it at the sharp edge of this difficulty. On the one hand, it is committed to the protection of women; it provides a service for which the backing of the state is required. On the other hand, Women's Aid is committed to feminist principles of autonomy and self-help and to mounting a continuing challenge to the gendered power structures of society.

This is not a problem that is exclusive to feminist initiatives. Many groups in Britain operate both insider and outsider strategies, depending upon which aspect of their political identity is in play. Such 'thresholder' groups, as political scientists call them, are uneasily situated in their policy communities, but they are nevertheless capable of considerable policy success.[9] Insider strategies became increasingly important during the 1980s, when the refuge movement played a growing role in local and national policy communities which were concerned about policy towards domestic violence. This work took a variety of forms, and was probably most sustained in the areas of law enforcement, housing, and social security. At government level, WAFE participated in working parties, presented evidence on legal reform, and made representations to the Home Office, the Law Commission, and the Department of the Environment.[10] In the regions, the most sustained interactions were with police authorities and in local authority multi-agency forums set up to deal with sexual violence.

## The Refuge Movement and the State: The Police

It is difficult to see how the refuge movement might avoid taking up issues of law-enforcement policy. From the days of the first refuges, issues about policing have been prominent. These were often dealt with locally. The Home Office took no interest in the work of the refuge movement when it first began, and the inclusion of the police and the criminal justice system within the domestic violence policy community was not envisaged. By the beginning of the 1990s, however, the Home Office was publicly concerned about the issue of domestic violence in general, and about the role of the police in particular. In the provinces, Nottingham, Manchester, West Yorkshire and Newcastle police forces, amongst others, initiated contacts with refuge workers.

There are several aspects of the role of the police in protecting

[9] Stedward, 'Entry into the System', 211–12.
[10] See WAFE, *Women's Aid into the 1990s.*

women from domestic violence which have been identified as important. These include the seriousness with which police treat the issue, and the degree and the kind of protection that they provide; their knowledge about domestic violence as a syndrome; the way in which they relate to feminist refuges; the problem of police racism; and the widespread perception that the police themselves number prominently amongst abusers of women. For a considerable period of time, the police tended to underestimate the violence of men and the need for police assistance by women and by refuges operated by women. The Domestic Violence Act of 1976 enabled courts to attach a power of arrest to injunctions restraining abusive men, but this power was not often used. Injunctions that do not include the power of arrest are widely regarded as ineffective when it comes to restraining violent men, although they have a value in 'entitling' women to rehousing.

Nor were the police much motivated by professional imperatives to prioritize domestic violence. Women who were beaten by their partners were notoriously reluctant to give evidence, and because these crimes were not likely to lead to convictions, individual police constables regarded such complaints as a waste of their time. Moreover, complaints about inadequate policing proved ineffective and sometimes counter-productive. SWA found that some women who complained about the policing they received were later charged with wasting police time when they requested assistance. Feminists were often philosophical about such treatment, taking the view that the police are no better than the society they serve, and that they reflect uncritically a social endorsement of domestic violence as well as racist perspectives on the protection of black women. The experience of the refuges made it clear that policing practice and ideology was not compatible with the needs of the women who experience domestic violence.

But even the most sexist institutions have the capacity to change. By the beginning of the 1990s there were some indications that the policing of male violence to women would be reformed. There were several reasons for this. First, and possibly most importantly, public attitudes towards the police were changing, becoming less trustful and more critical. Secondly, the Thatcher government sustained its support partly through an emphasis on law and order, increasing public expectations of personal safety. Thirdly, the women's movement was successful in bringing the issue of domestic violence on to the political agenda and keeping it there. The fourth development was the appearance of child sexual abuse on the public agenda after 1986.

A series of Home Office memos to police forces between 1983 and 1990 instructed them to take domestic violence more seriously. These memos were given considerable press publicity. Home Office guidance was issued to police forces in England and Wales in 1983. In 1986 the Home Office issued a circular reminding police of their powers under the 1984 Police and Criminal Evidence Act. A report the same year by the Metropolitan Police working party on domestic violence (attended by the Home Office) made extensive suggestions on training, referrals to refuges, and advice and information for women. This was followed up by a report from the London Strategic Policy Unit on police treatment of violence to women in the capitol. Police everywhere have been enjoined to take the problem more seriously; the Metropolitan Police has been ordered to do so. It is now a requirement that domestic violence complaints are fully recorded, and police receive training about domestic violence.[11] In 1991 the Home Office instructed police forces to set up data banks of women at risk.

The result is mixed, not least because of variations in the police forces themselves. Police forces are organized regionally in Britain, and they are jealous of their independence. Discretion is wide, and practice varies from locality to locality. Moreover, the police on the beat have considerable autonomy. Consequently, the policing of domestic violence now varies from very good practice in a few localities to dreadful (in other words, no change) in others. There are forty-two police domestic violence units in London, but few or none in some of the large provincial cities. Many police officers now accept that domestic violence is as serious a crime as stranger assault, and the tendency to encourage reconciliation as the stock response appears to have declined.

### The Refuge Movement and the State: Co-option or Co-operation?

These changes are not uniformly welcomed by feminists. Adjustments in police priorities to take on elements of the femi-

---

[11] G. Hague et al., 'Women's Aid: Policing Male Violence in the Home', in C. Dunhill (ed.), The Boys in Blue (Virago, London, 1989).

nist agenda may augur a loss of feminist control over the issue. The same problem is raised when feminists co-operate with the government at local and national levels. During the three Thatcher governments, the context of this co-operation was a series of social policy initiatives that consistently eroded the provisions which make it possible for women to leave violent men. Reductions in publicly owned housing stocks through the sale of council houses reduced the possibilities of being able to offer adequate accommodation for homeless women and their children. Changes in benefit payments reduced the rents that were paid for women in refuges. Cuts in local authority funding led to reductions in funding for refuges. The result was that refuge workers had to spend increasing amounts of time on trying to make ends meet, and bottlenecks occurred as refuges filled but no permanent housing was available for women to move into. Average stays in refuges increased, and it is believed that many women returned to violent relationships rather than endure long periods of living in a refuge. In 1990 WAFE estimated the provision of refuges to be one per 60,000 of the population, nowhere near the one per 10,000 of population that had been recommended by the parliamentary select committee on violence in marriage in 1975.

Yet housing authority co-operation is essential to the refuge movement. The powerlessness that women experience when dealing with the authorities that have to be mobilized when they try to leave home is often overwhelming. The very negative experience of black women when leaving violent men has been extensively described by Amina Mama. Her London-based study showed that it took as long as three years for women to be rehoused. Women were passed from one department to another, with little right or power to resist encroaching webs of coercive and punitive state interventions.[12] This is described here in words that vividly express the strength required to cope with bureaucratic obstructiveness:

Once they've made the enquiries, they're supposed to send you a paper called Section 64, which says they consider you homeless and will rehouse you. It took them six months to send me that paper. This paper is like a passport to lots of other things. You need it to feel secure, and they know you need it. Without it, you can't convince any other

---

[12] Mama, 'Violence against Black Women', 11.

borough or anywhere else that you have registered. It took six months and in the meantime I had to keep phoning, going down there. When I rang up they used to tell me to stop bothering them, that they would send the paper. Nothing arrived, so I went down there in person, and I was told not to make any enquiries until I hear from them. I rang again and he put the receiver down on me.[13]

Meanwhile, welfare professionals and local officials continued to seek control of the policies. Once they became aware of the radical nature of the feminist critique and of its implications for client–professional status, notably at a DHSS conference in 1981,[14] welfare professionals and experts became very wary of close association and developed arms-length strategies. The state employs professional carers who, although often radical as individuals, are impelled by the demands of professionalism to separate the status of client and carer. Inevitably, professional carers have an interest in imposing their own definitions of, and solutions to, violence to women in the home, and they develop strategies to do this. For example, local authorities have established their own women's refuges in Birmingham, London, Manchester, and other British cities. As with the police, these initiatives are often couched in feminist rhetoric and show sensitivity to many aspects of feminist analysis. Official refuges offer safety, but they do not encourage residents to become involved in the running of the refuge. They are not founded on an ethos of empowering women. The irony here is that although the refuge movement made the problem visible, unleashing a huge demand to which it offered a solution, that solution was a radical one that was unacceptable to many members of the policy community. The anti-authoritarian ethos of feminist self-help strategies is not compatible with the goals of the New Right, and its implied autonomy offends the welfare professionals and local officials. During the 1980s there was an increase in such tensions. Because the government wanted to reduce the powers of the state by devolving responsibilities to the community in the form of the voluntary agencies, the refuge movement was able to gain financial support from the state. This enabled refuge collectives to assert feminist values. In other words, as the form of the state

---

[13] Mama, 'Violence against Black Women', 11.
[14] See Stedward, 'Entry into the System'.

changed, space was created for feminist interventions. But the welfare bureaucracy was bound to contest the erosion of its authority. The resulting political struggle is at the heart of disagreements between feminist Women's Aid workers and welfare professionals.

Another way in which the refuge movement intervenes in the state is by monitoring policy, making representations to relevant bodies, and campaigning for policy changes. This activity is very much the responsibility of the federations, whose roles and skills are different to those of the local groups. Refuge workers and volunteers developed counselling and therapeutic skills which were not transferable to the campaigning and administrative tasks that turn their expertise into policy. Women's Aid policy development initiatives met with some success. The Home Office has taken an increasing interest not only in the area of policing, as we have seen above, but in the area of domestic violence generally. Following the publication of Home Office Working Paper 107, a review of the literature on domestic violence, the ministerial group on women's issues met in July 1989 to examine the issue of domestic violence. WAFE submitted a report to the group, and will monitor the progress of the initiatives that the group suggested: a review of civil law, guidance to chief officers of police, a project on the education of domestic violence offenders, and the development of good practice guidelines for health and social service staff.[15]

At the beginning of the 1990s the problem of violence to women in the home is visible and large; 25 per cent of all violent crime in Britain is domestic assault on women; over 1,000 women telephone the London police each week with complaints of domestic violence. The refuge movement is the primary agency for helping battered women. In any one year, about 12,000 women and 21,000 children experience refuge life. Feminists have placed domestic violence on the political agenda. Women's Aid has fought its corner and continues to emphasize the unique service that is offered by the refuge movement. The underlying principle that women's needs are best met by involving women in meeting those needs continues to be central to its work. Inevitably, Women's Aid (and the rest of the feminist refuge

[15] WAFE, *Women's Aid into the 1990s.*

movement) oscillates uncomfortably between its insider and outsider statuses and strategies. Like other voluntary organizations
concerned with welfare, Women's Aid is part of the welfare system. Every time its expertise is used by official bodies, every time
it is included in an inter-agency forum, control of the issue
becomes open to other contenders. Whatever the ambivalences
about engaging the state, the problem and its solution are, in all
important respects, political. And this is well recognized in the
movement. Refuge workers are certain in their affirmation that
creating space where women can talk and deal with their problems collectively in an empowering way is political work.
Bringing an issue out from the private sphere, making it visible,
and offering a social diagnosis and a public solution is the
essence of feminist politics.

## RAPE

Working on the issue of domestic violence made feminists
increasingly aware that, in practice, women have more to fear
from men whom they know than from violent strangers. The way
in which this perception was dealt with and understood in the
movement led to the split between those second-wave feminists
who came to believe that male sexuality was inherently violent
and those who did not. Action over rape was widespread by the
end of the 1970s as feminists organized in a number of British
cities. Groups such as Women against Rape (WAR) and
Feminists against Sexual Terrorism (FAST) organized 'Take back
the Night' marches from July 1977 onwards, when the first of
these marches took place in Edinburgh. An important part of the
context of this organization was the 'ripper' murders that took
place in the north of England. These murders and attempted
murders received widespread publicity in the national media and
had a particularly important effect on feminism in Leeds and
Bradford. On 27 November 1980, ten days after the death of
Jacqueline Hill (one of the victims), 500 women attended a conference on sexual violence in Leeds. The conference brought
together women who had been organizing around issues of sexual
violence. They were linked in a new campaign, Women against
Violence against Women (WAVAW), which planned campaigns

to combat male violence and asserted every woman's right to defend herself against it.

Actions included the occupation of the *Sun* newspaper offices to protest at the use of rape stories for titillation, the formation of local anti-pornography groups which leafleted family newsagents for stocking pornography, demonstrations outside cinemas showing 'Dressed to Kill', smashing the windows of strip clubs, putting glue in the locks of sex shops, etc. In Leeds a woman drove her car through the front of a sex shop. Women were angry about the failure to solve the 'ripper' murders, angry that the 'solution' was, in effect, a curfew for women, angry that the media coverage of rape seemed to have titillation as its objective. Susan Brownmiller's book *Against our Will*, published in Britain in 1975, became very influential. This book presented an enormous amount of information about rape, much of which was drawn from 'speak-outs' by United States feminists who had been raped. It demonstrated the shocking prevalence of the crime. Brownmiller argued that rape was the means by which all men kept all women in a state of fear, and that such fear was the basis of male oppression. It was a powerful message, one that was difficult to dismiss when so many women had experience of sexual coercion. Gradually, the belief that rape and wife-beating were the product of men's essentially violent natures gained support. The connections that revolutionary feminists made between male sexual violence and women's subordination led them to the view that all instances of sexual coercion (including pornography and sexual harassment) were forms of rape.

The issue developed in this way partly because of rage.[16] As the prevalence of male violence became more apparent, anger became more widespread. Reactions from the police, the media, the courts, the police, doctors, and other (mainly male) professionals exacerbated this anger by treating the issue with contempt. There is considerable evidence that the press used the 'soft pornography' of rape-case reporting to boost sales and circulation.[17] The reasonable and easily understood argument that crimes of sexual violence form a continuum, reflecting women's social subordination, was treated with derision by male opinion

[16] Segal, *Is the Future Female?*, ch. 3.
[17] See Keith Soothill, Sylvia Walby, and Paul Bagguley, 'Judges, the Media and Rape', *Journal of Law and Society*, 17/2 (1991), 211–33.

leaders, who wrote sneering articles which claimed that feminists were confusing courtship and seduction with rape.

Part of the source of women's anger was surprise. There is a huge and contradictory mythology that surrounds rape, and women born before 1970 were brought up in thrall to that contradictory mythology. We were led to understand that rape was a rare event, that *normal* men aimed to protect women from violence, that only women are raped, that rape was normally the act of strangers, that women lie about being raped to conceal their promiscuity—so much so that a woman claiming to have been raped should be disbelieved as a matter of course. We knew that women were only raped if they wanted to be, and that only psychopaths raped, but that male sexual desire was so uncontrollable that they could be driven to rape by our inappropriate behaviour. Feminist research exposes all of these myths and shows how they protect male aggressors.[18] Feminists offered two—opposed—explanations of rape. The first, and most widely publicized, is the Radical feminist view that the cause of rape (and other sexual violence) is male sexuality itself.[19] The basis of this explanation is the widespread incidence of male sexual violence to women, the considerable effect that the fear of sexual violence has on women's lives, and the notoriously unsympathetic attitudes of the mainly male officials who treat rape victims. This makes for a fairly simple politics: the problem is male sexuality, especially as expressed in heterosexuality. The solution is political lesbianism.

Lynne Segal is perhaps the most consistent advocate of the other explanation, which is that the problem is not maleness, but masculinity. Her work draws attention to the large number of men who do not coerce women, and she has attempted to explain the construction of masculinity in contemporary society in an effort to show that male sexual violence is about gender and roles rather than essential biological characteristics.[20] This is a feminist version of the nature–nurture argument, and it is likely to continue for some time yet. Its implications for feminism have been profound, both in organizational and theoretical terms. But

---

[18] Segal, *Is the Future Female?*, ch. 3.
[19] Susan Brownmiller, *Against our Will* (Penguin, Harmondsworth, 1975).
[20] Segal, *Slow Motion.*

the effect has been different in different parts of the country. Divisions in London are deep, continuing, and bitter, but feminists in Leeds are able to work around their differences. Feminists there stress the importance of the 'ripper' murders and the subsequent investigations as something that had a compelling local effect. Nevertheless, a split did occur in Leeds between revolutionary and Socialist feminists. One feminist recalls early discussions about male sexual violence:

we seemed to get a lot of opposition from particularly Socialist Feminists at even raising it . . . they were saying 'well you're making women feel frightened, and it's not as bad as this' . . . I suppose it was because it was saying that all men are potential rapists . . . rather than saying it was a class issue 'cos it obviously isn't . . . if you've got the money you can get a taxi but you can still be raped . . .

And race, too, became an issue in Leeds. Black community leaders have long argued that rape charges are one more opportunity for racist police to set them up. The black communities resented the Take back the Night marches through Chapeltown: black feminists repeatedly raised such issues in the women's movement. Some white feminists found the charges of racism difficult to understand. Why, they argued, were left-wing marches through ghetto areas regarded as demonstrations of racial solidarity, but feminists marches (which, after all, were expressions of solidarity amongst women) were regarded as instances of racism? Divisions eased, not least because some of the points that the Radical feminists made about male violence were partly accepted in Leeds. A lot of women were controlled by the 'ripper' murders: they gave up jobs and evening classes, women students left university and returned to homes in other parts of the country after Jacqueline Hill was killed. Their lives were altered. And some men took advantage of women's fears:

Local youths were jumping out of shrubs saying 'I'm the ripper' not funny, terrifying . . . Women were getting 'helpful' lifts from male colleagues who would then try it on in the car. Or under the guise of helpfulness, coming to collect their partners after classes, immediately after, so she could not go for a drink with her friends. Made to think that you need men's protection all the time.

Under these circumstances, women shared taxis, organized lifts for each other, and lent each other their guard dogs. Instead of a siege mentality, there was the development of a sense of collective strength, a sense of a shared experience, which continues to affect the attitudes of Leeds feminists to this day, however divided they might otherwise be.

## Rape Crisis

Feminist action about rape involved more than collective protection. Apart from the direct action of marches and demonstrations mentioned above, there were two other main strands of activity: the rape crisis groups, which offered telephone counselling on rape crisis lines, and feminist research on the nature, causes, and solutions to rape.

The appearance of rape crisis groups was very much a local phenomenon which occurred more or less spontaneously in different parts of the country. Although the groups are networked, in that members of their support groups attend conferences on sexual violence and are generally active in the sexual violence policy communities, there is no formal organization to link them. The links are shared feminist networks and commitments. The first rape crisis centre[21] opened in London in March 1976, and others appeared over the next several months and years in Leeds, Tyneside, Manchester, Edinburgh, Bristol, Newcastle, Nottingham, and elsewhere. The centres were influenced by the practices of feminists from the United States, where such centres appeared at the beginning of the 1970s. A group of about forty women began to meet in London in the early 1970s because they wanted to do something about rape. One group set up London Rape Crisis, and this became the London rape crisis group (LRG). A similar period of preparation before the opening of a rape crisis centre was a feature in other regions. In Birmingham the rape crisis group began meeting in 1979, but it was two years before they had a crisis line for calls. LRG took about 150 calls in the first year; by 1978 about twenty-five new callers telephoned each week. Over the years there was a shift from talking about old rapes, never reported, to detailing new ones as knowledge about the line spread and recourse to it increased. By the early 1990s

[21] The term 'rape crisis centre' normally refers to rape crisis lines. Experience and fear of attack by hostile men and the importance of survivor anonymity meant that 'drop-in' centres were not really feasible.

LRG was taking about 100 counselling calls per week, and on a Saturday night the line is permanently in use as one call after another comes in.[22]

The organization consists of a support group, a telephone line and arrangements to cover calls. LRG runs a twenty-four-hour service, which it regards as an essential feature of its work. The collective operates on three levels: as a sustaining developing collective, as providers of a service, and as a campaigning group. The themes of feminist political action are very apparent here. Decision is by discussion. Organization is kept to the barest minimum, and the collective takes care to support its members as well as rape survivors. Over time, LRG and other rape crisis groups have established their expertise on rape survival, and they have become involved both in the policy community and in public debate and discussion about policy.

Rape counselling has not developed in the same way as other feminist group-based service provision, because the use of the telephone makes the service an individual one. Telephone counselling has enormous advantages for the rape survivor. It is anonymous, the caller is in control—she can hang up or ring back as she wishes. It is also confidential in a way that a drop-in centre can never be. Counselling is central to the work of rape crisis lines. The pioneer group in London was very careful to seek training from other organizations with relevant experience, including the Samaritans, sympathetic GPs, other counsellors, and psychologists. And whilst callers were encouraged to join consciousness-raising groups, it was decided not to offer 'survivor groups' to the women who telephoned. Counsellor stress was less of a problem than might have been envisaged. Because the process was strengthening for the callers, it was also strengthening for the counsellors; and internal support groups worked hard on supporting each other.

Funding came from charitable foundations, local authorities, and the DHSS (because the twenty-four-hour line was a national service). It was important to the collective that it was not entirely state-funded. The fact that the funding came from a range of groups made its acquisition more time-consuming, but it gave

[22] For a full account, see Liz Kelly's interview with Romi Bowen and Bernadette Manning in *Trouble and Strife*, 10 (Spring 1987). This is the source of most of our account of LRG.

greater flexibility. However, the straitened financial climate of the 1990s meant that local authority funding became more important. In 1991 the London Borough Grants Scheme considered withdrawing LRG funding in favour of other rape crisis initiatives. LRG was able to argue that their woman-centred approach, their twenty-four hour-line, and guarantee of confidentiality were unique in London, and funding was maintained. Like other rape crisis groups, LRG is autonomous, and contacts with other such groups are mainly informal. Many people imagine that because LRG is in London, it must be a national headquarters, a misconception that causes resentment from provincial groups, and makes LRG a focus for foreign visitors, journalists, and much of the publicity that the movement receives. The decision not to have a national organization was taken at the end of the 1970s, and although the idea of a national co-ordinating structure was raised at various conferences on sexual violence in the intervening years, there appears to be no real sense that such an agency would be of value. Members of the group see no reason why there should be a consistent policy between centres, and they are unwilling to devote precious time to the arduous tasks of formal networking. Such strategies are regarded as forms of male power-building which are inappropriate to feminist service provision. Their charitable status prevented LRG from overt support of WAVAW, but ideas are exchanged through groups such as FAST and through bilateral exchanges with groups in other British centres. Other ways of networking include conferences about sexual violence, which are often organized by local authorities and local multi-agency committees which have been established by council women's committees to treat the range of crimes of sexual violence.

During the 1970s, feminist activists in WAR stressed the uniqueness of the rape issue, resisting attempts to combine strategies and policies on other forms of male violence as potentially deradicalizing. However, the view that all sexual coercion is a form of rape gained acceptance during the 1980s. The formation of the Incest Survivors' Group in 1981 was as a result of knowledge obtained through rape crisis work and was a rationalization of effort rather than a division of principle. Since rape crisis groups have been in operation, there has been a shift of emphasis from a focus on rape to sexual violence more generally. This is partly a result of what has been learned by listening to survivors, and partly a reflection of the course of debates amongst feminists. Rape crisis workers are themselves often rape survivors, and their direct and indirect experience of male violence seems to predispose them towards essentialist explanations of sexual crime. There is a widespread belief that sexual violence is the ultimate expression of male dominance: that it is men who cause rape. A member of a rape crisis support group in Leeds told us:

There is a lot of tinkering away at the edges of the problem as if rape is caused by bad street lighting . . . I mean bad street lighting may aid the rapist in his endeavours but it is not the cause. And its like we do away with the bad street lighting and we change the design of flats and that and everything will be all right . . . but the cause of the problem is untouched and women become more and more controlled.

Feminist direct action on rape continues. In July 1990 WAR protestors caused a sitting of the Court of Appeal to be suspended when they called for the judge, Lord Justice Watkins, to be sacked for his decision the previous week to clear a policeman of raping a teenage girl in his panda car.[23] In 1991 Take back the Night marches took place in a number of cities. In many respects, the feminist construction of work on rape is similar to the work developed in the women's refuge movement. The stress is on empowering women, on listening to and believing what they say, and on developing expertise as a result. The use of the word 'survivor' rather than 'victim' is a deliberate strategy of empowerment, product of the perception that casting women as victims underlines their subordination.

### Rape and the State: The Law, Rape Trials, and the Police

On 14 December 1991 the *Independent* carried reports of two trials. In one, a woman who strangled her husband and dumped his dismembered body in a nearby cornfield after eight years of violence and humiliation was placed on two years' probation. In another, two boys were freed by a judge who accepted that their rape of a 15-year-old victim was a childish prank. The juxtaposition of these two cases is interesting and raises a number of points about the way in which the law takes circumstances into

[23] The *Independent*, 10 July 1990.

account when it treats crimes of violence. What strikes us about
the two cases is their obvious inconsistency. In the first case, the
sitting judge took male sexual violence so seriously that only a
token punishment was required for the serious crime of a brutal
murder. In the second case, a different judge ruled that the sexual
violence meted out to a young woman was trivial—a 'prank'. The
decisions reflected the differing concerns of the two judges rather
than a coherent legal position. There are many such decisions in
cases of sexual violence that we might have cited here. They
remind us that at the beginning of the 1990s the law about violence between men and women is in some disarray, reflecting confusion as attitudes change more quickly than judicial personnel.

Feminist work about rape and domestic violence has been
instrumental in creating some of this confusion. It has challenged
dominant views of the way in which power is constructed in gender relations. This effect has been complicated by divisions
between feminists about the appropriateness of intervention in
different state arenas. Currently, there is at least an implicit feminist acceptance that it is not possible to work on the issue of
rape without taking account of the role of law and the problems
of policing. The most radical and separatist of feminist positions
implicitly supports the policing of the dangerous group. And
police forces themselves may facilitate service provision. Rape
crisis groups normally try to persuade statutory agencies to refer
women rape survivors to their helpline. This involves contact and
negotiation. Local government is important, at least as a source
of funding. Local authority social services also sometimes provide
links between rape crisis groups and the police.

Feminist attempts to understand and influence the law have
been of three kinds. First, feminists lawyers, criminologists, and
sociologists have made intellectual critiques of the gendered bias
of rape law, and especially of the conduct of rape trials.
Secondly, feminist activists have campaigned for reforms in the
law and in the conventions of rape trials. Thirdly, feminists have
worked with the police in some areas to alter police practice in
respect of rape complaints.

Feminists have several objections to the way in which rape trials are conducted. Rape is normally a matter of criminal law.
The requirements of proof are that the evidence of the raped
woman must be collaborated. In court, the woman is a witness to

the crime, subject to cross-examination, but not protected by any defence. Because there is rarely any collaborative evidence, because there are rarely any other witnesses, the trial will turn on the issue of consent. The accused will claim consent, and the defence will use almost any means to undermine the woman's assertions that she did not consent.[24] Her sexual history will often be regarded as relevant evidence, and there is a strong tendency to disbelieve her account. Part of the reason for this lies in the nature of criminal trials, but much of it is to do with the way in which male and female sexuality and consent is understood by the important (normally male) actors in the trial. The trial is offensive in other ways as well, and many feminists believe that the legal process itself is a sexual violation.

Carol Smart is prominent amongst feminists who have criticized the conduct of rape trials.[25] She offers what is basically a discourse analysis of such trials, an effort to reveal the mechanisms by which the law misunderstands accounts of rape. Her argument is built around a view of sexuality which says that male and female heterosexualities are differently constructed and understood, and that this is magnified in the rape trial. The dominant view of sexuality is a phallocentric construction which emphasizes the pleasures of penetration and intercourse. The context of the trial is a belief that rape must be pleasurable for women because it involves penetration. Actors in the trial share an understanding that female sexuality is problematic, that it is capricious or whimsical. The core of the trial is the woman's 'no'. This 'no' is automatically undermined by the culture of phallocentrism and is overlaid with contradictory meanings. As a result, her evidence may not be credited. The following remarks were made by Judge David Wild in December 1982: 'Women who say no do not always mean no. It is not just a question of saying no. It is a question of how she says it, how she shows and makes it clear. If she doesn't want it she only has to keep her legs shut and there would be marks of force being used.'

Not only is the context in which a raped woman must prove her non-consent one that infantizes her (she does not mean what

---

[24] The question of consent in rape trials is avoided only if the man says it is a case of mistaken identity, e.g., that he was somewhere else at the time.

[25] Carol Smart, *Feminism and the Power of Law* (Routledge and Kegan Paul, London, 1989).

she says), it also humiliates her. *Her* sexual history is relevant to the question of rape, but *his* is not. In practice, consent is assumed, and a raped woman may have to provide evidence of considerable force for her to be believed. One of the most important difficulties arises when a woman agrees to a certain amount of intimacy, but not intercourse. Smart points out that the rapist will argue a continuum, that she consented to be with him, therefore . . . if she submits rather than risk violence, her credibility is undermined. The issue of 'promiscuity' is also relevant. Many men believe that if a woman consents to one man, she has somehow consented to all men. A verdict of innocence for the accused is also a verdict of sexual complicity on the part of the victim. In this way, the phallocentric view of women's capriciousness is confirmed.[26]

Proving non-consent is not the only difficulty experienced by raped women during the trials. It is well known that trial and pre-trial events in the police station are found to be profoundly disturbing by many women who have been assaulted. MacKinnon has argued that women do not want to pursue charges of rape because the evidence that they have to give in court becomes a pornographic vignette in which the naming of the body parts is almost a sexual act. The public may gaze on this performance and re-enact her violation in their imaginations.[27] The woman must name parts of her body, use words which are heavily encoded with sexual meaning. As Sue Lees has observed, it is *her* intimate garments which are handed around, not *his*.[28] Prosecution rebuttals of the woman's claim that she did not consent, together with prevailing attitudes which associate sex and violence, obstruct the distinction that a jury must make between rape and seduction. The judicial view is often that a degree of violence is taken for granted; that quite a lot of violence is necessary to overcome genuine non-consent. Moreover, there are racist presumptions that a white woman would only have intercourse with a black man if she were forced to, and that black women are sexually more available. In Carol Smart's analysis, the rape trial is the particular legal expression

[26] *Feminism and the Power of Law*, 33–4.
[27] Catherine MacKinnon, *Feminism Unmodified: Discourses on Life and Law* (Harvard University Press, Cambridge, Mass., 1987).
[28] Sue Lees, 'Blaming the Victim', *New Statesman and Society*, 1 Dec 1989

of the dominant culture, and she is pessimistic about the possibilities for reform. She finds it problematic that reforms might make the trial tolerable enough to be endured, without any guarantee that its phallocentric assumptions have been altered. Like many feminists, she is uneasy about making alliances with agencies of law enforcement.

During the 1970s there were feminist-inspired reforms to prevent disclosure of the names of raped women in the press and to restrict the use of their sexual histories as evidence. The public nature of the humiliation was therefore modified, although trial judges are notoriously lenient in allowing details of the sexual past of raped women. The high degree of independence of the British judiciary makes it difficult to control their prejudices, so feminists have gradually sought ways of protecting raped women in court. Rape crisis workers attend trials with survivors in order to provide psychological support. Efforts have been made to reorganize courts so that rape survivors do not share waiting-rooms with their rapists. But many critics believe that more fundamental change is necessary.

There have been two important sets of proposals. One is that raped women should have an advocate in court to protect their interests. This system has been tried in Denmark and it might be worth trying in Britain. Danish police are required to inform all raped women of their right to free legal representation, which may begin from the moment of police questioning. Advocates may interrupt if questioning is improper, and ask questions, which are recorded, if important issues have not been covered. They have access to all statements, including the defendant's, although this may not be revealed to the raped woman. They cannot cross-examine, but they can object to defence questions, particularly those relating to the woman's sexual history. This reform was rejected by the male-dominated Criminal Law Revision Committee, an advisory group of senior jurists, who deemed it unnecessary in 1984. The advisory group thought that if witnesses were represented in rape cases, it would be difficult to refuse such represention in other kinds of cases.[29] Another suggestion has been to use expert witnesses to educate juries about rape trauma syndrome; this would enable them to understand

[29] J. Temkin, *Rape and the Legal Process* (Sweet and Maxwell, London, 1987).

such behaviour as delayed reporting, continuous crying, etc. on the part of raped witnesses. An obstacle to this reform is that the British judiciary is especially hostile to the expertise of the 'psy' professions. And, as Carol Smart points out, such a reform would not requalify women's accounts; rather, it would empower 'experts' to speak for them.[30]

Any demand by feminists to reform the conventions of rape trials will be resisted by one of the most powerful, independent, and unrepresentative sections of the British élite (see Chapter 5). It may be, therefore, that reform of the law itself offers a more promising strategy. For example, feminist campaigns in the 1980s to reform the law on rape in marriage appeared to have met with success by 1991. Early in 1991 the Law Commission reported its deliberations on the law on rape in marriage. Its recommendations were that such rape be criminalized. The report reviewed the history of the legal immunity of Englishmen from prosecution for raping their wives. It dates from a 1736 opinion given by a Chief Justice Hale, who asserted that: 'By their mutual matrimonial consent and contract the wife hath given herself up in this kind to her husband, which she cannot retract.' No authority was cited for this statement, but it became the accepted legal wisdom incorporated into common law and assumed in the 1976 Sexual Offences Act. The Law Commission made its case on the basis that modern marriage is a partnership of equals; rape is non-consensual sexual intercourse, and women are entitled to refuse to have sexual intercourse on any particular occasion. The Law Commission considered and rejected all the objections normally raised to the criminalization of rape in marriage as irrelevant to the fact that rape is a crime.[31]

The Law Commission's statement might best be seen as one of intent, a sign that attitudes are changing, rather than that rape in marriage will be prevented by legal change. It is likely that such a law will prove impossibly difficult to implement as evidential problems become apparent. Nevertheless, such a change is to be welcomed as an authoritative statement of social values and principles. Even if it does not bring immediate change in sexual behaviour, it adds to the resources that an individual woman may use when seeking her rights.

[30] Smart, *Feminism and Law.*
[31] 'Law Commission on Rape and Marriage', *Spare Rib*, Mar. 1991

Our third example of feminist–state interaction on the issue of rape concerns the police. This is political work, similar in many respects to the political work undertaken by the women's refuge movement, and its examination reveals many of the same difficulties, although there are some differences. Two differences between rape crisis and women's refuge work are that the police appear to be more interested in the issue of rape, and that rape crisis groups appear to feel less able to co-operate with local police forces than many refuge workers do. Otherwise, the parallels are striking. For example, the struggle over definitions is central. Feminist control over the definition of rape and its solution is one of the issues. As police attitudes to rape begin to change, they have a tendency to seek to control the way in which it is processed. Feminist success in altering definitions of the issue has led not to the acceptance of feminist principles, but to their modification and incorporation by an institution with its own imperatives. This is progress, and it is progress in a feminist direction, but it is also part of a political struggle in which feminists risk incorporation and must become ever more skilled in order to fight their corner successfully. Another similarity between the rape crisis and the women's refuge movement is that, in addition to the skills of campaigning and administration, the skills of counselling and support are acquired. Thus (and this is the third similarity), what rape crisis has to offer is its expertise, the knowledge that it has gained about raped women in the course of its work. The police want (for whatever reasons) women to report rape, and they want to prosecute rapists. Rape crisis workers know why women are reluctant to report such crimes, and what may help to change that.

For most of the 1980s, LRG had a remarkably unsatisfactory relationship with the police. During its first ten years of operation, the police thought that LRG dissuaded women from reporting rapes, and group members say that the Metropolitan Police obstructed negotiations to co-operate by demanding such things as the names and addresses of all the women working there. They say that the police issued a memo to its officers telling them not to co-operate with LRG.[32]

LRG learned about police attitudes from the women who came to them:

[32] See Liz Kelly, *Trouble and Strife*, 10 (1987).

At the beginning we just didn't know. We discovered all kinds of appalling things like women being left with no clothes, being driven home with only a blanket around them, being taken around the streets immediately after the rape to look for the rapist . . . we were wary of developing a relationship with the police because of these things. We didn't want to be associated with that kind of treatment of raped women.[33]

Other rape crisis groups had different attitudes and different experiences. Feminists became involved in police training, and local authority women's committees in Leeds and Norwich instituted committees in which rape crisis workers, Women's Aid workers, police, and welfare professionals concerned about violence to women regularly take part.

By the middle of the 1980s there were signs that the police were becoming more sensitive. Undoubtedly, the exposure of their practices by feminist action was part of the reason for this. And public outrage followed a television documentary by Roger Graef which was broadcast on national television in early 1982. The programme showed the hostile and brutal way in which the police treated a raped woman, who attempted to make a complaint to the Thames Valley police. In 1985 Metropolitan Police Superintendent Ian Blair wrote a book called *Investigating Rape*. This was a catalyst for revamping police procedures. In the same year the Metropolitan Police set up a working party on policing and rape. Blair has been at the forefront of the police drive to facilitate rape complaints by London women.[34] Following the working party's recommendations, the force organized four special rape suites in which to interview raped women. Women police officers were recruited and trained about rape trauma, women police surgeons were recruited, raped women were given a night to recover before their statements were taken, and better and more sensitive advice was given about the risks of pregnancy and venereal disease. The Home Office put pressure on other police forces to follow suit.

The differences between police and feminists remain. At the beginning of the 1990s, LRG members were sceptical about accounts of changes in police practice which were receiving widespread publicity. In reality, there were very few rape suites in

[35] See Liz Kelly, *Trouble and Strife*, 54 (1987).
[34] See Ian Blair's letter to the *Guardian*, 20 Dec. 1990.

operation, and for most women things had not really changed. For example, the Sexual Assault Referral Centre at St Mary's Hospital in Manchester, which is widely cited by the police as a model of provision, is rejected by feminists, who see the initiative as a 'medicalization of rape' and who are not involved in the centre, which is staffed by paid professionals. The fear is that feminist words and phrases have been incorporated into a professional rhetoric about rape, but that the empowering politics to underpin those words is absent.[35]

Similar objections are raised to Home Office initiatives to fund the training of counsellors on victim support schemes for rape survivors. This was regarded by rape crisis group members as a way of providing alternatives to rape crisis lines. And feminists are concerned that the medicalization of rape empowers medical professionals rather than rape survivors. It is a process whereby medical professionals try to establish themselves as the only appropriate definers and treaters of rape trauma. Such developments inevitably affect feminist capacities to deliver services, and must therefore inform their political strategies. As always, the struggle over definitions is crucial. The usurpation of rape by other experts may result in cuts in the funding of feminist initiatives and in the loss of the empowering element of feminist initiatives in rape counselling. 'The previously dominant definition of rape as an issue of crime and punishment left the field free for feminists to define the response of the woman who had been raped; because no one else was interested.'[36]

Rape crisis group members are not the only feminists in the policy networks. Local authority women's committees have looked for ways of providing support to women survivors of rape. NALGWC recommends that local authorities provide funding for rape crisis ventures, and that they facilitate liaison between the police and the voluntary sector. Progress has been made in some localities, including the provision of better facilities for the examination of rape survivors, liaison over training, and the encouragement of the police to inform raped women about rape crisis centres. Amongst the most important types of local authority initiatives in the 1980s and 1990s are the conferences

[35] Sarah Scott and Alison Dickens, 'Police and the Professionalisation of Rape', in Dunhill (ed.), *The Boys in Blue*.
[36] Ibid. 191.

on violence; these bring together the policy community and often lead to the establishment of continuing liaison groups. For example, the Crimes against Women conferences held in Leeds in the mid-1980s set the agenda for negotiations between feminists and the police which led to the establishment of the Leeds rape suite. Such conferences have been repeated all over the country. These are promising initiatives which may ensure the continuation of rape crisis group activity and feminist input into public responses to rape.

The problems facing feminists in reforming the law and the law enforcement of rape are enormous. Any demand concerned with sexuality risks being transposed into the language and policy of the moral purity campaigns (the relevance of this to the anti-pornography campaigns is discussed below).[37] There appears to be an intractable contradiction between the need to give due weight to a raped woman's complaint and the need to maintain the presumption of the innocence of the accused in rape cases. This means that reform of the trial procedure may be an ethical and political minefield. On the one hand, it is vital to establish that women's experience is valid, but, on the other hand, the requirement that guilt be proved is a major resource which we would not want to see eroded. Rapists have been protected over the years by the mythology of rape, especially by the presumption that accusations of rape are more likely to be false than is the case for other crimes. It is the mythology, and the cultural phallocentrism that supports it, which has to go, rather than the need to prove that the accused is guilty.

Although the path across this minefield has not yet been cleared, much has been accomplished. A major shift in the understanding of rape is apparent amongst some policy-makers. Rape is less likely to be conceived of now as stranger attack, and more likely to be reported; it has been shown that rape accusations are no more likely to be false than any other accusations. The struggle about issue definitions and control makes their work difficult for feminists, but it is also a sign of success, an indicator that the issue of rape is on the political agenda.

---

[37] Smart, *Feminism and Law.*

## SEXUAL HARASSMENT

Sexual harassment at work is another issue that is part of the spectrum of male sexual violence, but it has generated a rather different kind of feminist politics from the other issues in this chapter. Because it is a 'workplace' issue with important equal opportunities implications, we seriously considered placing our main discussion of sexual harassment in Chapter 6. But there are good reasons for including it here. Typically, instances of sexual harassment are evidence of the way in which men use sexuality to control women, and, as such, they are important to feminist explorations of sexual coercion. It has been recognized as a problem by feminists since the 1970s, and was raised in their discussions about the sources and meanings of male sexual violence. Sexual harassment includes a large area of behaviour ranging from verbal to physical abuse and rape. It is a salacious issue which often gets a lot of press coverage, but which was not recognized as an appropriate matter of concern in Britain until the early 1980s. It is a vexed issue for workplace managers and negotiators. Behaviour that most women would define as harassment is often considered to be harmless fun by many men. The problem is to gain acceptance of the perspectives that women may have of the issue. Once again, definition is very important.

Women against Sexual Harassment (WASH) was formed in 1984 and is the main feminist group campaigning on the issue. WASH defines sexual harassment as behaviour of a sexual nature which is unwelcome and unreciprocated and which might threaten job security and create a stressful or intimidating environment. The behaviour may include comments, looks, jokes, suggestions, pin-ups, and physical contact ranging from touching to pinching and rape. It is a widespread practice. A TUCRIC survey commissioned by the EOC found that, in 1983, 60 per cent of the women interviewed had been sexually harassed at work, most of them on more than one occasion.[38]

Perhaps because it is harassment in the 'public' rather than in the 'private' sphere, it has engaged different policy networks from

[38] See 'Sexual Harassment at Work', *Industrial Relations Review and Report*, 384 (20 Jan. 1987), 2–6.

other debates about sexual violence. Because it is a workplace problem, both the trade unions and the equal opportunities policy communities have developed strategies to deal with it. In the trade-union movement, it was the women members of NALGO in Liverpool who took the lead. The local equal opportunities working party initiated discussion in 1981. Nationally, NALGO put out a statement in 1981 entitled 'Sexual Harassment is a Union Issue', and NATFHE, prompted by its women's rights panel, followed with 'Fighting Sexual Harassment at Work: An Issue for NATFHE' in 1982. During the 1980s other trade unions took up the issue, which was consistently endorsed by the TUC after 1983. Sarah Boston attributes this to the increasing presence of women in the unions during the 1970s and 1980s. The efforts that unions made to attract more women workers and to negotiate benefits for them were clearly a factor.[39]

The EOC was also interested in the issue of sexual harassment by the early 1980s. Complaints and queries started around 1984, after which they came in at an increasing rate, but there was no statutory provision against such harassment. Characteristically, the EOC watched for an appropriate legal opportunity. The opportunity came in 1986, when the Scottish Court of Session found that sexual harassment constituted sex discrimination in *Porcelli* v. *Strathclyde Regional Council*. In giving judgment, Lord Emslie said: 'Sexual harassment is a particularly degrading unacceptable form of treatment which it must have been the intention of Parliament to restrain.' This decision was strengthened when the Court of Appeal ruled in *DeSouza* v. *The Automobile Association*, confirmed in 1986, that employers are liable for acts of discrimination by their employees. That the courts and tribunals will take the issue seriously is evident in the rising levels of compensation that were being awarded by tribunals at the end of the decade.[40]

Most feminists who write about sexual harassment are clear that it is about power. It is primarily a demonstration and assertion of male power which serves to 'keep women in an inferior position. Treating women as sexual beings rather than working

---

[39] Sarah Boston, *Women Workers and the Trade Unions* (Lawrence and Wishart, London, 1987), ch. 12.

[40] For a good review of the implications of early cases, see 'Sexual Harassment at Work'.

Most feminists agree that pornography eroticizes power and domination. The domination of women by men is the mainstay of most pornography. This (for a variety of reasons) arouses both men and women, which leads to the assumption that, in sex, domination by men and submission by women must be natural. If it is natural in sex (which is natural), it must also be natural in other parts of social life. There is also agreement that violent or sadistic pornography, which shows women and/or children as raped, mutilated, murdered, etc., is objectionable. However, the meaning of violent pornography, and its importance, are matters of disagreement. During the 1980s two basic views of pornography were developed by feminists. Beverly Brown[45] called them the 'pornography as violence' position and the 'pornography as representation' position. Revolutionary and Radical feminists take the former view, arguing that pornography is society's most significant means of subordinating women and that violent pornography reveals men's true sexuality.

Other feminists disagree. A group of Socialist feminist intellectuals is prominent in advancing the 'pornography as representation' position, citing feminist work on images and representation and its meaning and effects. Drawing on work by Ros Coward,[46] Annette Kuhn,[47] and others, the argument is that pornography is a 'regime of representation'. The representations show bodies, usually naked, in a sexualized way, or people involved in the sex act, according to certain conventions which are interpreted by society as pornographic. On this interpretation, nothing is intrinsically pornographic. Rather, there are codes of interpretation which we learn and apply. These are conditioned by context and circumstance. There is a growing body of scholarship which demonstrates that there is a pornographic 'genre' attached to the way in which women are portrayed. This pornographic genre is widespread. Many of the poses, expressions, juxtapositions of bodies, arrangements of clothes, even the vulnerability of the posed model—common devices in the advertising that makes use of images of women—may be shown to conform to this regime

[45] Quoted in Smart, *Feminism and Law*, ch. 6.
[46] R. Coward, 'Sexual Violence and Sexuality', in Feminist Review (ed.), *Sexual Violence: A Reader* (Virago, London, 1987).
[47] Annette Kuhn, *The Power of the Image* (Routledge and Kegan Paul, London, 1985).

people undermines them and helps prevent them being treated as workers on the same terms as men.'[41] Perceptions of feminist involvement in this issue vary. Melissa Benn wrote in 1985[42] that, despite its importance, she was able to find little enthusiasm for campaigns about sexual harassment. In 1988 she repeated this assertion in the *Guardian*, commenting that the sexual harassment issue had never really ignited or mobilized feminists. This is partly attributable to the fact that it is a quite technical campaign, but also, she suggests, it is because the sexual harassment campaign did not really come out of the autonomous women's movement. Rather, she categorizes it as an initiative by individual women within mixed, but male-dominated, organizations such as trade unions. Melissa Benn is very critical of the campaign, arguing that sexual harassment does not affect all women in the same way, and that those who are active on the issue show little awareness of the importance of racism. Other commentators see it differently. Sarah Boston[43] details the activities of both black and white women trade-unionists in her account of women's organization in British trade unions during the 1980s. Vicky Seddon's account takes a rather different line. She regards the questioning of male sexual power at work and on the street as an obvious development of the WLM.[44] In this sense, the politicization of the issue of sexual harassment did come from the autonomous women's movement.

## ANTI-PORNOGRAPHY CAMPAIGNS AND THE PORNOGRAPHY DEBATES

Pornography is another issue that has been processed in 'established' political channels. But feminist activity in this area is different again from other issues that are defined in terms of male sexual violence. Divisions among feminists about pornography are severe, and the argument about definitions is a continuing feature of the politics of pornography. There has been feminist

[41] Maryon Tysoe, 'The Sexual Harassers', *New Society*, 4 Nov. 1982.
[42] Melissa Benn, 'Isn't Sexual Harassment Really about Masculinity?', *Spare Rib*, July 1985.
[43] Boston, *Women Workers and Trade Unions*.
[44] Vicky Seddon, 'Keeping Women in their Place', *Marxism Today*, July 1983: 20–4.

interest in the issue since the early 1970s, but activity took off during the 1980s, when new campaigns about pornography attracted increasing popular support. But popular support for their campaigns has not established feminist definitions of the issue in the minds of the public, in the view of 'informed opinion', or amongst policy-makers. This is partly because many other groups have an interest in making pornography a political issue. But that is not the only obstacle. Definitions of the pornography issue are also contested within feminism, where there is disagreement about the causes, nature, effects, and responses to pornographic representations and their marketing. The most influential views are those that stress the violent associations of pornography. The very fact that we discuss the issue here, in a chapter about sex, violence, and institutions, is a recognition of the effect of feminist interpretations of pornography which have emphasized its violent and coercive dimensions. But some feminists would argue that the connections between violence and pornography are beside the point, part of another issue. They maintain that once the two issues of pornography and violence are separated, the futility and, indeed, the danger of censorship as a solution become apparent. But such arguments have not prevailed. The acceptability of censorship has provoked divisions between liberals and New Right both amongst feminists and in the wider political arena. Pornography therefore presents a complex pattern of politics in which different groups of feminists have allied with groups on the Right, the Left, and in the centre of the political spectrum. It is almost impossible to isolate the arguments and debates from the context in which they take place. Moreover, the absence of agreement about definitions, and the controversial nature of censorship as a proposed solution, set a framework in which feminist interventions might best be characterized as struggles over definitions. Our account of pornography therefore includes a considerable amount of background detail and an extensive discussion of different efforts by feminists to understand the nature of pornography and the discourse in which it is embedded.

Contemporary feminist debates about pornography really began in the United States, where the issue trundled along for some years before it took off with the publication of Andrea Dworkin's *Pornography: Men Possessing Women* in 1979, which

was published in Britain in 1981. Pornography is an issue which emphasizes many of the divisions between feminists. It also taps the ambivalence of women who find positions on one or the other side of these divisions difficult to sustain in the face of contradictory experiences and emotions. As we write, the debate is in full flow. It is a debate that has both popular and intellectual manifestations, and it is often bitter and sectarian. It is difficult to predict which views will prevail either in the women's movement or in British society generally.

It is possible to distinguish three kinds of problems in making policy about pornography: problems of response, problems of meaning, and problems of strategy. Each of these affects and is affected by each of the others. The main problem of response is affected by the extreme difficulty of trying to understand and analyse the extreme difficulty of trying to understand and analyse pornography from feminist perspectives. Feelings of anger, arousal, despair—sometimes all of these at once—are frequently reported. If feminists are to be true to their principles of empowering women, then each type of response must be confronted and understood. Problems of meaning include difficulties and disagreements about definitions, the nature of evidence, and literal effects. Feminists disagree both about appropriate definitions of pornography and about whether the construction of such a definition is an appropriate endeavour. This overlaps with disagreement about whether pornography may be identified by the specific images that it offers, or whether it is the context of the images and their offering which gives sexual images a degrading character. There is also an important argument about whether pornography causes rape and other sexual violence, or whether it simply represents it and elicits a response only at the level of fantasy.

There are two problems about strategy: one is what to do about pornography, and the other is what sort of alliances should be made to obtain a preferred solution. Should feminists ally with the Right to promote bans or licensing restrictions on pornography? Is it appropriate to increase state powers over the production of images and their display? Is it appropriate to seek protection from the state at all? In engaging the issue of pornography, feminists find themselves caught up in debates about censorship and state power that have been hotly and bitterly contested for some years.

of representation. The codes of pornography are fragmentation, submission, and availability, and these are apparent everywhere. The display of women's breasts in the daily newspapers, the arrangement of women's submissive bodies around motor cars, etc., is evidence that pornographic representation is now openly encoded. Both pornographers and advertisers promote a repertoire of images that promise certain kinds of pleasure. When a viewer is invited to desire a particular object, this is often done by making it appear available, submissive, and compliant. It is there to please. 'The object (whether a woman or a car) is ready and able to do anything, go anywhere you please. Any possible assertion of autonomy (i.e. saying no, breaking down) is excluded.'

It is this reduction to the level of commodities, the signification of women as having no autonomy, which constitutes the offensiveness.[48] To summarize: pornography is only one source of degrading images of powerless, submissive women. The political implications of the 'pornography as representation' position are twofold. First, nothing will be gained by banning pornography when so many other representations of women encode the same meanings; and, secondly, there is no reason why pornography should degrade women; it is possible to construct a non-sexist pornography, a feminist-inspired erotica.

That such an erotica is possible is denied by many Radical feminists, who are much more concerned about the association between violence and pornography, a concern which shows itself in two ways. First, their writing often concentrates on specific items of violent pornography rather than considering its full variety and its context. Secondly, at the heart of their political analysis is the contention that pornography is one of the main causes of male sexual violence. Indeed, some British Radical feminists accept unreservedly that pornography is the main cause of women's subordination.

The debate is difficult to assess, not least because it tends not to be conducted at the same intellectual level, over the same issues, or on the same political terrain. It is unusual to find the protagonists answering each other's arguments. More usual is a crossfire of parallel accusations which leaves each side convinced

---

[48] Coward, 'Sexual Violence and Sexuality'.

that their case is irrefutable. Matters are made more complicated by the fact that, as we described in Chapter 4, this is a three-sided debate for feminists. There were three main feminist campaigning groups at the end of 1991: Campaign against Pornography (CAP), Campaign against Pornography and Censorship (CAPC), and Feminists against Censorship (FAC). As their names imply, much of the debate was about censorship.

## The Political Context of the Pornography Debates

In order to provide an adequate contextualization of the feminist pornography debates, it is necessary to provide two brief background sketches. The first is an outline of the various positions in long-standing debates about censorship in Britain; the second is an account of the MacKinnon/Dworkin ordinance which many feminists in the United States have tried to incorporate into American law.

In Britain, feminist debates about pornography intersect—and therefore compete for attention and influence—with two well-entrenched positions on censorship: that of the liberal establishment and that of the moral Right. As is the case with feminist views, each position is a continuum, each contains contradictions and ambiguities. There is not enough space to explore all of this here, so we offer only a brief and somewhat simplified outline. Carol Smart wrote what, in our view, remains the best feminist-inspired summary accounts of the two positions.[49] She inferred the liberal establishment view from the 1979 report of the Williams Committee on Obscenity and Film Censorship. The strategy of the Williams Committee was to treat sexual matters as matters of individual taste, preference, and concern. The committee was not interested in the wider questions of sexual power and dominance. Their definition of pornography identified two components: intention to arouse sexually, and the explicit representation of sexual material. This two-part definition was constructed in order to protect 'art' from legal interference, and the individual from unwanted encounters with pornography. The idea was that such a definition would offer objective measurable criteria for classifying material as pornographic, and then the dis-

[49] Smart, *Feminism and Law*, ch. 6.

play of such material could be controlled. Both components needed to be present for the matter to be classified as pornographic. In practice, however, the two-part definition collapses into one, as only explicitness can be 'objectively' measured. Intention is always contentious, and, argues Smart, actual arousal may only be presumed. In practice, therefore, both will be read off from explicitness.

The Williams Committee did not find the evidence that pornography led to violence convincing, and therefore it did not think that censorship was necessary. Its general view was that censorship should be kept to the minimum possible level. The moral Right, on the other hand, faces no such difficulties. It is pro-censorship, and seeks the widest possible ambit of control. Its strategy is to expand the definition of pornography. In the context of British law, custom, and practice, such a strategy is fairly straightforward. The tendency has been to restrict the publication of materials deemed to be 'obscene' or 'indecent'. Both terms have working legal definitions: if an object or representation is obscene, it is likely to deprave. The general public are not regarded as uniformly depravable, and policy about obscene material normally restricts its scope to those likely to come into contact with it. 'Indecent' is a more flexible term, defined in the 'Clapham omnibus' tradition. It consists of 'anything', said Lord Denning in 1976, 'which an ordinary decent man or woman would find to be shocking, disgusting or revolting'. Leaders of the moral Right such as Lord Longford, Mary Whitehouse, and Winston Churchill have sought to substitute the wider notion of indecency for the more restricted notion of obscenity. They have had some success. The Indecent Displays Act of 1981 prohibits public display of materials which would be offensive to the general public. For example, pornographic magazines may not be kept at or below eye-level in newsagents. The moral Right believes that pornography is harmful and that it consists mainly of representations of sex. Their views would not preclude the banning of all representations of sex, including sex education materials. The moral Right tend to be sexual conservatives, and the liberal establishment tend to be sexual libertarians, a division that informs their views about censorship.

To understand the debates amongst United States feminists that became so influential in Britain during the 1980s and 1990s, it is important to start with the campaigns initiated by Andrea Dworkin and Catherine MacKinnon. City councils in the United States can pass local legislation as they wish. Such laws, called ordinances, must be constitutional, but otherwise they are unrestricted. Dworkin and MacKinnon inaugurated a new phase in the United States anti-pornography campaigns when they drafted an ordinance that was submitted to Minneapolis City Council in 1983. The ordinance enabled women to take pornographers to court on the grounds that pornography discriminated against women, denying them the equality to which they were legally entitled. The draft ordinance generated considerable controversy, as the city council considered its implications in a set of widely publicized hearings in which evidence was given by women who had been harmed by pornography, by academics, lawyers, and jurists. Minneapolis decided not to pass the ordinance; it was later passed by the Indianapolis City Council, but it was declared unconstitutional by the Supreme Court. Briefs (evidence) were presented to the court by opposing groups of feminists. Feminists who opposed the ordinance called themselves the Feminists Anti-Censorship Task Force (FACT). The signatories of the FACT brief were mainly feminist intellectuals and artists, including a few men. The censorship and pornography debate among American feminists is a very bitter one which shows no signs of subsiding. The point of the Dworkin/MacKinnon ordinance (or the Minneapolis ordinance, as it is sometimes called) is, its sponsors argue, that it categorizes pornography as a 'discriminatory practice based on sex which denies women equality in society'. It offers six alternative definitions of pornography which specify that it is images that are violent in various ways, that the images depict male domination of women and that they are degrading to women, and that they show women enjoying their degradation. Such images encourage men to believe that women enjoy violent and degrading sexual treatment, and the supporters of the ordinance assert that pornography is behind male sexual violence and that it is the chief cause of the domination of women by men.

The strategic thinking behind the ordinance is that it is the women who have been discriminated against, rather than law-enforcement officers, who may decide to take cases to court. This ostensibly avoids the problem of increasing the powers of state censors. Cases may be brought against producers or sellers of people undermines them and helps prevent them being treated as workers on the same terms as men.'[41] Perceptions of feminist involvement in this issue vary. Melissa Benn wrote in 1985[42] that, despite its importance, she was able to find little enthusiasm for campaigns about sexual harassment. In 1988 she repeated this assertion in the *Guardian*, commenting that the sexual harassment issue had never really ignited or mobilized feminists. This is partly attributable to the fact that it is a quite technical campaign, but also, she suggests, it is because the sexual harassment campaign did not really come out of the autonomous women's movement. Rather, she categorizes it as an initiative by individual women within mixed, but male-dominated, organizations such as trade unions. Melissa Benn is very critical of the campaign, arguing that sexual harassment does not affect all women in the same way, and that those who are active on the issue show little awareness of the importance of racism. Other commentators see it differently. Sarah Boston[43] details the activities of both black and white women trade-unionists in her account of women's organization in British trade unions during the 1980s. Vicky Seddon's account takes a rather different line. She regards the questioning of male sexual power at work and on the street as an obvious development of the WLM.[44] In this sense, the politicization of the issue of sexual harassment did come from the autonomous women's movement.

## ANTI-PORNOGRAPHY CAMPAIGNS AND THE PORNOGRAPHY DEBATES

Pornography is another issue that has been processed in 'established' political channels. But feminist activity in this area is different again from other issues that are defined in terms of male sexual violence. Divisions among feminists about pornography are severe, and the argument about definitions is a continuing feature of the politics of pornography. There has been feminist

[41] Maryon Tysoe, 'The Sexual Harassers', *New Society*, 4 Nov. 1982.
[42] Melissa Benn, 'Isn't Sexual Harassment Really about Masculinity?', *Spare Rib*, July 1985.
[43] Boston, *Women Workers and Trade Unions*.
[44] Vicky Seddon, 'Keeping Women in their Place', *Marxism Today*, July 1983: 20–4.

interest in the issue since the early 1970s, but activity took off during the 1980s, when new campaigns about pornography attracted increasing popular support. But popular support for their campaigns has not established feminist definitions of the issue in the minds of the public, in the view of 'informed opinion', or amongst policy-makers. This is partly because many other groups have an interest in making pornography a political issue. But that is not the only obstacle. Definitions of the pornography issue are also contested within feminism, where there is disagreement about the causes, nature, effects, and responses to pornographic representations and their marketing. The most influential views are those that stress the violent associations of pornography. The very fact that we discuss the issue here, in a chapter about sex, violence, and institutions, is a recognition of the effect of feminist interpretations of pornography which have emphasized its violent and coercive dimensions. But some feminists would argue that the connections between violence and pornography are beside the point, part of another issue. They maintain that once the two issues of pornography and violence are separated, the futility and, indeed, the danger of censorship as a solution become apparent. But such arguments have not prevailed. The acceptability of censorship has provoked divisions between liberals and New Right both amongst feminists and in the wider political arena. Pornography therefore presents a complex pattern of politics in which different groups of feminists have allied with groups on the Right, the Left, and in the centre of the political spectrum. It is almost impossible to isolate the arguments and debates from the context in which they take place. Moreover, the absence of agreement about definitions, and the controversial nature of censorship as a proposed solution, set a framework in which feminist interventions might best be characterized as struggles over definitions. Our account of pornography therefore includes a considerable amount of background detail and an extensive discussion of different efforts by feminists to understand the nature of pornography and the discourse in which it is embedded.

Contemporary feminist debates about pornography really began in the United States, where the issue trundled along for some years before it took off with the publication of Andrea Dworkin's *Pornography: Men Possessing Women* in 1979, which was published in Britain in 1981. Pornography is an issue which emphasizes many of the divisions between feminists. It also taps the ambivalence of women who find positions on one or the other side of these divisions difficult to sustain in the face of contradictory experiences and emotions. As we write, the debate is in full flow. It is a debate that has both popular and intellectual manifestations, and it is often bitter and sectarian. It is difficult to predict which views will prevail either in the women's movement or in British society generally.

It is possible to distinguish three kinds of problems in making policy about pornography: problems of response, problems of meaning, and problems of strategy. Each of these affects and is affected by each of the others. The main problem of response is the extreme difficulty of trying to understand and analyse pornography from feminist perspectives. Feelings of anger, arousal, despair—sometimes all of these at once—are frequently reported. If feminists are to be true to their principles of empowering women, then each type of response must be confronted and understood. Problems of meaning include difficulties and disagreements about definitions, the nature of evidence, and literal effects. Feminists disagree both about appropriate definitions of pornography and about whether the construction of such a definition is an appropriate endeavour. This overlaps with disagreement about whether pornography may be identified by the specific images that it offers, or whether it is the context of the images and their offering which gives sexual images a degrading character. There is also an important argument about whether pornography causes rape and other sexual violence, or whether it simply represents it and elicits a response only at the level of fantasy.

There are two problems about strategy: one is what to do about pornography, and the other is what sort of alliances should be made to obtain a preferred solution. Should feminists ally with the Right to promote bans or licensing restrictions on pornography? Is it appropriate to increase state powers over the production of images and their display? Is it appropriate to seek protection from the state at all? In engaging the issue of pornography, feminists find themselves caught up in debates about censorship and state power that have been hotly and bitterly contested for some years.

Most feminists agree that pornography eroticizes power and domination. The domination of women by men is the mainstay of most pornography. This (for a variety of reasons) arouses both men and women, which leads to the assumption that, in sex, domination by men and submission by women must be natural. If it is natural in sex (which is natural), it must also be natural in other parts of social life. There is also agreement that violent or sadistic pornography, which shows women and/or children as raped, mutilated, murdered, etc., is objectionable. However, the meaning of violent pornography, and its importance, are matters of disagreement. During the 1980s two basic views of pornography were developed by feminists. Beverly Brown[45] called them the 'pornography as violence' position and the 'pornography as representation' position. Revolutionary and Radical feminists take the former view, arguing that pornography is society's most significant means of subordinating women and that violent pornography reveals men's true sexuality.

Other feminists disagree. A group of Socialist feminist intellectuals is prominent in advancing the 'pornography as representation' position, citing feminist work on images and representation and its meaning and effects. Drawing on work by Ros Coward,[46] Annette Kuhn,[47] and others, the argument is that pornography is a 'regime of representation'. The representations show bodies, usually naked, in a sexualized way, or people involved in the sex act, according to certain conventions which are interpreted by society as pornographic. On this interpretation, nothing is intrinsically pornographic. Rather, there are codes of interpretation which we learn and apply. These are conditioned by context and circumstance. There is a growing body of scholarship which demonstrates that there is a pornographic 'genre' attached to the way in which women are portrayed. This pornographic genre is widespread. Many of the poses, expressions, juxtapositions of bodies, arrangements of clothes, even the vulnerability of the posed model—common devices in the advertising that makes use of images of women—may be shown to conform to this regime

[45] Quoted in Smart, *Feminism and Law*, ch. 6.

[46] R. Coward, 'Sexual Violence and Sexuality', in Feminist Review (ed.), *Sexual Violence: A Reader* (Virago, London, 1987).

[47] Annette Kuhn, *The Power of the Image* (Routledge and Kegan Paul, London, 1985).

of representation. The codes of pornography are fragmentation, submission, and availability, and these are apparent everywhere. The display of women's breasts in the daily newspapers, the arrangement of women's submissive bodies around motor cars, etc., is evidence that pornographic representation is now openly encoded. Both pornographers and advertisers promote a repertoire of images that promise certain kinds of pleasure. When a viewer is invited to desire a particular object, this is often done by making it appear available, submissive, and compliant. It is there to please. 'The object (whether a woman or a car) is ready and able to do anything, go anywhere you please. Any possible assertion of autonomy (i.e. saying no, breaking down) is excluded.'

It is this reduction to the level of commodities, the signification of women as having no autonomy, which constitutes the offensiveness.[48] To summarize: pornography is only one source of degrading images of powerless, submissive women. The political implications of the 'pornography as representation' position are twofold. First, nothing will be gained by banning pornography when so many other representations of women encode the same meanings; and, secondly, there is no reason why pornography should degrade women; it is possible to construct a non-sexist pornography, a feminist-inspired erotica.

That such an erotica is possible is denied by many Radical feminists, who are much more concerned about the association between violence and pornography, a concern which shows itself in two ways. First, their writing often concentrates on specific items of violent pornography rather than considering its full variety and its context. Secondly, at the heart of their political analysis is the contention that pornography is one of the main causes of male sexual violence. Indeed, some British Radical feminists accept unreservedly that pornography is the main cause of women's subordination.

The debate is difficult to assess, not least because it tends not to be conducted at the same intellectual level, over the same issues, or on the same political terrain. It is unusual to find the protagonists answering each other's arguments. More usual is a crossfire of parallel accusations which leaves each side convinced

---

[48] Coward, 'Sexual Violence and Sexuality'.

that their case is irrefutable. Matters are made more complicated by the fact that, as we described in Chapter 4, this is a three-sided debate for feminists. There were three main feminist campaigning groups at the end of 1991: Campaign against Pornography (CAP), Campaign against Pornography and Censorship (CAPC), and Feminists against Censorship (FAC). As their names imply, much of the debate was about censorship.

### The Political Context of the Pornography Debates

In order to provide an adequate contextualization of the feminist pornography debates, it is necessary to provide two brief background sketches. The first is an outline of the various positions in long-standing debates about censorship in Britain; the second is an account of the MacKinnon/Dworkin ordinance which many feminists in the United States have tried to incorporate into American law.

In Britain, feminist debates about pornography intersect—and therefore compete for attention and influence—with two well-entrenched positions on censorship: that of the liberal establishment and that of the moral Right. As is the case with feminist views, each position is a continuum, each contains contradictions and ambiguities. There is not enough space to explore all of this here, so we offer only a brief and somewhat simplified outline. Carol Smart wrote what, in our view, remains the best feminist-inspired summary accounts of the two positions.[49] She inferred the liberal establishment view from the 1979 report of the Williams Committee on Obscenity and Film Censorship. The strategy of the Williams Committee was to treat sexual matters as matters of individual taste, preference, and concern. The committee was not interested in the wider questions of sexual power and dominance. Their definition of pornography identified two components: intention to arouse sexually, and the explicit representation of sexual material. This two-part definition was constructed in order to protect 'art' from legal interference, and the individual from unwanted encounters with pornography. The idea was that such a definition would offer objective measurable criteria for classifying material as pornographic, and then the dis-

[49] Smart, *Feminism and Law*, ch. 6.

play of such material could be controlled. Both components needed to be present for the matter to be classified as pornographic. In practice, however, the two-part definition collapses into one, as only explicitness can be 'objectively' measured. Intention is always contentious, and, argues Smart, actual arousal may only be presumed. In practice, therefore, both will be read off from explicitness.

The Williams Committee did not find the evidence that pornography led to violence convincing, and therefore it did not think that censorship was necessary. Its general view was that censorship should be kept to the minimum possible level. The moral Right, on the other hand, faces no such difficulties. It is pro-censorship, and seeks the widest possible ambit of control. Its strategy is to expand the definition of pornography. In the context of British law, custom, and practice, such a strategy is fairly straightforward. The tendency has been to restrict the publication of materials deemed to be 'obscene' or 'indecent'. Both terms have working legal definitions: if an object or representation is obscene, it is likely to deprave. The general public are not regarded as uniformly depravable, and policy about obscene material normally restricts its scope to those likely to come into contact with it. 'Indecent' is a more flexible term, defined in the 'Clapham omnibus' tradition. It consists of 'anything', said Lord Denning in 1976, 'which an ordinary decent man or woman would find to be shocking, disgusting or revolting'. Leaders of the moral Right such as Lord Longford, Mary Whitehouse, and Winston Churchill have sought to substitute the wider notion of indecency for the more restricted notion of obscenity. They have had some success. The Indecent Displays Act of 1981 prohibits public display of materials which would be offensive to the general public. For example, pornographic magazines may not be kept at or below eye-level in newsagents. The moral Right believes that pornography is harmful and that it consists mainly of representations of sex. Their views would not preclude the banning of all representations of sex, including sex education materials. The moral Right tend to be sexual conservatives, and the liberal establishment tend to be sexual libertarians, a division that informs their views about censorship.

To understand the debates amongst United States feminists that became so influential in Britain during the 1980s and 1990s, it is important to start with the campaigns initiated by Andrea Dworkin and Catherine MacKinnon. City councils in the United States can pass local legislation as they wish. Such laws, called ordinances, must be constitutional, but otherwise they are unrestricted. Dworkin and MacKinnon inaugurated a new phase in the United States anti-pornography campaigns when they drafted an ordinance that was submitted to Minneapolis City Council in 1983. The ordinance enabled women to take pornographers to court on the grounds that pornography discriminated against women, denying them the equality to which they were legally entitled. The draft ordinance generated considerable controversy, as the city council considered its implications in a set of widely publicized hearings in which evidence was given by women who had been harmed by pornography, by academics, lawyers, and jurists. Minneapolis decided not to pass the ordinance; it was later passed by the Indianapolis City Council, but it was declared unconstitutional by the Supreme Court. Briefs (evidence) were presented to the court by opposing groups of feminists. Feminists who opposed the ordinance called themselves the Feminists Anti-Censorship Task Force (FACT). The signatories of the FACT brief were mainly feminist intellectuals and artists, including a few men. The censorship and pornography debate among American feminists is a very bitter one which shows no signs of subsiding. The point of the Dworkin/MacKinnon ordinance (or the Minneapolis ordinance, as it is sometimes called) is, its sponsors argue, that it categorizes pornography as a 'discriminatory practice based on sex which denies women equality in society'. It offers six alternative definitions of pornography which specify that it is images that are violent in various ways, that the images depict male domination of women and that they are degrading to women, and that they show women enjoying their degradation. Such images encourage men to believe that women enjoy violent and degrading sexual treatment, and the supporters of the ordinance assert that pornography is behind male sexual violence and that it is the chief cause of the domination of women by men.

The strategic thinking behind the ordinance is that it is the women who have been discriminated against, rather than law-enforcement officers, who may decide to take cases to court. This ostensibly avoids the problem of increasing the powers of state censors. Cases may be brought against producers or sellers of

in the mid-1980s. The one and only issue of a lesbian sex magazine called QUIM was banned from Sisterwrite and Gays the
Word bookshops (see Chapter 3). The meaning of fantasy and
the nature of lesbian sexual arousal became part of the debate
about pornography and censorship.

The terms of the debates between the opposing camps are
sometimes reasoned and careful, but more often polemical and
bitter. On occasion, they are simply vicious. Sheila Jeffreys
asserts in her essay in the *Feminism and Censorship* collection
edited by Chester and Dickey that what motivates anti-censorship feminists is not their convictions but their ambitions, their
desire to climb career ladders and thus avoid offending the powerful liberal establishment figures who control such ladders. Anti-
censorship feminists have been accused of being in alliance with
the pornographers, whilst pro-censorship feminists are accused of
being against sex. Elizabeth Wilson has remarked that the danger
of focusing campaigns on the sexually explicit and on literal
effects is that connections between pornography and other
degrading images of women are ignored, and the contradictory
uses to which the imagery is put goes unremarked.[51] Speech,
words, and images are simply speech, words, and images. What
matters is behaviour, and laws already exist to prohibit the violent behaviour that is objected to by pro-censorship feminists.
FAC warns against relying on the state not to misuse its powers,
and points out that the increasing strength of the right makes the
1990s a very bad time to call for any increases in state power.

In practice, the feminist pornography campaigns involve different sorts of people with different preoccupations. CAP and
CAPC are led mainly by people who have some experience of
sexual violence, either in their work or as victims, and they campaign mainly on the basis of information and evidence about sexual violence. The material that they oppose and analyse is
offensive, involving strong, violent images which they describe in
their debates. The fact that this evidence is episodic, and that the
evidence of literal effects is often anecdotal, is often obscured by
the sheer power of the images and the strength of the popular
emotional response to them. FAC, on the other hand, is led by

---

[51] Elizabeth Wilson, 'Against Feminist Fundamentalism', *New Statesman*, 23
June 1989.

academics, intellectuals, and artists, some of who are directly involved in the production of feminist erotica. They abhor the violent and degrading images of much pornography, but they are concerned to protect 'art' and to explore sexual imagery and representations. The result is that the two groups often do not address the same issues. What is taking place is not so much a debate as the telling of a set of parallel accounts by feminists who are separately engaged in working out their positions on the pornography issue. Their accounts will have to become a debate if feminists are to achieve any unity on the issue.

## CONCLUSIONS: FEMINISM AND MALE VIOLENCE

Our discussion shows that despite a significant cross-fertilization of feminist views about different aspects of male sexual violence, and despite considerable co-operation in particular campaigns, there are still many important disagreements over these issues. For over twenty years, concerns about male violence have been interwoven with other significant feminist issues. They were argued about and discussed in an atmosphere that was often uncomfortable, sometimes mistrustful and hostile, as British feminists became aware of the importance of the issues that divide them.

Some of the divisions have eased. By the early 1990s, as the arguments about racial difference and racism which were so bitterly fought during the 1980s begin to recede, black feminists were beginning to note the similarities between their circumstances and those of white women. For example, in a discussion of the violence of the 1985 Brixton riots, Anna Hearne argued that the sadism and racism of the British should not obscure the sexism of black men to black women, two of whom were raped during the riot by black youths. She complains that, too often, fear of racism led white women on the Left to keep silent about violence in the black communities. It is wrong, she wrote, for white women to corrupt their reasons for fighting racism with the idea that racial oppression excuses the sexual violence of the black male. Only when black women speak out against the violence that they received within their communities will things improve for black women.[52] By 1991, when we interviewed black

[52] Anna J. Hearne, 'Racism, Rape and Riots', *Trouble and Strife*, 9 (Summer 1986) 9 14.

feminists working in refuges, such implicit comparisons between black and white women were being made explicit.

Race was not the only 'difference' issue to feature in feminist work about male violence. Division about sexuality also persisted, this time expressed as a problem of how to understand male sexual behaviour. This disagreement continues to be sharp. Margaret Hunt recently pointed out in *Feminist Review* that a clear analogy could be drawn between the contemporary moral Right and past social purity movements. She found a striking parallel between the sexual views of the women in the nineteenth-century social purity movement and those expressed by the contemporary Radical feminist Sheila Jeffreys. She expressed concern that in allying with the moral Right, Radical feminists were ignoring the lesson of the past—that conservatives normally co-opt feminists, rather than the other way around. Jeffreys and her supporters continued to blame sexual libertarians for the growth of male sexual violence.[53] The implication of Jeffreys's arguments is that there is a correct feminist sexual practice, one in which only certain kinds of sex are acceptable. This was apparent in the Radical feminists' widespread rejection of attempts to produce a feminist erotica. Such rejections, and their accompanying calls for censorship, were rejections of difference and variety, the product of a notion, often unarticulated, of an essential female nature. From that notion, there was a relatively straight path to strategies of intolerance and control. In a climate of sexual panic such as that generated by the AIDS crisis, the consequences of such intolerance may be catastrophic.[54]

Socialist feminists were quick to criticize any feminist alliance with the political Right. They were especially mindful of the fact that feminist campaigners did not have the power to secure their definitions and priorities through the processes of law-making and law enforcement. They drew attention to the parallels between the social purity campaigns of the last century and the new anti-pornography campaigns. Such campaigns were always dangerous, because there could be no guarantee—indeed, there

---

[53] See Sheila Jeffreys, *Anticlimax* (The Women's Press, London, 1990), for a recent restatement of this position.

[54] Margaret Hunt, 'The De-Eroticization of Women's Liberation: Social Purity Movements and the Revolutionary Feminism of Sheila Jeffreys', *Feminist Review*, 34 (Spring 1990), 23–46.

was little likelihood—that censorship or social purity policies would be implemented by officials who are sympathetic to feminist values. It was not feminists who controlled the levers of state power.[55] Too often, Radical feminists appeared to be unaware of such dangers. Indeed, they sometimes appeared to believe the very opposite. For example, Sheila Jeffreys attributed an unrealistically large measure of political power to feminism when she asserted that it was the insecurities felt by men in the face of newly powerful women which made them crave images that assert male dominance and female submission—in other words, that the growth in the market for violent pornographic representations was an indicator of a dimunition of male power.[56]

Jeffreys's contention seems to us to be a somewhat optimistic and overly simple formulation. The feminist achievement in the politics of sexual coercion is a reformulation of the problem. Although much has been accomplished, this work is far from complete. Feminists have defined problems in terms of male violence, because it was possible to marshall a huge body of evidence which showed that this was a reasonable way of understanding the problems. That was a necessary beginning. Now the plausibility of such definitions should be examined and, if it is false, exposed. For feminists to do this, it will be necessary to look closely and courageously at evidence and ideas about maleness and the construction of masculinity and feminity, and the structures of thought which support that evidence and those ideas. Such exploration should be constrained neither by essentialist assumptions about sexual characteristics nor by gloomy prognostications about the political uses to which feminist work might be put.

We also take issue with the view that feminists are too weak politically to risk placing the pornography issue on the public agenda. The weakness of this argument—that feminists have insufficient power to risk imposing their preferred policy solutions—lies in its implicit assumption that feminist ambition should be commensurate with feminist political power. We dispute this understanding of political power. Although we are not convinced of the case for censorship, we do not agree that the

[55] Rosemary Betterton, 'How Do Women Look? The Female Nude in the Work of Suzanne Valedon', *Feminist Review*, 19 (1985), 3–24.
[56] Jeffreys, *Anticlimax*.

reason for its avoidance lies in asymmetric power relations. That would mean giving up the battle before it is joined, that ignores the power of ideas to alter political outcomes. The project to understand sexual coercion has its own (compulsive) dynamic, and the task now is to make further explorations of the significance of images and representations to constructions of identity and sexuality, whilst at the same time developing the practical policies that feminism has initiated. If the campaigns in favour of censorship are dangerous, and we believe that they probably are, then what will alter their focus is the open debate and the development of new understandings which come from a continuous exploration and contestation of dominant meanings of particular phenomena. The politics of the movements to alter the political treatment of domestic violence, rape, and sexual harassment are all proof that such a strategy, whilst difficult, is possible and productive.

# 10

# Conclusion

So far we have discussed, issue by issue, the emergence of the many kinds of politics that are features of contemporary British feminism. That their development since 1979 has been both rapid and complex is abundantly clear. British feminism of the early 1990s is a very different phenomenon to that of the end of the 1970s. And yet there are important continuities in the movement. Preoccupations with equality, autonomy, difference, and identity widened and became more sophisticated, but they continued as distinctive components of feminist thinking. Feminist achievements were considerable as both its activists and values found new and more numerous places in public life. If the WLM itself declined, this was neither universal nor uniform. Although activism around individual issue areas fluctuated, there has been no time since 1979 when feminists were not mobilizing over one issue or another. Although internal conflicts were often bitter and organizationally divisive, the high tide of feminism left a solid core of committed feminists established in a range of political organizations and with a good foothold in state institutions. This has given British feminism a purchase on public life that, at best, will grow over the coming years into a major political presence; at worst, it is there, working behind the scenes, able to offer continuity, experience, and professionalism when the next upsurge comes.

We argue, therefore, that feminism has once again made a political impact in Britain. But not all of its accomplishments are secure, not all of the prognoses are optimistic. If we attempt to write a list of the positive and negative aspects of the political position of British feminism in the first half of the 1990s, we get as many pluses as minuses. The balance is a fine one.

On the positive side, we can offer substantial evidence of a new and productive relationship between the women's movement and the state, into which feminists make a considerable input. A significant professionalization of feminist organization is apparent. The major political organizations of the Labour Party and the trade-union movement have taken up and accommodated important feminist principles, as have the Liberal and Social Democrats. The 1992 elections brought the 'closet' feminism of many Conservative Party women into the spotlight. Feminist ideas have found a place in popular culture that gives them a purchase on British political attitudes. All of this offers grounds for optimism. But our negative list is equally impressive. There has been a damaging fragmentation of the WLM, a decline in its organizations that was accompanied by 'burn-out' for many former activists, who have not been replaced in sufficient numbers by a 'following generation' of younger women. Deradicalization has occurred, dimming the shine of the liberation ethos of feminist activity and goals. When issues were successfully propelled into the political mainstream, feminists lost control of their definitions, because policy-makers and administrators inevitably muted the impact of radically conceived reforms.

None of these trends is universal, but all of them are present. Arguably, one side of our list is the obverse of the other. The integration of feminists into state and political institutions necessarily removes them from the grass-roots movements. The popular absorption of some feminist values, and the recycling of feminist ideas in a variety of contexts, almost by definition means their dilution. As we wrote in our introduction, such developments are partly, but not completely, a product of the natural life cycle of a successful social movement. In this concluding chapter we return to that assertion, and draw together our observations, discussions, and arguments to offer our view of what has become of the British women's movement. First, we review the major changes since 1979, then we consider how they might be explained. Finally, we consider the future of British feminism.

## CHANGES IN BRITISH FEMINISM

### Gains

*Institutionalization and Professionalization* We have traced an increasing involvement by feminists in state agencies since the end of the 1970s. During the 1970s the pattern was different. There was a strong ethic of self-help within the WLM, and emerging local campaigns tended to rely on their own fund-raising efforts and members' energies in order to help themselves or other women directly, rather than use an official agency. For example, a women's group might have set up a women's refuge by themselves, have organized a squat in an unused building, have operated a voluntary rota to run the refuge, and have raised any necessary funds through benefits, discos, and so forth. But such activity placed enormous demands on what were usually small groups of women. Moreover, their very success generated levels of demand that were impossible to meet without real resources. In such circumstances, arguments for accepting or, indeed, soliciting assistance from government and other public organizations became more urgent and persuasive, despite real (and well-articulated) fears about the consequences of compromise and dependency.

Many important changes began at local level. Initially, arrangements were made with local authorities, perhaps to secure premises for a refuge or a women's centre, or with local social services to ensure resources for the women who came there. Gradually (slowly), experience of working with a variety of public agencies was gained, and feminists became more confident of their ability to exploit the resources of particular institutions. Where local authorities became committed to some form of 'municipal feminism', ideological divisions between feminists and administrators and welfare professionals were less clear-cut. Though many feminists regarded municipal feminism with great suspicion, the boundaries between feminist activist and local council employee were blurred. During the 1980s, local authorities became more and more reliant on voluntary groups to cover gaps in service provision, a result of Mrs Thatcher's political and financial squeeze on local power. They became ever more willing (and obliged) to work with groups that offered services to particular sections of the community. Thus resources were offered to women's refuges and centres, Asian women's centres, rape crisis lines, child abuse survivor groups, etc. The forms that such experience took were many and various. An existing campaign might approach a local authority for assistance in the form of, say, a worker's salary or accommodation; a local authority or its women's unit or even a CHC worker might encourage, facilitate, or actually sponsor a great range of projects, self-help groups, campaigns, and so forth.

National-level interaction also became important, although this was inevitably more formalized. National feminist campaigns approached charities and central government departments for funding. In the case of both the WRRC and NCC, this meant setting up separate charitable trusts to receive the money. Out of this process came a variety of developments. Many feminists gained important knowledge and skills; charitable organizations and state agencies became more sensitive to feminists elements in their constituencies; campaigning groups became more professional and businesslike. Accepting public resources meant accepting conditions about their use. Activists had to adapt their organizations and modes of operation to an array of managerial requirements. Feminists in collectives had to work out difficult relationships with paid workers. There was a tendency to concentrate energy on those parts of a group's work that were funded. As the 1980s progressed, project success brought the pressures of increased public demand, a pressure exacerbated by public spending cuts. Our interviews with feminist volunteers in different projects repeatedly came up with the complaint that the workers felt that they had to do the work of the council, that they were too buried in day-to-day work and too restricted by the requirements of accountability to have time for the political campaigning and networking that once nurtured the WLM. Over time, such experiences became widespread, and later they were analysed in the feminist retheorization of the state that we described in Chapter 5.

Increased involvement with the government and other public institutions was accompanied by a growing feminist presence in established political organizations, notably the Labour Party and the trade unions, but also in the smaller parties and, inevitably, in the Conservative Party. The 1992 general election campaign was remarkable for the gloss that parties placed on their policies to attract women's votes. All the British parties offered policies on child benefits, maternity rights, women's rights at work, increased pensions for women, enhanced child care provision, enhanced educational opportunities, women-targeted health care, equal pay, and greater protection from violence. Labour, the SNP, and the Greens offered the establishment of a Ministry of

Women, and all except the Conservatives supported some version of parental leave for child care. All except the Conservatives had an explicit policy to increase women's political representation. This was a considerable change from 1979, when, despite the election of Britain's first woman Prime Minister, such issues were either not a matter of party policy or they were relegated to the bottom of the political agenda.[1]

The public commitment of the labour movement to a feminist platform has been a significant success for the British women's movement, and the signs are that this success will continue. In the summer of 1992 the Labour Party elected John Smith and Margaret Beckett as its leaders on an agenda that reasserted Labour's commitment to feminist values in general and to women's representation and empowerment in particular. They were elected with overwhelming trade-union support, suggesting that the conversion of the labour movement to feminism is secure. But with Labour's repeated electoral defeats, we need to ask how far such successes can actually take us. And with this, we are required to acknowledge that Conservative feminism has some way to go before it becomes a force to be reckoned with.

Other areas of public life have also seen a growing women's presence, although, as we emphasized in Chapter 5, we cannot assume that more women necessarily means more feminists. However, we can see an increasing impact of feminist ideas in those professional areas where women have long been numerous: social work (especially in the areas of child abuse and child care), community health (the encouragement of women's self-help groups), nursing and midwifery (ARM). In professions still largely dominated by men, notably medicine and the law, feminists and their arguments have begun to make headway. There is also a growing feminist presence in academic and cultural milieus. Individual feminist lecturers have disseminated ideas; researchers and writers have honed and strengthened feminist arguments; and women's studies courses have grown in number and popularity. Interaction between feminism and public institutions has brought beneficial changes.

*The Diffusion of Feminist Values* One such change is apparent in popular values. Ideas and attitudes about women's rights and

---

[1] Ros Morris, 'Who Is the Fairest of them All?' the *Guardian*, 7 Apr. 1992.

entitlements that seemed radical at the beginning of the 1970s are widely accepted today. There has been a steady diffusion of feminist values that is probably linked to the increasing presence of feminists in the political mainstream, but which has a much wider influence. Contemporary public opinion undoubtedly harbours negative images of feminists, but it has, nevertheless, gradually absorbed many feminist arguments. Thus, according to the report on British social attitudes for 1988–9, public support for abortion in all circumstances increased in all demographic groups between 1983 and 1987. The proportion of respondents who rejected traditional sex stereotyping for a range of selected occupations increased, as did the proportion who assumed in principle that partners should share general domestic duties. Between 1980 and 1987 the proportion of respondents who believed that women with children under 5 should not go out to work fell from 62 per cent to 45 per cent. But there were limits to this process. The valuation placed on lesbianism by Radical feminists was not echoed in public attitudes, which, affected in part perhaps by fears about AIDS, seemed to become more homophobic during the 1980s.[2] However, while reliable statistical evidence is not available, there is some indication that attitudes about sexual harassment, rape, and domestic violence have changed in ways that reflect much of the original Radical feminist analysis of sexual politics. British interest in the Anita Hill–Clarence Thomas controversy brought about by the latter's nomination to the United States Supreme Court highlighted arguments about sexual harassment in 1992. The rape trials of Mike Tyson and Stephen Kennedy Smith were also much reported and discussed. Overall, explicit support for feminism was higher than we thought. An ICM poll commissioned in early 1992 by *Elle,* a glossy women's fashion magazine, in conjunction with the *Guardian* found that the majority of both women and men viewed feminism positively (57 and 56 per cent respectively).[3]

It is likely that such changing attitudes have had a constraining influence on national government policy, and we have already discussed their impact in particular issue areas. Nevertheless, we

[2] See Roger Jowell *et al.* (eds.), *British Social Attitudes: The Fifth Report* (Gower, Aldershot, 1988). Especially relevant here are Stephen Harding, 'Trends in Permissiveness', and Sharon Witherspoon, 'Interim Report: A Woman's Work'.
[3] See 'Men and Women', *Elle/Guardian*, 9 Jan. 1992: 1.

would find it hard to argue that the Thatcher government itself
did much for women's employment rights. And what it did do
was largely the result of duress. Nor did it do much for child
care provision. But at least it never directly questioned women's
right, or even the right of married women with young children,
to work. In the field of reproductive rights, the government did
not yield significant ground to the moral conservatives on questions of abortion or contraception for the under-16s. In the areas
of rape and domestic violence, the influence of feminist values is
especially evident in the introduction of considerable improvements in police and legal procedures. Of course, it is hard to be
comfortable with all instances of the diffusion of feminist values.
The super-individualist, consumerist feminism embodied in
*Cosmopolitan* and *Elle* seems light years away from the movement's early idealism. However, to the extent that it offers arguments that women in all sorts of situations may use to assert
themselves, even this glossy magazine feminism is empowering.

## *Losses*

*Decline, Conflict, and Fragmentation*   As we noted in our introduction, the second half of the 1980s heard numerous assertions
that feminism had once again declined, that it was a spent force,
that many of its aims were met, and that those still outstanding
were ridiculous. The media was, at worst, scathing, at best, reluctant to run stories about feminist issues.[4] But events in the 1990s
suggest that this decline was overstated, perhaps, even, had not
taken place at all. How might we account for such contradictory
perceptions? Some of the confusion is probably the result of the
different focus of those who made the judgements. While we
think that there is little doubt that the WLM has experienced a
decline, the wider women's movement, now a carrier of feminist
values, appears to be thriving. Even so, there were new forms of
autonomous, broadly feminist mobilization throughout the
1980s—black women, Greenham, and the pornography campaigns. These new sources of energy, along with municipal feminism and the struggles of the miners' wives, were significant
political forces during the 1980s.

[4] Rosalind Coward, 'Name Calling,' the *Guardian*, 20 Dec. 1990.

But there is no doubt that the visible national feminist move-ment has declined. As we travelled to collect the material for this book, everywhere we went, except Scotland, we encountered a sense that numbers of activists were fewer, that old networks had broken down. Local women's centres were closing down, women's newsletters were folding. Many women questioned whether there was still an autonomous women's movement. Although there were some newcomers, we got little sense that large numbers of younger women were becoming involved in the movement. Those whom we did meet were usually there because of personal experiences of domestic violence or rape, or because they had been enthused by women's studies courses. Clause 28 was also, for a time, a mobilizer. Throughout the decade, *Spare Rib* acted as a valuable noticeboard for movement events as well as a forum (though not always an entirely open one) for debate. But it experienced growing financial problems and became harder to find in the shops. Public demonstrations, marches, and rallies are much less well attended than they were during the 1970s. For example, the numbers who protested against the anti-abortion bills of James White in 1975 and John Corrie in 1979 were much greater than they were for David Alton's bill in 1987–8. Though this is hardly a scientific measure, the average age of the 120 or so activists whom we interviewed was between 36 and 37. The distribution was roughly normal, and only a handful of women were in their 20s.

Such decline at a time when general support for many feminist values appeared to be growing requires some explanation. One important factor here was conflict. The early 1980s were marked by bitter rows and confrontations. We have described in detail two particularly debilitating splits: between Radical and Socialist femi-nists, and between white feminists and the black women's move-ment. These were not the only sources of division and mutual suspicion. There was a London–provincial division, as manifested over LWAC activities and the attempt to set up a national women's health network. There was conflict about working with state agencies, leading to bitter accusations of collaboration and selling out. Conflict between volunteers, users, and paid workers arose in collectives—for example, in the NCC, the NAC, and many women's refuges. There was enormous hostility towards women who made their way in mainstream institutions.

Conflict within the WLM accelerated a process of fragmentation already inherent in the diversity of its concerns, the characteristic participatory forms of decision-making, informality, and decentralization of feminist organizations. There were no movement-wide national conferences after 1978. The national coordinating mechanisms that had been established in the 1970s for abortion rights and women's aid survived only after a fashion. NAC split in 1983, and the National Women's Aid Federation split into federations for England, Scotland, and Wales, with the English one the most internally divided. The information newsletter WIRES had stopped by the end of the 1980s. The weakening of national co-ordination did not reduce local activity, of course, but here, too, there was fragmentation as straitened financial circumstances led activists to concentrate on their own particular projects.

Of course, fragmentation and decline are not necessarily synonymous. A corollary of geographical fragmentation is the diversity to be found not only between regions, but also between cities and towns. Perhaps the most striking difference that we encountered was in Scotland, where feminists had their own story to tell of movement decline and voluntary sector 'burnout', but where there was an evident resurgence from 1987 onwards as conferences of feminists were being organized throughout the country. And contrasts were to be found elsewhere. Leeds in 1989 still seemed to have a lively feminist scene, and old networks functioned well; activists in Birmingham reported that they felt isolated and despondent. Local factors may go some way towards explaining these variations. During the years of Conservative rule, political activists in Scotland cultivated its oppositional culture and regional identity, providing a milieu in which an oppositional social movement might thrive. Leeds had been important to the resurgence of British feminism at the end of the 1960s and it was the birthplace of revolutionary feminism a few years later. It was an attractive place for feminists of all persuasions to settle, and many of our interviewees were drawn there by its feminist subculture. Once there, they naturally sought to continue it. The city is relatively compact, there is a local university, and an alternative newspaper. And the grim proximity of the 'Yorkshire ripper' drew women together in networks of protection and support.

*Deradicalization* The dilution of its core values through fragmentation, the need to compromise and negotiate with public
agencies, and, no doubt, the passage of time and the ageing of
activists—all contributed to a deradicalization of the WLM,
whose boundaries became blurred with those of the wider
women's movement. This is apparent in a number of ways.
Members of feminist collectives whose idealism once fired action
now find themselves nominally running projects as paid workers.
Answerable to state agencies that have come to dominate the
agenda, they now have less say. When members of the collective
drop out, disillusioned or simply wanting a change, it is often
difficult to replace them. Women working in the projects in the
meantime increasingly form part of a kind of welfarism, often
indistinguishable from underpaid social workers. Similarly, feminist voluntary workers have had to deal with the women whom
they assist as 'clients', inexorably moving away from the egalitarian and encouraging strategies of empowerment and self-help.
The financial realities of public spending cut-backs and of more
competition for resources require that political campaigning is
more professional and businesslike. Groups learned how to
handle the media, devoted time to the production of glossy
brochures, and so forth. Success in getting important issues on to
the political agenda meant that feminists lost control over them.
A good example of this is the way in which the work of the rape
crisis collectives has led to the adoption of feminist rhetoric in
police rape work, with the loss of much of its accompanying
empowering strategy (see Chapter 9). Another example is the way
in which NCC demands were redefined as its issues were taken
up by new campaigning organizations. Ideologically, the cultural
feminism to which we referred in Chapters 3 and 8, with its
unthreatening concentration on a reassessment of maternity that
sometimes looks suspiciously like traditional valuations of motherhood, has been deradicalizing, and, politically, the relative
decline of Radical feminism itself has been a contributing factor.

Despite all this, radical analyses continue to set the terms of
feminist debate, especially in the areas of reproductive rights, violence, and pornography. And the angry mobilization around the
issue of pornography that began in the late 1980s is undoubtedly
an exception to trends of deradicalization. Moreover, the corollary of a deradicalization within the WLM is a radicalization of

the understanding of such issues as abortion, child care, domestic violence, and rape in mainstream institutions. Here, too, the directions of change are by no means uniform

## EXPLAINING THE CHANGES

Thus, the changes that we have traced are contradictory; for each trend identified, a substantial list of exceptions may be itemized. We are not analysing a single, clear set of developments, here. Nevertheless, we do have some ideas about the way in which the progression of British feminism might be explained. We choose to understand it as a product of the interaction between the internal dynamic of the women's movement and its changing political environment. This has many parallels with the patterns that characterize other NSMs, but we think that British feminism contains important particular features that have produced their own unique consequences. Although women's movements elsewhere have experienced bitter conflicts, and identity politics have created divisions in most NSMs, particular features of the British women's movement may have intensified such effects. Identity politics are bound to have more important and far-reaching effects on a movement that is actually based on identity, and many women's movements have experienced problems here. In Britain, however, the relative weakness of liberal or right-wing strands of feminism, and the concomitant strength of more militant Radical and Socialist feminisms, has made the formation of political coalitions more difficult than in the United States, Australia, or Sweden. And the black women's movement has been more significant in Britain than in most other European countries. Moreover, the movement has lived through a specific era, one characterized by important and relevant social and economic trends as well as by the more deliberate policies of Thatcherism. These, too, have had distinctive effects.

Many of the changes in British feminism do have counterparts elsewhere. After more than two decades of activity, many of the 'older' second-wave movements seem to have run out of steam. This may in part be a generational phenomenon. The first cohort of movement activists were mobilized between the end of the 1960s and the late 1970s, and they are now middle-aged. To a younger generation of women, who could be (and sometimes are) their daughters, these pioneers must seem strange and dated, carrying as they do, New Left or 'post-materialist' baggage with little resonance for those who have grown up in such a different political climate.

It is also possible to link these trends of closer ties to public agencies and increasing penetration of mainstream institutions to processes that are observable in most NSMs. As we noted in our introduction, Claus Offe has pointed out how all such movements face problems of 'receding movement enthusiasm' when victories are won and seem to make participation less urgent, or when lack of progress creates despondency. In such circumstances, *de facto* leaders will be under pressure to institutionalize and professionalize their organizations. First, they will adopt more formal elements of organization, and soon they will increasingly be drawn into official channels of participation.[5]

To some extent, this is what happened to the British women's movement. But the process was modified; it reflected the distinctive characteristics and particular circumstances of British feminism. Although there was a fairly concerted effort to enter mainstream institutions, apparent in the influx of Socialist feminists into the Labour Party at the beginning of the decade, we are talking otherwise about a highly fragmented process. Individual campaigns modified their organizations and became more dependent on state bodies, they but never fully integrated into them. Strongly imbued as they were with New Left and Radical feminist values, British feminists continued to be particularly mistrustful of involvement in state institutions. As a result, opportunities may have been lost.[6] But opportunities were not the same in Britain as they were elsewhere. The British political system is, by comparison with that in other liberal democracies, unusually centralized and difficult to break into. Some of the feminist attitudes to this state were simply realistic.

But the 1980s were a time of change. Not only was there the shock of the Conservative victory in the 1979 general election, but the establishment of Thatcherism altered the political opportunity structure; in particular, it made the labour movement more

---

[5] Claus Offe, 'Reflections on the Institutional Self-Transformation of Movement Politics', in R. Dalton and M. Keuchler (eds.), *Challenging the Political Order* (Polity, Cambridge, 1990).

[6] See Sophie Watson, 'Unpacking the "State": Reflections on Australian, British and Scandinavian Feminist Interventions', in M. Katzenstein and H. Skjeie (eds.), *Going Public* (Institute of Social Research, Oslo, 1990).

receptive to feminism. Political change in the Thatcher years combined with the impact of long-term social and economic trends to produce some paradoxical consequences for women. Long-term shifts in family structure together with expanded possibilities for part-time work and certain government policies tended to increase women's *autonomy* without necessarily making them more *equal* to men. At the same time, a large overall increase in unemployment as well as government measures to deregulate the economy, constrain public expenditure, and privatize state holdings made life harder for the majority of women while it provided new opportunities for some. It is difficult to determine precisely how these changes affected the women's movement itself, but there are some obvious probable consequences. First, the trend towards greater autonomy strengthened the resonance of many feminists arguments with women and, indeed, with the public at large. Secondly, economic hardship added to the constraints on feminist activists in the 1980s. It must have been more difficult for activists to find the time and the energy to continue, and the problems of drawing new women into campaigns and projects undoubtedly increased. In this sense, we believe, the arguments for a widespread 'depoliticization' under Mrs Thatcher are convincing and relevant to the fortunes of feminism. Thirdly, a widening gap between the majority of women and those benefiting from new opportunities may have exacerbated divisions within the movement. As they took advantage of new professional opportunities, it may have seemed to some women that feminism had achieved its goals.

We are largely unpersuaded by analyses that depict Thatcherism as some kind of anti-feminist backlash. Although groups and individuals on the Conservative Right repeatedly demanded the reaffirmation of traditional moral and family values across the full span of public policy, the government did not consistently take these up in its rhetoric, and it was still less inclined to act upon them in practice. Indeed, it is arguable that feminism might have gained from such an attack. Had Mrs Thatcher's government confronted feminism head-on, it might have helped to coalesce the fragmented movement, to give it a more united identity in the face of a clear common enemy. But while Thatcherism was not a form of anti-feminism as such, by shifting the fulcrum of public political discourse to the Right, it made it difficult for radical or left-wing views of any kind to be taken seriously. And there is no doubt that the government played to homophobic sentiments in the population at large, thus increasing the sense of marginalization that many lesbian feminists experienced. In these ways, Thatcherism surely contributed both to the deradicalization of feminism and to fragmentation within it.

On the other hand, the regrouping of the Left and the changed fortunes of the Labour Party and of the trade unions during the Thatcher years created important political openings for feminists. Here we have a major political party and a huge interest organization prepared to take some feminist ideas and objectives on board. This shift in the political opportunity structure provided channels of participation that would not otherwise have been available to the outsider groups that characterized feminist organization. And while the decreasing power of a labour movement haunted by the spectre of permanent opposition undermines the net gain that feminists made, the implementation of the skills and strategies derived from this experience of labour movement networks of all kinds is much in evidence in the feminism of the 1990s. Feminist networking is more formalized, better articulated, better established. The formation of organizations like NAL-GWC and the National Alliance of Women's Organizations indicates an acknowledgement of the need for a separate and distinctive women's voice in different public arenas. The validation of feminist knowledge and experience which is an important function of women's studies courses in further and higher education helps to keep in play ideas that might otherwise be lost as mainstream practices are adopted by activists.

As we have seen, there has been a diffusion of feminist values into public attitudes, even while feminism continues to be a term of abuse in the gutter press. There are grounds for concern about how such values will be sustained in the absence of a thriving, autonomous feminist movement. But for the moment, although it has declined, the WLM has not disappeared, and in many places it thrives. There is still a considerable incidence of characteristic feminist activity. Active feminists form a core of women who continue to work in projects and collectives in different issue areas in different parts of the country. Self-help, the provision of services, publications and campaigns are still a feature of feminist politics. Although the balance has changed, the relationship between this and other forms of feminist activity continues. In other words, as British feminism has developed and grown, the division of labour within it has gradually altered. During the 1990s the fortunes of feminist politics will depend on whether this division of labour proves capable of mobilizing and energizing a feminist-inspired women's movement.

# Bibliography

*Books and Articles*

ALEXANDER, SALLY, 'Women, Class and Sexual Difference', in Lovell (ed.), *British Feminist Thought: A Reader*.

AMOS, VALERIE, and PARMAR, PRATIBHA, 'Challenging Imperial Feminism', *Feminist Review*, 17 (1984).

ARDILL, SUSAN, and O'SULLIVAN, SUE, 'Upsetting an Applecart: Difference, Desire and Lesbian Sado-Masochism', *Feminist Review*, 23 (1986).

ARDITTI, RITA, KLEIN, RENATE DUELLI, and MINDEN, SHELLEY (eds.), *Test-Tube Women: What Future for Motherhood?* (Pandora, London, 1984).

AZIZ, RAZIA, 'Feminism and the Challenge of Racism: Deviance or Difference?', in Crawley and Himmelweit (eds.), *Knowing Women*.

BAKKER, ISABELLA, 'Women's Employment in Comparative Perspective', in Jenson, Hagen, and Reddy (eds.), *Feminization of the Labour Force*.

BANKS, OLIVE, *Faces of Feminism* (Martin Robertson, Oxford, 1981).

BARRETT, MICHÈLE, *Women's Oppression Today*, rev. edn. (Verso, London, 1988).

—— and MCINTOSH, MARY, *The Anti-Social Family* (Verso, London, 1982).

BARRY, JIM, *The Women's Movement and Local Politics* (Avebury, Aldershot, 1991).

BELL, PATRICIA, and MACLEOD, JAN, 'Bridging the Gap: Glasgow Women's Support Project', *Feminist Review*, 28 (1988).

BENHABIB, SYLVIA, and CORNELL, DRUCILLA (eds.), *Feminism as Critique* (Polity, Cambridge, 1987).

BENN, MELISSA, 'Isn't Sexual Harassment Really about Masculinity?', *Spare Rib*, July 1985.

—— 'Page Three and the Campaign against it', in Chester and Dickey (eds.), *Feminism and Censorship*.

—— 'Sisters and Slogans', *Marxism Today*, Apr. 1987.

BERER, MARGE, 'Whatever Happened to "A Woman's Right to Choose"?', *Feminist Review*, 29 (1988).

BETTERTON, ROSEMARY, 'How Do Women Look? The Female Nude in the Work of Suzanne Valedon', *Feminist Review*, 19 (1985).

BEURET, KRISTINE, 'Women and Transport', in Maclean and Groves (eds.), *Women's Issues in Social Policy*.

BOSTON, SARAH, *Women Workers and the Trade Unions* (Lawrence and Wishart, London, 1987).

BOYD, ROISIN, et al., 'Greenham Common', *Spare Rib*, Feb. 1983.

*Breaching the Peace* (Onlywoman Press, London, 1983).

BREITENBACH, ESTHER, 'The Impact of Thatcherism on Women in Scotland', in Brown and McCrone (eds.), *The Scottish Government Yearbook (1989)* (Unit for the Study of Government in Scotland, Edinburgh University, Edinburgh, 1989).

—— 'Sisters Are Doing it for Themselves', in Brown and Parry (eds.), *The Scottish Government Yearbook (1990)*.

BREUGEL, IRENE, 'Sex and Race in the Labour Market', *Feminist Review*, 1989.

BRIGGS, ANNA, 'Why Children?', *Spare Rib*, Feb. 1981.

BRITTAIN, SAMUEL, 'The Government's Economic Policy', in Kavanagh and Seldon (eds.), *The Thatcher Effect*.

BROWN, ALICE, and MCCRONE, DAVID (eds.), *The Scottish Government Yearbook (1989)* (Unit for the Study of Government in Scotland, Edinburgh University, Edinburgh, 1989).

BROWNMILLER, SUSAN, *Against our Will* (Penguin, Harmondsworth, 1975).

BRYAN, BEVERLY, et al. (eds.), *The Heart of the Race* (Virago, London, 1985).

BRYSON, VALERIE, *Feminist Political Theory* (Macmillan, Basingstoke, 1992).

BULPITT, JIM, 'The Discipline of the New Democracy: Mrs Thatcher's Domestic Statecraft', *Political Studies*, 4/1 (1986).

BYRNE, PAUL, *The Campaign for Nuclear Disarmament* (Croom Helm, London, 1988).

CAMPBELL, BEA, 'Feminist Sexual Politics', *Feminist Review*, 5 (1980).

—— *The Iron Ladies* (Virago, London, 1987).

—— 'Trading Places', the *Guardian*, 24 Oct. 1990.

—— *Unofficial Secrets* (Virago, London, 1988).

CARBY, HAZEL, 'White Woman Listen! Black Feminism and the Boundaries of Sisterhood', in Centre for Contemporary Cultural Studies, *The Empire Strikes Back*.

CARMEN, et al., 'Becoming Visible: Black Lesbian Discussion', *Feminist Review*, 17 (1984).

Centre for Contemporary Cultural Studies (Race and Politics Group), *The Empire Strikes Back* (Hutchinson, London, 1982).

CHARLES, NICOLA, 'Women and Trade Unions in the Workplace', *Feminist Review*, 15 (1982).

CHESTER, GAIL, and DICKEY, JULIENNE (eds.), *Feminism and Censorship* (Prism, Bridport, 1988).

CLARK, WENDY, 'Home Thoughts from not so Far Away: A Personal Look at the Family', in Segal (ed.), *What Is to Be Done about the Family?*

COCKBURN, CYNTHIA, 'Equal Opportunities: The Short and Long Agenda', *Industrial Relations Journal*, 20/3 (1989).

—— *In the Way of Women* (Macmillan, London, 1991).

—— *Women, Trade Unions and Political Parties* (Fabian Research Series 349, the Fabian Society, London, 1987).

COCKS, JOAN, 'Wordless Emotions: Some Critical Reflections on Radical Feminism', *Politics and Society*, 13 (1984).

COHEN, BRONWEN, *Caring for Children* (Family Policy Studies Centre, Edinburgh, 1990).

CONNELL, R. W., *Gender and Power: Society, the Person and Sexual Politics* (Polity, Cambridge, 1987).

CONNOLLY, CLARA, 'Splintered Sisterhood: Antiracism in a Young Women's Project', *Feminist Review*, 36 (1990).

CONOVER, PAMELA JOHNSTONE, and GRAY, VIRGINIA, *Feminism and the New Right* (Praeger, New York, 1983).

COOK, ALICE, and KIRK, GWYN (eds.), *Greenham Women Everywhere* (Pluto, London, 1983).

COOLE, DIANA, 'Patriarch and Contract: Reading Pateman', *Politics*, 10/1 (1990).

COOPER, DAVINA, and HERMAN, DIDI, 'Turning us Off', *Trouble and Strife*, 19 (1990).

COOTE, ANNA, 'Putting Britain to Rights', the *Guardian*, 24 Oct. 1974.

—— and PATTULLO, POLLY, *Power and Prejudice: Women and Politics* (Weidenfeld and Nicolson, London, 1990).

—— and CAMPBELL, BEA, *Sweet Freedom*, new edn. (Blackwell, Oxford, 1987).

——, HARMAN, HARRIET, and HEWITT, PATRICIA, *The Family Way* (Institute for Public Policy Research, London, 1990).

COWARD, ROSALIND, 'Name Calling', the *Guardian*, 20 Dec. 1990.

—— 'Sexual Violence and Sexuality', in Feminist Review (ed.), *Sexual Violence: A Reader*.

COYLE, ANGELA, 'The Limits of Change: Local Government and Equal Opportunities for Women', *Public Administration*, 67 (1989).

—— 'Going Private: The Implications of Privatisation for Women's Work', *Feminist Review*, 21 (1985).

CRAWLEY, HELEN, and HIMMELWEIT, SUSAN (eds.), *Knowing Women* (Polity, Cambridge, 1992).

CREWE, IVOR, 'Has the Electorate Become Thatcherite?', in Skidelsky (ed.), *Thatcherism*.

—— 'Values: The Crusade that Failed', in Kavanagh and Seldon (eds.), *The Thatcher Effect*.

CREWE, IVOR, and SEARING, DONALD, 'Ideological Change in the British Conservative Party', *American Political Science Review*, 82/2 (1988).

DAHLERUP, DRUDE, *The New Women's Movement: Feminism and Political Power in Europe and the USA* (Sage, London, 1986).

DAHRENDORF, RALF, 'Changing Social Values under Mrs Thatcher', in Skidelsky (ed.), *Thatcherism*.

DALTON, RUSSELL, and KUECHLER, MANFRED (eds.), *Challenging the Political Order: New Social and Political Movements in Western Democracies* (Polity, Cambridge, 1990).

DAVID, MIRIAM, 'Moral and Maternal: The Family in the Right', in Levitas (ed.), *The Ideology of the New Right*.

DOUGLAS, GILLIAN, 'Family Law under the Thatcher Government', *Journal of Law and Society*, 17/4 (1990).

DRIVER, EMILY, 'The Incest Survivors', *Spare Rib*, Mar. 1982.

DRYSDALE, LIZ, 'Black Resister', *Spare Rib*, May 1986.

DUCHEN, CLAIRE, *Feminism in France* (Routledge and Kegan Paul, London, 1986).

DUNHILL, C. (ed.), *The Boys in Blue* (Virago, London, 1989).

DURHAM, MARTIN, *Sex and Politics: The Family and Morality in the Thatcher Years* (Macmillan, London, 1991).

—— 'The Thatcher Government and the Moral Right', *Parliamentary Affairs*, Jan. 1989.

DWORKIN, ANDREA, *Pornography: Men Possessing Women* (Perigee Books, New York, 1979).

EDWARDS, JULIA, 'Local Government Women's Committees', *Local Government Studies*, July/Aug. 1988.

EGERTON, JAYNE, 'The Family Way', *Trouble and Strife*, 20 (1991).

EICHENBAUM, LUISE, and ORBACH, SUSIE, *What Do Women Want?* (Fontana, Glasgow, 1984).

EISENSTEIN, HESTER, *Contemporary Feminist Thought* (Allen Unwin, London, 1984).

ELLIOTT, RUTH, 'How Far Have we Come? Women's Organisations in the Unions in the United Kingdon', *Feminist Review*, 16 (1984).

ENGLISH, DEIRDRE, HILLIBAUGH, AMBER, and RUBIN, GAYLE, 'Talking Sex: A Conversation on Sexuality and Feminism', *Feminist Review*, 11 (1982).

EOC, *Annual Report, 1989* (HMSO, London, 1989).

—— *Equal Pay for Men and Women* (EOC, Manchester, 1991).

—— *Equal Treatment for Men and Women* (EOC, Manchester, 1988).

—— *Equality Bargaining: Why Not?* (EOC, Manchester, 1989).

—— *From Policy to Practice: An Equal Opportunities Strategy for the 1990s* (EOC, Manchester, 1988).

—— *The Key to Real Choice* (EOC, Manchester, 1990).

EPSTEIN, BARBARA, and ELLIS, KATE, 'The Pro-Family Left', *Feminist Review*, 14 (1983).

ERMISCH, JOHN, and WRIGHT, R. E., 'Welfare Benefits and the Duration of Single Parenthood', *National Institute of Economics Review*, 130 (Nov. 1989).

EVANS, JUDITH, *et al.* (eds.), *Feminism and Political Theory* (Sage, London, 1986).

Feminist Review (ed.), *Sexual Violence: A Reader* (Virago, London, 1987).

FINCH, SUE, *et al.*, 'Socialist Feminists and Greenham', *Feminist Review*, 23 (1986).

FIRESTONE, SHULAMITH, *The Dialectic of Sex* (Bantam, New York, 1971).

FLANNERY, KATE, and ROELOFS, SARA, 'Local Government Women's Committees', in Holland (ed.), *Feminist Action*.

FOSTER, PEGGY, 'Well Woman Clinics: A Serious Challenge to Mainstream Health Care?', in Maclean and Groves (eds.), *Women's Issues in Social Policy*.

FRANZWAY, SUZANNE, COURT, DIANNE, and CONNELL, R. W., *Staking a Claim* (Polity, Cambridge, 1989).

FRATER, ALISON, 'Twenty Years of Women's Choice', *Marxism Today*, Mar. 1987.

FREER, JEAN, *Raging Women: In Reply to 'Breaching the Peace'* (privately publ.).

FRIEDAN, BETTY, *The Second Stage* (Abacus, London, 1983).

GAMBLE, ANDREW, *The Free Economy and the Strong State* (Macmillan, London, 1988).

GARDINER, JEAN, 'Women, Recession and the Tories', in Hall and Jacques (eds.), *The Politics of Thatcherism*.

GARLICK, HELEN, 'Sex and the Single Parent', the *Guardian*, 5 Dec. 1990.

GIEVE, KATHERINE, 'Rethinking Feminist Attitudes towards Mothering', *Feminist Review*, 25 (1987).

GLENDINNING, CAROLINE, and MILLAR, JANE, 'Poverty: The Forgotten Englishwoman', in Maclean and Groves (eds.), *Women's Issues in Social Policy*.

GOMEZ, JEWELLE, and SMITH, BARBARA, 'Talking about it: Homophobia in the Black Community', *Feminist Review*, 34 (1990).

Greater London Council, *Annual Report, 1984/5* (GLC, London, 1985).

GREGORY, JEANNE, 'Equal Pay and Sex Discrimination: Why Women Are Giving up the Fight', *Feminist Review*, 10 (1982).

—— 'Equal Value/Comparable Worth: National Statute and Case Law in Britain and the USA', in Kahn and Meehan (eds.), *Equal Value/Comparable Worth*.

GREWAL, S., *et al.*, *Charting the Journey: Writings by Black and Third World Women* (Sheba, London, 1988).

HAGUE, G., *et al.*, 'Women's Aid: Policing Male Violence in the Home', in Dunhill (ed.), *The Boys in Blue*.

HALL, STUART, and JACQUES, MARTIN (eds.), *The Politics of Thatcherism* (Lawrence and Wishart, London, 1983).

The Hansard Society, *The Report of the Hansard Society Commission on Women at the Top* (HMSO, London, 1990).

HARDING, STEPHEN, 'Trends in Permissiveness', in Jowell *et al.* (eds.), *British Social Attitudes: The Fifth Report*.

HARFORD, BARBARA, and HOPKINS, SARAH (eds.), *Greenham Common: Women at the Wire* (The Women's Press, London, 1984).

HARNE, LYNNE, 'Reinventing the Wheel', in Sebestyen (ed.), *'68, '78, '88*.

HEARNE, ANNA J., 'Racism, Rape and Riots', *Trouble and Strife*, 9 (1986).

HENDESSI, MANDANA, 'In Conversation', in Southall Black Sisters, *Against the Grain*.

HENRY, ALICE, *et al.*, 'Greenham Inside and Out', *Spare Rib*, May 1984.

HERON, ELIZABETH, 'The Mystique of Motherhood', *Time Out*, 21–7 Nov. 1980.

HEWITT, PATRICIA, and MATTINSON, DEBORAH, *Women's Votes: The Key to Winning* (Fabian Research Series 353, the Fabian Society, London, 1989).

HILLS, JILL, 'Britain', in Lovenduski and Hills (eds.), *The Politics of the Second Electorate*.

HOLLAND, JOY (ed.), *Feminist Action* (Battleaxe Books, London, 1984).

HOOPER, CAROL ANN, 'Getting him off the Hook', *Trouble and Strife*, 12 (1987).

HUMPHRIES, JANE, and RUBERY, JILL, 'Recession and Exploitation: British Women in a Changing Workplace, 1979–1985', in Jenson, Hagen, and Reddy (eds.), *Feminization of the Labour Force*.

HUNT, MARGARET, 'The De-Eroticization of Women's Liberation: Social Purity Movements and the Revolutionary Feminism of Sheila Jeffreys', *Feminist Review*, 34 (1990).

INAM, MUNEEZA, 'Opening Doors', in Southall Black Sisters, *Against the Grain*.

JAMES, BARBARA, 'Ten Years of Women's Health: 1982–92', *Feminist Review*, 41 (1992).

JEFFREYS, SHEILA, *Anticlimax* (The Women's Press, London, 1990).

JENSON, JANE, and HAGEN, ELIZABETH, 'Paradoxes and Promises: Work and Politics in the Postwar Years', in Jenson, Hagen, and Reddy (eds.), *Feminization of the Labour Force*.

——, ——, and REDDY, CEALLAIGH (eds.), *Feminization of the Labour Force* (Polity, Cambridge, 1988).

JESSOP, BOB, *et al.*, 'Authoritarian Populism: Two Nations and Thatcher', *New Left Review*, 147 (1986).

JOWELL, ROGER, *et al.* (eds.), *British Social Attitudes: The Fifth Report* (Gower, Aldershot, 1988).

KAHN, PEGGY, 'Introduction: Equal Pay for Work of Equal Value in Britain and the USA', in Kahn and Meehan (eds.), *Equal Value/Comparable Worth*.

—— and MEEHAN, ELIZABETH (eds.), *Equal Value/Comparable Worth in the UK and the USA* (Macmillan, Basingstoke, 1992).

KATZENSTEIN, MARY FAINSOD, 'Feminism within American Institutions: Unobtrusive Mobilization in the 1980s', *Signs*, 16/1 (1990).

—— and SKJEIE, H. (eds.), *Going Public* (Institute of Social Research, Oslo, 1990).

KAVANAGH, DENNIS, *Thatcherism and British Politics* (Oxford University Press, Oxford, 1989).

—— and SELDON, ANTHONY (eds.), *The Thatcher Effect* (Oxford University Press, Oxford, 1989).

KELLY, LIZ, 'The New Defeatism', *Trouble and Strife*, 11 (1987).

—— 'Talking about a Revolution', *Spare Rib*, Aug. 1988.

—— 'What's in a Name? Defining Child Sexual Abuse', *Feminist Review*, 28 (1988).

KING, DESMOND, *The New Right* (Macmillan, London, 1987).

KUHN, ANNETTE, *The Power of the Image* (Routledge and Kegan Paul, London, 1985).

LAND, HILARY, 'Time to Care', in Maclean and Groves (eds.), *Women's Issues in Social Policy*.

LEES, SUE, 'Blaming the Victim', *New Statesman and Society*, 1 Dec. 1989.

LEVITAS, RUTH (ed.), *The Ideology of the New Right* (Polity, Cambridge, 1986).

LEWIS, GAIL, *et al.*, 'Talking Personal, Talking Political', *Trouble and Strife*, 19 (1990).

LIDDINGTON, JILL, *The Long Road to Greenham: Feminism and Anti-Militarism since 1820* (Virago, London, 1989).

LIEBERMAN, SUE, 'Women's Committees in Scotland', in Brown and McCrone (eds.), *The Scottish Government Yearbook (1989)*.

LISTER, RUTH, 'Future Insecure: Income Maintenance under a Third Tory Term', in Maclean and Groves (eds.), *Women's Issues in Social Policy*.

LOACH, LORETTA, 'Can Feminism Survive a Third Term?', *Feminist Review*, 27 (1987).

—— 'Is there Life after the GLC?', *Spare Rib*, Mar. 1986.

London Women's Liberation Campaign for Legal and Financial Independence and Rights of Women, 'Disaggregation Now! Another Battle for Women's Independence', *Feminist Review*, 2 (1979).

374 BIBLIOGRAPHY

Lovell, Terry (ed.), *British Feminist Thought: A Reader* (Blackwell, Oxford, 1990).

Lovenduski, Joni, 'Implementing Equal Opportunities in the 1980s: An Overview', *Public Administration*, 67 (1989).

—— 'Parliament, Pressure Groups, Networks and the Women's Movement: The Politics of Abortion Law Reform in Britain, 1967–83', in Lovenduski and Outshoorn (eds.), *The New Politics of Abortion.*

—— 'Toward the Emasculation of Political Science', in Spender (ed.), *Men's Studies Modified.*

—— *Women and European Politics* (Harvester, Brighton, 1986).

—— and Hills, Jill (eds.), *The Politics of the Second Electorate* (Routledge and Kegan Paul, London, 1981).

—— and Norris, Pippa, 'British Conservative Parliamentary Recruitment: Patronage, Liberal-Rational, Radical and Feminist Models', paper presented to the annual meeting of the American Political Science Association, Washington, DC, 29 Aug.–1 Sept. 1991.

—— —— 'Selecting Women Candidates: Obstacles to the Feminization of the House of Commons', *European Journal of Political Research*, 17 (1989).

—— and Outshoorn, Joyce (eds.), *The New Politics of Abortion* (Sage, London, 1986).

——, Norris, Pippa, and Levy, Catriona, 'The Conservatives and Women', in Seldon and Butler (eds.), *The Conservative Party, 1900–1990.*

McIntosh, Mary, 'Introduction to an Issue: Family Secrets as Public Drama', *Feminist Review*, 28 (1988).

Mackinnon, Catherine, *Feminism Unmodified: Discourses on Life and Law* (Harvard University Press, Cambridge, Mass., 1987).

Mackintosh, Mary, and Wainwright, Hilary (eds.), *A Taste of Power* (Verso, London, 1987).

Maclean, Mavis, and Groves, Dulcie (eds.), *Women's Issues in Social Policy* (Routledge and Kegan Paul, London, 1991).

MacLeod, Mary, and Saraga, Esther, 'Challenging the Orthodoxy: Towards a Feminist Theory and Practice', *Feminist Review*, 28 (1988).

Mama, Amina, 'A Hidden Struggle', *Spare Rib*, Feb. 1990.

—— 'Violence against Black Women: Gender, Race and State Responses', *Feminist Review*, 28 (1989).

Marsh, David, and Chambers, Joanna, *Abortion Politics* (Junction Books, London, 1981).

—— and Rhodes, R. A. W. (eds.), *Implementing Thatcherite Policies* (Open University Press, Buckingham, 1992).

MARSHALL, JANE, et al., 'What Future for the National Abortion Campaign?', *Spare Rib*, Oct. 1983.

MEEHAN, ELIZABETH, *Women's Rights at Work: Campaigns and Policy in Britain and the United States* (Macmillan, London, 1985).

—— and SEVENHUIJSEN, SELMA (eds.), *Equality Politics and Gender* (Sage, London, 1991).

MILIBAND, RALPH, et al. (eds.), *Socialist Register, 1987* (Merlin, London, 1987).

MILLETT, KATE, *Sexual Politics* (Abacus, London, 1972).

MITCHELL, JULIET, *Psychoanalysis and Feminism* (Penguin, Harmondsworth, 1974).

—— 'Women: The Longest Revolution', *New Left Review*, 40 (1966).

MOI, TORIL, *Sexual/Textual Politics* (Methuen, London, 1985).

MOORE, WENDY, 'There Should Be a Law against it, Shouldn't there?', in Chester and Dickey (eds.), *Feminism and Censorship*.

MORGAN, DAVID, *The Family, Politics and Social Theory* (Routledge and Kegan Paul, London, 1985).

MORRIS, ROZ, 'Who Is the Fairest of them All?', the *Guardian*, 7 Apr. 1992.

NALGWC, *Responding with Authority: Local Authority Initiatives to Counter Violence against Women* (The Pankhurst Press, Manchester, 1990).

NAVA, MICA, 'Cleveland and the Press: Outrage and Anxiety in the Reporting of Abuse', *Feminist Review*, 28 (1988).

—— 'From Utopian to Scientific Feminism? Early Feminist Critiques of the Family', in Segal (ed.), *What Is to Be Done about the Family?*

NORDEN, BARBARA, 'Campaign against Pornography', *Feminist Review*, 35 (1990).

—— 'City of Splits', *Spare Rib*, May 1986.

—— 'Many Visions—Many Hands', *Spare Rib*, Sept. 1985.

NORTON-TAYLOR, RICHARD, 'Old Values Die Hard', the *Guardian*, 13 Sept. 1989.

OECD, *Employment Outlook* (OECD, Paris, 1983).

OFFE, CLAUS, 'Reflections on the Institutional Self-Transformation of Movement Politics: A Tentative Stage Model', in Dalton and Kuechler (eds.), *Challenging the Political Order*.

PARMAR, PRATIBHA, 'Gender, Race and Class: Asian Women in Resistance', in Centre for Contemporary Cultural Studies, *The Empire Strikes Back*.

—— 'Other Kinds of Dreams', *Feminist Review*, 31 (1989).

PARTON, NIGEL, *Governing the Family: Child Care, Child Protection and the State* (Macmillan, London, 1991).

PATEMAN, CAROLE, *The Disorder of Women* (Polity, Cambridge, 1989).

PATEMAN, CAROLE, *The Sexual Contract* (Polity, Cambridge, 1988).

PERRIGO, SARAH, 'Feminist Politics in the 1980s', paper presented to the annual conference of the Political Studies Association, Warwick University, Apr. 1989.

—— 'The Labour Party and the Promotion of Women', paper presented to the workshop, 'Party Responses to Women's Demands for Political Entry', Essex University, Mar. 1991.

PETRIE, RUTH, and LIVINGSTONE, ANNE, 'Out of the Back Streets', *Red Rag*, 11 (1976).

PFEFFER, NAOMI, *The Experience of Infertility* (Virago, London, 1983).

PHILLIPS, ANNE, *Divided Loyalties* (Virago, London, 1987).

PRINGLE, ROSEMARY, and WATSON, SOPHIE, 'Fathers, Brothers, Mates: The Fraternal State in Australia', in Watson (ed.), *Playing the State*.

RANDALL, VICKY, 'Feminism and Political Analysis', *Political Studies*, 39/3 (1991).

—— *Women and Politics* (Macmillan, London, 1987).

—— Women and the Left in Europe: A Continuing Dilemma', *Western European Politics*, 9/2 (1986).

REEVES, ROSANNE, 'A Welsh Patchwork', in Sebestyen (ed.), *'68, '78, '88*.

RICHARDSON, J., and JORDAN, GRANT (eds.), *Government and Pressure Groups in Britain* (Clarendon, Oxford, 1987).

REDDLE, SHEILA, 'Hell No—We Won't Glow', *Spare Rib*, June 1982.

ROELOFS, SARAH, 'Can Feminism Win?', *Spare Rib*, Sept. 1983.

ROWBOTHAM, SHEILA, 'More than Just a Memory: Some Political Implications of Women's Involvement in the Miners' Strike, 1984–1985', *Feminist Review*, 23 (1986).

—— *The Past Is before us* (Penguin, Harmondsworth, 1990).

RUTHERFORD, JONATHAN (ed.), *Identity, Community, Cultural Difference* (Lawrence and Wishart, London, 1990).

SACKS, VERA, 'The Equal Opportunities Commission Ten Years On', *Modern Law Review*, 19 (1986).

SAHGAL, GITA, 'Fundamentalism and the Multi-Cultural Fallacy', in Southall Black Sisters, *Against the Grain*.

SAVAGE, WENDY, *The Savage Inquiry* (Virago, London, 1986).

SCOTT, ALAN, *Ideology and the New Social Movements* (Unwin Hyman, London, 1990).

SCOTT, SARAH, and DICKENS, ALISON, 'Police and the Professionalisation of Rape', in Dunhill (ed.), *The Boys in Blue*.

Scottish Women's Aid, *Annual Report, 1989–90* (Edinburgh, 1990).

SEBESTYEN, AMANDA (ed.), *'68, '78, '88: From Women's Liberation to Feminism* (Prism, Bridport, 1988).

SEDDON, VICKY (ed.), *The Cutting Edge: Women and the Pit Strike* (Lawrence and Wishart, London, 1986).

—— 'Keeping Women in their Place', *Marxism Today*, July 1985.

SEGAL, LYNNE, *Is the Future Female?* (Virago, London, 1987).

—— 'Lynne Segal Interviews Diane Abbot', *Feminist Review*, 27 (1987).

—— 'Pornography and Violence: What the Experts Really Say', *Feminist Review*, 36 (1990).

—— *Slow Motion: Changing Masculinities, Changing Men* (Virago, London, 1990).

—— (ed.), *What Is to Be Done about the Family?* (Penguin, Harmondsworth, 1983).

SELDON, A., and BUTLER, D. (eds.), *The Conservative Party, 1900–1990* (Oxford University Press, Oxford, forthcoming).

SERTUC, *Still Moving towards Equality: A Survey of Progress towards Equality in Trade Unions* (SERTUC, London, 1989).

SKIDELSKY, ROBERT (ed.), *Thatcherism* (Blackwell, Oxford, 1989).

SMART, CAROL, *Feminism and the Power of Law* (Routledge and Kegan Paul, London, 1989).

SOMERSET, JO, 'I Was a Teenage *Jackie* Reader', in Sebestyen (ed.), *'68, '78, '88*.

SOOTHILL, KEITH, WALBY, SYLVIA, and BAGGULEY, PAUL, 'Judges, the Media and Rape', *Journal of Law and Society*, 17/2 (1991).

SOPER, KATE, 'Feminism, Humanism, and Postmodernism', *Radical Philosophy*, 55 (1990).

SOUTH, JULIA, 'And at the End of the Day, who Is Left Holding the Baby?', *New Statesman*, 15 Nov. 1985.

Southall Black Sisters, *Against the Grain: Southall Black Sisters, 1979–1989* (Southall Black Sisters, Southall, 1990).

SPENDER, DALE (ed.), *Men's Studies Modified* (Pergamon, Oxford, 1981).

STANLEY, LIZ, and WISE, SUE, *Breaking Out* (Routledge and Kegan Paul, London, 1983).

STEDWARD, GAIL, 'Entry into the System: A Case Study of Women in Scotland', in Richardson and Jordan (eds.), *Government and Pressure Groups in Britain*.

TARROW, SIDNEY, *Struggle, Politics and Reform: Collective Action, Social Movements and Cycles of Protest* (Cornell University, Western Societies Paper 21, Ithaca, NY, 1991).

TEMKIN, J., *Rape and the Legal Process* (Sweet and Maxwell, London, 1987).

TEN TUSCHER, TESSA, 'Patriarchy, Capitalism and the New Right', in Evans *et al.* (eds.), *Feminism and Political Theory*.

TOBIN, ANN, 'Lesbians and the Labour Party: The GLC Experience', *Feminist Review*, 34 (1990).

TSOULIS, ATHINA, 'Heterosexuality: A Feminist Option', *Spare Rib*, June 1987.

TUC, *Black and Ethnic Minority Women in Employment and Trade Unions* (TUC, London, 1987).

—— *Trade Unions Working for Equality* (TUC, London, 1990).

TUCRIC, 'Sexual Harassment at Work', *Industrial Relations Review and Report*, 384 (20 Jan. 1987).

TYSOE, MARYON, 'The Sexual Harassers', *New Society*, 4 Nov. 1982.

VALLANCE, ELIZABETH, *Women in the House* (Athlone, London, 1979).

WAINWRIGHT, HILARY, *Labour: A Tale of Two Parties* (Hogarth, London, 1987).

WALBY, SYLVIA, *Theorising Patriarchy* (Blackwell, Oxford, 1990).

WANDOR, MICHELENE, *Once a Feminist: Stories of a Generation* (Virago, London, 1990).

WATSON, SOPHIE (ed.), *Playing the State: Australian Feminist Interventions* (Virago, London, 1990).

—— 'Unpacking the "State": Reflections on Australian, British and Scandinavian Feminist Interventions', in Katzenstein and Skjeie (eds.), *Going Public*.

WEBSTER, BARBARA, 'A Woman's Issue: The Impact of Local Authority Cuts', *Local Government Studies*, Apr. 1985.

WEBSTER, CHARLES, 'The Health Service', in Kavanagh and Seldon (eds.), *The Thatcher Effect*.

WEEDON, CHRIS, *Feminist Practice and Poststructuralist Theory* (Blackwell, Oxford, 1987).

WEEKS, JEFFREY, 'Causes for Concern', *Marxism Today*, Feb. 1987.

Welsh Women's Aid, *Annual Report, 1989–90* (Cardiff, 1990).

WICKS, MALCOLM, 'The Battle for the Family', *Marxism Today*, Aug. 1990.

WILLETTS, DAVID, 'The Family', in Kavanagh and Seldon (eds.), *The Thatcher Effect*.

WILSON, AMRIT, *Finding a Voice* (Virago, London, 1985).

WILSON, ELIZABETH, 'Against Feminist Fundamentalism', *New Statesman*, 23 June 1989.

—— 'Thatcherism and Women: After Seven Years', in Miliband *et al.* (eds.), *Socialist Register, 1987*.

WITHERSPOON, SHARON, 'Interim Report: A Woman's Work', in Jowell *et al.* (eds.), *British Social Attitudes: The Fifth Report*.

Woman's Aid Federation England, *Women's Aid into the 1990s: Annual Report, 1989–90* (Bristol, 1990).

*Newspapers and Periodicals*

*America Political Science Review*
*Cosmopolitan*

*Elle*
*Everywoman*
*Feminist Review*
*FOWAAD*
The *Guardian*
The *Independent*
*Industrial Relations Journal*
*Industrial Relations Review and Report*
*Jobs for a Change*
*Journal of Law and Society*
*Local Government Studies*
*Marxism Today*
*Modern Law Review*
*New Left Review*
*New Statesman and Society*
The *Observer*
*Onward*
*Outwrite*
*Parliamentary Affairs*
*Peace News*
*Political Studies*
*Politics*
*Politics and Society*
*Public Administration*
*Radical Philosophy*
*RAGE*
*Red Rag*
*Revolutionary and Radical Feminist Newsletter*
*Salisbury Review*
*Sanity*
*Shrew*
*Signs*
*Spare Rib*
The *Sun*
*Time Out*
The *Times*
*Trouble and Strife*
*Western European Politics*
*WIRES*
*Women's Abortion and Contraceptive Campaign Newsletter*

# Index